GIVING BLOOD ENDORSEMENTS

For those of us who bemoan the lack of appreciation of current communication theory in homiletics, this is the book. Finally, something that moves beyond a linear understanding to a broader perspective incorporating the digital and image. 5 stars!
—*Dale Keller, Professor of Corporate Communication, Taylor University*

Dietrich Bonhoeffer once said: "The time when people could be told everything by means of words, whether theological or pious, is over." In this, his latest work, Dr. Leonard Sweet challenges today's "heralds of hope" to communicate old truths in new ways. His passion for Christ and his church can be found on every page of this book. This is a must read!
—*Donald Hilliard Jr., Lead Pastor, Cathedral International, and Assistant Associate Professor, Doctor of Ministry Program, Drew University*

Leonard Sweet is an atypical theologian and one of the most insightful spiritual thinkers of the twenty-first century. In this book he has accurately diagnosed the spiritual condition of our contemporary culture and found it in need of life—the life that is in the blood. He has detected the inability of spiritual physicians to dispense the very life-blood needed by their patients, those who fill the pews and the corridors of our culture. Dying men and women come to the emergency room of the church in need of trauma specialists. Sweet invites us to go with him on rounds as we hone our skills in dispensing life.
—*Bishop Kenneth C. Ulmer, DMin, PhD, Senior Pastor/Teacher, Faithful Central Bible Church, Los Angeles*

Label this book "O Negative." It is rare and urgently needed. Good for all types.
—*Heather Murray Elkins, Professor of Worship, Preaching, and the Arts, Drew University*

In *Giving Blood*, arguably his most magisterial work, Leonard Sweet keeps one hand on the pulse of the culture, one hand on the heart of ministry, and two eyes on the Great Physician. Drawing from a typically eclectic cavalcade of sources, Sweet has pieced together a master class in twenty-first century homiletics. Along with a winning appeal to preaching that is truly participative, readers will find here many skill-building interactivities and a wealth of sheer artistry that delights and inspires. Any seasoned or would-be homiletician who does not come across something in this book to stir his or her blood had better check their pulse.
—*Alan Rathe, author of (the forthcoming)* Evangelicals, Worship, and Participation: Turn-of-the-Millennium Readings

Len Sweet provides a fresh and much-needed perspective of preaching that goes far beyond the reductionist approaches dominating homiletics today. He helps preachers see and communicate scriptural truths in far more holistic, understandable, memorable, and moving ways. The New Testament shows us that Jesus' own approach to preaching was filled with narrative and metaphor. Sweet taps into long-forgotten, yet indispensable, communication tools and provides a comprehensive manual that is valuable for those starting out in ministry as well as experienced preachers who see the need for a fresh approach to reach today's listeners.

—*Alan Ehler (DMin, George Fox Evangelical Seminary), Dean, College of Christian Ministry and Religion, Southeastern University, Lakeland, Florida*

When I think of my friend Len Sweet, I think of two words: creative and communicator. This book is vintage Len—he is both creative in the way he presents his material and his communication is par excellence. To every preacher and communicator who wants to be more effective, this is the book to read.

—*James Merritt, Lead Pastor at Cross Pointe Church*

Simply put, *Giving Blood* is *the* primer for the art of semiotic preaching and is destined to become a true preaching paradigm shifter.

—*David Wahlstedt, StoryShaper | Crosspointe*

Len Sweet has done it again! *Giving Blood* offers a much-needed transfusion both for those in the pulpit and those in the pew. Len is the Duke Ellington of homileticians: his intricately woven metaphors inspire us away from preaching models that are incompatible with culture and toward the relational, improvisational ones we find Jesus embodying on the pages of the gospels. This kind of preaching offers lifeblood to preachers and their churches. You'll want to read this book—it's good to the last drop!

—*Dr. Jay Richard Akkerman, Professor of Preaching and Pastoral Theology, Northwest Nazarene University, Nampa, Idaho*

Bold and accessible, *Giving Blood* will revitalize pastors and communities suffering the deadly effects of stale preaching and pump new life into the twenty-first century church. Refreshing!

—*Wendy J. Deichmann, PhD, President, United Theological Seminary*

Len Sweet's latest book is an ingenious and insightful look at the process of preaching for a postmodern reality. Preachers of all experience levels will benefit greatly from reading it. Sweet does what he does best—he integrates significant learning for the reader and invites the preacher to try EPIC new things for the twenty-first century. A true red-blooded gem!

— *Dr. Karyn L. Wiseman, author of I* Refuse to Preach a Boring Sermon: Engaging the 21st Century Listener

a fresh paradigm for preaching

GIVING BLOOD

LEONARD SWEET

ZONDERVAN

Giving Blood
Copyright © 2014 by Leonard I. Sweet

This title is also available as a Zondervan ebook. Visit www.zondervan.com/ebooks.

Requests for information should be addressed to:

Zondervan, 3900 *Sparks Dr SE Grand Rapids, Michigan 49546*

Library of Congress Cataloging-in-Publication Data

Sweet, Leonard I.
    Giving blood : a fresh paradigm for preaching / Leonard Sweet.
        pages cm
    Includes bibliographical references.
    ISBN 978-0-310-51545-6 (hardcover) — 1. Preaching. 2. Postmodernism—Religious
aspects—Christianity. 3. Blood—Miscellanea. I. Title.
    BV4211.3.S94 2014
    251—dc23   2013034566

Cover design: Michelle Lenger
Cover photography: Veer; iStock
Interior design: Matthew Van Zomeren & Ben Fetterley

Printed in the United States of America

14 15 16 17 18 /DCI/ 20 19 18 17 16 15 14 13 12 11 10 9 8 7 6 5 4 3 2 1

I dedicate this volume to Ken Ulmer
whose preaching provokes in me dreams
with enough magic
to stir the blood

Contents

Acknowledgments

Everything is flowing—going somewhere, animals and so-called lifeless rocks as well as water. Thus the snow flows fast or slow in grand beauty-making glaciers and avalanches; the air in majestic flood carrying minerals, plant leaves, seeds, spores, with streams of music and fragrance; water streams carrying rocks.... While the stars go streaming through space pulsed on and on forever *like blood* ... in Nature's warm heart.

—John Muir's *Yosemite Journal*, 1872[1]

THE SOUND OF GREAT PREACHING is not applause, but the creaking of doors in heaven and hell, and sometimes even in the back of the church. The dirty little secret of preaching is that people expect to enter heaven every week. The doorway is the sermon, and the preacher buzzes the congregation in.

This book is written for those "called" to do the impossible: make the incredible "good news" credible without losing its incredibleness. In a famous passage from Romans 8,[2] Paul names those "called" the "firstfruits of the Spirit"—people who groan while awaiting the full redemption of their beings. Preaching is the "groanings" of those whose full redemption awaits the fulfillment of their calling. Paul believed he would fall under divine judgment if he did not carry out his "call" to preach: "Woe is me if I do not preach the gospel."[3]

This book is the story of those "groanings." It has gone through the groaning pains of creation as much as any birthing rite. My biggest "groaning" was the metaphor of blood itself. I did everything I could to use another. My preference was a metaphor based on the Greek word for worship, *proskuneo*, which means literally "to kiss toward." The English word "worship" is the shortened form of *worthship*, which means to give worth, a "bowing down." In other words, if worship is bowing down to kiss the earth, preaching is a rising up to kiss the joy as it flies. Every sermon should be as enlivening as fresh air and as passionate as a first kiss.[4]

11

Acknowledgments

But try to escape blood as I might—these pages groaned in disobedience and took longer to come together than any other book I have written. Something kept pulling me back to this biological symbol for life and the organizing symbol of the Christian faith. The metaphor kept me in its grip no matter how hard I tried to wrestle free. What you hold in your hands is my surrender and my limping free of that street fight.

In my struggle with this material, my own blood has been mingled with those of others who have influenced me and nourished me along the way. These blood brothers and sisters include Betty O'Brien, who worked for years on the endnotes and never complained once; Teri Hyrkas, a weekly lay participant in sermons who gave me the best feedback; Lori Wagner, who wouldn't let me leave this book behind and rescued it from oblivion on numerous occasions; my doctoral students in semiotics at Drew University—Zavette Smallwood, Byron Kaiser, Larry Oksten, Nichelle Nelson, Alyvia Rae Smith, Alexander Houston, Roderick Merritt, Thomas Gregg, Paul Hutchison—and at George Fox University—Scott Ness, Norbert Haukenfrers, Robert Parker, David Sebastian, Paula Champion Jones, Kevin Glenn, Daniel Russell, Leonard Calhoun, Timothy Willson, Richard Callahan, Matthew Thomas, Douglas Witherup, Bryce Ashlin-Mayo, Patrick Sehl. There is also a long line of preachers who modeled for me their refusal to become laborers of points rather than painters of pictures and tellers of stories, starting with my preacher mother Mabel Boggs Sweet; my high school pastors Lawrence Snow and Walter J. Whitney; Joe A. Harding, a preacher who never failed to stir my soul; and the American Bible Society's Deputy General Secretary Arthur P. Whitney, who introduced me to the rich preaching tradition of New York City (e.g., Bryant Kirkland, David James Randolph, David H. C. Read, William Sloane Coffin Jr.) while I was researching my doctoral dissertation at the Schomburg Library.

I was taught by the academy that a preacher must refrain from playing on the register of feelings. With an intellectual arsenal second to none at their constant command, Samuel DeWitt Proctor, H. Beecher Hicks Jr., Buster Soares, Otis Moss Sr., Amos Brown, Suzan Johnson Cook, Vashti McKenzie, Cecelia Williams Bryant, Bishop John R. Bryant, Cynthia Hale, Daryl Ward, and Frederick D. Haynes III taught me to listen instead to Ernest Hemingway's call for art to "make people feel something more than they understand."[5]

At the same time, *Giving Blood* is written as an act of praise, a song and a supplication for the lifeblood of the Spirit that grants those "called to preach" the humble grace to claim our birthright as Christ-bearers. It was said that in Winston Churchill's World War II speeches, he "marched the English

12

Acknowledgments

language into battle." William Quick, friend and master pulpiteer, taught me that a preacher's speeches do something far more important: they march the body of Christ into mission and ministry. Thanks for teaching me, Bill, that only our "calling" enables us to proclaim the Word with undivided powers and undiminished strength.

My current colleagues Donald Hilliard Jr., Kirbyjon Caldwell, Alan Ehler, Gary Simpson, Dale Keller, Heather Elkins, Jay Akkerman, Claybon Lea Jr., and Ken Ulmer remind me that our songs are never solos. Paul's *omnia in bonum* is a reminder that preaching is never a game of solitaire but a multiplayer game—or better yet, a song around the campfire. We may begin the song, but it is the voices of the many who give it beauty, power, and harmony. Like Jesus' parable of the mustard seed, a good song will spread like vines, enlivening everyone who accepts its invitation to join the chorus. I thank a long line of unheralded, unnamed camp-meeting preachers who have taught me over the years that loving God means most importantly sharing the indwelling Christ, the life source that energizes you, with others until everyone around you is singing their combined songs of praise.

The founder of my tribe, John Wesley, in his sermon on "What Is Man," describes human beings as filled with arteries and veins that circulate blood through the body. Wesley, in his attempt to describe what pumps the blood through the body, says that a vital fire is mingled with the blood, a fireball of spirit, without which no life could be possible.[6] One of the most Wesleyan creatures I've ever known, the late Steve Sallee, showcased every week at Cokesbury United Methodist Church (Knoxville) that no great sermon could be given or constructed without the fire of the Holy Spirit. The Holy Spirit of Christ gives us the life source that quickens our creativity and activates the connections to God and to each other, which make possible acts of creation. In the missional art of preaching, we encounter God. What begins as one act of giving blood soon becomes a blood stream, allowing the body of Christ to become alive and vital.

A teacher correcting examination papers received from one candidate a sheet of paper that was blank except for the words "*Macbeth* Acts 2 Scene 5 Line 28." He could hardly contain his curiosity, so he went to the library, found the collected works of Shakespeare, looked up the reference to *Macbeth*, and found that the line read: "I cannot do this bloody thing."

Every preacher feels the same way. And everyone who has ever attempted to write a book on preaching has felt this doubly, quadruply, or more. What kept me writing in the midst of feelings both of humility and futility was this: if God calls you to do something, like preach or write, you must have the courage to do it badly, even when you can't do it well. But there is no excuse for not doing it as well as you can do it. Besides, we have the apostle Paul as a model: "Pray also for me, that whenever I speak, words may be given me so that I fearlessly make known the mystery of the gospel, for which I am an ambassador in chains. Pray that I may declare it fearlessly, as I should."[7]

Introduction

"The Blood Will Be a Sign for You"[1]

> I give you this charge: Preach the word; be prepared in season and out of season; correct, rebuke and encourage—with great patience and careful instruction.
>
> —2 Timothy 4:1–2

SIGNING UP TO GIVE BLOOD is our license to preach.

I cut my homiletic teeth on two literary giants—the liberal Presbyterian Frederick Buechner and the evangelical Baptist Calvin Miller. In my mind, they were the two master wordsmiths of the pulpit in the last half of the twentieth century. They modeled for me the art of great preaching, which brings together first and last things, which explores life and death in the common places of human life, which shows the dusting and washing side of love as well as entering the holy of holies of sacrifice, which sets memory against time, which showcases the strangeness of evil and the even greater strangeness of grace.

On July 22, 2012, Calvin Miller preached his last sermon at First Baptist Fort Lauderdale as part of a summer preaching series.[2] A month later, he would hand his life over to the Gracious Mystery. Ironically, Calvin began his last sermon quoting Buechner on the story of Buechner's daughter's illness. According to Miller, Buechner confessed that during the time his daughter was in the hospital with feeding tubes in her stomach, the Buechners didn't go to church to find someone to tell them what happened to the Hittites, or who could parse Greek and Hebrew phrases, or who could give them the best three points. They said, "We wanted to find someone who would stand up there and bleed with us."

"Bleed with us."

Jesus preached only one sermon in his lifetime—the Sermon on the Mount—and it began with the word *blessed*. *Blessed* is from the Old English word *bledsian* or the Proto-Germanic word *blodison*. Both these words come from the root word *blod*, from which we get our word *blood*. Blessing involves

15

blood. No blood, no blessing. To drink blood or to have blood poured over you was to be blessed by whatever it was the blood came from.

The most famous journalism saying of all time is "If it bleeds, it leads." Ironically, bleeding has not been leading in the church. The Beverly Sills of homileticians, Fleming Rutledge, was invited to preach at an Episcopal church in suburban Connecticut on Good Friday. When Dr. Rutledge was greeted by the rector, the first words out of his mouth were, "I hope you're not going to say anything about the blood."[3]

My preacher mom, Mabel Boggs Sweet (licensed to preach in the Pilgrim Holiness Church), defined a bad sermon as one with no blood on the pulpit. "There's no blood on the pulpit this morning," she would mutter to herself, sometimes in the midst of the sermon being delivered.

It is hard not to say anything about the blood when a preacher is someone who gives the blood of Christ to the body of Christ. It is hard not to talk about the blood when the primary colors of a Christian are red and white, as the blood of the Lamb dyes our souls white as snow. It is hard not to speak of blood when it is the magical fluid that courses through every cell of your body, the scarlet thread that weaves together every warp and woof of the Bible. Take away the blood from your brain and you pass out. Take away the blood from your lungs and your body can't get oxygen. Freeze the blood in your feet and you get gangrene and your toes fall off. Take away the blood from the Scriptures and they stop breathing.

At the same time we have declared a moratorium on speaking about blood in church, the culture is drenched in blood. After eight years without producing a novel, Tom Wolfe reemerged on the scene with *Back to Blood* (2012). Gore-steeped gothic films have become a genre of their own with a flourishing academic industry built around them.[4] Of course, the House of Horrors has always been the most visited part of Madame Tussauds Wax Museum. But this culture revels in blood like a waving flag. We can't imagine a heaven not tinged with Hitchcock.

The August 18, 2010, cover of *Rolling Stone* magazine featured a bloody mess—and it was a huge hit, creating a big stir, selling lots of copies. Wearing nothing but dripping, smeared, puddling blood, the three young stars of *True Blood* posed in all their fresh and fleshy bloodiness.[5] *True Blood* is only one of a bumper crop of teenage vampire soap operas. Anne Rice sold 80 million copies of her Vampire Chronicles to boomers and Gen Xers in the late 1970s, '80s, and '90s. But the first decade of the twenty-first century belonged to Stephanie Meyer, whose red-hot Twilight series reignited vampire mania among newer generations, especially those twenty and under. The bloodthirsty, blood-sucking "undead" have become the darlings of young adults everywhere. Vampires aren't creepy; they're cool. Or in the bad-is-good

Introduction

language of pop culture, *Vampires Suck* (another movie). In fact—as mere mortals in all these "love stories" come to believe—vampires are "to die for." But wait a minute: it is not just Vampirism that is alive and well.

The ancient religion of Mithraism that competed with Christianity in the first four centuries also celebrated initiates with blood. The original "blood bath" was a sacred ritual in the Mithras cult, whose elevated god was symbolized by the bull. New initiates into the Mithras cult would stand under the neck of the bull as it was sacrificed. When the animal's neck was cut, the "newborn" member of the cult would be baptized in the lifeblood of the bull as it poured out. In Mithraism, you were washed in the blood of the bull.

Mithraism is still alive and well—on Wall Street. Like Vampirists, Mithraists also sacrifice everything on the altar. But the Mithraic worship of Wall Street is not the bull, but the bull market. We will give up everything for fortune, for fame, for success. In this consumer culture, where we buy our way into the salvation of brands and experiences, we get drenched in the blood of the bull all the time. Putting the two bulls of Vampirism and Mithraism into the pen of today's TGIF (Twitter, Google, Instagram, Facebook) culture together is like putting two bulls into a pen with a cow in heat.

★   ★   ★

"The People's flag is deepest red...."
—Socialist hymn (1899)

"Are you washed in the blood of the Lamb?"
—Christian hymn (1878)[6]

★   ★   ★

You can't escape getting washed in the blood of something. The only question is whether that something will be the blood of bulls, the blood of vampires, or the blood of the Lamb. Every congregation wants its pound of pure flesh. Every congregation is owed its drop of true blood.

Preachers bleed the love of God. Jesus warned his disciples that to journey with him meant carrying the bloody cross every step of the way. This applies most of all to preachers. Ever since that first gospel sermon was preached by Peter (standing "with the Eleven") after Pentecost,[7] to follow Jesus into the preaching life has meant a willingness to sacrifice even life itself for the sake of the gospel.

To participate in the new covenant, Jesus said, we must drink his blood.[8] In Scripture a covenant is always "cut,"[9] that is, a cutting or a sacrifice is involved in the making of a covenant. That is why when Jesus inaugurated the new covenant after his last Passover with the disciples, he said, "This is

Introduction

My blood of the new covenant, which is shed for many for the remission of sins."[10] In the Eucharist, the history of redemption is told in the language of life, which is the language of flesh and blood: "Whoever eats my flesh and drinks my blood remains in me, and I in them."[11]

The sacrifice for sin has been made "once for all."[12] The Lamb has been slain. "Lamb" is a favorite symbol of Christ in the book of Revelation, where Christ is called "Lamb" twenty-eight times. In the eternal purposes of God, Christ was "the lamb who was slain from the creation of the world."[13] A lamb was cut in the legal covenants of the First Testament, and the first sacrifice ever offered by a human was a lamb.[14] Foreshadowing Christ's sacrifice, a lamb was used in the Passover,[15] and lambs were used in the daily sacrifices of the tabernacle[16] among other sacrifices.[17]

Christ was also called a Lamb in Old Testament prophecy — "He was led like a lamb to the slaughter."[18] And in the New Testament, Philip confirms that Jesus is the fulfillment of that prophecy when he finds an Ethiopian eunuch reading Isaiah's words: "He was led like a sheep to the slaughter, and as a lamb before its shearer is silent, so he did not open his mouth."[19] John the Baptist called Jesus a sacrificial lamb, exclaiming, "Look, the Lamb of God, who takes away the sin of the world!"[20]

The slaying of the Lamb of God was once for all. Jesus spelled the end of animal sacrifice. Rather than the blood of animals, the wine of communion with Christ is the "blood of grapes" treaded out. When Jesus, the Lamb of God, offered himself as the final and complete sacrifice for the sins of the world, his gift to us was eternal life. Jesus banished the need for bloodletting by breaking the power of death. The gift on the other side of the cross is eternal life. Eternal life does not feed off lifeblood; it is the lifeblood of God.

Through Christ, the new lifeblood of all his disciples is love.

The ultimate question every preacher asks is this: So what will it be?

Will you be washed in the blood of bulls?

Will you be washed in the blood of vampires?

Or, will you be washed in the blood of the Lamb?

Only the blood of the Lamb is true blood.

Worship is a communal feast, and wherever we worship is "a banquet hall"[21] that hosts celebratory responses to a God-initiated relationship and a manifestation of a living relationship with Christ. The sermon is the wine of worship.

Preaching is the discipline and craft of turning water into Cana wine[22] and decanting the old, aged-to-perfection Jesus wine into new bottles. Preaching is the primary means whereby the miracle of Cana continues, as Jesus turns our life from water — tasteless, colorless, odorless — into homemade vintage wine, known for its vibrant flavor, vivid sparkle, and alluring aroma.

18

Part 1

INTRODUCTORY WORDS FROM THE LAB

Chapter 1

Under the Microscope: Preaching in a Google World

PREACHING IS A SACRIFICIAL ACT. America's greatest choral conductor, Robert Shaw (d. 1999), liked to tell his musicians that every note they sang was a drop of their blood. Singing, he claimed, is shedding blood. The one whom critics call "the greatest live performer of all time," Judy Garland, called it "giving blood."

On April 23, 1961, 3,100 people packed Carnegie Hall to be a part of what is now known as "the greatest concert ever given." Among those present for "Judy Garland at Carnegie Hall" were Carol Channing, Rock Hudson, Spencer Tracy, Hedda Hopper, Henry Fonda, and Julie Andrews. Everyone present adored Garland for her belting voice and moving performances. Everyone knew that each evening on stage Garland would sing until exhausted and depleted. Everyone knew this artist never sang the same song the same way, not even her signature songs "Stormy Weather" or "Over the Rainbow." Everyone knew "Hurricane Judy" believed she owed everything she had to her every audience.

Capitol Records captured the evening's twenty-six songs live, an album that received five Grammy awards. But just before walking out on stage, the superstitious Garland ritually repeated to herself, and anyone else within earshot, an unusual charge. It was not the time-honored "Break a leg." Rather, it was this: "Time to give blood."

Give blood she did. With every song she sang, she offered her fans a fleck

21

of her flesh, an intimate piece of her life. Her authenticity was as transparent and fragile as Cinderella's glass slipper.

In preaching, each speech act must be a baring and bearing of the story of Jesus in what is less a performance art than a participation art. Preaching today takes place without audiences, only with participants and partners. Giving blood is not a matter of donor and recipient but of donor and participant. Of course, participation art can become performance art. When that happens, preaching moves from being a relational discipline and craft and becomes merely a solitary performance.

True participation is not just meeting another Christ follower but is becoming Christ for the other. Self-sacrificial participation vivifies the body with the blood of revelatory story and sacramental embodiment of the living Christ. Giving blood serves as a means of grace for a body in need of continuous transfusions of the Holy Spirit. A movable feast (there are no chairs at the Lord's Table: the posture of faith is not sitting but walking toward, kneeling down, standing up), a sermon that makes the body "so happy" that "I can't sit down," is both artisan bred and Christ bread. Sacrificial and sacred, incarnational and iconic, the sermon is born of death and rises resurrected to whisper "Christ in you" to a community of faith.

Sermons that point to Christ through stories and images make use of "semiotics." Semiotics is best defined as the ability to read and convey "signs," where a "sign" (be it an image, gesture, sound, object, or word) is something that stands for something else.[1] Semiotics is about pointers, not points. You can't point to Jesus if you're trying to make Jesus fit your point. Semiotics is important because it's the language of the human body. When asleep, and your body needs to tell you it's time for a bio break, how does it communicate that to you? You dream of water. Even in your state of sleep, you "read the signs" and interpret the "sign" of water, wake up, and head for the bathroom.

A semiotic sermon reads the signs of what God is up to in the world, connects those signs in people's lives with the Jesus story, and then communicates the gospel by connecting people in relationship to Jesus through stories, images, and gestures. A semiotic sermon is a search for that holy grail receptacle that conveys Christ's incarnational presence from giver to receiver. And every preacher knows how often that semiotic receptacle can feel just as elusive and unobtainable as the Holy Grail itself.

Before we can offer a sermon that bleeds, we need to prepare our blood in the lab. This book invites you into a homiletics lab where you can experiment with a new paradigm for preaching called "semiotic preaching." The semiotic method connects biblical narratives to indigenous cultural landscapes and their native languages of signs and symbols. Semiotic preaching differs from traditional sermon building in its insistence on seeing the sermon itself as an incarnational medium. Traditional textual exegesis is based on mining the ore of words to excavate the gems of "biblical principles," a biblical panning for nuggets of wisdom in one massive stream of words. Biblical semiotics, by contrast, is a form of spelunking the Scriptures while surfing the Spirit for resonant images and stories by which to live and for which to die in Christ. Semiotic preaching is as much liturgical as it is exegetical. Are words the best conveyers of the divine? Or are experiences, intuitions, emotions, images, and stories more reliable and memorable? For Jesus, parables were the most trust-worthy purveyors of truth. Semiotic preaching, really a new form of expository preaching, seeks to reconnect us with the stories, images, relationality, and resonance of the Scriptures as they were told, written, and intended to be received. In semiotic preaching, we return to the roots of our faith and to a method of conveying truth favored by Jesus himself.

*　　*　　*

"The time when people could be told everything by means of words, whether theological or pious, is over."
—*Dietrich Bonhoeffer*[2]

*　　*　　*

In the creative space of the "lab," this book serves to heighten and hone the preacher's semiotic skills and then to show how to use those skills to build identity from narrative and metaphor and to cultivate what I like to call an EPIC style—an experiential medium (E) that allows for participatory engagement (P) with biblical images and stories (I) that connect the congregation with what Christ is already doing in their midst (C). In the course of our lab time, I will also introduce you to what I call the *transductive* or *transincarnational* method of preaching truth, a missional mode of preaching that acts as a "means of grace," connecting people relationally to Christ on a level that encourages not just passive reception but active incarnation of the heart and spirit of Christ. Transincarnational (transductive) preaching is preaching that mediates the revelatory power of the Holy Spirit; it points to God in the midst of the congregation, in the midst of lives. Semiotic exegesis, EPIC delivery, and a transincarnational theology of relational "knowing" create a kind of preaching that engages and changes lives.

Lifeway Research conducted a study of seven thousand churches under the supervision of Ed Stetzer and Thom Rainer. One of the most surprising findings? Passivity reigns. The majority of people in the majority of churches are not engaged in any significant ministry or mission. Christians have become passive spectators in worship rather than active participants. By and large, we come to church to "watch the show" rather than to engage and participate. We consume a service rather than serve Jesus in his mission in the world.[3] If we want to engage Christians as participants in worship, sermons fit for the twenty-first century must offer more meat on their bones and blood in their veins than higher criticism's word-based exegesis has allowed for.

★　★　★

"Do you rest each moment in the Crucified?
Are you washed in the blood of the Lamb?"
—*Elisha A. Hoffman*[4]

★　★　★

Why "Giving Blood"? The metaphor of blood is not politically correct, even though we live in a world where some of the great diseases of the day are blood disorders and the most dangerous animals on the planet are blood-sucking insects.[5] Indeed, blood is a fluid that makes us shudder. When was the last time you sang "Washed in the Blood of Jesus" or "There Is a Fountain Filled with Blood," or "There Is Power in the Blood" in one of your services? Whenever someone protests my use of blood language, I can't help but think of Heinrich Himmler, the officer in charge of the Nazi death camps, who fainted dead away at the sight of real blood.

Yet to be squeamish about blood is to develop an aversion to our own life source. Even more, blood symbolism is central to the Christian faith. In our banning of the blood, we've lost the theological power that allows us to revel, awestruck, in the salvific mystery of Christ's blood shed on the cross, the remaking and restoration of the "human" in baptism, and the sacramental presence of Christ's body and blood.

Christianity is a revolutionary faith, but it's not a bloodless revolution. The church's century-long experiment in a bloodless Christianity has left the body of Christ plasticized and ossified, a fossil of its former self. A living faith requires a healthy circulation of the blood of God's creating, redeeming, and sustaining covenant for the world. The mystery of life in Christ is both corporeal and *corporal*.[6] From trough to cross, the blood of the covenant is the life source that ensures our resurrection hope.

The ecclesial organism called "church" is a body with blood coursing through its veins—a dynamic and holistic life force that flows with multiple coordinated interrelationships. What gives the body life is the constant nourishment of the Word of God, the Spirit of life that breathes dynamically through its mind and members, imparted through the blood of Christ.

The church's failure to tell stories in a culture that talks in stories is a story in and of itself. But stories and images are more than just tools and techniques for communicating in today's TGIF (Twitter, Google, Instagram, Facebook) culture. They have become the very essence of communication itself. Stories are the lifeblood of the body, and the blood of Jesus is the Life of all life, the Story of all stories. To be "washed in the blood" is to be bathed in the stories of Jesus' missional beauty, relational truth, and incarnational goodness. If you cut preachers, they bleed the Scriptures, and their bloodletting is healing, a balsam of the body, a balm of the soul.

*   *   *

"Love is that liquor sweet and most divine,
Which my God feels as Blood; but I, as Wine."
—*George Herbert (1593–1633), Welsh poet and Anglican priest*[7]

*   *   *

I can think of no better definition of preaching than "giving blood." Of the three traditional ways of making a living—mud, blood, and grease—preaching involves all three: the mud pies of creativity, the blood bank of living in the Word, and the grease pit of hard work and dirty hands. But of the three, giving blood is the defining metaphor. The blood of Christ is the prime bearer of the gospel's message and meaning. Or to adapt for the preacher what Red Smith, the premier sportswriter of the twentieth century, used to say about writing: "[It's easy:] all you do is sit down and open a vein and bleed it out drop by drop."[8]

If blood is the liquid bearer of incarnational life, preachers are homiletic hemophiliacs, hereditary bleeders of the Word. If you've never bled, you have no material for preaching. If when you're finished preaching you're not finished, spent, wiped out—if you haven't "given blood"—you haven't really preached.[9]

George Bernard Shaw was a critic of the church all of his life. Perhaps his most insightful criticism was about preaching: "Some is like coffee, stimulates but does not nourish; some is like wine, has sparkle but no lasting value; some is like seltzer water, a big fuss over nothing; some is like spring water—good but hard to get."[10] I would say preaching is like giving blood, the transfusion of Christ's resurrection power into the body of the Church. Without the giving-blood preaching that brings together body and spirit, the body is only "dem dry bones."

Preaching is both discipline and craft. Semiotic preaching seeks to revive the art and craft of the potter. Creativity and practice must play together in the mud, sometimes for many hours, before an image or metaphor (or the combined form of image and story that I will define later in the book as a "narraphor") emerges from the clay to reveal the incarnational Word of Christ. In the craft of pottery making, often colored dyes, sands, or stains are added to the clay. When the pottery is baked or glazed, the colors will "bleed" or ooze out of the clay to form beautiful and unique designs. Each pot becomes a unique piece.[11] The better the bleeding, the more dynamic the experience of the pottery medium. In similar fashion, a semiotic sermon does more than hold water: it bleeds Jesus.

Yet pottery is not designed merely to sit on a shelf or to be admired from afar. A Jesus vessel is an everyday, down-to-earth, meant-to-be-used-by-all kind of vessel — for nourishment as well as for beauty. Each clay piece baked in the lab is only as powerful as the participants who hold it in their hands, feel its character, recognize its defects, celebrate its color, mete out its message.

Artists say that art delivers an experience in multiple dimensions to its receiver in a way that no mere words can do. The semiotic sermon, as potter's clay, hands over the body and blood of Christ for others to partake of. Preaching is an imaginative and participatory medium — only powerful when dynamically and tactually experienced. A gifted pianist doesn't practice hours per day only to play music for herself. She presents the fruit of her prodigy as a gift to her listeners. Hours and hours of preparation and play yield a brilliant, revelatory, uplifting experience that touches the soul. Semiotic preaching must also be EPIC preaching — each sermon an experience of God that is image rich, participatory, and connectional. Each moment, a life-giving, Christ-infusing beat of the heart of God in the body that is the church.

* * *

"We are standing on the brink of a mind makeover more cataclysmic than anything in our history."
—*Susan Greenfield[12]*

* * *

Preaching today takes place while driving the sharp bends of history. It is an exhilarating experience but not one for status-quo steering or faint-of-heart turning. Anyone who isn't confused doesn't understand what's going on. Social media has replaced print as the dominant communication choice. The nature of the presumed contract between preacher and people has changed. Even at concerts, people expect participation, not mere performance. Metallica starts out its concerts with a mantra: "There are four of us up here. The fifth member of Metallica is out there. You know that."[13] Television shows revolve around "real-life" nonprofessionals and invite audience interaction.

Cultural critic Seth Godin says that the average person is exposed to three thousand ad messages a day.[14] Each of these ads is a sermon in disguise. Messages bombard us in more channels and frequencies than Girl Scouts have cookies. White noise emits everywhere. In such a noisy world, preachers need to preach a sermon that can talk, walk, shake hands, and invite someone to dance.

Semiotic preachers in our current culture need EPIC blood to surge in their veins, not printer's ink. While traditional preaching still echoes a "smash the icons" Gutenberg mentality that privileges words, points, and principles over images and stories, images are the bread and butter of semiotic preaching. Part of creating an EPIC sermon is dynamically and relationally to introduce metaphors, images, and stories (narraphors) that "make the familiar strange," that catapult the participant into a realm of the unexpected, unusual, and mysterious. A great metaphor takes a familiar image and gives it a twist in order to introduce an unfamiliar vision. Great metaphors or narraphors (extended metaphors) made EPIC take a semiotic sermon and make it accessible and powerful.

Semiotic preaching revels in the mystery of life itself. It reveals truth in all of its beauty. It invites all to the table to follow Jesus where he will take us—into new places, uncharted territory, unfamiliar landscapes. It doesn't seek to nail down, firm up, work out, or objectify the Bread of Life. It serves the Bread of Life piping hot, fresh from the ovens of suffering and sorrow, joy, and celebration. It celebrates the leaven that is faith, the mystery that is Christ. Only through images, metaphors, and stories (narraphors) can profound truths be understood or conveyed to others. Philosophy may be the language of the mind, but narraphor is the talk of the soul, the music of the heart, the stuff of memory, dreams, and faith.

If you've taken a course in preaching, you've no doubt learned a method of doing exegesis that examines the text, looks for context, searches the words, and lines up authorities with insight into the meaning of the verses. But the Bible was never written in verses. Jesus never taught in points, whether three, five, or ninety-five. Jesus wasn't known for touting propositions or praised for the clarity of his teachings. Jesus wasn't known for his well-prepared lesson plans, or for having disciples who could pass quizzes on his parables. Jesus was best known as a master of metaphor, a legendary storyteller, and a powerful healer who communicated in signs, images, and gestures. Therefore, to understand Jesus and the Scriptures, we need to train ourselves and others not to exegete more words but to exegete images. The semiotic sermon is the art of exegeting not the words and principles, but the images, metaphors, and stories (narraphors) of Scripture.

Jewish traditions had a way of finding meaning on four levels.[15] The first was the *peshat*, the literal and simple understanding of Scripture as found in the Mishnah (the oral interpretations of the Torah and Writings). The second was the *remez*, the more complex typological meaning, represented by the studies of well-known rabbis in the Talmud or gemara. The third was the *derash*, the metaphoric or parabolic meaning and in-depth exegesis associated with the studies of the midrash. The *sod* was the fourth and deepest level of meaning. The most spiritual in nature, it contained the very secrets of Truth itself, requiring intuitive and creative interpretation. The meanings of metaphors, parables, and mysteries had to be discerned and understood in levels that would touch the innermost reaches of one's mind and heart, as much transformational as informational. Not everyone had the depth of discernment needed to reach the levels of meaning denoted by the *sod*. But if you did, that experience could confront and challenge the very foundations of your soul, similar to the experience of meeting God face-to-face within the space of the *shekinah*.

Jesus was the world master at parables, stories, metaphors, and images. "That's why I tell stories," Jesus said: "to *nudge* the people toward receptive insight."[16] He spoke in different ways to different audiences. To some he spoke in images. To others, in parable and story. He took his disciples aside and removed for them the secret coverings of some stories and parables. As disciples of Jesus, we need to enter into the stories and images of Jesus, to "dig in" and "dig down" into the levels of meaning Jesus portrayed to his most trusted disciples. Semiotic preaching is a new form of biblical preaching, but what is being exegeted are age-old stories and images, or what we might call "narraphors" — narrative metaphor.

To preach with narraphor is to practice discernment, looking for meaning in everything you see. Therefore, I invite you to enter into the homiletic blood lab — to explore this new concept of preaching with narraphors. To get started, I'd like to immerse you in the elements of narraphor firsthand. Let's take a look under the homiletic microscope.

We begin with two slides: an image and a story.

Slide A—The Image
"A Pelican's Love Feast": A Semiotic Exegesis of a Metaphor

The image of the pelican in Christian art, sometimes called "Pelican in Its Piety," appears everywhere in the late Middle Ages—in paintings, icons, drawings, misericords, altar cloths, and stained glass.[17] The image is based on a legend of the pelican sacrificing itself for the sake of its children. It's a legend that predates Christianity, but early Christian writers linked the story of the pelican to the sacrifice of Jesus on the cross and his continued nourishment of his "little ones." The image of the bird plucking its breast and spilling blood for its young reminded Christians visually of Christ's love, devotion, and sacrifice for all people.

Several medieval writers used the pelican as a literary metaphor as well—an image in words. Lyricist Master Konrad von Würzburg (thirteenth century) referred to the legend of the pelican (*der vogel Pellikan*) in a German poem.[18] Dante mentioned the *nostro pellicano* as an allusion to Christ in his *Divine Comedy* (*Inferno* 25).[19] Thomas Aquinas also used the symbol of the pelican to refer to Christ in his *"Adoro Te"*: "Pelican of Mercy . . . / Cleanse me, wretched sinner, in Thy Precious Blood."[20] Catholic mystic St. Gertrude of Helfta wrote that she saw Christ in a vision in the image of a pelican.[21] St. Augustine referred to the pelican fable in his commentary on Psalm 102:6: "I am like a pelican of the wilderness": "These birds are said to slay their young with blows of their beaks, and for three days to mourn them when slain by themselves in the nest: after which they say the mother wounds herself deeply and pours forth her blood over her young, bathed in which they recover life."[22]

The pelican legend in the Christian retelling comes from a second-century adaptation of animal legends found in the *Physiologus*.[23] According to the legend, young pelicans flap their wings heftily at their parents so that the father (sometimes noted as both parents), in anger, kills the pelican children. After seeing that they have died, the mother (though sometimes indicated as the father) then pierces her breast so that her blood flows upon them, and she revives the young pelicans with her lifeblood. Popular medieval bestiaries record not the flapping but the pecking of the children at the parent bird. In medieval texts, the piercing of the pelican's breast is called "vulning" (related to our word *vulnerable*).[24] In some illustrations, both blood and water are depicted, in harmony with the crucifixion account.[25] Other mentions of the pelican include Pliny the Elder (*Natural History*), Isidore of Seville (*Etymologies*), Guillaume le Clerc (*Bestiaire*), and Bartholomaeus Anglicus (*De proprietatibus rerum*). All of the medieval bestiaries mention the pelican not only in a descriptive sense but as a metaphor to symbolize Christ.[26] In the medieval mind, the natural world was filled with signs and symbols that pointed to Christ's work of salvation. Hence the pelican is often depicted with other animals symbolizing Christ, such as the phoenix, the lion, and the eagle.

The later Christian adaptation of the pelican legend often leaves out the death of the pelicans, focusing on the nourishment of the young by the mother's blood. One reference speaks of the mother pelican nourishing her children with her blood in a time of famine. For most medieval Christians, the doctrine of the atonement and the liturgy of Communion were conceived and conveyed through the pelican image. In the latter Middle Ages, this image would become an official icon, a symbol for the Holy Eucharist and the spiritual nourishment of the sacrament. The Redeemer's shedding of blood to revive us was a theme popular not only in medieval art and literature but in many of the icons of the church.

Additionally, the fable's images of death and resurrection echoed Christ's act of sacrificial grace. As the pelican is known to be extremely devoted to its children, so is Christ's life-sustaining blood a symbol of God's abounding grace and love.[27] To "love like a pelican" came to be seen as the deepest love possible. Although humanity struck at God in sin, Christ's death on the cross revives us to new life.

The image of the pelican is not only a Catholic image, but it is also a universal reminder of the love of Christ and human reconciliation to God. The "gift of blood" is an incarnational, relational, and missional exchange. The church is the *corpus Christi*, the sacramental image of Christ in the world. The sign of the pelican signifies the church as a nurturing giver of life to the congregation and of love to the world. Just as the community of Christ receives the ultimate gift of life from the Creator, so also must those children grow up themselves to become givers of life. The pelican gives life so that life can be passed on. Biblical themes of lineage, covenant, flesh, and embodiment all flow together in the early image of the pelican's tale.

The metaphor of "giving blood" carries with it powerful stories of sacrificial love and selfless living. In the pelican's fabled act of boundless love for her children, she not only loses all thought of her own welfare; she loses herself in others. She embodies the formation within herself of a new image, just as Jesus followers embody in ourselves a new image, a new manifestation of God's covenant of *imago dei* in the human spirit. In the ultimate act of transformation, pelican piety takes on a new identity—from female pelican to parent, from simple symbol to complex metaphor and image of Christ, from hungry pelican to sacred purveyor of the love feast of creative redemption.

Slide B—The Story
"You Can't Squeeze Blood from a Stone": A Narrative
The Inspirational Story of Ken Medema and Briar Patch Music

Introductory Words from the Lab

When Ken Medema decides to tell a story, everybody listens, because Ken's stories are everybody's stories. Ken doesn't just tell them; he sings them. He sings them from the heart—straight from the briar ("br'er") patch.

If you're a fan of Uncle Remus tales, you may know the story of Br'er Rabbit and Br'er Fox. If you don't know the story or you've forgotten it, let me tell you briefly how it goes.

Ol' Br'er Fox always had it in his mind to make a stew out of Br'er Rabbit. Now, br'er means briar, as in "briar patch," a prickly field of thorns, but it also can mean brother. I'll let you decide if both meanings can apply to our tale today. But back now to the story. Anyway, try as he might, Br'er Fox could never quite catch Br'er Rabbit. The two were a match of equal wits. So when Br'er Rabbit is finally caught, he begs Br'er Fox to do anything—anything at all—except throw him into the dreaded Br'er Patch. But you see, Br'er Rabbit's plea is an act of pure genius, because that's exactly what Br'er Rabbit wants Br'er Fox to do. Br'er Fox, thinking he is dooming Br'er Rabbit to pain and suffering, tosses him gleefully long and far into the briar patch—where Br'er Rabbit quickly makes his escape. Br'er Rabbit has triumphed again. He has tricked Br'er Fox into returning him to his native home.

Often, the places and situations that seem most unlikely to us are exactly where we find God taking up residence. Jesus lived a very thorny life, and when we missionally take up the cross with Jesus, we follow him into some very thorny thickets. When Ken Medema launched his music company, Briar Patch Music, he intentionally named it after Br'er Rabbit's home. In Medema's own words, "Brer Rabbit lived in a place not comfortable for anyone else … and we have decided to follow him there."[28] And follow him he did.

Ken was born in Michigan in 1943 with extremely limited sight. He can distinguish only between light and dark and can see fuzzy outlines of large objects. That's it. Not readily accepted as a "normal" child by others, he spent much of his time alone and learned to lean on music for consolation and creativity. Ken learned to play piano by Braille and soon by ear. He also had a teacher who taught him how to improvise to any style of music.

After studying music therapy and working at a psychiatric hospital in New Jersey, Ken realized that he could help people by writing songs about their lives. In 1973 he began a career as a performing and recording artist, and in 1985 founded Briar Patch Music. "Briar Patch creates musical expressions that celebrate all aspects of the human experience, with an emphasis on spirituality and such universal concerns as peace, justice, and the environment," says Medema.[29]

Ken's music is story, homiletic, humor, and theology. From classical to rock, ballads to blues, sacred to profane, Ken is "always searching for ways in which people can connect to each other, enabling them to sense the sacred within themselves and in surprising places."[30] Without his eyes, Ken "sees" in ways and with insights that allow him to grasp the story within a message or person as well as the shared stories of congregations. What really sets Ken apart, however, is that he understands that for people to see Christ within any context, they must participate and become part of that message. They must embody the music, and the music must incarnate Jesus for them. Using his spellbinding skills in story composition and spontaneous improvisation, Ken Medema literally creates on-the-spot songs that narrate a person's dreams, desires, and most sensitive faith-filled stories. He takes a personal story and creates around it a faith experience that is embodied, ritualized, and customized. Personal experiences become community experiences, as those stories are sung and celebrated within the body of Christ.

Ken Medema is my favorite *preacher*. Oh, I know Medema is a musician and a poet—an artist of Jesus' presence in the world. But through the gift of musical storytelling, Ken links people's lives to biblical faith and inspires them in the way of Christ. He is one of the first "preachers" to understand the EPIC shift of our digital culture and to successfully transition his "preaching" (aka "concerts") from performance art to participation art.

Ken preaches by conducting a concert of participation art. Ken will begin with a song and story from his own life then link that song and story to a biblical passage and image. In one instance I personally witnessed, for example, Ken shared a time in his life when he felt God's hand on his shoulder like David did when he shunned Saul's armor for a sling. Ken asked everyone present to think back on their own lives when they may have felt the weight of some divine touch and anointing. Then he asked people to come to the microphones scattered throughout the auditorium and tell their story of when God touched them in a transformational way for mission in the world. I will never forget my amazement as hundreds of people filed out of their seats to form lines behind the microphones to tell their story. After each personal storytelling, Ken sang an original song that captured that person's witness, which became a gift to them at the end of the concert. He can do this for hours, and I have seen concerts go on long after more traditional "performers" would have left the stage, with no one leaving and everyone clamoring for more. I have also seen Ken Medema wrap a church in a patchwork quilt of songs that showcased its uniqueness and singularity. When stories of a community turn to songs, the symphony that is created is unlike any other witness—a true Ebenezer moment.[31]

Ken sees himself first and foremost not as a musician but as a story catcher, story builder, and storyteller.[32] When Ken Medema makes music, he is not just evoking emotion but playing, as he says, with a hermeneutic—creating a theological statement or sermon in song that serves the direction of discipleship. He is more interested in making music for the current moment and the pressing needs of those present than in playing and replaying a repertoire of compositions created to address his own needs. Medema strives to play music in the "mother tongue" of each congregation, which varies according to anything from geography to theology.[33] So his first task as a missional musician is to learn the language of each community to which he has been called. Most of all, Ken Medema believes that God can be found in every venue, whether labeled sacred or secular. Indeed, the gospel can be heard sometimes in the most unusual and unexpected of places. One has to be ready to improvise, to bring out that gospel moment within a space of time and place of service and to call attention to that divine moment within the lives of people—to help people tell the story of Christ within the stories of their lives.

For Ken Medema every concert is an original, organic composition from the ground up. To make up the music as he goes along is an expression of his creativity and trust. With his incredible gift, Medema most often highlights the presence of Christ in the uncomfortable places in people's lives. Most of all, he embodies the image of Christ in his own personal journey. Some people have viewed the traditional and beloved songs and hymns of the church as the stones in the mortar of faith. I rather like to think of Ken's songs, not as those stones, but as vinesongs: the truth of the vine in song. Ken Medema is the voice from the briar patch. He sings the victory of Christ over all that is patchy and thorny, the power of the Spirit to make music of our lives that is in tune with that of Jesus.

Chapter 2

Blood and Water: Narraphor—The *Ars Combinatoria* of Narrative and Metaphor

The main benefit that is obtained by preaching is by impression made upon the mind in the time of it, and not by an effect that arises afterwards by a remembrance of what was delivered.

—Jonathan Edwards[1]

DO YOU REMEMBER THE FIRST SERMON you preached? Can you remember enough to tell about it? Do you remember the content, the points, the illustrations, the metaphors, the title, the kind of audience you were speaking to?

Jesus began with his listeners. He asked the Samaritan woman at the well for a drink, then told her about living water. He resurrected, then told his disciples, "I am the resurrection and the life." Jesus was master of the "teaching moment." More than half the time, Jesus derived his preaching from the people more than delivered a message. They set the agenda. Ralph L. Lewis calls it the "Jesus' start-from-scratch, listener-centered attitude."[2]

As the early church gathered to tell the stories of Jesus. They varied their style depending on the audience. The church's first preachers were bicultural: they had to speak to Greco-Roman linear thinkers and to Hebrew nonlinear, more right-brained types. The apostles and disciples later wrote down those stories of Jesus in the symbol- and metaphor-filled narratives of the Gospels. By the third century, the simple storytelling of the early church—"gossiping the gospel"[3]—had changed into rhetoric. And out of this shift, what we know as homiletics—the discipline of preaching—was born.

Somewhere along the way, we lost the art of storytelling. Even worse, we have lost the art of story casting—finding our identity in the Jesus story, along with how to understand, interpret, and find meaning and the truth of Jesus in story. And we've lost the art of passing that storied identity along to others.

★　　★　　★

"I am not a theologian. I am a Christian, a feminist, and a writer: a fictionalizer, a liar in Plato's definition. I rather incline to the definition of theology as (1) the art of telling stories about the divine and (2) the art of listening to those stories."
—*Sara Maitland, poet, novelist, and "theologian"*[4]

★　　★　　★

Francis Bacon once observed how "Some books we read, others we admire, and a few we flat out love."[5] More often than not, the books we "flat out love" tend to be fiction novels or childhood books. But why? Because they have the best stories. A story can convey more wisdom than a bookshelf of philosophy. Yet stuck in a Gutenberg paradigm, we consign stories to the children's wing of the church and reserve the sanctuary for points and propositions.

Children's authors understand the importance of stories better than anyone. Children need stories like they need milk, and they gravitate to the most exciting storytellers they can find. They were always flocking to Jesus, much to the dismay of his disciples. Today they gravitate to television, video games, movies, and iPads, all of which are in the storytelling business. In the meantime, the church is busy passing out seven principles for this and three ideas about that. Is it any wonder that the *Jesus Storybook Bible* by Sally Lloyd-Jones[6] has become such a bestseller (and one of the cherished treasures on my bookshelf)?

A recent study testing brain activity found that the brain is most active when the subject is telling a story. As award-winning children's author Philip Pullman puts it: "All stories teach, whether the storyteller intends them to or not. They teach the world we create. They teach the morality we live by. They teach it much more effectively than moral precepts and instructions.... *Thou shalt not* is soon forgotten, but *Once upon a time* lasts forever."[7] The semiotic sermon begins by identifying and creating stories and images that fuse into our memories and allow for sensory experiences of a different world—not a world of fiction but a world of greater truth. As I said in chapter 1, together images and stories create what I call "narraphors," extended metaphors. And they are the hallmark building blocks of semiotic preaching. In the slides in chapter 1, you experienced both an exegesis of an image (pelican) and a narrative (story) about Ken Medema. In exegeting the image of the pelican, we discovered its metaphorical power. In the story of Medema's preaching, Ken uses the image and metaphor of the briar patch to inform us about his theology of storytelling and faith. When we combine images/metaphors with narrative (story), we create a narraphor. Like a parable, a narraphor contains the power of a metaphorical image with the accessibility and approachability of a story.

As Paul Ricoeur has taught us, narratives and metaphors are inseparable. A narrative, or story, is nothing but an embellished and embroidered metaphor. By the same token, we could define a metaphor as nothing but a dense and distilled narrative. Therefore, when we speak of narraphor, we are simply naming a form that Jesus used in his preaching and teaching. "He did not speak to them except in parables."[8] *Parable* literally means "alongside of," and Jesus built his stories alongside of the native images, reports, and experiences of the people to whom he was speaking. He spoke to those who wanted to understand, who needed to think about the larger meaning of the story and how to apply it to their lives: "Let those who can see, see; those who can hear, hear." To "get it" the listener had to be an active and willing participant in the story and in relationship with Jesus, to enter into the story and apply it personally, but also to enter into a relationship as a disciple with the Master.

In Jesus' storytelling, meaning is layered and "lessons" are conveyed in a kind of code. Deciphering these images and lessons takes time, commitment, and engagement with the Storyteller to delve into his deepest meanings. Some images are easier to decipher than others. They are not meant to thwart or throw off those who invest in their meaning. Rather, they are designed to reveal the secrets of God and reward those who hunger for the truth enough to seek relationship with Christ. Jesus was not interested in going deeper with those who just "came for the food." With those who sought to follow him in discipleship, he spent time discussing and engaging with them in the deeper meanings of the stories (the metaphorical and spiritual meanings of the parables). No matter what image, metaphor, or story Jesus used, the result was a lifting of the listener from the surface of the literal and a plunging of them into a surprise encounter with deep meaning and divine revelation. As the parable was revealed, the listener-participant's heart was also revealed.

Because a narraphor is a story made from metaphor, it narrates with meta-phorical meaning. The combining of story and image creates a reality into which the listener enters: a narrative that touches life contextually and layers of meaning that offer depth, breadth, and height.[9]

Semiotic preaching builds on the tradition of "preaching as storytelling." But if we want to be good storytellers, we must first be good listeners. "Let those with ears, hear, and eyes, see." If we want to tell the stories of Jesus, we must first see in them the stories and metaphors that reveal the living Jesus. David Martin explains:

> If sign and image are central to the New Testament, then it has to be read as a kind of narrative poetry. In the Scripture, we encounter types and symbols and emblems of transfiguration, and that is how the early Church, which created the New Testament, understood its own creation. What stands in the way of that are, first, the so-called critical method, which disintegrates the text into a thousand pieces without seeing it steady and seeing it whole, but also its mirror image in fundamentalism, which understands the New Testament about as much as a flat-earther understands the expanding universe.[10]

So how do we exegete images, stories, metaphors? How do we find Christ alive in the Word and in the world? Preachers need first to have the wonder-filled eyes of a child, the imaginative mind of an artist, the pilgrim devotion of a saint, and the serious humor of a comedian. Boredom is the deadliest sin of a preacher. Better a preacher with a weird imagination than a humorless, tedious mind.

★   ★   ★

**"There once lived a man called Oedipus Rex.
You must have heard about his odd complex.
His name appears in Freud's index
Because he loved his mother."**
—Tom Lehrer[11]

★   ★   ★

The most powerful metaphors both create and destroy. Austrian-American economist Joseph Schumpeter developed a theory of innovation termed "creative destruction."[12] The theory proposes that innovation rises phoenixlike from the ashes of destruction. And the most powerful metaphors do exactly that. They draw you close, inviting you in, only to subvert meaning. They destroy your prior worldview and usher in a new one in a moment of revela-tory epiphany.

Not by Might but by Metaphor?
The Sphinx and Oedipus Rex

One of the best (but not quite serious) illustrations of the seriousness and importance of metaphor can be found in the myth of Oedipus. As part of the myth, Oedipus arrives in Thebes where he finds that a monster, called the sphinx, is guarding the road to the city. She poses riddles to everyone on their way to Thebes and devours them if they are unable to solve the riddles.

Everyone has been devoured when Oedipus arrives on the scene. The sphinx asks him a riddle: "Which is the animal that has four feet in the morning, two at midday, and three in the evening?" Without hesitation Oedipus answers, "Man, who in infancy crawls on all fours, who walks upright in maturity, and in his old age supports himself with a stick." The sphinx is defeated and kills herself. Oedipus thus becomes the king of Thebes.

How was Oedipus able to solve the riddle? He had the ability to think in metaphors. Two conceptual metaphors operate in figuring out the riddle. The first is the metaphoric idea that *the life of human beings is a day*. Morning corresponds to infancy, midday to mature adulthood, and evening to old age. Since he knew these mappings, he offered the correct solution. Another and somewhat less important metaphor is that *human life is a journey*. This conceptual metaphor is evoked by repetition and the important role of feet in the riddle. Feet evoke the concept of journey, which provides a clue to the successful solution of the riddle. This is reinforced by the fact that much of the myth is a tale of Oedipus's life in the form of a journey. In other words, Oedipus's life is saved, at least in part, by his facility with metaphor. Perhaps C. S. Lewis was right when he said that what the church needs is not better arguments but better metaphors.

We can take this one step further by looking more closely at the sphinx and then comparing her with Oedipus. The sphinx is a hybrid creature, neither one thing nor another. She is part lion, part eagle, part full-breasted woman. Her reign of terror is ended by Oedipus. Yet Oedipus, the one who saves Thebes, is also the one who pollutes Thebes. He is a man guilty of incest, who kills his father and marries his mother. He needs to have both of his eyes opened to his powers of salvation and his powers of destruction. The creature he meets therefore can be seen as a reflection of his own inner life.

Think now about how you might create a semiotic sermon using this story. How would you connect this story to the story of Jesus? To the story of your congregation? How can you see the metaphor of the sphinx as a metaphor for "metaphor"?

Jesus was a master at this kind of storytelling. His use of parables, narratives, and metaphors can be seen as a subversive strategy. Narraphoric preaching breaks down resistance, enters the unconscious quickly, and causes the participant to fall into the lap, or trap, of truth. Narraphors get us thinking about something we may not want to think about. They force us to look at life in new ways, and they outwit our reasoned defenses.

Paul Ricoeur uses the term *rupture*,[13] or "the inexhaustible capacity of the parable to speak with the grain and against the grain."[14] A good metaphor or a good narrative can't have rapture without rupture. "Metaphor produces new possibilities of imagination and vision. When the reader is seized by this 're-figured world,' the narrative effects become revelatory and transformative."[15]

In the same way, a narraphor should lift language, thought, and reality and point to God first from the realm of experience and then beyond experience to revelation. I call these revelatory types of metaphors, the ones Jesus most often used, supermetaphors. Supermetaphors create a relational reality. They are Christ-bearing change agents. They are a living semiotic carrying incarnational presence. They twist or turn what we know about life and living, and they surprise us with truth that is new to us. Jesus was an artist of the metaphorical turn or twist. He was able to change, not just thought or opinion, but a disciple's entire worldview. His parables and relational power led people to turn around (*metanoia*), or "repent." The goal of the narraphor is the same: the "breaking down" that allows for that turn or twist, moving from metaphor into metamorphosis.

The founder of Methodism, John Wesley, spoke often of the need for followers of Jesus to engage in "means of grace," those communal channels and relational delivery arteries that would bring one, if not directly "face-to-face" with God, then at least near the backside of God's glory. Supermetaphors can also be "means of grace" — powerful mediators of Christ's incarnational presence that can stun people with God's grace and turn lives around. It is one thing to know the 23rd psalm; it is another to know the Shepherd of the psalm.

*　　*　　*

"Unto whom much is given, much is required."
—Jesus[16]

*　　*　　*

Points are sharp and cutting. They are hard to pick up. Metaphors are fuzzy and embracing, which is their blessing and their curse. Metaphors can take on a life of their own, which is why literary critics recognize the text as "alive" and "independent" with a reader's right to interpret.

Yet the Bible, while literary, is more than literature. It is the inspired story of God. As preachers, we are endowed with great responsibility both for our interpretation of the Word and our delivery of it. Russian novelist and physicist Aleksandr Ilichevsky, who won the Booker Prize in 2007, describes metaphor as "a pollinating bee." Preachers are in the business of pollinating the planet with metaphors that fill the mind with truth, thrill the heart with beauty, and chill the gates of hell with goodness.

The symbol of the 1950s and early '60s is often encapsulated in the unrealistic image of the housewife in pearls. The image is inspired by the character of June Cleaver of *Leave It to Beaver* (1957–63) fame, who always wore pearls even when washing the dishes. Barbara Billingsley (d. 2010), the actress who portrayed June, revealed in interviews that the reason she wore either pearls or a high collar was to hide a cleft in her neck that she feared would not show well on camera. Her practical wardrobe choice was misconstrued as a sociological statement about 1950s America. Sometimes pearls are just pearls.

In the same way, our interpretations can sometimes create their own realities that have nothing to do with the original intent. You can outfit a metaphor with so many accessories that it gets lost and you can't see where it's going. It may have been for this reason that the Puritans so distrusted metaphor: "metaphors make us blind."[17] Puritan divines insisted that the New Testament used no metaphor, none being needed once revelation was complete and "plain." Since all metaphors are lies, they argued, parables were really similitudes.

Yet to be true to the stories of Jesus, we need to approach them as the life-changing stories they were meant to be. We need to "pollinate" them with the anointing grace of God and the blood of the covenant flowing through us: "I am with you always, to the very end of the age."[18] It is not the preacher's role to help the Scriptures come alive. The Scriptures are already alive. If they are not alive in our life, it's not a problem with the Scriptures — it's a problem with us. Our role as preachers is to help people come alive in new ways to the living Word, "the only force that has the power to change the human heart: The Holy Spirit working by and with the Word in our hearts."[19]

Chapter 3

Blood Work:
Making Narraphors EPIC

DOCTORS ARE PRACTITIONERS OF MEDICINE. Preachers are practioners too. The are practitioners of incarnation. "Giving blood" reveals what God has done in the texts and traditions of our faith; "giving blood" reveals what God is doing in the lives of others; "giving blood" points out Christ's incarnated, pulsing presence within the life of the body; "giving blood" opens all the senses to receive the narraphors of grace and truth.

The practice of giving blood requires knowledge of the body — its symptoms, strengths, vulnerabilities, and idiosyncrasies. As a preacher, you need to know your culture's and your congregation's peculiar storyboard and find ways to connect those story lines with the story of Jesus in ways that allow them to participate in and connect with Christ's powerful and life-changing presence. This is what I refer to as "blood work." Blood work is the practice of preaching. It is semiotic preaching gone EPIC (experiential, participatory, image-rich, connective).

In the chapters that follow, we will look at the various stages of lab work that will take you from the first steps of preparing the sermon (knowing yourself, your sources, and your method of delivery), to the challenge of building your sermon (constructing creative narraphors; using image and metaphor; embedding style, depth, and passion; and supplementing with humor and participatory apps), to the nuts and bolts of delivery (involving your congregation creatively, using altar calls, embedding sacramentality, and ensuring powerful impact), to problems you have encountered (including preacher's block, criticism, nervousness, the propensity to be too rough or too sugary, agendas, heresies, and ideas that don't come off), to lessons that come from experience (maintaining humility, learning from peers, interpreting response, and feeding your sheep more effectively). From here we will move from the lab into the life of your congregation, from blood work to actually giving blood.

★   ★   ★

"More often than not, life imitates craft, for who among us can say that our experience does not more closely resemble a macramé plant holder than it does a painting by Seurat."
—*Fran Lebowitz*[1]

"Space speaks."
—*Edward T. Hall (1914–2009), "proxemics" anthropologist*[2]

★   ★   ★

As we saw above, EPIC stands for the four hallmarks of the interface that works in a digital culture.[3] Preaching in an EPIC style is the mix of craft and craftiness, practice and creativity, tradition and innovation required to create an atmosphere of receptivity and play. It squares the power of a narraphoric message with hands-on participation and story sharing.

EPIC preaching is somewhat akin to John Wesley's field preaching. When Wesley first preached out in the open to crowds, those in authority considered it shocking and vulgar. But today visitors to England take tours of Wesley's preaching sites: Wesley's tree, Wesley's thornbush, Wesley's lodging house. EPIC preaching encourages firsthand experiences of God, taking into account the unique time and place of the experience.

EPIC preaching is a new form of "field" preaching. In the highly charged field between the preacher and the people, each listener makes the message his or her own. Jesus spent the bulk of his ministry in the "field" with "vulgar people," the "folk" of his day. He took the gospel through, not past, that field; and in the midst of the field, he connected with people in ways that sparked the lowest and the forgotten to experience God afresh, to apply the Scriptures in new ways, to experience forgiveness, healing, and change of heart. Jesus practiced the art of the heart not in the appointed sites or sacred spaces but in the out-of-doors, in the fields and hills of Galilee.

The Bible says of Jesus, "The large crowd listened to him with delight."[4]

The worst thing to befall a preacher is to lose the common touch.[5] The majority of the crowds that followed Jesus were the "common people." Jesus' disciples, even those of his inner circle, were not the most learned and educated of the temple. Divine things come to those most willing to experience something new, to open wide the senses, learn hands-on, and take risks to chart new life courses. The religious establishment condemned Jesus for his "vulgar" associations, folk healing, and "common" communication. But nothing deterred Jesus from an arts and crafts homiletic that put the cookies on a low shelf.

Why is it that so often the very churches that talk the most about the poor are the ones with worship in which the poor would feel least at home? The semiotic homiletic is about reclaiming the common touch and not the spinning of threads so fine, as Robert Burns once put it, "that it is fit for neither weft nor woof."[6] It's about communicating in ways that those within and without our stained-glass windows and big-screened warehouses can hear and comprehend. It's about releasing the church from its homiletical autism as we are safely ensconced inside our various bubbles, spending God's money to keep our preferred bubble inflated so we can luxuriate in the breath of self-referential discourse. We could take a lesson from poet Marie Ponsot, who learned something from a great musician affectionately known as "Pops": "Louis Armstrong taught me that unless what you write has a contact with the common and everyday, you haven't done anything."[7]

★　　★　　★

> "You are not your own; you were bought at a price.
> Therefore honor God with your bodies."
> —*Apostle Paul*[8]

★　　★　　★

EPIC preaching is embodied communication truth in a disembodied world. Pamela Ann Moeller, professor of worship at Toronto's Emmanuel College, talks about "embodied" preaching or a "kinesthetic homiletic" that is "full-bodied." Preaching, she argues, is best defined as communal dance.[9]

> The point is not to turn the brain off but to turn the body on, to enable it to be a full partner in the *pas de Dieu*. The point is not to throw away all the wonderful schemes and processes we have learned for exegesis and sermon formation but to use them to check and support our body-work. The point is not to replace the preached sermon with a wordless dance but to create the preached sermon out of the dance choreographed by the text.[10]

Preaching must embody the gospel. What Moeller says about kinesthetic preaching goes for EPIC preaching as well: "Yes, we may need to move mountains in order to help the people in the pew into this new world. Yet many of those mountains will be the obstacles we create for ourselves. As for the rest, a mustard grain of faith and our best educational footwork will go a considerable distance toward accomplishing our goal."[11]

If we want to engage the body, we need to make our narraphors EPIC. A body is meant to move and be moved. Narraphors are meant to be held, felt, and touched. Join me now for a closer look at the components of EPIC preaching.

EXPERIENTIAL

The core issue of preaching is not "getting something said"; it is not even "getting something heard"; it is getting something experienced that can transform your life for God and the gospel.

What is the fastest-growing Christianity in the world right now? Pentecostalism. It is sometimes called the "third force" or "third stream" of Christendom. In my personal encounters with Pentecostal preachers in places as diverse as Latvia and Indonesia, they share one thing in common: each one has become an author of experience. Each preacher is a participation artist. And their preaching is artisanal. Preaching is the artistry of evoking transforming experiences of the transcendent. Sorbonne professor Anne-Marie Duguet, head of the Centre de Recherches d'Esthétique du Cinéma et des Arts Audiovisuels, defines the creators of interactive arts as the "authors of experience."[12]

If I were to ask you, "Are you experienced?" you might not know, at first, what I was referring to. But in Seattle, for example, that phrase takes on a whole new meaning. "Are you experienced?" means "Have you been to Paul Allen's memorial museum for Jimi Hendrix called The Experience Music Project?" Designed by architect Frank Gehry to look from the air like a smashed electric guitar, it's less a museum to rock and roll than a series of immersion experiences in which you can simulate a concert. You can sing or play instruments in front of an audience complete with smoke, hot lights, and screaming fans.

In the modern world, the phrase "Are you experienced?" means something quite different: are you skilled, are you good, are you rationally and technically equipped to control a challenge or a project? What rational was to the Gutenberg world, experiential is to the Google world. In the ongoing battle between Aristotle and Plato, Aristotle wins in the twenty-first century. It's the difference between sermons that evoke the response, "You really gave me something to think about, Preacher" and those that garner "That message really moved/touched me." Plato insists that philosophy reigns supreme; Aristotle makes a place for drama, the arts, poetry, and experience.

In our day, the challenge is not belief but authenticity of faith. You can "believe" that Jesus is Savior of the world or "believe" the resurrection is true and still not give your heart to Jesus. But to "trust in" Christ is another matter entirely. Faith is "trusting in" Christ and allowing Christ to live in you. *Trust* and *faith* are EPIC words. Faith is not just accepting propositions about Jesus. Faith is being in a grace relationship with Jesus. And that four-letter preposition *with* defines the experiential aspect of EPIC.[13] The essence of faith is the suspension of our knowledge and belief systems to trust in Christ with mind and heart. This means taking risks, "listening" to God's voice, spending time with God in relationship, experiencing God's healing touch, following Jesus not out of proof but out of love—practices that together constitute discipleship. Experiencing Christ does not make us irrational. But it allows for truth that goes beyond knowledge. It allows that there are truths in life that we cannot know. When we realize that we cannot nail down, define, or rationally contain Jesus—or faith—we take the first step toward God. God cannot be found in the realm of the rational but dwells in the mysterious realm of grace. Jesus' parables were not given to be "understood" but to reveal. And what was revealed was the grace of God and the truth of the human heart.

When Jesus called Nathanael, he not only "called him" but he "called him out" from under the fig tree. He "saw" who he was, the sum of his life. When Jesus offered the woman at the well a drink from the water of life, he revealed to her the circumstances of her life. From the beginning of time, Adam and Eve tried to "hide" from God, but God "called them out." Experience is allowing ourselves to be "called out" and "revealed," to bare our hearts to Jesus for him to see our lives, our motives, our sorrows, our pain, our issues, our joys. Experiential preaching does the same; it "calls to" and "calls out" the flock to see and be seen.

Marketing is the art and science of getting people to want what they don't need. Preaching is the art and craft of getting people to want what they don't know they need but can't truly live without: daily experiences of Christ. In their watershed book *The Experience Economy* (1999), James Gilmore and Joseph Pine II show how in our lifetime we've migrated through various economies: from commodities to goods to services to experiences to transformations. People today are interested in buying experiences, not goods or services themselves. If you buy a "good" after having an experience, you are purchasing an artifact that helps you remember the experience.

Introductory Words from the Lab

We can call these artifacts, the objects that bring to mind an experience, icons. And in our preaching, the icon is the narraphor. A good narraphor helps people remember, and it functions as a sensory icon—like the touch of Jesus' robe. For people to remember sermons, they must experience Christ within them—not just intellectually but "bodily" with the senses. And they must experience Christ not just individually but communally, as a "body."

The decline of establishment churches and the rise of a "spirituality culture" derives in part from this hunger for sensory experience. Craving for a more experiential encounter with God is what draws people to yoga, to Taizé, to Reiki, to everywhere except our rationalist churches where the primary sweet spot is a head nod over a heart skip.[14]

★   ★   ★

> "They may forget what you said, but they will
> never forget how you made them feel."
> —Carl W. Buechner, Presbyterian pastor[15]

★   ★   ★

Of course, it is possible to go too far too fast in rejecting the rational, just as the Gutenberg world went too far too fast in the direction of the individual. When we prefer spending time under our own "fig tree" rather than reveling all together in God's garden, when we don't experience God together as a community of faith, when in place of Jesus' stories we hear only our own voices, we quickly go wayward. What makes experience so rich is that we do it in common with others in shared spaces, whether in cyberspace (e.g., Twitter, Facebook, Google) or around the corner at Starbucks. Our experiences of God are checked, corrected, and bettered by the presence of those who came before us, those with us, those around us, and even those in front of us.

To worship "in the Spirit and in truth"[16] is less an individual experience than a community experience. In the Gutenberg world, worship became sanctuary; in the Google world, worship must become communion again—a debanalized, resacrilized experience of relationship, of connectedness, of eucharistic union. EPIC preaching does not throw reason out the window, but it secures worship in Scripture without straitjacketing the senses or the Scriptures. Body and blood sermons do more than reproduce the preacher's personal experiences of God; they make God's truth the preacher's experience. Experiencing God's truth requires both reason and emotion. That's why every sermon should give people something to see, something to hear, something to touch, something to taste, and something to smell. EPIC preaching makes you think and feel at the same time.[17]

We find this emphasis on experience in the Armenian rite, when the priest anoints with oil the newly baptized, and the newly baptized receives the sacrament of confirmation with these words:

Forehead: Sweet ointment in the name of Jesus Christ is poured upon you as a seal of incorruptible heavenly gifts.

Eyes: This seal in the name of Jesus Christ enlighten your eyes, that you may never sleep unto death.

Ears: This holy anointing be for the hearing of divine commandments.

Nostril: This seal in the name of Jesus Christ be a sweet smell from life unto life.

Lips: This seal in the name of Jesus Christ be for you a guardian for your mouth and strong door for your lips.

Hands: This seal in the name of Jesus Christ be a cause for charity and for all virtuous deeds and behavior.

Heart: This divine seal may confirm in you a pure heart and renew within you an upright spirit.

Back: This seal in the name of Jesus Christ be to you a shield of strength thereby to quench all the fiery darts of the Evil One.

Feet: This divine seal direct your steps unto life everlasting that you may not be shaken.[18]

$\star \quad \star \quad \star$

"Piskies, Piskies, on their knees,
Hopping up and down like fleas.
Presbys, Presbys, too stiff to bend,
Sitting down on man's chief end."
—Author unknown[19]

$\star \quad \star \quad \star$

Reformed theologian and Presbyterian leader Tim Keller says that the church must come out of its cognitive bias and move into more experiential modes of worship: "If even I see this, then maybe it's here."[20] It is not enough simply to give Christ intellectual assent. We must "taste and see that the LORD is good."[21] Even at the height of the Enlightenment, Jonathan Edwards differentiated between believing that God is good and experiencing God's goodness. We tend to forget how those Calvinist psalms generated energy and aroused emotions. Not hick emotions, but high emotions, and the urgent invitation to experience the divine.

Modern preaching prided itself on lucid reasoning, coherent organization, performative presentation, focused structure, formal elegance. No more. The days of the "pulpit prince" with "golden tonsils" and oratorical fluorescence are over. EPIC preaching is nothing more, nor less, than helping people experience God. Every study of churches that are "healthy" and "alive" comes to the same conclusion: they mediate transforming experiences of God.

Moderns have been as unnerved and embarrassed by Jesus' penchant for parables as were the original disciples. The Twelve could not figure out why Jesus used parables in the first place.[22] They complained that too many in the crowd simply didn't "get it" with Jesus' teaching style. Why couldn't he make things as clear as a point and not as murky as a parable? Too often they said, "We don't understand what he is saying."[23] The disciples wanted Jesus to think straight and say it like he meant it, just as we expect sermons to lay out "truth" in black and white, putting it all "on the line" and drawing lines that don't squiggle and sway.

But Jesus preached toward the prize of something higher than clarity: conversation, relationship, and participation. Jesus' goal in preaching was not that everyone understand him, but that everyone experience him and interact with his message.[24] He knew he would reach those willing to lay their souls bare and their hearts wide open. But even though he knew he wouldn't reach everyone, he invited everyone to hear God's story, become part of God's story, and to learn about other pilgrims who joined God's story. Jesus taught people to experience truth within their own lives, to "rise to the occasion" of God's glory and grace. Preachers need to create an experience in preaching that will allow people to experience that truth of the living Jesus in their lives still today.

PARTICIPATORY

Participation is the mediator of experience and the animator of narraphor. While experience can be passive, participation turns people into active agents of initiation and response. It is not enough to listen to the message; listeners become hearers and hearers become doers when they "take part" in the message. Semiotic preaching moves from a listening paradigm to a participation paradigm.

In the shift from representation to participation, the black church is light-years ahead of the Anglo traditions. In the African-American tradition, the greater the quality of interaction, both verbal and physical, the greater the quality of preaching. The research of Dr. Lyndrey A. Niles, however, makes the case that what seems like "feedback" is more than that.

> In several instances, the audience participation precedes the words of the speaker, and preachers often respond in their preaching to the prompting of the congregation. Thus call and response may not be the call of the minister and the response of the congregation, which is the way this signature act of the black church has often been written about. It may be the opposite with the audience stimulating (calling) the minister to new heights of oratorical excellence and insightful sermonizing.[25]

Participation is the essence of what we will call the "transductive (or trans-incarnational) method"—focusing less on *taking apart* passages and more on finding ways for the congregation to *take part* in the message dynamically. I discuss this in more depth in chapter 5, "Blood Types and Blood Screening." At this point, it is enough to say that participatory preaching requires relationship building and adaptability. It involves taking on the stories of all participants, who will themselves begin to "cowrite" the story. Authentic participation creates and modifies experience.

The TGIF culture we live in is a karaoke culture. The success of social media has proved passivity passé and turned a performance culture into an age of participation. Of course, this is nothing new. But our ability to be hands-on in the "everything" of life is increasing at warp speed, more and more adeptly and abruptly with each new innovation of digital technology. The revolution that we call the "digital age" may be more aptly termed the "age of interactivity." No longer are people satisfied with stimulating their minds. They expect holistic stimulation: mental, emotional, physical, spiritual.

* * *

"Today we are no longer passive observers of a cosmos created by a Clockwork God but full members of a participatory universe.... We now know that only those systems which are open and responsive to their environments will, in the long run, survive.... In this new world we are all responsible, all participators. And so the rest is up to us."
—F. David Peat[26]

* * *

A parable is by definition participatory—an animated experience whose ending is left open. Preaching is a collaborative process between pulpit and pew. A sermon isn't a sermon until it is received, and its success is based not solely on the preacher but as much if not more on the congregation. Hence Jesus' call for active listening: "Let anyone with ears to hear listen!"[27]

Even traditional preaching requires participation, so much so that some homileticians have argued, "The skills of the hearers are more important than the skills of the preacher."[28] What we must recognize is that preaching is not just a one-way communication; it is a two-way street. The preacher must also be an active listener. A true sermon is written with the ear, and skilled preachers are always listening to the voice of Christ to give voice to the church. Consecrated lips require consecrated ears.

★　　★　　★

"A sermon is a work of the church and not
merely a work of the preacher."
—*Thomas G. Long*[29]

"God is in us, we are in God by way of mutual participation."
—*Attributed to John Wesley*

★　　★　　★

In participatory preaching, the congregation is not a passive consumer of content but an active author of experience and creator of participation. The congregation is part of the homiletic team and is involved in the process of sermon composition and design. The *P* in EPIC is not just being responsive to content but is itself constitutive of it. The participation is less fill in the blank than flesh out the story. In fact, participatory preaching brings us closer to the way Jesus communicated. In a content analysis of the 125 incidents of Jesus' encounters with people, Ralph L. Lewis has found that "roughly 54 percent of those encounters are initiated by His hearers. Instead of standing up and proclaiming the message He wanted the people to hear, He responded to His audience's questions, objects, doubts. He allowed and welcomed their involvement."[30] In traditional pulpit-centric preaching, great labor is spent on writing better opening sentences. But in participatory preaching, time is spent on creating better opening (and closing) interactions.

IMAGE RICH

"Sinners in the Hands of an Angry God" is perhaps the most famous sermon in American history. If people know about a sermon, it's this one. But why do we remember it? It's not the content that is often remembered. It's Jonathan Edwards's unforgettable imagery of people as spiders held dangling over the flaming chasm of hell.

Images are the thoughts of the heart. You grow a soul by the cultivation of an image garden. People today are like the Israelites in the desert. They follow the pillars of fire and the cloud, not abstract commands and disembodied voices. Image-rich preaching moves beyond literacy to imagacy. Literacy is the ability to read, write, and think critically about words. Imagacy is the ability to read, use, and think critically about images and stories. The art of imagacy is what makes narraphors memorable. In an image-rich sermon, imagacy invites people to participate in the incarnational power of the Christ narraphor.

Semiotics, especially EPIC semiotics, excels in the art of exegeting and animating images. One of the shifts we need to make from traditional preaching to semiotic preaching is to realize that the power of the Word isn't in the words—it's in the images, the stories, the music of the text. In traditional pulpit-centric preaching, we learned how to exegete words. Semiotic preaching exegetes images. Preachers must take up the poet's tools—image and imagination, rhyme and rhythm, simile, metaphor, and story. Jesus was a master builder (*tekton*) of metaphor. And in his metaphors lay metamorphosis. The metaphors we learn to live in will be the reality we will learn to live out of.

*   *   *

"As God hath spangled the firmament with starres,
so hath he his Scriptures with names and
metaphors, and denotations of power."
—*John Donne (1572–1631), English poet and cleric*[31]

*   *   *

The Hildegaard of homileticians, Barbara Brown Taylor, writes, "The church's central task is an imaginative one. By that I do not mean a fanciful or fictional task, but one in which the human capacity to imagine—to form mental pictures of the self, the neighbor, the world, the future, to envision new realities—is both engaged and transformed."[32] The prevailing homiletic approach encourages preachers to identify the "main principle" or the "key idea" or the "big point." So, for example, if I were preaching about the flood of Noah, I would identify the "main principle" as God's judgment and mercy. This is not the goal of EPIC preaching. In EPIC preaching, we look for the "master metaphor," the leading or controlling image that reframes the conversation or concept. This metaphor can be a character, a key moment in the story, an artifact or artifice, even a word that functions as an image. Metaphors are not the sermon's seasoning; they're the very meat of the sermon itself, and they are the mediators that carry the incarnational story of Jesus.

Most preachers today have noticed that we live in a visual culture. No one can miss that advertisers spend billions of dollars a year not to bombard us with words but to bathe us in images. But the solution for many preachers has been to remedy that gap by using charts, graphs,[33] and PowerPoint, where the power is still in the point — not in the image. Image-rich EPIC preaching acknowledges that no point or proposition can explain the feeling and insight of knowing in one's heart that one belongs to God. Image-rich preaching sears the image and living presence of Christ into the hearts of his followers.

CONNECTIVE

Harvard fellow (and former lyricist for the Grateful Dead) John Perry Barlow once presented a University of Chicago audience with a challenge. If an angel were to descend into this room, he said, and give everyone present one minute to decide, "Give up all your assets or give up all your relationships," which would be your choice?

The result? Astonishingly, all agreed to give up their assets. Why did no one give up his or her relationships? The unanimous answer was this: "I know I can rebuild my assets from my relationships, but I can't rebuild my relationships from my assets."[34]

★   ★   ★

"The only gift greater than the air you breathe is the hand you hold."
— *Old Irish toast*

★   ★   ★

Humans are a relational species, and we live in a relational world. In fact, this is less an age of information than an age of connection. People are desperate to connect with God, with each other, with creation, with their culture, and with their community. Yet the worlds of the academy and the church remain forums for disseminating "information" to or at people rather than involving people in the process of connecting with each other in a "network" of experiences. Most sermons still involve preaching to a passive audience in

54

a world resistant to being passive—a world where people every day navigate their way through congested crowds of choices and connections.

*   *   *

**"The character of a man depends on
his connections to the world."**
—*Horace*[35]

"None of us is as strong as all of us."
—*Old IBM tagline*

*   *   *

Networking is the central metaphor of the new economic system. The path forward is not a ladder of success but a web of connections. It's no wonder the Internet has been the "great equalizer" of societies East and West. The hierarchical systems of the past with their command-and-control structures and top-down "authorities" cannot withstand the social networking mind. Whereas hierarchies channel communication into conduits (trust the process), networks connect people to each other (trust the connection). An age of connection deserves an introduction to Jesus' relationship-first theology.

I once had a conversation with a preacher friend about the need for the content of preaching to be more interactive and relational. I will never forget his response: "You just make me mad, Sweet. That's why I went into ministry—so people would listen to me." I appreciate his honesty, but in EPIC preaching, there are no rock stars.

Preachers are bodybuilders. One of the surprises to emerge from the Second World War was that when an Allied or Axis city came under attack, no matter how savage the assault, both alcoholism and suicide declined significantly. When a community rallies together behind a common cause, even a defensive one to ward off catastrophe, it diminishes personal problems. Binding together with others in community releases positive impulses toward the future.[36]

But connective preachers are not just in the business of building communities or even of forging personal relationships with Christ. Preachers are in the bodybuilding business of forming the body of Christ. Preachers are not lovers of community for the sake of community but lovers of people for the sake of embodying the gospel. Jesus' prime directive was to love God and love one another. When love is at the heart of the body, the body is whole and healthy in Christ. Connectional preachers invite people to connect with each other so they can better connect with Christ's healing power and life-giving presence.

ON-TAP PREACHING

I am a member of the Wesleyan tribe. My early ancestors created the Method-ist movement that turned England and America upside down. They were not concerned about preaching literary masterpieces. What engaged their artistic energies was crafting sermons that hit the bull's-eye of the human heart and changed lives. When they used notes to assist them in preaching, they stuffed them "up the sleeve" where it would appear to the people that they were speaking "off the cuff." They were masters of on-tap preaching.

Over time things have changed. The more culturally "respectable" Methodism became, the more these storytelling ancestors were ridiculed, and those who produced closely reasoned, tightly argued treatises that appealed mostly to the intellect were celebrated. Preachers turned in their homespun patchwork quilts for the latticework of a literary production or the rational rungs of a ladder, symbolized by triple-decker sermons pro-claimed from double-decker pulpits. The people in the pews often protested the move from an "orascript"[37] to ladderly or latticelike manuscripts, say-ing, "How can you expect us to remember it when you can't remember it yourself?"

★ . ★   ★

"Those who are in love with community, destroy community; those who love people, build community."
—*Dietrich Bonhoeffer*[38]

★   ★   ★

The craving for respectability and professionalism in the pulpit meant a move away from the oral ways of the ancestors, who aimed not only to reach the upper-crust pews in the front, but to "reach the back row,"[39] the place where the "backsliders" convened and the dregs of the cup most often congregated. One of the most cutting slurs to sling at a scholar was "How common!" Still the worst thing that can be said of an academic is that he or she "plays to the galleries." To be "common" is to be inferior and weak. But Jesus prized the "common," especially the "common people" and the "com-mon touch." In fact, when you start pleasuring in your crème de la crème status, you've likely become too creamy for Jesus. Jesus trumped the cream of the crop with the curdled and skim milk of the earth, or what poet Johan Ferreira would add were "the sour cream and chives of society." And as his parables made plain, Jesus relished the burble of everyday life, the bauble of everyday things. The Master's touch was the common touch, and it must be every preacher's touch as well.

Interactives

1. Watch the YouTube presentation on social media by Eric Qualman, author of *Socialnomics*, by searching for his name.[40] What impact do you think social media has had on the church? How can you use social media effectively in order to make your sermons more EPIC?

2. Look at the first stanza of the lyrics below for the song "The Red Flag":

   > The people's flag is deepest red,
   > It shrouded oft our martyred dead,
   > And ere their limbs grew stiff and cold,
   > Their hearts' blood dyed its ev'ry fold.

   What is the metaphor of the song? What do you think it's about? How might you adapt this metaphor in a sermon about Christian faith?

   http://www.marxists.org/subject/art/music/lyrics/en/red-flag.htm

3. Blood has had various cultural connotations. There used to be a thriving German trade in dried blood: "Dragon's blood (derived from trees in Africa and the Canary Islands); animal blood was used for various medicinal purposes; medieval pharmacopoeia also contained blood; unguents had potions made of powdered blood and human tissue, a witches' brew that might include rendered fat from executed criminals, and most notoriously mummia, powdered Egyptian mummy."[41]

   Although these types of practices may seem barbaric, the significance of blood in our culture has gained in popularity, as evidenced by the onset of vampire movies and books. In fact, there is a new energy drink called Blood Energy Potion (designed to increase the consumer's iron level) that looks like blood and comes in an IV bag. The Christian church has a long, blood-rich history in art and metaphor. And our highest ritual contains the language of blood and body. Why are churches today so squeamish about the language and metaphors of blood?

http://www.xoxide.com/blood-energy-potion.html?gclid=COTEzNSo
oKoCFUHc4Aoden7XmQ

4. Fleming Rutledge, in her book *Help My Unbelief* (2000), compares her experience in the Connecticut Episcopal Church, where the rector didn't want her to mention blood, with her experience in a black Baptist church in South Carolina, where she says, "I was struck by the number of references in the songs to the cleansing blood of Jesus, and the unabashed way that the preacher referred to sin." Then she talks about the central theme of reconciliation of sinners in the black tradition — with "no squeamishness about the blood" and "their intense rejoicing that God in Christ is cleansing us, sanctifying us, counting us as righteous even in the midst of our sin."[42] She goes on to say that is why forgiveness is so much a part of the black church.

Does her experience sound familiar to you? Why do you think there is such a dichotomy between black churches and Anglo traditions regarding blood? How can your preaching become more joyful about being washed in the blood of Jesus?

5. The words *blood* and *blessing* are related words. In fact, the word *blessing* is unique to the English language. The proto-Germanic word *blodam* meant "blood," or that which bursts out. *Blothisjan* meant "to mark with blood." The Old English word is *blotham*, and the Old English *bloedsian* meant "to consecrate, make holy" ("to bless"). In the Old Testament Jacob and Esau story (Gen. 25), it is more correct to translate the "blessing" stolen from Esau as the "bloodline" (the covenantal privilege). Blood is the essence of the covenant, the sacred bloodline, and God's covenant was made with all flesh — that which has blood. In fact, the only proper way to make a covenant in the Hebrew tradition was to "cut the covenant," a process in which sacrificial blood was spilled.

Find the passage in the Bible in which God "cuts the covenant" with Abraham (Gen. 15). What do you think was the significance of this ritual? The Hebrew word *berith* means "covenant," and it was often "cut" with blood. What other significant covenantal rite in the Hebrew and Jewish tradition signifies this cutting and spilling of blood? What is its significance for us today?

6. The French words *fête itinérante* ("movable feast") and *fête de l'amour* ("love feast") represent two significant metaphors for the church. What are they? In what ways might they still be significant today?

7. Many Protestant churches, especially more recently built ones, are far more devoid of art, icons, stained glass, and symbols than the sanctuaries of older cathedrals and churches. What have we lost in not retaining those symbols and traditions? How can we learn imagacy? How might we regain a better understanding of the metaphors, images, symbols, and stories of the early church today? In what ways can technology help us to do that?

8. In the book *Eat, Pray, Love* (2006) by Elizabeth Gilbert, a woman, confused and depressed with her life, goes searching in Rome for a place to eat. She takes the advice of a friend to visit a small Italian café and is accompanied by a new friend. In her experience of tasting the food, she undergoes a transformational experience. At the end of her meal, she says that in the mirror she sees "a bright-eyed, clear-skinned, happy and healthy face."[43]

    What is the metaphor Gilbert has used so effectively? What themes of life and theses of transformation does this metaphor suggest? How can you connect with this story in a sermon? Go online and identify five to ten helpful resources for using this metaphor in relationship to Jesus.

9. Check out the lyrics to "Kryptonite" by Three Doors Down on their album *The Better Life*. Listen to the refrain: "I really don't mind what happens now and then as long as you'll be my friend at the end." How can you relate this song to the need for EPIC experience?

10. Do you think George Bernard Shaw's narraphor of preaching, "Some preaching is like wine: it has color and sparkle, but it does no permanent good; some is like drinking coffee: it stimulates, but does not nourish; some is like carbonated water: a fizzle over nothing; some is like pure spring water: good, but hard to get"[44] is better than that of simply "Cana wine"? Or is there value in simplicity?

Part 2

"A+" POSITIVE PREP

Chapter 4

Blood Stream: Scriptures

[God's] divine power has given us everything we need.
—2 Peter 1:3

PIERCE A BODY AT ANY PLACE. The same thing comes out: blood. The same should be true for a sermon. Every sermon needs to bleed the same thing—the love of Jesus. Whether you preach from a Scripture, preach to a Scripture, preach through the Scriptures, or preach around the Scriptures, the sermon and the Scriptures are in symbiotic relationship.[1] Or in the words of Charles Haddon Spurgeon about Puritan preacher John Bunyan, the preacher's "bloodline" is "Bibline": "Bunyan is a living Bible! Prick him anywhere; his blood is Bibline, the very essence of the Bible flows from him."[2]

John Wesley was adamant that no matter how intense our personal experience of Christ, Scripture must always be the mud and sticks that hold the edifice of preaching all together—the first and last stops in our search for the voice and presence of Jesus. I once heard Yale Divinity School dean Leander Keck echo Wesley when he claimed, "The preacher who neglects the Bible as the bread of his or her own life may find that regardless of how many attractive delicacies one serves each Sunday, one may be suffering from malnutrition. On the other hand, the one who preaches the Bible biblically usually finds himself confronted by more bread than one can say grace over."[3]

Scriptures are the red blood cells of our message. They carry the oxygen of divine presence into our lives. Scriptures and sacraments are the soul's bread and butter. In Scripture we find the stories and sacramental identity of Jesus that courses through the blood. This is what the "authority" of the Word means: the stories are alive and "at work in you who believe."[4]

Preaching is not voicing thoughts from ancient texts. Preaching is giving voice to God—the sound of whose voice can break cedars, heal broken hearts, repair relationships, transform commitments, alter lifestyles, overturn philosophies. The aim of preaching is not to make the Scriptures come alive but to awaken oneself and help one's people come alive to the Scriptures, to be alive to the living story, to increase our capacity for pleasuring in the Word, and for embracing and experiencing Jesus: "The text is being fulfilled today, even as you listen."[5] Someone once described Wendell Berry's writing as the land given voice. The Bible is simply the Spirit given voice.

But what voice would the Spirit have? It's not a propositional voice, but a storytelling, poetic voice. That's how you know when Christ is in your midst or when it's merely the preacher. Sometimes, at the end of a sermon, the preacher says, "This is the Word of the Lord." And sometimes I want to yell, *"Not!"* The role of the preacher is not merely to provide commentaries on current events or even meditations on texts. The role of the preacher is to point prophetically to Christ in the midst of the congregation and to encourage people to open themselves to fuller portions of the presence of the Holy Spirit in their lives. In a sense, it is waking people up to the morning watch.

Likewise, the Holy Spirit reveals Scripture. The disciples grasped the meaning of a passage only after Jesus "opened their minds so they could understand the Scriptures."[6] The Scriptures have authority over the follower, and Jesus has authority over all. Therefore, the blood of Jesus needs to be in the veins of every sermon.

*   *   *

"Now let me and everyone who speaks the word of Christ freely boast that our mouths are the mouths of Christ. I am certain indeed that my word is not mine, but the word of Christ. So must my mouth also be the mouth of him whose word it utters."
—*Martin Luther*[7]

*   *   *

The Mozart of homileticians, Charles Haddon Spurgeon, who has 3,500 sermons in print (sixty-three volumes), looked for Christ in every passage of Scripture. When criticized for his exegetical liberties, he retorted: "I would rather see Him where He isn't than to miss Him where He is!"[8] African-American preachers often interrupt their preaching with, "Do I have a witness?" or "Can I get a witness?" What they are really saying is, "Do you hear what the Spirit is saying to the church?"[9] Do you hear the ring of that "voice of one calling in the wilderness"?[10] Preachers are voices calling in the wilderness, witnesses to Christ. Preaching is giving voice to Jesus, the *Deus loquens* ("speaking God").

SERMONS NEED TO BE BIBLICAL

Jesus was the greatest communicator who ever lived, a grand master at the linguistic arts. His messages were just that: art. He was not a rhetorician, but an artist, an imagesmith (*tekton*), who constructed parables filled with truth, with narraphors—stories, metaphors, signs, questions, parables, twist endings, wordplays, poetry. All works of art.

Some people are arguing that the day of the sermon is over, but everyone who has counted preaching out has been wrong. Preaching does need, however, to be more authentically biblical and christological. That means more artistic and less dogmatic, more slanted and less straight, more participatory and less performative, more pilgrimage and less checklist, more formational and hand grenades and less informational and hand-holding. We need to preach to our zip code. We need to give people what they didn't know they needed until that moment when Christ's story begins to resonate within their own life story and they recognize truth. We need to dispel the delusion that people come and sit there wanting to know what the church or the preacher think about a subject. It's that delusion that has led us to the point where, according to a 2010 survey, more than one-third of people who style themselves "born again" confess to "rarely or never" reading the Bible. Among "unaffiliated" people (people not belonging to any religious congregation), more than two-thirds say they don't read the Bible.[11]

It is up to us to make the connections between a Sunday faith and a Monday world. As Haddon Robinson puts it, we need to "walk the bridge, and not jump the river."[12] No parent comes to church wanting to know how 1 John 4:8 relates to John 3:16. A father comes to church wanting to know how to relate to a daughter who has just told him, "I want your money, I want your car, I want your name, but I don't want your counsel, your companionship, or your love."

To preach from the Scripture is to bleed the truth of Christ, to let people know that no one is beyond Christ's reach. Even preachers. We forget that when Luther said, "Sin boldly," he was speaking directly to preachers. And we always forget to quote the whole passage: "If you are a preacher of grace, then preach a true and not a fictitious grace; if grace is true, you must bear a true and not a fictitious sin. God does not save people who are only fictitious sinners. Be a sinner and sin boldly, but believe and rejoice in Christ even more boldly, for he is victorious over sin, death, and the world."[13]

Preachers can approach the Scriptures in a variety of ways. For some it is *lectio selecta* (the lectionary tied to the liturgical calendar). The lectionary contains most of the important Second Testament sections.[14] But it mangles and omits the First Testament. In spite of its drawbacks, the increased use of the lectionary in the late 1970s and '80s led to a renewal of biblical preaching in oldline churches. For over twenty years, I have contributed a sermon a week to a lectionary-based preaching resource.[15]

Those not using the lectionary may opt for *lectio continua* ("consecutive preaching" of books or passages). Martyn Lloyd-Jones preached on Romans for fourteen years. (Don't try it!) This is increasingly popular in Reformed circles, where whole seasons of the year (fall, winter, summer, spring) are devoted to one book of the Bible.

Still for others, it's *lectio semiotica*, looking at the stories, metaphors, and images of the scriptural texts. As I show in this book, this can be combined with any other lectio method.

No matter which "lectio" you choose, preaching connects text to context in such a way that people will never want to be without their daily bread. Henry Wadsworth Longfellow once went to hear a sermon by John Ware of Cambridge and wrote these words when he got home: "I heard a good sermon and I applied it to myself." That's the best a preacher can hope. There is a certain physicality to the Bible that we lose at our peril. Whether the Bible is in book or digital form, preaching should so awaken a hunger for the narraphors of faith that we will always want its physical presence with us.

SERMONS NEED BOTH TO DEFAMILIARIZE AND RESONATE

An old Cameroon proverb says, "If familiarity were useful, water wouldn't cook fish." Nothing deadens like the drumbeats of familiarity.

Western culture has privileged the connection between seeing and knowing; to a lesser degree, hearing and knowing. But "knowing" comes from all the senses: touching and knowing, tasting and knowing, smelling and knowing. Scripture needs to be known in every way possible.

Multisensory knowing requires that we both "estrange" the texts and at the same time connect them to people's lives in multisensory ways that resonate with real-life problems and situations. In fact, emotions can be more discerning, more perceptive, than reason. The buzzing of old saws, the rattling of moldering bones, is all too often heard in sermons. Karl Barth said we domesticate Scriptures when we look for confirming clichés and convictions rather than daring to enter "this strange new world of the Bible."[16]

Preaching is nothing less than the craft of making the familiar strange. When we make the familiar even more familiar, we find ourselves on homiletic cul-de-sacs. When our usual ways of "knowing" the Scriptures have become too cozy and comfortable, only defamiliarization enables us to hear the challenging stories of judgment and the hope that lies within and behind the texts. When we open the Scriptures up to new angles and locate them in different contexts, we allow people to become reacquainted with texts that can shine new light into their shadowed doubts and dilemmas.

$$\star \quad \star \quad \star$$

"Among the many excellent gifts which God has adorned the human race, it is a singular privilege that he deigns to consecrate to himself the mouths and tongues of men in order that his voice may resound in them."
—*John Calvin*[17]

"His word is in my heart like a fire,
a fire shut up in my bones.
I am weary of holding it in;
indeed, I cannot."
—*Jeremiah 20:9*

$$\star \quad \star \quad \star$$

The hardest texts to preach on are familiar texts like we preach at Christmas and Easter. Martin Luther called these "little Bibles." We've become so used to preaching the same messages over and over again that we ourselves often fail to see the "new" and the "sparkle" in those texts.

Defamiliarization forces us to look with different lenses and to preach familiar texts with a new prophetic voice—one that gives a new edge to the story and provides a new bloodline for connecting with Christ. Some successful preachers contend that it is best to choose "emotionally neutral subjects." The only problem with limiting yourself to emotionally neutral subjects is that what it is for you, it will be for others. You cannot connect your whole self to that which has been emotionally stripped. I'm not even sure you can be neutral and neural at the same time. If you're alive, you're on some side of something.

Jesus took on emotionally charged or "difficult" subjects. His parables were not exercises in mental prowess but emotionally gripping revelations about how we should live our lives. Narraphors do more than tell the truth; in Jesus' hands they are the truth. The very use of parables is an incarnational device—a vein that pumps and plugs in directly to the heart.

In 1751 Charles Wesley heard a sermon by Methodist lay preacher Michael Fenwick. This was his response: "But such a preacher I have never heard, and hope I never shall again. It was beyond description. I cannot say he preached false doctrine, or true, or any doctrine at all, but pure, unmixed nonsense. Not one sentence did he utter that could do the least good to any one soul. Now and then a text of Scripture, or a verse quotation, was dragged in by head and shoulders. I could scarce refrain from stopping him."[18]

Preaching must be true to the story of Jesus—as true as the preacher can be. We must never use Scripture halfheartedly, absentmindedly, or flippantly. This is the danger in using the lectionary. If you chop a bit here and splice it there, you create a biblical collage that runs the risk of inventing the Scriptures in your own agenda, or worse, rendering them utterly meaningless. Jesus, Jonathan Edwards, Dwight L. Moody—none of them were "verse-by-verse" preachers. The way we have defined it, traditional expository preaching is "too easy." What's hard is taking the stories of the Bible and connecting them to the stories of your zip code.

We don't preach the Scriptures; we let the Scriptures preach through us as they point to Christ. True preaching starts when the Scriptures start preaching themselves. After Vatican II the bishops of the Roman Catholic Church instructed its preachers to "dwell in the word." By this they meant, "The homily is not so much on the Scriptures as from and through the Scriptures."[19] Or, as interpreted by James A. Wallace, "The homily is not so much an explanation of the scripture as a process of first entering their world (thus speaking *from* them) and then using this world as a lens to look out onto our world (thereby speaking *through* them)."[20] In this sense, "all true Christian preaching is expository preaching. If by an 'expository' sermon is meant a verse-by-verse explanation of a lengthy passage of Scripture, this would be a misuse of the word."[21] But if exposition "refers to the content of the sermon (biblical truth) rather than the style (a running commentary)," then to "expose" or point to Jesus and facilitate people to "experience" him through Scripture must be the goal of every sermon. "Whether it is long or short, our responsibility as expositors is to open it up in such a way that it speaks its message clearly, plainly, accurately, relevantly, without addition, subtraction or falsification."[22]

With a proper understanding of "expository" in mind, let us look now at how to "expose" those Scriptures in a way that is most EPIC for our context. Let us look at the blood type most suited to the narraphoric sermon.

Blood Types and Blood Screening: Deduction, Induction, Abduction, and Transduction

> What is the use of a book, without pictures or conversations?
> —Alice, in *Alice in Wonderland* by Lewis Carroll

BEFORE YOU CAN BUILD YOUR SERMON, you need to know what type of sermon you want to build. There is no one right way to preach, and in the course of your lifetime as a preacher, you will need to change preaching styles many times (I'm on my fifth and working on my sixth). Like Picasso, whose artistry went through various "stages," so will your ministry and your preaching go through various stages.

There are many architectural styles from which to choose, and different time periods have blessed some styles over others.[1] What is excellent communication to one culture is execrable communication to another. For example, the early church's simple storytelling became in the third century classical rhetoric (which is still being taught in some quarters and is gaining increasing attention in European and North American universities).[2] It was "baptized" by Augustine in part 4 of his *De Doctrina Christiana*, which provided advice for the giving of homilies. A content analysis of Augustine's work shows the equivalent of over one hundred footnotes to Cicero's *De Oratorio*, leading some to claim that "homiletics was born as the stepchild of rhetoric."[3]

What is tenderloin to some cultures, however, is gristle to another. Those supporting narrative theory argue for a homily as story. The Thelonius Monk of homileticians, Eugene Lowry, posits "homiletical plots" that involve the creation of dramatic tension followed by resolution of the tension, which takes place through five stages: upsetting the equilibrium, analyzing the discrepancy, disclosing the clue to resolution, experiencing the gospel, and anticipating the consequences.[4]

Others advocate for a sermon based in cultural studies and view cultural studies as intrinsic to biblical studies. Cultural studies sermons seek to understand the context of the writer, or what Ernest Best called the "loam" from which the text is grown. In that vein, LeRoy E. Kennel proposes that "cultural counterpointing can transpose a hermeneutical crux into a homiletical crucible."[5]

The more traditional distinction divides all sermons into three types: topical, textual, and expository. *Topical* preaching elaborates on a specific topic or theme and seeks to relate it to life. Scripture is deployed to back up the topic or theme. Topical sermons derive a text for delivery. *Textual* preaching delivers a sermon from a text. A textual preacher chooses a passage from the Bible and then attempts to use it as a jumping-off point to discuss a particular theme or thrust.

Expository preaching speaks on Scripture passage by passage in order to allow the text to determine its own point or to allow Scripture itself to speak authoritatively and prophetically. Larger portions of Scripture are used in this case than the single line and may include a *lectio continua*, or a series of sermons that continue through an entire book of the Bible.

Some homileticians, such as Haddon Robinson, have argued that Jesus used an expositional style,[6] which is hotly debated. To be sure, Jesus respected Scripture. Almost everything—if not everything—recorded of his words references Scripture in some way. Yet he rarely quoted exactly from the Bible. He paraphrased it and placed it in his context. He cited Scripture in one way to the scribes, Pharisees, and religious leaders but in another way when speaking with crowds of common people.

Jesus brandished biblical authority most of all when dialoguing with those who professed the greatest faith in it.[7] Even then, however, his usage of Scripture went far beyond simple quotation. Jesus chose texts for specific contexts and hearers. His comprehensive understanding not just of the Scriptures but of their varied interpretations, symbolisms, metaphors, meanings in Hebrew history, and layers of rabbinic exegesis meant that his sermons flummoxed some and landed with laserlike precision on others.

Jesus also had a different method of teaching and preaching to his inner group of disciples. How did they remember so much of Jesus' teaching? Because Jesus was master of the "teaching moment." He did more than quote or comment on Scripture. In fact, his teaching was not based, as all teaching was before him, on authoritative rabbinic interpretations. His teaching was self-authenticating: "You have heard it said ... but I say." And he frequently created interactive, real-life, hands-on situations in which he and his disciples could engage in the act of learning together.

*   *   *

"Mature leaders give the congregation wise blood."
—*Peter L. Steinke, systems consultant*[8]

*   *   *

We have almost as little scholarship devoted to the oratorical life of Jesus as we do to the imaginative life of Jesus. But one of the few things biblical scholars agree on is that the kingdom of God was the cornerstone of Jesus' preaching. The "kingdom of God" is an interesting phrase, because it not only denotes a theological meaning but an exegetical method expressed in the acronym PaRDeS, representing the third of the four basic types of Jewish exegesis used during the first century. To review what we learned in chapter 1, these methods were *peshat* (simple inquiry), *remez* (hinting, typological), *derash* (complex metaphorical midrash), and *sod* (intuitive, revelational).

Of the four layers of meaning in the Hebrew PaRDeS, Jesus used all four. The *peshat* is a literal reading; the *remez*, typological. The *derash*, however, indicates the layers of meaning represented by parables that reveal the nature of the "kingdom of God." The word *midrash* derives from the word *darash* or to "inquire," the origin of the word *derash*. At this "midrash" level of interpretation, the rabbi is making his own interpretations of the truth. But Jesus told his disciples even deeper, more "secret" interpretations related to his messiahship and to the underlying inspirational and revelational meaning of life—the *sod*. Whereas many times our exposition might stop at the second level of Jewish interpretation, the *remez* (the method of hinting at meaning that goes beyond the literal—the *peshat*—and is dependent on simpler and more traditional interpretations), we must dig more deeply into the innermost layers of meaning to reap the richness of interpretation. Laying the sod of God in the rich and fertile landscape for a hillside sermon.

The methodologies used to understand meaning that most closely echo the PaRDeS Hebrew exegetical method might well be described as the methods of deduction, induction, abduction, and transduction. The first three are well known as knowledge-producing methods. The last, which I add here, transcends traditional means of knowledge making and allows for a depth and interplay only possible in the relationship between divine and human. Whereas a deduction shows a simple conclusion according to a law or principle, induction determines value. Inductive conclusions are drawn from gathered evidence or propositions. Abduction, often thought to be a subtype of induction,[9] is more creative and imaginative because it forms explanatory hypotheses or suggestions based on intuition that must be subsequently proven by action or experience.

The fourth, and one I add here, I call "transductive" (or "transincarnational"). Transduction is the interactive unfolding of internal revealed meaning, revealed truth. Like abduction, it includes intuitive right-brained inquiry but adds reception and animation. The origin of transductive knowing is interactive and relational. It originates within the relationship between knower and known. It involves a search for truth, not fact or proof. While in abduction, the seeker of meaning forms a creative but reasonable hypothesis that is later proven in experience and action, in transductive knowing, the seeker of meaning engages in relationship with the disseminator of revelatory knowledge and immerses in a story and/or image that bears on and bares the soul. Reveling in revelation rather than grounded in reason alone, transincaration transforms meaning and truth through the relational engagement of faith itself.

While this level of meaning would be rejected by philosophical, mathematical, or scientific means of knowing that demand external and concrete proofs, transduction (or transincarnation) instead is an internal transformational and incarnational experience, proven only by confession of faith, conversion of spirit, and repentance or change of heart. Transincarnation invites visual, auditory, kinesthetic, and other sensory experiences. It is relational truth that is discovered within questions rather than answers, in probes rather than proofs, through opening windows rather than shutting doors. It is not designed for "texterminators"—only "questians."

Transduction not only creates meaning but transfers meaning and transforms through meaning. It is not just meaning created through Q&A, but meaning transformed to a higher or deeper level by the quest itself. It is an incarnational "means of meaning." Not just a simple dash of *derash*; rather, more the *sod* of God. In the Hebrew PaRDeS, this would be the level of knowledge considered hard hitting, life changing, mind blowing, and most closely related to the divine, revelatory experience. It was not knowing "about" God but was about "knowing" God.

* * *

"If we cannot in some measure understand God's mind, all science must be a delusion and a snare."
—*Charles Sanders Peirce, founder of semiotics*

* * *

Best used in partnership with abduction, and often in conjunction with elements of deduction and induction, the addition of transincarnational meaning to the means of knowing transports the sermon out of a merely rational or philosophical discourse and places it within a faith-filled, full-flavored interactive experience of truth that admits that faith cannot be philosophically or rationally "known" but must be embodied communally, engaged holistically, and impressed deeply into both mind and heart.

Jesus used a combination of all of these methods in teaching. And as preachers, I would assert, so should we.

Charles Sanders Peirce, philosopher and semiotician, has been called the most original and important American philosopher in US history, equaled in history only by Aristotle and Gottfried Wilhelm Leibniz. Like Leibniz, Peirce hoped to write a "theory of everything" or the Ultimate Hypothesis. Peirce is known as the founder of semiotics (the study of how meaning is communicated) and philosophical pragmatism.[10] He famously defined a sign as "something which stands for somebody to something in some respect or capacity." He was also the first experimental psychologist in America. He originated the use of light waves in the measurement of length. He designed the first electric switching-circuit computer. I could go on and on.

Who Was Charles Sanders Peirce (1839–1914)?

Peirce led a tragic life. Although brilliant—he wrote a history of chemistry when he was only eleven years old. In his later years, he suffered from facial neuralgia, which he treated with ether, opium, and morphine, most likely cocaine as well. He appears also to have been manic-depressive (bipolar). One example of the odd dialectic between his philosophy and his life might be seen in his personal encounters. Peirce married Harriet Melusina Fay (Zina) in 1862. Melusina was a feminist Christian who believed that the Holy Ghost was the feminine force in the universe. She influenced Charles to become an Episcopalian. Peirce made clear that he didn't like sex and saw marriage as a platonic ideal. He even advocated death as punishment for adultery.

Yet in 1875, on a trip to Paris, he got caught with his pants down. Melusina left him and eventually divorced him. In 1883, two days after the divorce was final from his first wife, he eloped with a mysterious "dark lady" from Europe named Juliette Pourtalai who claimed to be a Romanian princess. In the eyes of his peers and public, he did the unthinkable.

It was one thing to have a mistress yet another thing to marry her. This offended the Boston Brahmins, and he was ostracized from his peers.

Peirce's professional life reflected this same turbulence. Peirce taught at Johns Hopkins, but students like John Dewey (philosopher and psychologist) and Thorstein Veblen (economist and sociologist) found him so hard, they dropped the course. Peirce was known to be ungracious and ill-tempered. He was eventually barred from Johns Hopkins, as well as from Harvard, and his only living came from what he received from book reviews written for the magazine *The Nation* and the largesse of William James. Peirce's last academic appointment was in 1884.

Peirce openly admitted his character flaws: "For long years, I suffered unspeakably, being an excessively emotional fellow, from ignorance of how to go to work to acquire a sovereignty over myself." Peirce's pragmatism (or pragmaticism) required him to argue that ideas had to be judged on the basis of their impact on one's life: an idea's value "lies exclusively in its conceivable bearing upon the conduct of life … and deliberate conduct is self-controlled conduct." By his own measure, his ideas had little value.

Peirce found himself destitute in his later years. Without a teaching post since 1891, the last twenty-three years of his life were spent jobless and penniless, with nothing to eat for days on end but oatmeal and crackers. He begged for money to buy food but spent the food money to hire workers to maintain his 2,000-acre estate in Milford, Pennsylvania. Even when he suffered greatly from illness, or as he put it "suffering at every mouth through which a man can drink suffering," still he and his wife went for days without groceries while they kept maintaining their home. In his final days, to keep warm during the Pennsylvania winters, they were reduced to burning his precious books as firewood. When William James credited him as the founder of pragmatism in 1898, he was sleeping on the sidewalks of New York City. Peirce published only one book in his lifetime (*Photometric Researches* [Leipzig, 1878]) but left behind more than eighty thousand pages of unpublished manuscripts. A few of the scholars who confess debts to him include Noam Chomsky, Ilya Prigogine, Jacques Derrida, and Umberto Eco. In 1914 Peirce died of cancer at his estate, Arisbe, and his wife Juliette became a recluse, surviving him by twenty years.

For Peirce knowledge had to be contextualized by experience. Peirce insisted that faith in God comes first, not from propositions or beliefs or ethics, but from the sheer beauty of faith itself: "A man looks upon nature, sees its sublimity and beauty, and his spirit gradually rises to the idea of God. He does not see the divinity, nor does nature prove to him the existence of that being, but it does excite his mind and imagination until the idea becomes rooted in his heart."[11]

In his later years, when his body was racked with neuralgia and he couldn't write down his ideas because the ink was frozen from the house being so cold from lack of fuel to heat it, he managed to scribble, "As a matter of opinion, I believe that Glory shines out in everything, and that any aesthetic odiousness is merely our unfeelingness resulting from obscurations due to our own moral and intellectual aberrations."[12] Peirce defined God in aesthetic terms like those of Jonathan Edwards, his only major competitor in the history of philosophy in America: God is beauty, and the divine is found in beauty.

The worse life got for Peirce, it seemed, the better his writings and ideas. The more his peers sneered at him for writing on religious topics, the more he wrote on them. He had no one to share his philosophical discoveries with in his lifetime except for Josiah Royce, who negotiated Harvard's purchase of his papers upon his death. Peirce believed that Royce was the only contemporary who understood him or his work.

Peirce recoiled in horror from the "if-it-works-for-you" subjectivism that William James seemed to be taking from pragmatism. So he coined the neologism *pragmaticism* to distinguish his realism from that of James, who had coopted the term *pragmatism*. Peirce argued in 1883 that true pragmatism was a continuation of Jesus' teaching in Matthew 7:16: "By their fruits you shall know them" (my paraphrase). Peirce even labeled his cosmology the doctrine of "Christian love."[13]

Peirce didn't think much of the concept of "originality." But he himself made original contributions to a staggering number of disciplines: chemistry, physics, astronomy, meteorology, cartography, experimental psychology, philology, statistics, mathematics, logic, phenomenology, philosophy, and theology. According to Peirce, "We can't know whether an idea is a good one unless we take a chance on it. Life is the only test of belief we have."[14]

Musement was one of Peirce's favorite words.[15] For a logician to make a case for intuition, imagination, entailment, entrainment, and "melted continuity" was as startling as a strategic planner making a case for "on a wing and a prayer."[16] For Peirce the "fuzziness" and vagueness" of God-talk was logically defensible. Aside from countless other "firsts," Peirce was the first advocate of "fuzzy logic."

Furthermore, Peirce came to see deduction, induction, and abduction as distinct but interdependent "stages of inquiry."[17] Lowest in Peirce's scale of mental processes is "deduction." At the core of an issue, analytic, deductive reasoning leads to no new information, only elaboration and a restating of the facts. Next up the ladder is "induction," a synthetic form of cognition that issues in a creative insight of generalization and classification ("therefore") but that does not entail the hypothetical leaps and explanatory power of "abduction."[18] The mind works first deductively and inductively. Deductive conclusions are drawn from close and sustained scrutiny of principles. Inductive conclusions are drawn from empirically gathered evidence.

The highest level of thought, according to Peirce, is the abductive process: only the "hypothesizing" of the abductive process "most closely imitates the divine Mind, for that Mind is, at its most playful and musing, feeling, sporting here and there in pure arbitrariness."[19] Our abductive moments of risk and exploration "put us into direct, imitative contact with this abducting Divine Mind."[20]

Peirce claimed that deduction is the language of mathematical logic while induction is the language of scientific empiricism. Abduction is creative philosophic inquiry, proven through experience and action. Hypothesis or inference is a posteriori, not a priori. A priori knowledge is conceptual and independent of experience, based on reason alone. A posteriori justifies a hypothesis, proposition, or assertion and is based on experience. A posteriori arguments cannot be based only on reason but must be proven through experience, or in a phrase Jesus used that Peirce liked to quote, "You may know them by their fruits."[21] You cannot reasonably assume that those who claim to have their hearts rooted in God live the life of the incarnated Christ unless their "fruit" is edible and ethical.

Jonathan Edwards called this "remanation." As God emanates the light of Christ into one's life, one reflects back to God the light of Christ within. In other words, one's life is a "sign," a visible sign of the invisible presence of Christ in the heart. Jesus often told his disciples to stay awake and pay attention to the signs of God's presence. To help us read the "signs" of God's presence, Jesus told multiple parables describing the "kingdom," which Christ himself has signaled by his own presence in the world.

For John Wesley his entire ministry was "proven" by the ripeness of the "fruit" of his converts. This experiential "evidence" backs up the inferences of abduction. For Peirce faith resides within the abductive imagination that experiences God as beautiful. However, abduction for Peirce could not be considered a valid means of knowing or a valid expression of belief ("faith") unless "proven" through right actions ("fruit").

While the logic of mathematical deduction proves through formula, and the science of induction shows value through the triad of observation-interpretation-application,[22] abduction measures the truth of a theory in relationship to experiences of its results. For Peirce conception must have some conceivable "apps," some observable effects of its applications. In abduction, the "gate of perception" meets the "gate of purposive action." Experience yields purpose yields action. In a sense, abduction is the semiotic signpost of Luther's doctrine of justification by faith: one is justified by faith alone, but when filled with the presence of the Holy Spirit, one's heart is necessarily provoked to acts of love and mercy. Fruits follow faith a posteriori. One first experiences Christ but then acts on that experience of grace with one's own fruitful living.

John Wesley took this idea a bit further by insisting that it is an ongoing process of "sanctification," whereby the means of grace motivate a follower to mission to bear the fruit of the Spirit. Likewise, one's life is a visible sign experienced by others of the incarnational presence of Christ living within. Peirce maintained that the experience of Christ (as intuitive, imaginative, perceptive, insightful) may be fallible, according to the limits of reason. Therefore, purposeful action (change) must be present as "proof" of that faith. According to Peirce, "Any flight of imagination is allowable, as long as it ultimately alights on possible, practical effect. This may or may not be fully conscious."[23]

What Peirce does not allow is a definition of faith that goes beyond concretized imagination, the insight that leads to perception by the mind. Proof of faith resides in visible signs. There can be no hidden or invisible signs secreted in what the Hebrew exegetical method would call the *sod*. For Peirce the pilgrim's search for God is not immersion but inquiry, not truth but still a form of knowledge. Though freed from analytics and linearity, abduction still remains without "proof," a fallible knowledge and a faulty reason. The inquiring mind is still in control and self-authenticating. Peirce said that in the abductive process the seeker still initiates the purposeful change. Abduction seeks answers and strives to prove results (concretized truth) rather than to provoke questions and probe mysteries (incarnated truth).

A person of faith can intuit or experience God, but only as an inquiring mind. The abductive process does not allow for any relationality or interiority of the *imago Dei*. A communal, open-grained experience of the transcendent that receives and remanates revelatory experience remains outside the abductive framework. In abduction there is no "metaphorical break," that pivotal moment in which a transformational shift occurs (repentance, turnaround) that is affected internally before it initiates change of action. In transduction a significant internal or relational metamorphosis takes place that is marked by relinquished control and repeated revelation in life's spaces of nonrational mystery and nonconcrete meaning.

For Peirce abduction must be ultimately proven by the visible signs of purposeful action: "Nothing is in the intellect that is not first in the senses."[24] In transduction (or transincarnation), the moment itself is revelational. It discloses truth not yet through action but through trust, insight, relationality, intuition, and healed perceptions. It is John Wesley's "strange" feeling of a "warmed heart," an experience not yet differentiated in action but distinguished by what chaos theory calls the "strange attractor"[25] that constrains and directs what is missional, relational, and incarnational (MRI). It is an inner experience of the whole being—mind, body, spirit.

Here is where John Wesley can help. In his sermon "We Walk by Faith and Not by Sight" (1788), he details the progression from "enlightenment" to "inner light." As people of Christ, we do not measure only by what we see with our sight but by what we perceive with our insight through the eyes of faith. If deduction is the language of mathematical logic, induction the language of scientific empiricism, and abduction the language of philosophical proof through a posteriori experience, then transduction (or transincarnation) is the mind-bending, heartrending, body-spending language of MRI faith—the grafting of the covenant onto a soul continuously cleansed by EPIC engagements. It is a bone-deep, blood-born, whole-body encounter— not just cognition of God, but a re-cognition of God's cognition of us, recognized as truth. Transincarnational preaching doesn't aim to "influence" the hearer, but to imbed in the hearer that recognition of truth, a re-cognition that is felt in the core of our being, as our humanity is ever after defined in and redefined by our relationship with our Creator.

As with Jesus, one cannot dig into the roots of the garden without first noting the presence of the plant. The Hebrew PaRDeS is intended as a four-fold exegetical method, all four parts necessary to a full and comprehensive homiletics. For John Wesley a believer could not have "enthusiasm" without reason, nor anything without grounding in the Scriptures. For Peirce all three of his categories need to work together for the mind to gain the fullest understanding. Likewise, in the sermonic method outlined in this book, the "blood types" are examined not in order to separate out their parts, but to appreciate their synergy and contributions to the whole.

In transductive (or transincarnational) preaching, the best of all forms of knowledge and understanding are employed to approach truth. In a sense, the transductive moment is the experiential prompt that opens relational space, allowing the participant to ask the imaginative questions necessary to provoke an abductive response. The "proof" is eventually in the pudding, but it is the kind of pudding that is especially important.

It is time to examine more closely the four "types" of preaching: first, the two most commonly referred to in classical preaching texts, deductive and inductive. Then we will add those experiential and narraphoric preaching styles, the abductive and the transductive (transincarnational).

TYPING AND SCREENING

If we take the four means of expressing meaning and think about the ways in which we can experience the Scriptures as the blood of Christ, we can also see four ways of "giving blood"—of connecting the lifeblood story of Jesus to the life of the congregation. We need to know the blood type in order for a transfusion to take place. Noncompatibility with a donor is the number one reason why blood transfusions fail. If we want to infuse blood into a body in need of Christ, we need to know the best kind of preaching to build on. Let's look under the microscope now and screen these four blood types—five, in fact, if you choose a method that combines the first two.

Type A. Deductive preaching: red blood cells with the presence of A and with an antibody against B. I call type A blood deductive. I name this the *peshat* of preaching, or expository preaching.

Type B. Inductive preaching: the reverse of type A—red blood cells with the presence of B and with an antibody against A. I call type B blood inductive. I name this the *remez* of preaching, or the narrative method of preaching.

Type AB. Deductive-inductive preaching: AB contains no antibody against anybody, but red cells contain both A and B substances. I call type AB blood the combination of inductive and deductive preaching. Since AB has no antibodies, it can receive any of the four types of blood. An AB is a universal recipient. AB is a combination of *peshat* and *remez*: it shares both rational and sensory knowledge.

Type O. Abductive preaching: red cells contain no substance, but the blood can form antibodies against either A or B. I call type O blood abductive. Type O can be given successfully to almost any person. An O is a universal donor. I call this the *derash* of preaching.

Type ABO$^\Omega$. Transductive (transincarnational) preaching: This blood type is really the name of the entire blood networking system. And it is the one I am using here to describe a method that takes the best of all three ways of expressing meaning and elevates them to "incarnational power." This is the *sod* of preaching—revealing and experiencing the incarnation of Christ within the body. It is partaking in the dance of life as choreographed by the Lord of the Dance.

$\star \quad \star \quad \star$

"The inner life of God, which is bound up inextricably with
the redemptive, justice-making activity of God in
the world, is characterized at its core by a dance or chorus,
a dance that is the ground and end of all beauty. Notice
that at this deepest level of God's being, an aesthetic image takes precedence over abstract terminology. For ...
this comes closest to expressing the mystery that is the life
of God ... which means they [texts/images] are to
be practiced rather than simply understood—or, better,
they will be understood only when practiced."
—William Dyrness, theologian[26]

$\star \quad \star \quad \star$

Closed, causal logic is comprised of three kinds of reasoned argument: abduction, induction, and deduction. The fourth, transduction, transcends argument and encourages participation as it points to truth. In a sense, our use of these terms in preaching already reveals a given: we will assume that preaching is a representational and participatory (semiotic) medium that points (as a sign) to God. It reveals God symbolically through Scripture and symbiotically through narraphor in an ABO$^\Omega$ way of preaching that issues in an EPIC style.

TYPE A: DEDUCTIVE PREACHING

Deductive preaching has something to declare. From that "big idea" or "central thesis," it then deduces points and subpoints. Like the deductive argument, it is almost algebraic in nature, conceptually clear and memorably formulaic—or for those of us who flunked algebra, obscure and out of range.

The deductive sermon sets out to demonstrate the validity and reliability of a truth. It often consists of an introduction, multiple points, and a conclusion. Deductive reasoning is the primary form of the "expository" method. Its chief proponent is Haddon Robinson, the Johann Sebastian Bach of homileticians. Robinson defines deductive preaching as "the communication of a biblical concept, derived from and transmitted through a historical, grammatical, and literary study of a passage in its context, which the Holy Spirit applies first to the personality and experience of the preacher, then through him or her to the listeners."[27] Robinson admits that "it is more a philosophy than a method."[28] Like Jacob's ladder, the deductive method yields a linear sermon laddered with propositions and latticed with points that connect heaven and earth.[29]

In the expository sermon, points and propositions are the skeleton; illustrations are the "fleshing out" of the structure, the add-ons. The strengths of deductive homiletics are obvious: studied, sturdy, sharply pointed. But the weaknesses of deductive homiletics are also obvious. You can't hug a skeleton. You can't hold hands with a bone. And points are hard to pick up without getting cut, and that cutting can seem at times like the splitting of hairs on the heads of angels dancing on the heads of pins, or what Sigmund Freud called "the narcissism of small differences." In this not much has changed since the "plain preaching" tradition of the Puritans, when a sermon was made up of diligent exegesis, a rigorous theological framework, and a worked-over and drilled-down proposition or principle.

Those who have defended the deductive (e.g., expository) over the inductive (e.g., narrative) approach to preaching have made their case partly on the need to preserve the teaching function of preaching, which is lost in a world that emphasizes feelings, experiences, and relationships.[30] To be sure, more now than ever people need teaching from their preaching. But what kind of "teaching"?

Teaching now takes into account EQ (emotional intelligence) as well as IQ, not to mention experiences and relationships.[31] Walter J. Burghardt, Jesuit theologian, preacher, and editor of *Theological Studies* for over two decades, talked honestly before his death at ninety-three about his grooming in the deductive method but his increased conviction that preaching needs to "grab the guts": "When I began to preach five decades ago, the Catholic stress was on the clear and distinct idea. From seminary on, we were dispassionate searchers for truth, cool critics of error and heresy: beetle-browed, lynx-eyed, hard-nosed, square-jawed. Imagination was for poets. We did not show our emotions. Emotions were for women, and women could not be ordained."[32]

Twenty-first-century listeners can't tolerate long investments in linear reasoning anymore. "For effective preaching [today]," Burghardt concluded, "the analytic mind is not enough by half."[33] There must be the experiential as well as the analytical, the perceptual as well as the conceptual, field thinking even more than linear thinking. Harvard's Harvey Cox, who studied the rise of Pentecostalism in the twentieth century, calls this "massive return of ecstasy in contemporary Christianity" an eruption of "primal spirituality."[34] And "primal spirituality" calls out for primal preaching.

*　*　*

"Human beings, vegetables and cosmic dust,
all dance to a mysterious tune intoned in
the distance by an invisible player."
—*Albert Einstein*[35]

*　*　*

In the Gutenberg world of print, preachers assumed that if they gave their people the right thoughts, if preachers rightly divided the Word of Truth, people would come to faith. Right thoughts would inevitably lead to right tasks. In this TGIF world, a right relationship comes before right thinking.[36] Or as it is more popularly put, the experience of belonging comes before the logic of believing.[37] A deductive sermon appeals to the mind but not the heart. It expresses faith not in felt terms or felt needs but in nuggets for the noggin.

Did Jesus come to give us points and propositions? Or did Jesus come to restore us to a covenant relationship with God? If we want to experience Jesus in relationship, we need to move from exclusively deductive and expository styles into different forms of preaching.

TYPE B: INDUCTIVE PREACHING

Inductive preaching is more of a journey than an arrival and is often manifested as narrative preaching.[38] With the inductive sermon, we move from literalisms and linearisms to storyboards, character development, and plotlines. The inductive sermon can still be expository, especially when referring to specific biblical narratives. But most often the journey of discovery and dot connecting typical of the inductive sermon privileges a narrative style.

Unlike the prefabricated precision of the deductive model, the inductive sermon mimics the empirical sciences, which are based on observation, interpretation, and application. The value of the sermon lies in the discovery that comes as a result of the buildup of increasing clarity of evidence. The inductive sermon moves from predictability to surprise. It doesn't so much *provide* an answer as *suggest* an answer, gather a response, imply a solution, narrate a reply. I wish I could preach as inductively as Winston Churchill (or was it W. C. Fields?), who, while intoxicated at a party, told a woman he detested, "You are ugly." To which she retorted, "And you are drunk!" "But," he responded, "in the morning, I'll be sober." That's inductive communication.[39]

The Handel of homileticians, Fred Craddock, has argued best for the inductive form of preaching. But he also recommends that the "forms of preaching should be as varied as the forms of rhetoric in the New Testament."[40] The inductive way of preaching is concerned with "How do you make your case?" Or "How can you assemble 'evidence' to prove a thesis or make a point?" Like the Hebrew *remez*, it intimates an answer. It is not launched from a predetermined point but gathers evidence until the unstated is inescapable. The inductive sermon argues a line of reasoning, stacking one brick at a time, climbing one rung of the ladder after another. This is the kind of "logic" that concludes that cottage cheese makes you fat, so everyone eating cottage cheese is fat or cottage cheese thighs are never thin.

Both deductive and inductive methods are useful if you are looking for a linear way of constructing a logical argument or need to argue convincingly on a central point and key doctrine or must land your sermons with absolute precision. The deductive method begins with a general introduction followed by specific (often anecdotal) backups, and ends with a general conclusion that summarizes or restates the main idea, which by now is unassailable. An example of a deductive sermon used to celebrate Communion could begin with the thesis that "Jesus, out of sheer grace, receives us into his friendship and family, and thus transforms our lives with power and significance."[41] The main points could focus on the fact that all aspects of Communion are peculiar and unusual, and Jesus' grace gives everything significance. A conclusion should draw together the uniqueness of God's grace and the unique qualities of disciples living out the Christian life.

The inductive approach is trickier because it doesn't begin with a foundational thesis on which a rational structure is constructed. Instead, it begins with a field and not a line. Like a river that takes its course, it journeys forward (and sometimes backward) with unexpected twists and turns. This approach may begin soliciting common agreement through a folk wisdom or cultural trend. Then, through a series of "moves,"[42] it rocks and rattles that premise. When people begin to feel uneasy about the shifting sand under their cherished assumptions, the sermon introduces a new idea, often one that would have seemed absurd or strange a few moments ago but that now offers new hope and resolution of the tension.

For the preacher, there is always a Sunday coming. The inductive and deductive possibilities for "bringing it home" every week are legion. You can begin with your conclusion then work backward. You can deliver well-told stories. You can use the story behind a hymn as a transition from the sermon to the hymn itself. You can ask a question and then answer it (another inductive method) or point out specifically the sermon's point and then paint that point in many colors. You never hesitate to rephrase and summarize main points to make sure people "get it." The "constructive" ease of building deductive and inductive sermons has made them enormously popular. For this reason, some still adamantly hold to a method that uses one or the other or some combination of the two.

TYPE AB: DEDUCTIVE-INDUCTIVE PREACHING

Some scholars argue that there is very little "distance" between an inductive and a deductive homiletic. In the words of Richard L. Eslinger, "Both seem to be bound to a rationalist hermeneutic."[43] The advantage of using a combination of both is, for some, that very linear, logical, and constructive hermeneutic. The difference between the two is one of deployment. The deductive method declares an intent and fulfills it. The inductive method leads the listener by the hand and arranges the place where minds meet. A combined method might give an organizing thesis but use a more narrative style. Or it might use induction with a more argumentative style. But whether you are moving from (deduction) or toward (induction) a proposition, you're still traveling in the world of propositions. You are still mounted on a rationalist motherboard.[44]

Eugene Lowry is the most potent voice against propositional preaching, which "distorts and even deforms the experiential meaning" of the gospel. Since the Bible is mainly "nonpropositional," he argues, only narrative forms are faithful to the "aesthetic communication" intrinsic to the Scriptures.[45]

Thomas G. Long, Bandy Professor of Preaching at Candler School of Theology, says that both camps are guilty of profound half-truths:

> The "main idea" crowd was half right about this—texts say something and therefore express ideas—but they were only half right because they over-

looked the fact that texts say what they say in order to cause something to happen.... The "aesthetic" crowd was half right as well—texts do create experiences—but they were also only half right because they downplayed the conceptual content by which texts create those experiences.[46]

The problem with every profound half-truth is the other half. How can we keep what is important to the deductive and inductive processes but move into the more right-brained realms of creativity, intuition, and conversation? How can we do the following?

1. Move from linear to nonlinear thinking, engaging both sides of our brains.
2. Ask more questions instead of giving all the answers.
3. Encourage people to think more creatively and not be afraid of mystery.
4. Make and see revelatory connections between Scripture and life, between our stories and God's story.
5. Make the sermon a holistic, multisensory experience.
6. Allow people to feel the presence of Christ in the message and facilitate faith responses.
7. See meaning in image, metaphor, signs, and symbols.
8. Allow Jesus to dwell within us, become stunned by his grace, be transformed by his love, beholding his glory instead of looking for ways to nail down Jesus.
9. Craft an EPIC architecture for our sermons.

For this we need to look at a third kind of sermon: the abductive sermon.

TYPE O: ABDUCTIVE PREACHING

The only way to hit a moving target is to give it a lead. This is what it means to "lead" forward. In the abductive method, you lead forward through hunches, hypotheses, and intuitions. You leave behind lines of battle for fields of dreams. In the words of Peirce:

Looking out of my window this lovely spring morning I see an azalea in full bloom. No, no! I do not see that; though that is the only way I can describe what I see. That is a proposition, a sentence, a fact; but what I perceive is not proposition, sentence, fact, but only an image, which I make intelligible in part by means of a statement of fact. This statement is abstract; but what I see is concrete. I perform an abduction when I [do so much] as express in a sentence anything I see. The truth is that the whole fabric of our knowledge is one matted felt of pure hypothesis confirmed and refined by induction. Not the smallest advance can be made in knowledge beyond the stage of vacant staring, without making an abduction at every step.[47]

In abductive preaching, the truth is not something we deduce but something we lean into, something we reach for beyond the confines of our limitations. Abduction uses the creative mind to make inferences, decipher signs, connect relationships, reframe images, change directions. The key to abduction is the ability to unsettle and surprise, which comes from diligent inquiry.

The *derash* of the PaRDeS comes from the Hebrew *derosh*. Ancient Hebrew scholars prized and counted every word of the Torah. In a word count of the Torah, the last word of the first half is *darosh* and the first word of the second half is darash, both words forming the expression *darosh darash*, or "diligently inquired" as found in Leviticus 10:16: "Moses [diligently] inquired." This was not a historical happenstance to the rabbis.[48] We must all aspire to be like Moses, who practiced a *darosh darash*, or "diligently inquired."

Sherlock Holmes was good at both deductive and inductive reasoning, although most Enlightenment minds preferred inductive to deductive. But both deductive and inductive methods can lead to bad conclusions. For example, scholars have observed that the preponderance of shipwrecks are along shorelines. They induced from the evidence the principle that ancient sailors hugged shorelines when sailing. They deduced from principle that ancient ships didn't cross open water. The truth of why the majority of wrecks are found along coastlines is far different from what the "inductive" or "deductive" methods suggest. Ancient mariners learned the hard way that to be close to a lee shore is the most dangerous place to be in a storm. It was experience of shipwreck that taught sailors the necessity of sailing out to sea and away from land to ride out a storm. Nothing is more dangerous in heavy winds than hugging harbors and squeezing coastlines.

Worship in a TGIF world needs to claim an abductive semiotic that moves worship beyond the inductive and deductive slugfest that has for too long been the hallmark of homiletics. Abduction leaves behind mathematical precision and scientific empiricism and moves into the realm of semiotic more than hermeneutic imagination. While still requiring "proofs," the abductive sermon is nonlinear and nonformulaic. It encourages right-brain creativity, "field" thinking, and Scripture-enhanced imagination.

In our current culture, knowing proceeds through field thinking more than linear thinking—through imaginative leaps, loops, and lurches that come to life in story form almost holographically around performative metaphors. "To be sure," in the words of Princeton education professor James E. Loder (1932–2001), "such leaps are not totally blind to observation or reflection, but in the discovery of new knowledge. The facts do not determine the theory. Instead, the theory creates the facts, and it is contradiction that creates theory through an act of imagination."[49] Replace "theory" with "story" and you have it about right.

Abduction is the process of forming an explanatory hypothesis, or what we are calling a narraphor. In Peirce's own definition, "It is the only logical operation which introduces any new idea, for induction does nothing but determine a value, and deduction merely evolves the necessary consequences of pure hypothesis."[50] Abduction ("creative," "inspirational," "imaginative," "feeling," "intuitive") doesn't exclude either induction or deduction ("scientific," "logical"). In fact, according to Peirce, "hypothesis produces the sensuous element of thought, and induction the habitual element."[51]

Abduction is "a feeling kind of knowing" not sufficient in and of itself but indispensable in the whole-brained representation and apprehension of the sacred. It is a more primal form of reasoning than deduction or induction because the function of deduction and induction is to test abduction. Abduction is the key that unlocks holistic knowing. The mind works less by mechanical calculations than by creative hops and hunches. Abduction occurs when old ideas are combined in new ways, when opposites collide, when relationships between things are reconfigured, when metaphors are mixed to yield moments of insight. For Peirce abduction is the very flashpoint of insight: "Oh, I see!" "I get it now!" "Finally, it makes sense!" "So that's what you mean!" "I've caught on." "It all fits together now"—although this insight will be, willy-nilly, "extremely fallible insight."[52]

The difference between the left-brained deductive and inductive methods and the right-brained abductive method[53] is the difference between approaching the Bible as God's rulebook versus God's storybook, God's handbook versus God's handiwork, God's homework assignment versus God's home page.[54] In David Storey's novel *A Serious Man* (1998), we find this memorable exchange:

> "What," I enquired, "is the point of it all?"
> "Isn't the point of the point," he ingenuously persisted, "that the point of the point is a circle?"[55]

Peirce insisted that faith in God comes not inductively or deductively but abductively, as the beauty of God opens in the imagination a leap of faith: "A man looks upon nature, sees its sublimity and beauty, and his spirit gradually rises to the idea of God. He does not see the Divinity, nor does nature prove to him the existence of that Being, but it does excite his mind and imagination until the idea becomes rooted in his heart."[56]

"Semiotics" was the name Peirce gave to the theory of signs. In Peirce's sign/object/interpretant triad, according to one of Peirce's most astute interpreters, Robert Corrington, "signs are always about both other signs and partially hidden objects. The term 'object' refers to anything whatsoever, from a solid space-time particular, to a possibility, to an empire, to a puff of smoke, to a gesture, or to anything that can be pointed to by human beings. What we are seeking are those dimly grasped objects that promise to show us the way toward a true understanding of the world."[57]

Abduction differs from induction in that propositions and laws do not define the sign, but one "has to posit the code at the same time as making the inference."[58] As Thomas Aquinas saw long before quantum physicists did, "The act of the believer terminates in the reality, not in the proposition. For we formulate propositions only in order to know things by means of them."[59] Classical physics is now known to be wrong, replaced by quantum physics. Science is no longer about natural laws, unbending principles, or absolute principles. Quantum theory is all about inputs, experiences, relationships, and propensities for experience. And what led to the change from classical physics to quantum theory and now string theory? According to Roger Penrose, the Rouse Ball Professor of Mathematics at the University of Chicago and "one of the world's most knowledgeable and creative mathematical physicists,"[60] it is by metaphors that true thinking is done and that science moves forward: "Rigorous argument is usually the last step."[61] Perhaps a better name for those famous "thought experiments" of Einstein and other scientists is abductive imaginings.[62]

Abductive imaginings were suppressed in the modern world for more rational calculations and left-brained considerations. The receptivity of TGIF culture toward abductive methods makes abduction the most important communication skill of the three at this time of history. In fact, we are in the midst of a pedagogical revolution as abductive learning is quickly becoming the basis of many visual, auditory, and kinesthetic educational styles. Just as induction and deduction were foundational in the Gutenberg world of print, abduction is quickly becoming the firmament in which Google culture is being built.

According to Peirce, the first person in history who fully developed and deployed the abductive method was Jesus of Nazareth.[63] One key element of Jesus' parabolic style of communication was surprise. Herein lies our problem. Gutenberg culture didn't like surprises: "The best surprise is no surprise." Holiday Inn used this slogan in the late 1970s and early 1980s to promise "no surprise" experiences—everything predictable, standardized, and franchised. People today are looking for more than the assurance of clean linens and toilets in their spiritual life. They're looking for ambushing surmises, big sunrises, and lurking surprises that God loves them even in the midst of their messiness, confusion, and pain.

This is what a preacher owes a congregation: passion, excitement, engagement, and just possibly, surprise.

Preachers work hard to say the same things differently. But in a world where change is exponential and not just incremental, it is now equally important to say different things using the same ways and words—to retain the revered language, to revel in the traditions, and to realize that every time Scripture speaks (whether read out loud or referenced in preaching) it also finds the same old way to say a different thing. The narraphor in its mysterious self speaks. We take it seriously precisely by trusting the story to speak directly to us and engage us on its own terms just as it did to its first hearers and as it has to every hearer since.

But we must let narraphors speak to us as story. We must let the story surprise us. "We do not try to plant the flag of Scripture in the ground in order to establish for all (or even any) time what it means. We carry the flag of Scripture with us, and at each new encampment on the shifting ground of context and meaning, we fly it from the center pole of the tent and marvel at how, against every new landscape, it surprises us with new colors and hues."[64] A "homiletics of surprise" celebrates that things are never the same. We walk under scaffolding fully aware of the danger. And we trust God to surprise us when the same words and metaphors say a brand-new thing that speaks to a brand-new reality in our always-changing culture.

This surprise may be part of the narraphoric twist or turn. Or it may be the stunning re-cognition of God's grace. But the surprise within the abductive sermon allows for the full engagement of the listener in and within the message as well as their subsequent "bearing of fruit" as inductive/deductive evidence of their new knowledge of God. Murray Frick divides every congregation into three parts: (1) those who respond visually and often sit in the back to see the big picture; (2) those who respond audibly and sit in the middle so as not to miss anything; (3) those who respond kinesthetically, preferring to be drawn into an experience by participating physically; they sit in front and engage with bodies as well as minds.[65] It is the third group that is sometimes called "holistic listeners."[66] The abductive sermon encourages people to engage holistically with the message.

If Christian faith comes to us in two forms—the "story mode"[67] and the "doctrine mode"[68]—for the majority of Christian history the doctrine mode has dominated. Even the church fathers quoted Paul and the Psalms and the Prophets more than the Gospels. In fact, references to the Gospels by theologians are conspicuous by their infrequency. When they are made, they are often turned into illustrations and proverbs and allegories.

It is now time to rediscover the story mode of faith. We are faced with a culture that no longer thinks in a linear manner but in fields and narraphors. It is based more in imagacy and graphicacy than literacy. It is captivated by metaphor and image and story more than by dogmatics. It is more open to emotion and intuition and mystery than ever before. If we are to reach people with messages that "give blood," we need to begin to embrace abductive ways of preaching.

But then we must reach beyond abduction to the most powerful form of preaching—the transductive, transincarnational method. Transduction is the experiential, in-depth knowledge of God that Jesus imparted to his closest disciples. It is the kind of communication that forms identity as followers: God's incarnational presence, the sacramental, sacrificial, sacred art of receiving and giving the blood of Christ within and among the body of Christ.

TYPE ABO$^{\Omega}$: TRANSDUCTIVE PREACHING (TRANSINCARNATIONAL PREACHING)

In the modern world, preaching was informational. It was designed to inform people of what and whom they should believe. It produced good citizen Christianity and "believers" with a "worldview."

Abductive preaching is formational and inspirational. It encourages the formation of a Christ identity within people. But transductive preaching is also transformational and incarnational. It enables people so to experience "the truth" (through sight, sound, touch, smell, hearing, but also intuition, revelation, and relationship with the divine) that they can be set free from various captivities by a love relationship with Christ and with the world.

This is the role of the transductive or transincarnational sermon: to get people to embrace the Way, the Truth, and the Life in the very core of their being. Jesus preached inductively. But most often he preached abductively and transductively. It isn't enough inductively to "just tell a story." It was not enough for Jesus' inner circle of disciples simply to experience Jesus' parables. They were expected to engage Jesus in deep knowing of the divine through an intimate relationship with the story. They were summoned to inherit and inhabit the incarnational power of the Holy Spirit.

The transductive sermon is not just to animate, much less illustrate. The transductive sermon orchestrates the whole being in the narraphor. Like the abductive method, this means in part not to supply right answers but to ask better questions. But even more it means to revel in the mystery of life, to accept that not every question should or must be answered, to embrace something deeper than knowledge and certainty: faith and assurance. Or as Eugene Lowry sums it up so beautifully, every sermon is "dancing on the edge of mystery."[69]

★　　★　　★

"When grace enters, humans must dance."
—W. H. Auden

★　　★　　★

A transductive sermon is a collage of narraphors and interactives, moves and plays, answers and questions, thrusts and trusts in which the homiletic experience changes and grows as it incorporates the responses of the congregation, takes on the stories of others, adapts to the questions of others, and allows for pause and "space" in which the body of Christ can immerse itself in Christ's incarnational presence. The transductive method aims not at "doing" a sermon but "being" a sermon.

In short, the transductive or transincarnational sermon is a never-ending song in which all take part. It invites all to join in God's creative and redeeming presence and encourages full participation in the dance of life.

PAS DE DEUX AND *PAS DE DIEU*

The phrase "new homiletic" was first introduced by David James Randolph.[70] In his *The Renewal of Preaching* (1969), which was honored with a thirtieth anniversary edition in 1998, he argued for a "new homiletic" to go along with the "new hermeneutic." The basic thesis was as simple as it was brilliant: what if we designed homiletic presentations that dovetailed with biblical formats? For example, if the text is story, the sermon ought to be in narrative form. If the text is poetry, so too the sermon, one which "does not so much state a thesis as create an effect." If the biblical form is an essay or personal reflection, so too the sermon. Ditto oratory. It was a thesis more talked about than tried.

Randolph saw four biblical forms as most used in the new communication: *concern, confirmation, concretion,* and *construction.* All would make the sermon "an active part of the theological enterprise, and would at the same time necessarily engage itself in the field of the world."[71] Most significantly, Randolph yoked the sermon as event with the text as event. Or in his words, a sermon should carry "forward the intentionality of the biblical text by following the arc of action called for by the biblical work to its point of intersection with the contemporary congregation."[72] It is in this sense that Randolph could call "every sermon a safari."[73] It is not an end but a journey.

The movement of homiletics from a "proposition-centered" focus to a "person-centered" approach[74] required preachers to find a "new voice."[75] Randolph instructed preachers to focus on the sermon's "eventfulness." The issue is not what the sermon "is" but what the sermon "does."[76] But as much as Randolph saw the need for a changed homiletic, he still focused on creation of the sermon as performative event rather than participatory experience.

Randolph would agree with Lowry that preaching is "dancing at the edge of mystery." ABO^{Ω}-transductive preaching takes it further: preaching is dancing with Christ in communion with others within the mystery of faith. Preaching is not a dance for one, but a dance for "two or three," as Jesus put it. Preaching is a circle dance.

Pas-de-deux ("dance-for-two") preaching is abductive preaching. *Pas de deux* allows people to engage in the sermonic experience, to participate actively, and to fully and sensorially immerse in the incarnational dance with God. *Pas de deux* is a circle dance, a ballet dance, an artistic and beautiful movement with the Lord and Savior of life and with each other. It does not have a beginning or end but revels in the mystery and the story of life itself.

Both abductive and transductive preaching create space for the *pas de deux*. But *pas-de-deux* preaching requires a new theory of the congregation. The issue is no longer how you become a better preacher, but how your people become better participants and how you can create a better congregation. If the "company with the smartest customers wins," the church with the smartest/deepest/most empowered congregation wins. The new standard of excellence for preaching is not the quality of the performance but the quality of the participation. Preaching now is more a participation art than a performance art.

Narraphors invite conversations and contributions; points invite assent or arguments. In transductive preaching, the sermon is a communal act in which the congregation becomes an essential part of the sermon composition. Not just in the sense that each person gets the feeling that the sermon "hits" them, but that the sermon belongs to them and is part of their creativity. The real content of a sermon is not the information but the "indwelling" interaction by which "the Word made flesh dwells among us and we behold his glory."[77] This is the "value" of preaching—its true content is "indwelling" interaction. Above all else, worship is an interactive pattern of "indwelling" that makes the familiar strange even as it is open to strangers. In the old homiletics, preachers used to have performance anxiety. In the new homiletics, preachers now have participation dread.

If the congregation is in some ways more central to the preaching craft than the preacher, the need to exegete the congregation is more pressing than ever. In this participant-observer transductive model of preaching, there are of course times when people must cease being participants and start being observers. But even in the role of observer, everyone needs to have ringside seats. There are no more "spectators." We are all participant-observers.

In the Gutenberg world of "seeker-sensitive worship" of the past decades, the prime directive was nonparticipation. Check out any old etiquette manual and you'll see that nonparticipation applied to all aspects of life: don't ask a famous person for an autograph in a lavatory; don't crush a walnut in the crook of your arm in a restaurant; don't applaud in church. Today, in this Google world and karaoke culture, a participatory or interactive homiletic is based on the priesthood-of-all-believers notion that the whole community is called to collaborate in the ministry of Word and story. It takes a village to raise a sermon.[78]

Novelist/playwright Carlos Fuentes, who died on May 15, 2012, believed that the essence of his success as a playwright was that everything he wrote was "unfinished": "The audience actually finishes writing the play for me. They recreate it in their own mind. My play opens up windows for them into their memory and imagination."[79] A narraphor is a work of imagination. As such, it needs to leave something to the imagination.

Without participation, how is the preacher to know what is being preached? This homiletic of interactivity can take many forms. In fact, the language of preaching needs to learn from the language of the Native American Pueblos (Tewa), in which everything has a different name depending on its state of interactivity. For example, wood that is the trunk of a tree has a different name than wood burning in the fireplace or wood legs on a chair or wood leaves that we call paper. For the Pueblos, everything is defined not solely in terms of its inherent properties but primarily in terms of its interactional properties.[80]

Interactivity is the opening up of spaces in which people can respond and participate. An authentic homiletic of interactivity means more than a " 'rhetoric of listening' through which the biblical interpretations and theological insights of the congregation find a voice in the pulpit."[81] Abductive and transductive interactivity are when you (1) actually alter the content of the experience by your participation and (2) leave behind evidence that you were part of the experience.

Too often interactivity is like checking out of a motel room: once you leave, no one would ever have known you were there. That's why, perhaps, musician Brian Eno is correct when he argues that the word *unfinished* is better than *interactive*.[82] If you can get someone to finish your sentence, it's no longer your sentence. Since they got there before you did, it's now their sentence. If preachers can get participants to "finish" their sermon, it's no longer their sermon.

Besides, participation finishes your thought in both senses of that word *finish*. There is a completion, and there is an added sheen that improves your own thought. For example, I tweeted this thought: God didn't make you to be a key that fits in the lock of every door it tries. Immediately Barry Laughton tweeted back: "So make the most of the door that opens." Barry's "finishing" of my thought brought a whole new sheen and luster to the thought itself. Interaction enhances every action.

The challenge here is that interactivity is beyond the preacher's control, challenges tidy minds, and necessitates that the preacher be willing to be educated in public. An abductive and transductive homiletic is fundamentally an out-of-control homiletic. Everything about modern worship said control: bulletins with their "orders of worship," lockstep ushers, people sitting straight in even rows.[83] In fact, we chose to control rather than to create. We have conceived preaching within a logic of control rather than a logic of creativity and risk.

To embrace participation is to embrace imperfection over control, to leave lots of breathing room for God's Spirit to work, to go in directions you did not plan to go. Transductive worship is more slot machine than gumball machine: worship where you never know what's coming up next versus putting a quarter in and the same thing comes out except in different colors. "Seek-thy-face"[84] worship is now "in-your-face," down-your-throat, out-of-control, off-the-cuff worship.

African-American preaching that has not pulled up its oral roots and call-and-response interactions for pulpit-centric manuscript speech has much to teach the wider church about communication in a Google world. One of the preachers I have learned much from is J. Alfred Smith. Dr. Smith has pastored the Allen Temple Baptist Church in Oakland, California, for more than thirty years. He has concluded:

> A classic three-point sermon will not do in this culture [occupied by a new generation of black youth]. Reasoned arguments with a few poems added will not communicate to this group. It seems to me that, among other things, preaching has to have more of a rhythmic quality. It also needs to be a form of communication that has room for spontaneity. One way to think about it is to imagine preachers incorporating some of the strengths of jazz musi-

cians.... The jazz musician develops a rhythm, a certain cadence with the audience. In like manner, the effective preacher develops a cadence with his or her listeners.... In this way, the congregation becomes an active participant in the sermon: you respond to them, and they respond to you.[85]

The transductive sermon does all this and more. The highest moment of the transductive message is when the *pas de deux* becomes a *pas de Dieu*—not just a dance together as a community, but a dance of the community with the incarnate Spirit of Christ. A renewal and rejoicing of the covenant relationship in all of its beauty and holiness. A transformative, transcendent dance with the resurrected Lord of life. Transductive sermons open up abductive preaching to the "incarnational power" of Christ's presence. The body of Christ comes "alive," stepping in time and singing in tune to the *pas de Dieu* of the risen Lord.

Interactives

1. Mark Driscoll cut his homiletic teeth listening to Chris Rock tapes and videos while he wrote his sermons. It's "my therapy," he says, laughing. God uses all sorts of "instruments" to help us do the "blood work" of Jesus. What is your favorite time and place for sermon preparation? What's your favorite background music? In ten sentences or less, how would you describe yourself as a "called preacher of God"?

2. Sometimes when we get discouraged and disheveled in spirit, we need to "preach to ourselves." It's a spiritual practice preachers need to learn and even teach to their congregations. Jeremiah did this when he said, "This I call to mind and therefore I have hope."[86] What are your practices of self-preaching? What faithful practices do you uphold to keep your passion for Jesus alive and vital?

3. Jesus instructed us not to put old wine into new wineskins. How can you prevent your sermons from being draped in heavily worn research and yet make use of adequate sources to support your message?

4. In the children's book *Stone Soup*, a simple stone is put into a pot, and all are invited to participate in the meal. Each contributor brings something for the pot: carrots, celery, potatoes, and so forth, until a very hearty soup is shared with all. Explain how your sermon can be that stone. What stone metaphors can you find in the Bible? Choose one, and tell about it. How can you use that metaphor as "stone soup"?

5. Choose a passage from the Bible that contains a metaphor. Find another two or three with similar themes or metaphors. Choose a psalm that reflects that metaphor. Now find three songs or hymns that also contain those images and metaphors. What visuals would you choose to go with your passage? What images stand out? How would you "exegete" those images?

6. Michael J. Prerau created a dance called the "Pas de Dieu." The dance, a type of ballet, features one human dancer and one virtual or "invisible" dancer. The dance is sublime and spirited.

http://music.columbia.edu/~mike/projects/pasdedieu/

96

Prerau says, "My goal for the music of this performance would be to create the illusion that the dance was choreographed to the music when in actuality it would be the music that would be dynamically fitting itself to the dance." How can this metaphor describe the twenty-first-century sermon?

7. Using Scripture, give examples of how you might plan a sermon using the (1) deductive method, (2) inductive method, (3) abductive method, and (4) transductive (transincarnational) method. What would the sermon look like? What would it feel like? Act like? How would you describe the reception of each sermon?

8. Interactivity can be as simple as monitoring the reaction and resistance of your congregation with feedback loops like "I see some smiles" or "I feel some scowls out there." Nonthreatening interactivity includes callbacks like "Will you repeat after me?" or "Turn to your neighbor and say …," or safe karaoke sermons like "letters from home," pageants, or dramatic monologues and dialogues ("duet sermons"). Or it can include high-risk karaoke sermons like "brown bag sermons," mediated sermons, talk-back sessions, sermon seminars, or what John S. McClure calls pre-sermon "round-tabling," where the dynamics of roundtable conversation actually midwife the sermon.[87] Break up into groups and share experiences you've had in your own ministry in which you have encouraged or experienced interactive preaching.

9. African-American novelist/playwright/poet James Baldwin's (1924–87) most famous book-length essay, *The Fire Next Time* (1963), appeared first as an essay in the *New Yorker*. Its title? "Letter from a Region in My Mind."[88] Which title packs a bigger punch? Why?

10. Discuss David Buttrick's critique of narrative preaching as follows: "I do not embrace the notion that preaching should tell stories because the gospel is essentially a 'story.' The language of faith is a 'horizontal' narrativity, but it is also 'vertical' symbolic-reflective language that grasps symbols within the hermeneutic of a 'being-saved community.' Thus, I stress the notion of plotted mobility rather than narrativity."[89]

11. Poet Robert Frost argued that metaphor was "the whole of thinking" and that it was the business of poetry to teach the science of metaphor.

Unless you are at home in the metaphor, unless you have had your proper poetical education in the metaphor, you are not safe anywhere. Because you are not at ease with figurative values: you don't know the metaphor in its strength and its weakness. You don't know how far you may expect to ride it and when it may break down with you. You are not safe in science; you are not safe in history.[90]

Do you think Frost is taking poetic license here? Or is metaphor indeed "the whole of thinking"?

12. In 1667 church authorities in Bern, Switzerland, instituted the Bern Preacher Act, which required preachers to give their sermons extemporaneously. It stipulated "that they must not read the same in front of congregation from notes on paper, which is a mockery to have to watch and which takes away all fruit and grace from the preacher in the eyes of the listeners."[91] Have you ever tried preaching extemporaneously? Share your experiences.

13. What are the bestselling movies in the world? Three series: Star Wars, Lord of the Rings, and Harry Potter. All are epic stories, all are fantasy fiction, and all deal with basic issues of good and evil. Is there anything preachers can learn from this?

14. Biblical scholar Joel B. Green proposes a new biblical hermeneutic: he says, in place of a modern "scientific hermeneutic of neutrality, the effect of which was to objectify the biblical text in order to hold it at arm's length for examination, the alternative I want to suggest is a hermeneutic of relationship or connection, oriented in relation to a theological affirmation concerning the nature of the Bible as Scripture."[92]

Have you been taught a hermeneutic of neutrality? If so, how has it affected your preaching? What are your reflections on this "hermeneutic of relationship"?

Part 3

"B+" BLOOD
BUILDING

Chapter 6

Blood Flow:
Bicameral Preaching

Facts go straight to the head; stories go straight to the heart.
— Ingmar Bergman, Swedish filmmaker

CHANGE THE STORY, change the world. Preaching is a revolutionary act.

Jesus' favorite expression was "Pay attention." We most often pay partial attention or selective attention. But we can train ourselves to better attend to attention — to pay attention to the story of the Scriptures as it is lived in our lives, in our postal code, in our world.[1]

Christianity expects so much of the heart yet speaks so much to the head. Jesus spoke to both as his hands brought head and heart together for a full encircling of truth. Narraphoric preaching turns acoustic space into embodied space. It engages the whole being in ways that open up new conduits of creation, cognition, and re-cognition, which can lead to change of heart and thoroughfares to truth. It embraces the body in as many ways as possible to know the story sensorially and thereby experience increased awareness of the divine.

★ ★ ★

"The story is the picture which is the text."
—Fred Craddock[2]

★ ★ ★

To create such transincarnational preaching, however, preachers need to discover how to engage the right side of our brains. Or as Harvard neuroanatomist Jill Bolte Taylor would put it, preachers need to "step to the right."[3]

The story of Dr. Taylor's massive stroke is now famous because of her 2008 TED Talk video and the bestseller that followed from it, *A Stroke of Insight* (2009). In the midst of that stroke, Taylor was able to study her left- and right-brain functioning "from the inside out." Her conclusions stunned the world. While the left side of her brain was shutting down, so was her ability to comprehend numbers, analyze, and verbalize. Additionally, as her right brain emerged the stronger, her sense of individualism decreased, and her relational sense of connection to the world around her increased. As her cognitive abilities decreased, her sense of joyous well-being and abstract imagination remarkably increased. As her urgency and self-awareness decreased, her sense of shared reality and peace increased.

Dr. Taylor discovered through her own experience that although we are trained through our industrial-era educational systems to approach the world from left-brained angles (objectively, critically, departmentally, disciplinarily), this one-sided approach can hamper our ability for relational engagement and holistic embodiment.

* * *

"We do not know the worth of one single drop of blood, one single tear. All is grace. If the Eternal is the Eternal, the last word for each one of us belongs to Him."
—*François Mauriac*[4]

* * *

To be sure, we need left-brain faculties to hack our way through life's jungle of detail and jumble of facts. Faith is not a thought-free zone. But God gave us separate hemispheres for a reason. Each one of these two hemispheres is very different structurally, physiologically, and psychologically.[5] The right hemisphere makes connections and loves possibility and novelty. The left hemisphere pins things down and loves maps, charts, and laws. The two different realities dance in creative tension, a choreography of *complexio oppositorum*, that is the spark of all human creativity and imagination, especially the highly charged intimate-distant tango of participant-observer scientific methodologies.

The Gutenberg world thought that being left brained was being spiritual. The Google world is prone to think that being right brained means being spiritual. The truth is that only a whole-brained being is spiritual. Our right brain lies largely unmoved and untapped through left-brain lectures, where we end up with theology without wonder, dogmas without silence, and creeds with cataracts. What is more, TGIF culture increasingly resides in a right-brain neighborhood. We live in a world grown leery of taking things apart. In order to reach people missionally, we need to design experiences of unity that draw upon both brain faculties.

For the preacher, the worship music and musicians are "the preacher's preacher." But why do some worshipers claim the music of the service is more of a "message" for them than the preaching? Music enables people to "experience" Christ and even theology. How? The right brain turns the entire body into a lyre on which the winds of the Spirit can play the chords of truth. Music turns our being into a theremin that can give off "good vibrations," vibes that are true and beautiful as well as good. Without engaging our right brains, we are left flat, able to analyze, to categorize, and to theorize but without sound or significance. We are left only with signifiers. Without right brains, there would be no Mozart quintet, Donne sonnet, Ming vase, Tiffany lamp, Huggler Black Forest carving, or Harley Davidson motorcycle.

⋆　　⋆　　⋆

"The metaphoric tease has no tease at all
without the discursive pole."
—*Eugene Lowry*[6]

⋆　　⋆　　⋆

Left- and right-brain thinking might be seen as the difference between knowing about God intellectually and "knowing" God relationally,[7] between discursive knowledge and narraphoric knowing, between simple signs and complex metaphors, between the scriptorial and pictorial. The left brain thinks as the crows fly; the right brain thinks as the rivers flow. Left-brain shepherding is watering the flock and feeding the sheep in barns. Right-brain shepherding is walking the flock and feeding the sheep in meadows. Oxford literary scholar and psychiatrist Iain McGilchrist, in a path-breaking book called *The Master and His Emissary: The Divided Brain and the Making of the Western World* (2010), explains:

> Though speech is principally a left-hemisphere function, the production of words in song is associated with wide activation of the right hemisphere. Following a left-hemisphere stroke which leaves the patient unable to speak, he or she may be able to sing the words of songs without difficulty. Damage to the right hemisphere, by contrast, can lead to a condition known as amusia, in which the ability to appreciate and understand, or to perform, music may be lost. Right-hemisphere lesions may leave the understanding of speech

relatively unaffected, while the perception of nonverbal sounds (including music) is profoundly disrupted.[8]

McGilchrist summarizes the differing functions of the right and left sides of our brains in this way:

> The left brain is focused, rational, and goal-directed. The right is concerned with the whole picture, the surroundings and the context. The essential difference between the right hemisphere and the left hemisphere is that the right hemisphere pays attention to the Other, whatever it is that exists apart from ourselves, with which it sees itself in profound relation.... I do not wish to leave the impression that it might be a good thing if the entire population had a left-hemisphere stroke.[9]

The left brain is linear, differentiating, and time oriented. The right brain is intuitive, creative, connective, the home of emotional and spiritual intelligences. The left seeks to concretize and separate; the right seeks to merge and join. The right brain is the source of many of the human characteristics we value most: love, reverence, the experience of art or literature, affection, companionship.

Transductive preaching alters worship, and particularly the message, to integrate our right-brain faculties. Music and the arts have kept the right brain from being wiped out of worship. But the time is long overdue for preaching to tap directly into right-brain resources to create a holistic experience of worship. Because we have spent so much time (five hundred years of Enlightenment culture) pumping up our left-brained muscles, we must deliberately set about now to "exercise" our right brains and to get them moving and jiving to the beat of the primal heart of creation.

So how do we beef up our right brains?

If you have ever seen a human brain, you know it is made up of two distinct and unconnected halves except for a cord of fibers called the corpus callosum, which bridges the base of the two cerebral hemispheres. When our two hemispheres work together as partners, we gather various types of knowledge through various perspectives and create a dazzling diamond view of our world. When one side dominates, we see the world through distorted eyes. The way we "educate" ourselves, the way we train our mind to "read," will affect our ability to see the world.

The Gutenberg world spelled the takeover and tyranny of the left brain. The Google world is rediscovering the right brain. McGilchrist argues that pre-Socratic Greece, the Renaissance, and the Romantic period were primarily right-brain triumphs in history, which released all sorts of creativity into the historical bloodstream. He goes on to argue, however, that the past several centuries have thrust us into a world tyrannized by left-brain dominance. In the words of medical historian W. F. Bynum, "The Renaissance allowed the right brain to flourish, whereas the Reformation turned out to be a left-brain disaster. For the most part, so was the Enlightenment.... Worst of all, though, was the Industrial Revolution, the ultimate triumph of materiality, exploitation, and greed."[10] We are now coming out of, in McGilchrist's graphic words, "the left-hemisphere's most daring assault on mankind."[11]

When most of us read the Scriptures, we read with our left brains cranked to full tilt. The preference for the abstract, the rational, the propositional was credentialed by the Protestant Reformers. In his preface to the New Testament, Martin Luther offered an evaluation of the New Testament canon. In a section called "Which Are the True and Noblest Books of the New Testament?" Luther wrote, "John's gospel is the one, fine, true, and chief gospel, and is far, far to be preferred over the other three and placed high above them. So, too, the epistles of St. Paul and St. Peter far surpass the other three gospels, Matthew, Mark, and Luke."[12] Luther's reasoning was simple. Anything in Scripture that tells the story of Jesus was far less helpful than books describing explicit doctrines about Jesus.

No wonder today we can be found approaching the text in an attack mode: "unlock" the passage; barrage the Bible with a variety of hermeneutical and exegetical strategies. We analyze texts, dissect passages, take apart words, construe points, principle-ize concepts. We make the stories of Jesus add up like $1+1=2$. Or at least $a+b=ab$. And we take those locked and loaded, solution-packed answers, download them into a lecture, count "one, two, three" for good measure, and randomly shoot our points at unsuspecting parishioners, hoping for some bull's-eye hits. The problem is, for all our attempted impact, the next day most parishioners couldn't repeat any one of those sermons, or the points and/or principles, for the life of them. And it is their lives that are on the line.

The church deserves a whole-brained homiletics. In many ways, the heart itself is the best symbol of a whole brain. One of the greatest eureka moments in the history of medicine was William Harvey's description of the circulation of the blood—*De moto cordis and sanguinis / The Movement of the Heart and Blood* (1628). Before 1630, paintings of the crucifixion often depicted the split side of Jesus on the right side. Later painters generally moved the wound to the left side. Why? Because in this book, William Harvey argued from empirical evidence that the heart was on the left and the circulation of the blood was circular. It is also obvious from this book that Harvey didn't see the heart as a mechanical pump or muscle, but almost as a metaphysical entity.

It was Descartes who made the heart a machine and in so doing enthroned thought while diminishing emotion. The truth is, the heart is covered in neurons, making it a little brain, a whole mind, a head at the same time a heart.

For the church to embrace a heart homiletics, it must discover again its right brain. How can we create a more right-brained homiletics for a right-brain world that thinks in narraphors and pictures? Shouldn't preachers be homiletic hemophiliacs, giving blood for a world in desperate need of the love of Christ? Perhaps we need to go backward and forward at the same time, back to the source that is right at our fingertips and forward to the resource that will lead us into the future.

Jesus taught differently from other rabbis.[13] One time Jesus' friends even asked him, "Why do you speak to the people in parables?"[14] It's a good question. Have you ever wondered why some of Jesus' stories seem to complicate or even cloud truth rather than clarify or simplify it? Perhaps God, who knows us better than we know ourselves, is not content to speak simply in bullet points, PowerPoint, or "Just-the-facts, ma'am!" but forms and informs us instead through imagination, intuition, and epiphany.[15] Perhaps God wants to reach us through both sides of our brains. If the left brain is enthralled with the letter of the law and the right brain by the spirit of the law, then no wonder Nicodemus could not understand what Jesus was talking about when he said, "You must be born again." But there is hope for left-brain dominant thinkers, and Nicodemus is their patron saint.

★ ★ ★

"The mystery of one's relationship to God cannot be captured
in proposition form and passed directly from one human
being to another—not even if the sermon is impeccably logical and flawlessly delivered. It must be wrapped, like faith
itself, in the paradoxical distance and intimacy that stories
provide, in the grandeur of myth, the lilt of songs, the memory
of legend, and the seductive disorientation of parables."
—*Robin R. Meyers*[16]

★ ★ ★

In the beginning was the Word. In the end was the commercial. In a culture that thinks and traffics in images, right-brain dominant people hold the keys to the future. In the discipline and craft of preaching, words come last. Metaphors create a culture. And biblical metaphors create a biblical culture.

Blood Flow: Bicameral Preaching

As in Jesus' own time, people are hungry for relationship, touch, participation, story. They are craving for the carving of wonder, meaning, and mystery from the monotony of their stressful lives. The world's cities understand that the future belongs to right-brained people, even if churches don't know what to do with them. The pursuit of what Richard Florida calls "the creative class"[17] has become the holy grail of urban growth and development. The difference is that cities are chasing the creative class "as if it were a high-stakes, zero-sum game," whereas the church is ostracizing and outlawing its creatives and artists. In a culture that every year spends billions generating competing, contrasting images to the gospel, almost every one of which is a lie, it is imperative that preachers offer alternative images of beauty, truth, and goodness.

In fact, the creative arts and crafts have erupted into an entire "folk" culture. Whereas today left-brain functions are increasingly being outsourced to computers (this is happening already in countries like India, soon to be the largest English-speaking country in the world), right-brain creativity is on the rise to the point that it's being franchised. Tully's Coffee is now distinguishing itself from Starbucks by putting hand-made signs in its windows claiming, "We serve hand-crafted coffee." McDonald's has gone from the unvarying "Do you want fries with that?" to "What can we cook for you today?" as they invite you to try their new McCafé gourmet coffee and drink choices.

This cultural paradigm shift mandates a retrieval of the Jesus mode of metaphorical communication. "Other rabbis want to speak so that their words can reach the sky," used to be rendered as, "I want to speak so that my words will reach the stomach."[18] Jesus spoke so that his words would reach all body parts on their way to the heart. To do this, he used multiple methods of communication, but the most dynamic method was the parable.

Poet and Harvard biblical scholar Amos N. Wilder called a parable a "narrative metaphor,"[19] or what we are calling a "narraphor." Like all narraphors, a parable is a literary form designed less to convey concepts than to platform interactive experiences with contraband meaning. In his classic book on the parables, C. H. Dodd speaks of Jesus' parables as "interaction metaphors." His definition of a parable is famous: "A parable is a metaphor or simile drawn from nature or common life, arresting the hearer by its vividness or strangeness, and leaving the mind in sufficient doubt about its precise application to tease it into active thought."[20] According to biblical scholar and former priest John Dominic Crossan, parables offer not abstractions but experience. Jesus invented parables that invited participation. Jesus' metaphors "demanded participation and personal decisions from listeners."[21] In the words of Amos Wilder, "A true metaphor or symbol is more than a sign;

it is a bearer of the reality to which it refers. The hearer not only learns about that reality; he participates in it. He is invaded by it. Here lies the power and fatefulness of art."[22]

Franz Kafka understood the open-endedness and the "fatefulness" of parables when he wrote, "If you only followed the parables, you yourselves would become parables."[23] In other words, a "hearer" of the Good Samaritan parable truly becomes the Good Samaritan. That's the ultimate in participation. This interactive component, by the way, is one of the things that irritated people most about Jesus' parables: they didn't want their minds teased into active thought.

★   ★   ★

"In contrast to the spoken and written word, a picture can be understood anywhere in the world. It can bridge the chasm created by differences of language and alphabet. It is a means for universal communication. It is the language of One World."
—Andreas Feininger (1906–99), German photographer[24]

★   ★   ★

Parables have the power to change the world. Jesus communicated in parables because God talks first to the world of imagination and faith rather than the world of intellect and information. Jesus was so skilled at using parables (fifty-three of them, each only about 100 to 150 words) that he was known as a "parabolist."[25] The power of these parables was such that you might even call them the "The Fifty Stories That Changed the World." But within and through those parables, Jesus used a variety of "techniques."

SOME NARRAPHORIC TOOLS TO INCREASE THE BLOOD FLOW

1. METAPHOR

The Pony Express lasted only nineteen months (1860–61). Shortly after it started, the telegraph, not the train or armed robbers, killed it. Yet what a legend it became, and what a lasting legacy it bequeathed to every generation—not because of what it accomplished but because of the metaphorical power of the story of the Pony Express. Pony Express is still being used for a fund-raiser for churches. And the expression "Pony Express" is still used today to indicate an urgency of desire to reach people.

Is metaphor little more than "figurative language," or is something deeper going on? Is metaphor an ornamental figure of speech? Or is metaphor a figure of thought? Aristotle was not the first to tell us that "the soul never thinks without a mental image."[26] Metaphors are buckets in which truths are held, although all handles ultimately snap from the weight they are supposed to carry.[27]

For Jesus metaphors were not smokescreens to be cleared away but filters through which we comprehend truth and healing instruments. Jesus used metaphors as a curative medium. His metaphors left divine imprints on the smithy of the soul. He authored phrases and metaphors that won't go away until we do. Metaphors such as kingdom, mustard seed, and leaven fuse into our minds an image of a new kind of world driven by love and human dignity.

Jesus drew heavily on the Hebrew love of metaphorical animations. His metaphors gave a depth and breadth to his parables that transported them far beyond the literal.[28] Poet Denise Levertov confessed to the human need for metaphors "grounded in dust, grit, heavy carnal clay."[29] Jesus got down and dirty with his metaphors, many of which were those of a gardener. You might even define a parable as another way of talking about the metaphorical nets Jesus was always casting through which he sieved palatable truths.

*   *   *

"Metaphor consists in giving the thing a name that belongs to something else."
—*Aristotle*[30]

*   *   *

Even when Jesus wasn't speaking in parables about the "kingdom of God," his favorite subject, the very metaphor of the "kingdom" may have been Jesus' most powerful change agent. Still today, it enables and indeed encourages us to think of the world not just as it is but as it might be.

I have already argued that Jesus was well versed in the Hebrew method of exegesis, the PaRDeS, the four levels of interpretation—literal (*peshat*), typological (*remez*), metaphorical (*derash*), and revelatory (*sod*). The metaphorical level was called the "kingdom level," in which the metaphors could facilitate one's understanding of God's kingdom in everyday life. The metaphorical mode of interpretation (the *derash*) is likely the layer of meaning that Jesus alluded to when he "explained" the parables to his inner circle. The revelatory level (*sod*) is most likely the level on which "he opened their minds so they could understand the Scriptures."[31] While the first two levels of interpretation (literal, typological) require distinctly left-brain functions, the latter two require the facility of the right brain.

Jesus' parables always hit a nerve, employing what I will call later the "metaphorical turn" or "metaphorical twist."[32] They not only instructed and informed, but they functioned as change agents of incarnation and innovation. Metaphors make things happen.

★   ★   ★

"The first time, the Logos made the flesh; this time the
Logos was made flesh, so that he might change our flesh to
spirit, by being made partaker with us in flesh and blood."
— *Gregory of Nyssa*[33]

★   ★   ★

Perform a dazzling leap of logic, and Gutenbergers are adoring while Googlers are snoring. Perform a metaphorical stunt, and the Googlers are left breathless while the baying of rumblings and grumblings begin from the Gutenberg pack. Such are our "appointed times" in this overlap of cultures.

2. PROVERBS OR APHORISMS

A Korean proverb speaks of the power of proverbs. In Korean the proverb sings linguistically. In English the proverb seems awkward and strained. Here is ancient Korean wisdom about the explosiveness of epigrammatic power: "it's less than the blood in a bird's leg."

Proverbs are slow-won, time-worn maxims, sound bites that often function as bits in the mouths of the foolish and reins in the hands of the wise. Our communication is becoming more and more parenthetical and more aphoristic at the same time, as any political campaign will attest. We love double direction, the pithy tweet with the density of poetry but the spaciousness of prose.

Our love of aphoristic modes of expression is part and parcel of the love of silences and the whirligig of wordlessness. Proverbs and epigrams themselves go in double directions — they have an air of confidence and finality to them while at the same time they are reticent and halting, nuggets of dense truth encased in silence that glow with a more than earthly light.

Jesus was a powerful speaker who rolled his own phrases as he roiled the authorities with artfully formulated symbolism. He left room for those casings of silence. But his one-liners were so dynamic that they would leave people relatively speechless: "The last will be first, and the first will be last."[34] "No one can serve two masters."[35]

Moses compared divine teaching to both rain and dew: "Let my teaching fall like rain and my words descend like dew, like showers on new grass, like abundant rain on tender plants."[36] In agrarian cultures, farmers pray for the rains to come "in their due season," as expressed in the second paragraph of the Shema.[37] When the rains fail, it is catastrophic. But it is also disastrous if they fall too heavy or are too prolonged beyond their season. The gentle dew, on the other hand, is always welcome. As the rabbis put it, rain is sometimes required and sometimes not, but the abundance of dew is required at all times.

Doctrine is needed on life's great occasions, especially for rites of passage. But the everyday speech of proverbs, or distilled doctrines, is what is needed in the daily grind, the daily round of living. Twitter is a great discipline to help you turn doctrine into dew.[38]

3. RIDDLES

Jesus frequently used riddles. A colleague once said that Jesus was a master of the "riddle wrapped in an enigma."[39] He didn't want his listeners to nod their heads agreeably but absently through every sentence he spoke, or to feel like God was patting them on the head and telling them how good they were. His preaching riled people up by design, and riddles were darts of daylight that pierced the darkest corners of life. Even his generalizations were riddled with exceptions and provocations. Jesus' riddles challenged the mind and the heart, such as the riddle of the seeds falling on four kinds of earth (Mark 4:1–12).

Jesus wanted people to think, to ponder, to contemplate, to search their hearts, and to flesh out the message he was giving them with their own lives. When they embraced the mystery of God at work and at play, life shone with added luster.

4. IRONY

Jesus used irony quite frequently in his parables and in his teaching, especially when winkling out the cussed ironies of existence. But his ironic twists were not ironclad. They did not exist for the sake of irony itself or for ironing out the wrinkles and creases of life, but were eminently versatile and immanently imaginative ways of reframing what it means to be human.

When arguing with the Pharisees, Jesus could be blatantly parasitic of their genres while at the same time ironically distancing himself from them. He spoke of the signs of the times, using the irony of the common knowledge of the skies. In a parable, Jesus had the master of a wedding remark to the bridegroom that typically the "cheaper wine" would be saved until the guests had had too much to drink, but this groom instead saved the best wine for last.

Jesus' use of irony allowed him to make sharp comparisons between the expected and the exceptional, the forces of life and the deputies for death. Jesus' life itself was ironic. It is the ultimate irony that Jesus died at the hands of those he came to save.

5. PARADOX

Jesus was prone to argue both ends against the middle. In fact, Jesus almost always comes in surround sound.[40] A major theme of his teaching showed people how to hold their contradictions together. At the same time he steadied them, he left his listeners giddy with dazzling paired opposites or double rings (paradoxes like Lion/Lamb, Alpha/Omega, first/last, saint/sinner, Prince of Peace/Swordsman). That is why he so capably wriggled out of every straitjacket. His everyday practice of paradox didn't spring from some philosophical sense of absurdity's beauty. Rather, he practiced paradox from a Trinitarian mind-set in which only contradictions make it possible to apprehend the real within its confounding totality.

The tensile strength of paradox is what makes Jesus' parables so compelling. A seeming contradiction is juxtaposed in a way that reveals a higher truth. Jesus' paradoxes are often the kernels of his metaphors that pop open unexpectedly and infuse the air with revolutionary ideas, bits of astounding truth that burst from the story and tantalize the hearer. Paradoxes topple our belief systems and hoist us into new territory. Disjunctive thoughts throw us off balance just enough to allow us to grasp hold of new perspectives and to land on different ground. Metaphor and paradox dance together to create powerful and life-changing parables.

For Jesus a love for something may sometimes be gauged by one's disgust at it. Jesus loved Jerusalem and the temple enough to cry over it. And yet he was sickened by it enough to display his anger and create a scene. For Jesus the imperishable is found in the midst of change and all that changes. A "Well-Curve" world[41] makes it all the more mandatory for preachers to move from conflict to conversation about the extremes and opposites that exist side by side in stark, unmediated lordliness.

This means preachers must become bipolar extremists.

*　　*　　*

"A man does not show his greatness by being at
one extremity, but rather by touching both at once."
—*Blaise Pascal*

*　　*　　*

6. HYPERBOLE

Jesus didn't bother with theological pillow fights. But when the stakes were high, he rolled out the hype. This flair of rollicking exaggeration allowed him to use elements of humor to cushion a blow while still countering the punches of those with a more pugilistic piety. "It is easier for a camel to go through the eye of a needle [narrow city gate] than for someone who is rich to enter the kingdom of God"[42] was a typical Jesus way of jerking people into seeing things afresh. It's the equivalent of 1940s comedian Fred Allen claiming, "You can take all the sincerity in Hollywood, place it in the navel of a fruit fly and still have room enough for three caraway seeds and a producer's heart."

*   *   *

"Preaching cannot be true to itself if it is a series of abstractions or a string of exhortations, because most fundamentally preaching is prayer."
—*Patricia Wilson-Kastner (1944–88)*[43]

*   *   *

Jesus' occasional use of this pump-priming trick of overstatement stood in the great tradition of Hebrew grandiloquence. For example, when he said one must "hate father and mother,"[44] he did not mean that literally but was making an emphatic point about loving God more than anything or anyone else. Such overstatements, popular in Hebrew literature, contributed to the impact of Jesus' stories and grabbed the attention of somnolent listeners.

7. SIMILE

"The kingdom of heaven is like...." Jesus was a huge fan of simile, a device he used to make his hearers sit up and take notice. His similes platformed his narraphors and distilled his teaching into aphoristic opulence.

At times similes allowed Jesus to venture safely and creatively into extremely provocative territory and served as spiritual fumigation more potent than any concrete statement. He told some Pharisees, "You are like whitewashed tombs, which look beautiful on the outside but on the inside are full of the bones of the dead and everything unclean."[45]

8. PUNS

A pun is a peg on which the preacher hangs a perception. A pun is a playful means of accessing memory and makes easy the retrieval of stored experiences in the unconscious mind. Of all the embarrassing "offenses" of your right brain, your left brain finds puns the most repugnant.

★   ★   ★

"Oratory: The art of making deep noises from the chest that sound like important messages from the brain."
—H. I. Phillips[46]

★   ★   ★

Poet W. H. Auden believed that "good poets have a weakness for bad puns"[47] (perhaps thinking of Shakespeare, who loved bad, dig-in-the-ribs puns). Whether wordsmiths are wordplayers or not, Jesus' punditry was not based on puns, but he did occasionally use them. In fact, he founded the church on a pun, punning Peter's name (Cephas means "rock") with the metaphor of rock: "On this rock I will build my church."[48] While puns were not one of the more common devices Jesus used, when he did, he used them surgically and humorously, proving that the iconic need not be uncomic. Jesus brought giggles with the gospel.

So should the preacher bring back the gurgle of shock and the giggle of play.

9. POETRY

Jesus did a lot of things that we know nothing about. For example, how many people did he disarm by his singing Hebrew poetry, which we know as the Psalms, at key moments? And beyond his chanting of the beloved poetry found in the Jewish hymnbook, Jesus frequently employed bits of poetry and verbal arabesques within his teaching. In his greatest scenes and gravest themes, he used beautifully descriptive language within a Hebrew style of poetic prose.

> If you do that,
> You will be like your Father in heaven,
> For he makes his sun to rise,
> On the bad and on the good alike,
> [Your Father in heaven] ... sends the rain
> On the saint and sinner.[49]

Jesus used poetic lines to buttress and beautify his parabolic illustrations and metaphors.

The Franz Liszt of homileticians, Walter Brueggemann, contends that when the language of homiletics and liturgics becomes prose rather than poetry, "there is a dread dullness that besets the human spirit, and we all become mindless conformists."[50] Why the dullness of our spirits and dryness of our souls? Could dull, dry, prosaic preaching have anything to do with the state of our souls? Might bland speech blanch our spirits and deflate our churches? Maybe we need more poetry in our preaching, replete even with a small portion of poetic license.

10. QUESTIONS

Jesus spoke in public through parables. But Jesus conducted private tutorials with his disciples. During these teaching sessions, Jesus often asked questions to judge whether they were "getting it."[51] And vice versa, his disciples asked him questions. They wanted further clarification about the parable of the sower.[52] They wanted to know the difference between "clean" and "unclean." Jesus answered them but not without registering his frustration at their dull-headedness and dim-wittedness.[53]

In these tutorials, Jesus "explained everything" to them.[54] Most likely, his explanations addressed the depths of interpretation that would have made connections (1) between metaphors and stories, (2) between traditions and the past, (3) between signs and occurrences, and (4) between Scriptures and his fulfillment of those Scriptures. When one is connecting the dots, there is no better way to follow new paths than to ask questions.

*   *   *

"Music, poetry, painting, the arts ... are a dwelling
in and a breaking out which lie somewhere
between science and worship."
—*Michael Polanyi (1891–1976), philosopher*[55]

"The event of preaching is an event in transformed
imagination. Poets, in the moment of preaching,
are permitted to perceive and voice the world
differently, to dare a new phrase, a new picture, a
fresh juxtaposition of matters long known. Poets are
authorized to invite a new conversation, with new
voices sounded, new hearings possible."
—*Walter Brueggemann*[56]

*   *   *

11. STORYTELLING

If I could translate John 1:1 any way I wanted, I would render *Logos* this way: "In the beginning was the Story, and the Story was with God, and the Story was God." To be a people of the book doesn't mean simply that words are important. It means that the story is also important. The story is sacred.

Jesus is God's Story. And God's Story is a master storyteller. His parables and even his short comments all either tell a story or relate his comments to a story. Jesus knew that the telling of stories, as well as the stories themselves, pull people together. Narrative discourse is accessible to virtually everyone and connects people relationally to the Scripture, to the story, and to Christ. Stories unite the linear to the nonlinear and the analytic to the abstract. They transgress boundaries and create alternative realities.

Jesus was a master of the linguistic arts. His "sermons" were not didactic lessons but "works of art." Stories, metaphors, questions, parables, surprise endings, word plays, and poetry are art. In contrast to those voices calling for the end of the sermon, we need sermons that are more biblical, more inspired by Jesus. That means more artistic and less dogmatic, more real and less accomplished, more provocative and less pietistic, more challenging and less soothing, more life-giving and life-altering and less informative and predictable.

Jesus communicated with us using a whole-brain diet of food for living (not just food for thought). To experience the incarnational Spirit of Jesus within the Scriptures — and within the sermon — you first have to approach the Scriptures with an open mind and take a "step to the right."

When you read the Scriptures with both eyes open and both brains booked, you read differently. You see signs and patterns and connections. A depth within the story pops out that was hidden by your monocular reading. You read "semiotically" when you read texts as stories animating truth, not a document disseminating facts or points.

Remember the four levels of Hebrew Scripture? You need all chambers of your brain to comprehend the multidimensionality of the biblical drama. The first literal reading will be very left-brained. The second typological reading — still quite left-brained. But when you move into the third level, the metaphorical or perceptual reading (the kingdom meaning), you will begin to tap your right brain. Finally, the incarnational reading that connects you to God in an EPIC way[57] will require your right brain to create and connect with your left brain. When both sides of your brain are on the same wavelength, you will not only understand but experience the story on several levels. You will be able to connect the dots of the greatest story ever told to the dotted lines of your own story. Say the word *story* and people think of either something written (left brain) or oral (right brain). It's time to think of story as something EPIC, or whole-brained.

⋆ ⋆ ⋆

"A man is always a teller of tales; he lives surrounded by his stories and the stories of others, he sees everything that happens to him through them; and he tries to live his own life as if he were telling a story."
—*French philosopher Jean-Paul Sartre (1905–80)*[58]

⋆ ⋆ ⋆

Preaching preparation requires reading with both sides of your brain. Implementation requires preaching in a way that enables others to make their own connections in a similar interactive journey. How do we read with "both eyes open" and "both brains booked"? Let's use the story of Jonah as a test case.

Lab Practicum
EXEGETING THE STORY AND IMAGES OF JONAH

The following lab practicum shows what a whole-brain method of exegesis might look like in praxis. Reading the story of Jonah, the exegesis explores the text with four different ways of reading. It links the four levels of Hebrew exegesis (literal, typological, metaphorical, revelational) with the four ways of knowing discussed in chapter 5: deduction, induction, abduction, and transduction. The first two, as will be discussed, are strictly left-brained ways of reading. The second two are presented in a way that adds two right-brain readings (depths of reading that we usually neglect), which create for the reader a holistic and multidimensional reading of the text, more akin to its nature as Hebrew story. Each section has both a "reading" and an "interpretation" of the story. You will find the readings of the Scripture set in sans serif. This is the "way" you would read the text, depending on which level of your brain you are employing. When we read with our left brains, we pay attention to different things in the story than we do when we read with our right brains. When we read with our left, the story sounds very linear and straightforward. The right-brain readings are ways we pay attention to the story that allow certain metaphors, truths, and connections to "jump out" at us. Thus we will discover that these readings are not linear; instead, we will begin to visualize, interpret, make connections, and expand metaphors as we read. In the fourth reading, we will apply the story to our lives and the world as we read. So the readings themselves, not just the interpretations, will reflect the ways our brains are engaged with the story.

The subsequent interpretation sections for each reading demonstrate the conclusions and connections our minds make from those readings. For example, in the literal reading, we come to a conclusion that is almost directly opposite what we discover by the time we contemplate the fourth reading. This is the beauty of the fourfold reading/exegetical method. The method allows us to discover a richness and depth to the text and an unveiling of truth—revelational and relational—that we miss by refusing to use our right brains.

LEFT-BRAIN READING #1
(THE LITERAL OR DEDUCTIVE READING)

God calls Jonah to warn the pleasure-seeking people of Nineveh of destruction if they do not repent. Jonah fears this mission to the capital city of the Assyrian Empire and flees to Tarshish on a boat. God causes a storm to rock the boat, and Jonah is eventually thrown overboard. God then arranges for a giant fish to swallow him up, where he languishes in the fish's stomach for three days and nights. After the three days, God commands the fish to pitch Jonah onto the beach. Once again God instructs Jonah to go and warn the wicked people of Nineveh.

At last Jonah does God's bidding. The people of Nineveh repent, and God spares them from judgment. But Jonah gets angry with God for showing mercy to God's enemies. Wasn't that, after all, a mockery of his mission? So Jonah storms off in a funk and finds a tree where he can sit and pout. God protects him for a day with a leafy plant. But at dawn God sends a worm to destroy the plant. When Jonah shows more concern over the loss of the plant than with the plight of the people of Nineveh, Jonah gets another reprimand from God.

In the literal version (Heb. *peshat*), we have the bare bones of the story. We understand the story's words and can relay them as a fun and interesting tale. But just as in fairy tales or fables, on the literal level we tend to see the story as a documentary that can serve as a cautionary tale for children. And a dark one at that. If we stay only with this left-brain version, we never get past the shabbiest parts of the story—the vomiting overboard of what was making everyone on the ship sick, the gruff intestinal rumble that hurled Jonah back on land. We end up arguing over the truth of the story (what fish swallows humans whole?) not the story of truth.

When we try to push deeper with this version, we get pushback. Why is Jonah acting so childish? Why doesn't he want to talk to the Ninevites? Why does God act the way he does? What's the real lesson here? How can we apply this story to our lives? In the literal version, this pushback often leads to dead ends. It's easy to see God as judgmental and disciplining should we choose to disobey. In a literal reading, our direction is legalistic, linear, cause and effect, deductive, and definitive. Literal readings identify and define, but the danger is that they can force the story to fit into a simplistic, prescribed deductive formula. This literal reading, however, does give us the tools to dig deeper. We now have a sense of the unfolding of the narrative, and we can identify the main characters, chief plot, and central theme.

Or can we? Who is the main character—Jonah or God or the people of Nineveh? The theme of repentance pops up quickly from such a linear reading. But not all in the story are required to repent. And repent from what? Our literal interpretation may look like a comparative between Nineveh and Jonah, proving that because Jonah refuses to do God's bidding, he is punished. But does that lesson make sense if the heathen sailors are only secondarily converted? And does it make sense with what we know about how Hebrew stories are written?

To leave our reading here at the literal level is to draw a plant with no roots. The interpretation remains simplistic, incomplete, and inorganic. To learn more, we must keep on digging.

LEFT-BRAIN READING #2
(TYPOLOGICAL OR INDUCTIVE READING)

As soon as Jonah hears God's call to Nineveh (which means "House of Fish"), this wealthy city that united the East and the West by its unique place on the highway between the Indian Ocean and Mediterranean Sea, he flees to Tarshish on a ship. God causes a huge storm to rise up. When the storm becomes unbearable, the sailors confront Jonah. He tells them to throw him overboard in order to spare themselves. Yahweh arranges for a fish to swallow Jonah, and Jonah laments and sings a psalm. After three days, the whale belches Jonah on the beach.

Jonah goes to Nineveh, and with one simple, perfunctory sentence, he tells the Ninevites, "Only forty days more and Nineveh is going to be destroyed." Jonah offers no hope, only judgment. Yet the Ninevites, to his dismay, immediately repent in hopes that God will be merciful. And God is. Enraged at God's compassion to Nineveh, Jonah stomps out of the city to stew and pout in a desertion to the desert. God creates a shade plant to cool his anger but then causes it to wither the next day, exposing him to the scorching hot sun and wind. Jonah's foaming fury at God continues unabated, now for removing the plant and his perilous consolation. God addresses Jonah's anger over the plant in comparison to his vengeance toward the innocent people and animals of Nineveh.

A typology (*remez* reading) brings to the fore what is behind a story. According to Charles L. Campbell, who has done the best work on figurative or typological preaching, By "nurturing a figural imagination," as Campbell puts it,[59] typology forces us off well-worn paths, which we tend to tread no matter how unique or novel the journey. It also can reveal a lot about a character and infuse significant humor into the narrative (as in *Aesop's Fables*). By bundling a simple word with a more complex *cluster* (a "type"), it brings a story to lesson if not to life.

The typological interpretation goes beyond literal translation to elevate the comparative, connect the figurative, and unify the narrative. But its function remains distinctly allusive and anecdotal. The story "hints" at meaning representationally and then defines an answer. It is an inductive method of knowledge. A typological reading uses a simple symbol (e.g., character, figure, event) to represent another word, idea, or principle. For example, a dove can be an emblem of peace; an eagle can be representative of the United States; being swallowed by the whale can be a divine banishing to the doghouse. Using the left brain, typologies simply equate one "type" with another to illustrate a point and leave a lesson. They require a predominantly left-brain capacity, even though they often speak symbolically and mask as right brained.

To flesh out the typological a little further: the word *Tarshish* in the Jonah story means in Hebrew "the ends of the world." Rather than a specific city or place, Jonah is fleeing into the "wild, blue yonder" to "anywhere but here." The typological reminds us that Jonah is not just deciding to go to a different city to defy God. He is attempting to run away from God's presence completely by sailing into oblivion with no specific goal but to flee into nowhere land where the "fish" reign supreme.

The typological lends a humorous bent to the story, as we realize Jonah is panicking and running like a scared rabbit in a pen, thinking he could actually outrun God. This humor continues as we see the sailors' reaction to Jonah's distress. Convinced that God must be punishing Jonah terribly, after they hurl Jonah into the sea, they all make perfunctory vows to Yahweh for good measure. We continue to laugh at Jonah for his rather amusing rendition of a psalm of ascent after God has provided a fish to swallow him up. The advantage of typology becomes evident in the comparison of Jonah's personal psalm to that of psalms such as 30, 31, 88, and 130.

Although an initial reading assumes the "psalm" to be a prayer of repentance, a typological look tells us that his ending is less than admirable and is rather self-serving. Rather than enemies at his throat, it is seaweed. As in Psalm 31, rather than being persecuted by idolatrous captors, he is pouting in the belly of a fish.

Jonah splices together his best attempt at a psalm of praise and grudgingly fulfills his mission in the simplest and least arduous way he can. Even Jonah's address to the Ninevites is humorous, and we begin laughing at his stubbornness. Then he goes to sit, most likely arms crossed, outside the city. The leafy plant may be seen as a type for God's mercy, a mercy Jonah deems to be fickle or unfair toward himself. In fact, the hearer of this story might "type" Jonah's behavior as that of a two-year-old. Defenders of the typological reading will be drawn to the exclusivist and self-serving attitude of Jonah as an Israelite wanting God's full attention.

The typological reading reveals a rather narcissistic leading character on the surface. But we do see Jonah saving the sailors in what appears to be a self-sacrificial event. Is that not a "type" of something else? What is the moral of the story? That Israel is not God's only concern? The problem with leaving our interpretation at a simple typological interpretation is that we are still only using our left brains to infer an answer that we pretty much already have seen and concretized in our linear reading.

But what if there are other messages and signs within the story, or narraphor, that we have missed? At best, typology and/or allegory are thin incarnation. Metaphor is thick incarnation. What if we begin to use our right brains to dig for metaphors?

RIGHT-BRAIN READING #3
(DIGGING FOR METAPHORS, OR ABDUCTIVE READING)

The most prominent metaphors in the story seem to be the ship, the storm, the sea, the fish, the plant, the worm, the sun, and the wind. The ship is Jonah's first escape method. It is a manmade vessel used to navigate the seas. The sea on the way to "Tarshish" (never-never land) may be that primordial, creative, genesis-like wellspring of God; and the depths of the sea, especially with the presence of the fish, a womblike experience. The ship is a method of journey, in this case, flight. And although we use the ship as a metaphor for a discipleship journey, Jonah's journey is not one of learning but of fleeing. The fish might be compared to Leviathan or simply to the womb, the inner self, or the contemplation of the mind and heart. Likewise, the storm itself may be a metaphor for the forces of nature, the power of God, or the creative energy of the organic and God-made world versus that of manmade shelters. We see that relationship come out again in the difference between Jonah's manmade "shelter" and that of the castor bean plant. Jonah's did not shield him, but God's could. The plant can also be seen as a vine rooted in God. This brings up the theme of dependency and covenant, selfishness versus putting one's faith and trust and humility in God. The plant also hearkens us back to the Genesis story, along with its demise by the "worm" or serpent. The serpent theme (whether Leviathan or the worm) can represent sin or separation from God, a breaking of covenant relationship. And our attention is called toward Jonah's attempts to separate from God in various and continuing ways. He seems almost angry at his utter dependence on God. The sun and wind likewise remind us of the authority and power of God. And similar to the story of Job, we might see the centrality of God to all living things, sinful and human, and we are put in awe of God's forgiveness, patience, compassion, and power. In the metaphors, we find both the relationality and omnipresence of God along with the vast power, awe, and transcendence of God brought together in Jonah's encounters with these metaphorical images and experiences.

God speaks to us in different voices and volumes and venues. There are some powerful metaphors in the Jonah story. Metaphors require us to use a part of our brain that we have been taught not to use. Most of us have been trained to determine knowledge factually and empirically, whether deductively or inductively. The left brain privileges the part, the fragment, over the whole. Using our right brains allows us to enter the whole garden of meaning and to seek (Heb. *derash*) and discern underlying connections we may have missed. A metaphorical reading is an abductive way of knowing. We look for signs, images that allow us to imagine beyond the reigning formulas of literal knowledge and to find new meaning, truth, and knowledge about God within it.

When you read a scriptural story literally, you define the characters and God. But when you read a scriptural story metaphorically or narraphorically—or semiotically—you reveal the characters within their relationships with themselves, others, creation, and God. Metaphorical knowledge does not define God but tracks relationships that point to God and God's attributes within those relationships. It adds felt truth to factual truth.

Metaphors urge us to think creatively and relationally. We treat the text less like an object and more like a subject. We ask the subject questions, and we relate what we know about Hebrew storytelling to the images and metaphors that we find in the text. By digging into the roots of the Scripture, we seek a richer, more experiential interpretation. The question "How does this relate to my life?" is clearer in the metaphorical interpretation. Perhaps the better question is "How does my life connect and contribute relationally to the kingdom of God?"

When we look at the metaphorical meaning of the story, the Bible's central themes of covenant, relationship, love, mercy, and humanity emerge much more prominently than the more literal and merely typological themes of repentance, exclusivism, or narcissism. A field of "humanness" begins to unfold within the horizon of the narraphors. Our primary comparison seems to turn to God's sovereignty as Creator, Redeemer, and Sustainer versus the human propensity for selfishness, independence, stubbornness, revenge, and control.

A metaphorical reading takes us back in some way to the beginning, the origins, the "garden." In fact, in Jonah 4:11, Hebrew tradition says that Jonah falls on his face in reference to Daniel 9:9: "Govern your world according to the measure of mercy, as it is said, 'To the Lord our God belong mercy and forgiveness.'" Jonah's "prayer" to God is an angry one: "That is why I fled to Tarshish: I knew that you are a gracious and compassionate God, slow to anger and abounding in love, a God who relents from sending calamity."[60] He even asks Yahweh to strike him dead. Whereas the typology of Tarshish only told us it is a symbol of a place out of the reach and realm of God, the metaphor of Tarshish reveals that to be out of the realm of God is to be dead. Life comes together when we are in relationship and "in mission." Life falls apart when we are out of relationship and "off mission." We find in the metaphor of Tarshish the relational struggle between humans and God, and the human thirst for justice versus God's unmitigated—and to Jonah, infuriating—mercy.

The metaphorical reading with its visuals and vibrations also allows us to connect this story with the metanarrative of the Bible where similar images are found. Examples include the story of the vineyard and its paid workers, the story of the woman with the alabaster jar, the story of the stoning of the adulterous woman; and other stories laced and loaded in the human response "That's not fair." Or what about metaphors of sin and separation (leviathan and worm and plant); the covenantal symbol of womb (sea and storm, and fish); the breathings of human life as well as Cain's rebellion (sun and wind); the primal story of vengeance and lust, mental thrashing, uncontrolled anger, selfishness, and rebellion by history's first family? All these connections serve to weave a rich tapestry out of the Jonah story with far more weft and weave than possible by left-brain stitching alone.

But more than that, whereas the literal reading assured us that we were reading a story about God's justice and the perils of disobedience, our metaphorical reading leads us into a more profound and sparkling story of the immensity of God's mercy and grace. To feel and experience that grandness of grace, we need to dig down yet one final level within our exegetical garden — into the revelational realm of Holy Spirit perception.

Let us take one more look at the Jonah story with our most intensely focused right-brain functioning. Let us step into reading number 4: an open-curtained, Spirit-driven knowledge of fugitive truths and divine mysteries. This is our transductive reading (or transincarnational), or Holy Spirit reading. Most simply, I like to call it our "faith" reading, since this blood-from-stone reading is less a test of skill than will, less technique than trust.

In a faith reading, we not only read and seek wisdom from the story, but we are read and scanned and healed by God from within the story. God takes our pulse, and we discover the diagnosis of what William Butler Yeats once called "the fury and mire of human veins."[61] If the metaphorical reading stings the soul, faith reading is the balm in Gilead that "heals the sin-sick soul." We open our veins and receive the biblical transfusion whereby we become the story and go face-to-face with the Divine. The revelational reading is EPIC: experiential, participatory, image rich, and connective. In the revelational reading, we leave the realm of words altogether to enter the Word — to allow God's message to make us whole with Christ or God. We stand under the story to understand the story: "Then he opened their minds so they could understand the Scriptures."[62] We also never separate revelation from redemption, remembering that revelation is "a noun of action" dealing with "a divine activity, not as the finished product of that activity."[63]

RIGHT-BRAIN READING #4
(THE REVELATIONAL ENCOUNTER OR TRANSDUCTIVE READING)

Reading the story once more, with right brains full throttle, we must not only examine and explore the text but enter the story until it washes over us, engulfs us, and takes root in us. At this level, we are even conductors of messages we do not fully understand. We are telling tales stronger than their tellers.

When we read the Jonah story transductively, we open secret closets of meaning and magic wardrobes of wonder about ourselves, each other, and eternity. If Shakespeare can promise sharpened sensitivities until we can find "tongues in trees, books in the running brooks, sermons in stones and good in everything,"[64] think how much more the Holy Spirit can do than Shakespeare.

Let's look again at those metaphors.

What if we allow those metaphors to serve not just as signs but as transformational change agents within the soul? When we become the story, when it is our hearts (not the Scriptures) being laid out on the slab for dissection, we find that the metaphors reflect our own spiritual and emotional journey of humanness as we "wrestle with God" what it means to live out our mission. Much like the Jacob story, the Jonah story is a "wrestling" with God to understand the whys of life — Why do good things happen to bad people? Why do bad things happen to good people? — and the reading echoes our cries for justice to a God who cares not just for "me" but for all people.

As our right brain moves us from left-brain "me-ness" to right-brain "we-ness," we become transformed by the truths of this struggle. When Jonah flees to Tarshish, we can feel his frustration and anger, his desire to be a "free agent," and his fear of his neediness. Like Jonah, we want a God who meets all our needs, who takes away our neediness, especially our need for God. We were made for a relationship with God and a mission in the world. We are like Jonah, wanting to do anything, hide anywhere, where God cannot "see" us, find us, use us, make us dependent.

In an inverse mirror of the Noah story, Jonah flees onto a ship (not with the innocent children and animals, which God reveals are back in Nineveh). Unlike Noah, Jonah thinks only of himself. He does not want to be bothered or responsible for the lives of anyone else, especially those he deems not as special as he is. And off he goes. But his soul cannot escape the turmoil. If we see God's "metaphors" within the story as physically created reflections of Jonah's own inner turmoil, we find that God is showing us that we cannot save ourselves. The tempest on the sea may well reflect Jonah's (and our own) anger, the struggle and panic that he takes out on everyone around him.

And yet even in his headlong race from God and his headstrong rebellion, he knows and feels God is still with him. He cannot escape from God. Sometimes God does not make it God's business to stay out of ours. In utter despair, Jonah pitches himself into the sea (into the depths of depression, into the abyss of hopelessness). But yet again, God saves Jonah from himself and gives him still another chance to face his true self within the belly of the beast, and he finds himself in contemplation with God in the womb of his tomb (but again, within God's primal care). Jonah stews and simmers, laments and groans within the "belly" of his most primal state in all of his utter and original humanness—until he at last gets to a place where he "spews out" an unwilling but partially relenting prayer.

Though grudging, it is a step toward reestablishing his relationship with God. He cannot escape the realization that he is utterly dependent on God no matter how much he wishes otherwise. But he has not surrendered yet. Jonah decides to do what he "should" but not with any turn of heart. We all know what that feels like. So he goes off and utters the most ineffectual words of prophecy one can imagine to the sinful Ninevites.

Lo and behold, the Ninevites actually repent. That's all it took—a ridiculous one-sentence warning? Now he is really seething. Even his attempts to thwart God through his cold admonishment have failed. Even his attempts to trick God with unheartfelt obedience, a fake sacrifice—a superficial sermon—have backfired. No matter how mundane his utterance, it has been given the unction of God. God's voice has communicated to the Ninevites through him regardless of how hard he tried to prevent it. He realizes that he is not in charge. He knew ahead of time (and therefore didn't want to do this mission to begin with!) that God wanted to forgive these Ninevites. But they don't deserve forgiveness. Jonah doesn't want them forgiven; he wants justice. And here he is put upon to be the vehicle of mercy.

Boy is he mad! He's been used! And he doesn't like it one bit. He goes off to fume, but God still won't leave him alone. God is one annoying God. The story turns now to where Jonah is not just fleeing, not just in turmoil, but combative and argumentative. In other words, Jonah is reengaged in a relationship with God.

The human array of reactions and emotions Jonah is going through cuts to the heart of each one of us. Jonah attempts to make himself a makeshift shelter, but God again has the upper hand and arranges for a leafy plant to grow up over Jonah to give him shade and chill his anger. Even in Jonah's anger, God remains caring and merciful. Jonah is so focused on his anger over God's mercy to the Ninevites that he can't see how merciful and patient God is being toward him in all of his humanness and rejection. Jonah needs to recognize his own humanness before he can understand the love and mercy of God.

Jonah still doesn't get it. He enjoys the comforting shelter of his shady plant and starts to feel happy and rewarded under God's protective cover. Just when his anger begins abating and he senses that perhaps he could put recent events out of his mind and enjoy the moment, just bask in God's favor and not have to think about his earlier conflict any longer, God removes the cover. Perhaps Jonah thought that he had indeed done what God had asked him and deserved a reward. After all, he had spoken the prophetic word as he was supposed to do. He had done what was required. He had gotten away with his pitiful noncommital token of obedience to the covenant.

But he had not changed his heart. He had "weathered" the storm outside, but the weather inside was still raging. It wasn't until the plant had withered and the "heat was on" that Jonah faced up to the scorching harshness of his own heart. In his selfishness and his lust for justice, Jonah's heart had pushed God out and rejected the garden relationship. He wanted to enjoy the favor of God but without living up to his covenant relationship within it. A covenant requires two sides. Jonah must choose either to live in relationship with God or to suffer the pain and separation of living apart from God. His refusal and anger at the end of the tale are still keeping him from becoming the kind of human that God in his mercy is calling him to be.

Like Cain and Adam before him, Jonah has by his own doing "cast(ored)" himself out of God's nourishing and nurturing relationship. And yet the last image in the story is one of the innocence of creation, the covenantal bond with humans and animals that signifies God's unending mercy toward all creation. The story leaves us to ponder our own relationship with God. And to choose our next steps carefully.

As we read with our right brains, we not only map the metaphors within the scriptural story, but we make the story our story. The fourth reading is an identity reading and a transincarnational experience (Heb.

sod). We trust the Spirit through the Scriptures to touch our spirit and to incarnate Christ within us, to turn our minds, and to penetrate our hearts with the unsparing truth of the divine covenant and the reality of our own humanity. We identify with Jonah in our humanness, and we feel all of the anger and indignation of unfair or forced treatment. Perhaps we feel the hesitancies of our call or the need to seek justice for unfair neglect or revenge for rejection. Perhaps our blood boils at the prosperity of those who deserve punishment instead. Perhaps we lament the trials we put ourselves under.

But as we contemplate our lives, we realize that God has been with us all along. Like every parent, God prefers a negative relationship with God's children over no relationship, patiently and mercifully allowing us to "act out" in all of our humanness and approach him in all of our weakness. Far from being the punishing God of our literal reading, we realize experientially that God showers us in mercy, even when we are at our vilest. When we read ourselves into the story, allowing the trans-incarnational power of God to connect with us and open our minds to the revelational truth of the Scripture, we are stunned by God's mercy.

This is the mystery of true encounter and what we might call in John Wesley's terms a "means of grace." It is our moment of transformational and incarnational realization, the highest form of knowledge. It is our moment of glory within the *shekinah*. And we emerge from the chrysalis of transincarnation changed. We not only contemplate or identify in the garden; we encounter the garden. We not only see the image of the serpent; we feel that serpent writhing within ourselves.

To bypass the Holy Spirit reading of the text is to bypass life. To be sure, this is the most intense and most difficult reading. It requires us to harness our critical, doubting, analytical left brain and to "step to the right" and experience God in living color. The story of Jonah becomes our story, our story within the story of God, as a third testament is being written: the Third Testament of You.

"Why are you angry?" God is asking you and me, not just Jonah. Only at this fourth level of the story do the narraphors of the Scripture take flight and become living and organic agents of change. They have become "supermetaphors" and "shape shifters." They have led us into divine space, moving our minds from an exegesis of flat words and images to a real-life, revelatory, and life-altering encounter with God.

When you "exegete" with your right brain, you exegete not just with words but with images. Readings 3 and 4 require you to delve into your creative space and to interact with the metaphors in a way that allows you to make connections, see relationships, and experience truth. Right-brain preaching likewise excels in design, synthesis, images, aesthetics, and interactivity.

Whereas the dominance of left-brain, pulpit-centric preaching has provided us primarily with logical, sequential, performative, step-by-step, point-by-point, zoom-in-on-the-right-answer homiletic styles, right-brain preaching does away with the time-space continuum and ventures into unknown territories where people encounter and experience Christ coming to life within them. We live in the fiery furnace of affliction, the lion's den of abandonment, the whale's belly of rebellion. The difference between left-brain and right-brain preaching is the difference between arrivals and itineraries, conclusive formulations and alluring possibilities.

Twenty-first-century consciousness involves a sea change in human cognition. "Points" no longer make points. People are beginning to think in brand-new ways, which are creating whole new experiences that move from knowing God with our left brain to knowing God with our whole brain; from faith formation through catechism to faith formation through proverbs, metaphors, music, images, imagination, and dance; from teaching through disquisition to teaching through narration by artists, mentors, coaches, and directors. People today aren't hungry for new information or brilliant messages; people are hungry for fresh experiences of faith and for experiences of a God who loves them. German philosopher Hans Georg Gadamer argues that the difference between experience and thought is the difference between dancing and talking about dancing. People today do not just want to talk about dancing; they want to dance.

To preach narraphorically is to teach people to "dance" with the Lord of the Dance, to move from a "damn the dawn" ennui of life to a "dance the dawn" exhilaration. To do that, you need to create not a skeleton with three bony points, but an organic architecture that will craft a network of meanings, a labyrinth of veins to deliver the blood of Christ to the body, warm and pulsing with energy, vitality, and meaning.

Chapter 7

Blood Cells:
Organic Architecture

The true "unpardonable sin" is to write something that "fails to live."
—Edmund Wilson, on writers[1]

TO FIND A FORM that accommodates the message and the mess we each make of the message is the task of every preacher.

What did Jesus do for a living? Jesus was a master builder. The word *tekton* in Greek has multiple connotations. It can mean a master builder, as in masonry, carpentry, metalwork, and so forth. It can also mean one who constructs, a master architect, including a scholar who crafts a literary edifice.[2]

Jesus was an architect of narraphors. Some have claimed shades of meaning to *tekton* that extend to one who constructs masterful literary "architecture," such as parables. Jesus was a master not only of building physical structures, which he sometimes referenced in his parables—"He did not say anything to them without using a parable"[3]—but a master of building multileveled stories that portray how to build a life.

Jesus' stories were filled with metaphorical lushness, surprising turns and twists, human foibles, and open endings. Most of all, they were postmortems of the heart and premortems of the Spirit. They were powerful organic structures, teeming with flesh and blood and bone.

Made up of blood cells, each part of a story carries with it the identity of Jesus and the invitation to be part of the anatomy of incarnation. In life it's all about story. For preachers of the gospel, it's all about God's story, the lifeblood of community. You might even call such stories "bloods," as they sometimes were in the past.[4] Truth is revealed in "blood." "True blood" preaching carries within it the ID markers, the metaphorical stem cells, the divine DNA, the narraphors and supermetaphors that allow the body to access that means of grace that incarnates Jesus within every life and within the communal body of Christ.

Narraphors are the leaven of heaven. They have the power to change lives and transform people from within the deepest levels of their being.[5] People's lives are built in storied stories—cell by cell, inch by inch, size by size, metaphor by metaphor. Each life is an organic mosaic made up of memories, and those memories are not of principles, points, or equations but of stories with (his)tories and, for the disciple of Jesus, relationship with (His)tories. We imagine and dream, not in viewpoints and values, but in narraphors, moving and meshing within horizons of hope. Our dreams for the future play out in alternative stories, scenarios, and signs that we wish to live within. When it comes to life, it's all in the story.

The dreams of humanity are stored in story and metaphor. Humans are, indeed, imaginal beings, "such stuff as dreams are made of." Stories are some of the highest achievements of organisms who think with organic minds that dream organic dreams with an organic capacity for organized complexity that is astounding. Why then are our organizations so *not* organ-ized? Why then are we so intent on delivering mechanistically structured sermons that disincarnate truth into distilled points delivered in lecture styles that challenge the eyelids of the most caffeinated? We have been trained to deliver left-brain theological algebra to people with EPIC cravings. We have defined what is "real" in abstract, scientific Enlightenment terms that spell endarkenment for twenty-first-century participants. We have "industrialized" faith into prepackaged and "tested" dogmas wrapped in paper and coded in words and wonder why the divine ends up in the dust heap.

In short, we have taken away the living Christ and have substituted a bobblehead. Like first-year medical students over a cadaver, we have spliced God's story, diced it, classified it, and proudly laid it out in technical and orderly jargon that's just short of legalese. But we are not called to study dead birds in pans or dead bodies on tables or dead texts on desks.[6] We are called to preach the good news of Jesus, a risen presence who can take up residence in beings yearning to breathe free and seeking to soar.

An organic sermon is in a sense not crafted but grafted from the lifeblood of Jesus, the "true blood" of the gospel. This labyrinth of vessels must deliver the blood to the body with pulsing vitality. How do we graft such a network of connections? How do we know it is vital and true?

The organic form must first come from narrative (Jesus' stories linked to our stories). Second, we must infuse the narrative with its intrinsic meta-phors. It's the metaphors, like parables in the Gospels, that break the closure of stories.[7] Third, we graft an organic architecture that carries a Jesus-DNA identity—and that identity comes from those metaphors that are the meat, not the sweets, of those narratives. An organic sermon is not dead meat. It is a transincarnational experience that can take hold of a life and heal.

As a writer, I'm also in the race horse business. I stable stallions—some I show; some I race. I breed them then raise a barn full of them, ten to twenty at a time. Every day I must feed them water and oats, groom them, and take them out for walks. Eventually I mount them when they (and I) are ready. I have no idea which ones are going to get strong and healthy enough until they start kicking down the door to be let out and race.

Every horse is a book/sermon/blog/podcast. Each must be fed, watered, and groomed. But when they are freed, they take on a life of their own. You don't own them. You raise them to race, and they take it from there. The sermon must do the same.

★　　★　　★

"Whoever listens to you listens to me."
—Jesus[8]

★　　★　　★

The human race is on a race of truth, which is a grace race to Christ. Preaching must be true to itself, to the heart of Christianity, to the chatelaine of every church: Christ, and Christ crucified.[9] Christianity betrays its mission when it lifts up anything other than Christ, no matter how true those other things seem to be. People need to hear the voice of Christ. They need to experience the presence of Christ that can lead them to the preeminence of Christ. One of the most famous quotes from Charles Haddon Spurgeon to a young preacher is this:

> Don't you know, that from every town and every village and every hamlet in England, wherever it may be, there is a road to London? ... So from every text in Scripture there is a road to the metropolis of the Scriptures, this is, Christ. And, my dear brother, your business is, when you get to a text, to say, "Now what is the road to Christ?" and then preach a sermon, running along the road towards the great metropolis—Christ.... I have never yet found a text that had not got a road to Christ in it, and if ever I do find one ... I will go over hedge and ditch but I would get at my Master, for the sermon cannot do any good unless there is a savor of Christ in it.[10]

133

Each of us begins life with a learning disability. We are hard of hearing ("You are dull of hearing")[11] and slow of learning. At least nine times the Gospels record Jesus saying, "Whoever has ears, let them hear."[12] For people today to "hear" the voice of Christ, they must feel that their own voice can be heard. An old saying goes, "It's all in the telling." I have said instead, "It's all in the experiencing." Further even than "Show, don't tell," an organic sermon lets someone hold it in their own hands and take it wherever it may go: "It's all in the participating."

"When you come together [in *ekklesia*]...."[13] When you encounter the word *ekklesia* in the writings of the early church, you are likely to meet two others: *isonomia*, which means "equality," and *eleutheria*, which means "freedom." In the *ekklesia* of the early church, all people were equal participants with the freedom to be heard.[14] Homileticians have typically read the data to prove the need for more illustrations and stories. The documentary data of text and context prove more than that: the need for animations and participations.

When a baby is born, we don't just want to be told. We don't just want to be shown. We want to hold the baby: "May I hold her?" we ask. We want to cherish the child close to our hearts — connect with her, play with her, bond with her. The same is true for the gospel. We cannot know Jesus only by being told. Not even only by being shown. We need to experience Jesus and feel our hearts beat in sync with his.

Early church worship was marked by spontaneous and collaborative efforts to remember and reveal the "rising Christ."[15] Today at best we conduct artfully constructed worship and preaching but without a glimmer of spontaneity and with carefully controlled participation. The best participation is not controlled. People are tired of control. They want the real thing in all of its messiness, and they expect direct participation in the real thing themselves. Representation is not enough.

*   *   *

"Chaos, trusted, becomes a dancing star."
—Friedrich Nietzsche[16]

*   *   *

Every narraphoric preacher is an architect whose work is to craft and graft a living, breathing meshwork for the body.[17] Preachers are God-moment makers, experience designers, imagesmiths, spirit *tektons*, participation artists. Preaching itself is the disciple and craft of story and song. In our exegesis of Scripture, we looked for the backstory and listened for the undersong. Now we need to start telling it, showing it, and singing it.

How do we craft and graft an organic sermon? We first need to know what it's made of.

ROOTS AND WINGS

There are only a handful of human responses to the world. German philosopher Walter Benjamin (1892–1940) once observed that all storytelling emerges from two fundamental experiences: the state of being rooted to a particular place and the act of traveling. The two types of stories are (1) "moving in" stories (roots, home), and (2) "moving on" stories (wings, journey, pilgrimage). Everything else falls somewhere in between staying home and pilgrimage.[18]

Narraphoric preaching has both roots and wings. It grows in two opposite directions at the same time. It is grown, not built, by its roots going downward into the ground. But at the same time, it grows upward with honey-filled flowers that fuel the living into flight. You cannot structure it into a certain number of points. Organisms require "organic architecture," a web of connections and network of meanings that exegete holistically and engage transincarnationally.

Jesus chose parables with images of both rootedness (mustard seed, garden) and movement (vineyard, talents).[19] In most stories, you can find elements of both roots and wings. Both are organic images of homeland and pilgrimage. Rootedness tells us that we have a sacred story of the past and a place to call "home." Wings tell us we have a sacred story yet to come and remind us to be on our way, although all pilgrims proceed to the future en route to their roots. The life of a pilgrim reflects both our past and our future, our memory and our dreams. Every preacher must garner his or her wings.

The power of a narraphoric sermon is that it connects people in the present to their past life story (and that of the scriptural story of Jesus) as well as to their future story within Christ's story (hope, resurrection, and transformation). The organs of roots and wings give a story both of life and longevity. The preacher anchors the story in the texts and traditions of the faith and then prepares for the Spirit to carry it and to release it in incarnate form long after the storytelling has finished. When telling the stories of Jesus, we remember the Clovis G. Chappell axiom "Context is part of text"[20] while trusting the story to take flight in current culture. An organic story bakes both personal and communal bread. The best organic sermons allow the body to finish the story on its own.

Hebraic storytelling was a rich, colorful, and complex art. Hebrew narrative was highly visual and image intensive. The organic metaphor of the garden, for example, permeates almost all of the First and Second Testaments in some fashion. The metaphor goes back to the creation story with the Word of Yahweh and its genesis in the garden. This is the image from which emerges the PaRDeS, the Hebrew exegetical method. The Scriptures of both testaments are highly organic. Their metaphors form an interlacing network of intercontextual and interrelational beauty. For architects to do justice to the Scriptures, we must respect the garden — both its Hebrew roots and its flowering in Jesus, its greatest storyteller.

MAKE THE FAMILIAR STRANGE: THE SWERVE

With every memorable story, there is a tweak in the telling — a twist, a turn, a veering. An organic story is like a vine: you never know where it will go or in what shape it might next appear.

But its stem cells are those of Jesus. The architect of the organic sermon doesn't seek out the ordinary and inorganic but seeks to connect with the living and changing, to grow along with the story, and to allow the story to take on its own special twist. Preaching re-creates life in a way we recognize but may not have seen before in quite that way. Through this new way, we experience an enhanced perception of truth.

*　　*　　*

"What is familiar is not known."
— *Georg Wilhelm Friedrich Hegel*

*　　*　　*

A school in Virginia offered a course called Home Economics for Boys. No one signed up. Then the dean renamed the course Bachelor Living, and 120 signed up. You've heard the quip "Reality is stranger than fiction." To make the familiar strange is to allow life in all of its mystery and eccentricity, all of its uniqueness and surprise, to live out through your stories in a new way that will catch the attention of your participants.[21]

Too many sermons are straightforward to the point of banality. Jesus was a master of "the swerve":[22] "You have heard it said, but I say...." To overcome the deadening effects of habits and to swerve the truth, it is necessary to defamiliarize: to portray familiar things in unfamiliar ways; to approach the subject crabwise, trawling assumptions and surmounting obstacles. Creative preaching is a fertile combination of difference and similarity: so similar that we can recognize it and see ourselves in it, so radically different that we can learn from it and grow beyond ourselves from it.

Some of the hardest things to see are those that stare us right in the face. Emily Dickinson talked about always telling the truth but "telling it slant." In making truth "slant" or "strange," you make it fresh so that it can become familiar again. The slanting toward strangeness, the veering off course, "the swerve," is the key to all creative communication.

Ever nod off while you're driving? Just for an instant? It's called "micro-sleep." I can tell you that the average microsleep is just under four seconds. Or I can tell you that at 60 mph you've just traveled the length of a football field dead to the world. By making the familiar strange, I've just imprinted on your mind an image you'll never forget.

*   *   *

"If it were not for this swerve, everything would fall down-wards like raindrops through the abyss of space."
—*Roman poet/philosopher Lucretius (99–55 BC)*

*   *   *

We use phrases like the "bottom billion" (who live on a dollar a day) and "billionaires" in such a casual manner. But a billion seconds ago, it was 1959. A billion minutes ago, Jesus was alive. A billion hours ago, we were living in the Garden of Eden. A billion days ago, no one was walking on two feet on planet Earth. A billion dollars ago was only eight hours and twenty minutes ago—that's the rate the US government is spending your money. By giving an image full of fruitful dislocations, a meaningless number becomes memorable.

REVEAL COMPLEXITY SIMPLY

God's world is amazingly complex. Ask any biologist. Take a look at fractals, and you will see the most beautiful patterns and designs, intricate in their complexity yet simple in their form. Organic architecture must be like those fractals, revealing the complexity of God in the simplest of ways. The more complex the message, the simpler your words need to be.

Jesus taught in parables. And those with varying "ears" heard them differently or heard them on different levels. The most powerful words in history were addressed to us simply in the language of husbandry and fishing. Yet we still need to read them over and over again to plumb their deepest meaning. The more complex the world, the more simplicity we need.

Metaphors are examples of revelatory complexity condensed in a single word. Just as there is no such thing as a "simple cell," there is no such thing as a "simple word." If every word can be a book, the thin, simple words write the longest books. Why? Because it's the simple words that unify the complexities. My only question is, why are life's first, simple words the last things in life we get to?

★   ★   ★

"You don't have to be fat to drive fat oxen."
—*Old Jewish proverb*[23]

★   ★   ★

In chapter 8, "Blood Bank," we delve more deeply into the grafting of metaphors. These are the lifeblood of your sermon. These are the fertilizer of your soil, what makes your sermon truly organic so that it can grow the best souls.

CULTIVATE IMAGACY AND POESIS

Poesis is the art of making images. "Image" is different from "symbol." A symbol stands for something else and points to something else. An image is something that stands for itself and may or may not be a symbol. The most powerful images are those that are embodied experiences. There is a revolution going on in our understanding of cognition ("grounded cognition") that demonstrates the priority of bodily states, ritual motions, and situated actions to the very act of cognition itself.[24]

Whereas the world of mechanization and industrialization focused only on literacy, today's world is a world of what I like to call "imagacy."[25] As a good organic architect, you need to be "poetic"—to cultivate an image garden, to grow and water the images that feed your congregation. It is these images that will carry the stories and allow your metaphors to flower and bear fruit. They are the color and song in the life of your sermon. They allow for an experience that not only serves the mind but is sensory, embodied, and grounded in practice.

ORGANIC DOES NOT MEAN DISORDERED OR DISORGANIZED

Beauty consists in amplitude and arrangement, Aristotle tells us in his *Poetics*.[26] The word organic means to have an organ-ized order, an ordering structure that is moving and living. The sermon with heart is an organ, a living organism, grafted without synthetic fillers. It is a complex and beautiful structure. Like that fractal, it is moving and changing as it breathes and speaks. When it comes into contact and interacts with the body, it moves and changes. This does not make the sermon disorganized, only more organic and organ-ized. Organic preaching is vectoral preaching—always in motion, always evoking emotion.

Some preachers feel that to make a sermon organized and "tight" is to bind it up in points, tie it together with applications, and wind it down in enclosures. But what is bound will not fly. And what will not fly will not reach the heart.

What distinguishes any house of theology is not its tenets but its tenants. As the "head of the household," how the preacher handles the pots and pans of living communicates truth more powerfully than the carefully prepared propositions served up in homiletic form.

For example, when you feel you have prepared enough for your sermon, you need to be able to pass what the George Gershwin of homileticians, Bryan Chapell, calls the "3 a.m. Test." The 3 a.m. Test requires you to imagine a spouse, a parent, or a parishioner awakening you from your deepest slumber with this simple question: "What's the sermon about today, Pastor?" If you cannot give a crisp answer, Chancellor Chapell insists, you know the sermon is probably half-baked. "Thoughts you cannot gather at 3 a.m. are not likely to be caught by others at 11 a.m."[27]

When you feel you are ready, practice your sermon with someone listening, or record yourself to watch the ways that you engage your people. Look at your expressions, your body language, your posture, your carriage. Listen to the intonation of your voice, your inflections, your volume. If you want to tell a story, you have to be a good storyteller.

Every sermon should have a good beginning. The best metaphor for what a good introduction feels like comes from Princeton communications professor G. Robert Jacks (1934–2002), who described a good introduction as a police ambush where you are arrested, handcuffed, and dragged before the bar to be booked.[28] If you want people to participate in the experience of your sermon, you first need to get their attention.

An introduction should pull (not push) people into the alternative, narraphoric realities of the Bible. By engaging them from the start with an invitation into "conversation," you also allow them to leave their role as "listeners" and enter into a new role as partners in creation. Once you have enticed them to put a first foot forward, you can teach them next how to join Jesus on this journey of life.

Every sermon should have a good closing. In organic preaching, to close "properly" means something different than to have the sermon signed, sealed, and delivered. Life is not a closed system but an ever-moving, always-opening journey. Our very resurrection message is one of law-breaking life. Why do we feel the need to "wrap things up" and tie them in a pretty bow and ribbon?

★   ★   ★

"Great is the art of beginning, but greater the art of ending."
— *Henry Wadsworth Longfellow*

★   ★   ★

The conclusion should not be the climax of the sermon. The participation is the climax of the sermon. Don't even think "conclusion." Think closure — but a "closure" that isn't an enclosure but a portal with you as the porter. The greatest sermon is an unfinished sermon, a sermon of everlastingness. Of course, there is a sense in which preaching is ever only unfinished business, or business that has to be begun all over again. For preachers there's always a Sunday coming.

The ending of an organic sermon is more like a *fermata*, or "hold" sign, the pause when the trumpets stop playing and the strings get ready to launch into ecstatic and fervent harmony. French philosopher Paul Ricoeur asked, "[Is not] the mutual exchange and mutual aid in the dialectic of openness and closure the essence of the pastoral act? ... Life is open at both ends ... we are always in process of revising the narrative of our lives."[29] The architecture of organic homiletics allows for endings to flow into the hands and lives of the people ... as new beginnings.

The closing of your sermon, although it may vary, must leave your congregation feeling nourished, refreshed, changed, and charged. There is nothing worse than a kite that nosedives and hits the ground in a silent thud. That's why some homileticians have argued that two-thirds of prep time should be spent on the last one-third of the sermon.[30]

An "altering" close keeps your people riding on the wings of the Spirit even after they leave the church. Here is where the long tail comes in. In a truly EPIC sermon, lives are changed, and people leave knowing and feeling the hope-giving resurrection presence of Jesus. The body of Christ becomes vital, moving, trembling, joyful. Only Jesus can say, "It is finished." No great sermon is ever finished. Sermons are everlasting. They go beyond the message's end, beyond the benediction, beyond the doors of the church to incarnate Jesus in the world. Here are some "altering" questions:

What do I want people to experience?
What questions do I want to tantalize them?
What images do I want them to keep sensing all week?
What healing do I want to take place?
With what part of discipleship do I want people to be challenged?
With what truth of Jesus do I want them to be stunned?

* * *

"Better the end of a speech than its beginning."
—*Ecclesiastes 7:8*

* * *

You could come up with hundreds of similar questions. But you should at least focus on two or three. By giving your hearers an "aftertaste," you supply a "foretaste" of their week as followers of Jesus. However you choose to close, challenge people to turn their lives toward Christ in even more earnest and joyful ways, to keep them dancing in the never-ending song of life. As John Wesley said, we must experience the means of grace as often as we can in order to keep perfecting ourselves in sanctifying grace.

ORGANIC IS ANIMATION MORE THAN ILLUSTRATION

Most homiletics texts will tell you that illustrations bring life to sermons. To "illustrate" literally means to "bring light," and illustrations may decorate a logical thesis just as Christmas lights decorate a tree. Many pastors have been trained in the "one illustration per point" formula. But it is just that—a formula. While illustrations bring light to a sermon by clarifying concepts, animations bring a sermon to life.[31] You illustrate points; you animate experiences.

Fred Craddock started us on this startling path of rethinking Jesus' use of "illustrations," and whether they were illustrations at all: "In good preaching what is referred to as illustrations are, in fact, stories or anecdotes which do not illustrate the point; rather they are the point. In other words, a story may carry in its bosom the whole message rather than the illumination of a message which had already been related in another but less clear way."[32]

Those homileticians who argue that 75 percent of Jesus' teaching is illustrations[33] are therefore confusing illustrations with animations. Jesus animated, not illustrated, his messages. In fact, Jesus is not the illustration of

God's nature. When the Bible says that the Son "made known" the Father (John 1:14, 18), the wording translated "made known" (*exegeomai*) means "to draw out in narrative."[34] Jesus is the extended animated narrative of God. The primary medium of biblical communication is narraphor. In fact, the Bible is most precisely a storybook. Seventy-five percent of the First Testament is narrative. Twenty percent of the Second Testament is the words of Jesus—the equivalent of twelve sermons thirty minutes long—but many of these words are spent telling stories.[35] The Bible is a unified whole. How it hangs together in an integrated fashion is that it presents the greatest story ever told. I like to translate the opening words of John's gospel like this: "In the beginning was the Story, and the Story was with God, and the Story was God."

Through EPIC animations, the preacher enables the experience of the Word to become enfleshed in accordance with the incarnational imperative: the "Word" wants to become "flesh" and "dwell" among us, taking on a life of its own. It is only in that embodied dwelling and indwelling that we can "behold his glory." The semiotic preacher learns to see everything as a potential animation—every song, sparrow, surprise, and sortie holds narraphoric promise—hence the need for preachers to be "globalists" rather than "specialists" in their reading and interests.

Lab Practicum
HOW TO GROW A POPPY

A metaphor is like a poppy. It looks beautiful already from the outside, but its seeds inside are even more astounding. Full of transcendent and revelatory surprise, they will take you places you have never been.

Creating organic architecture is like growing a garden. You need to find the narraphoric seeds that grow best in the native soil and then plant those seeds so they can germinate in the hearts and lives of your people. Preachers sow the seed and wait with hope—for God is responsible for the harvest.[36] But continued cultivation—feeding and weeding—after germination is the preacher's responsibility.[37] Following are thirteen steps on how to create an organic architecture using the metaphor of the poppy.

*   *   *

"In science as in every area where the combinatory play of metaphor applies, analogy comes only after the facts."
—*Richard Feynman, physicist*

*   *   *

1. First you begin with a seed—a scriptural story.
2. Then you read that story not just once but at least five to seven times. Out loud. The vibrations of the words help the story resonate in your mind and heart. Read it until you are living the story and it becomes your story. Then read it again until you know it "by heart" without reading it.
3. Exercise the discipline of historical context. Read the story in the context of its culture, and get the historical facts of the story right. Make sure you know the story "by head" as well as "by heart." If there is to be a careful selection of interpretive signs and symbols, you don't reach for the metaphor until you have fully grasped the data of the drama.
4. Next map the images. If you forget how to do this, go to the lab work in the introduction to this book. Or go to chapter 6, "Blood Flow," and review the text of Jonah. Dig deeply into the soil of your garden.
5. Start exegeting the images while you keep looking for metaphors. Highlight them in your Bible. The more you make this story your story, the more its images and metaphors will come to the fore.
6. Think about where else in the Scriptures you have found the images or metaphors. Use a Bible dictionary to help you. Compare the stories. What do you know about metaphor within Hebrew tradition? Where else has it appeared it the wider literature and how? What does it mean to you in your own life?
7. Go to your sources. Find those images and metaphors on the Web, in your online sources, in your commentaries, and in other texts. Look at all the pictures and images you can find. What do

you notice that you missed? What do they remind you of? What connections can you make between those images and the Scriptures? Between the scriptural images and your life?

8. How many meanings and connections can you find for each metaphor? Do they take you down other paths? In other directions? Do they open up new windows of thought or tasks? What emotions do they evoke in you? Do they have sacramental value? How do they connect with what you know about Jesus?

9. How can you connect these metaphors to other metaphors that appear in your life that carry the same emotions? In the lives of your parishioners? How can you portray them in the stories of their lives?

10. Take, for example, the poppy. Where in literature or in Christian symbolism does the poppy appear? What meanings has it had? What can the poppy be used for? What does the color red signify? What can this tell you about the way in which you could use the poppy in your life story? In the stories of others? Have you ever celebrated Pentecost by everyone wearing red? At football games they wear the colors of the team. What if we were to try this at church?

11. How can you create an organic architecture with the narraphors you have assembled? What images emerge from your exegesis? What sensory and emotional power do they have? How can you relate those metaphors to Jesus and his message for us?

12. What "slant" on the scriptural text has emerged through your exegesis of these powerful metaphors? Has the rubber hit the road in your own life? If so, what traction do these metaphors have for the long haul?

13. What will your organic architecture look like? Supposing you have just thirty seconds with which to capture your congregation, how will you introduce your narraphor? How will you infuse it with life?

Thomas Long has noted that "a sermon's form, although often largely unperceived by the hearers, provides shape and energy to the sermon and thus becomes itself a vital force in how a sermon makes meaning."[38] How can you tell if your sermon's architectural form is dead or alive? You can "test" it. Here are some tests of organicity.

★　　★　　★

"The story is the picture which is the text."
—Fred Craddock[39]

★　　★　　★

LAB TEST

1. DNA

Do a DNA test on your sermon ... an ID exam ... a blood test. This is your identity test: Does your sermon have a Jesus identity? Do you "lift him up"?[40] Have you connected the sermon in some way to Jesus? Does it help someone to find the ways that their own identity is found in Jesus? Every organic sermon must have within its stem cells Jesus DNA.

2. MRI

An organic sermon is missional, relational, and incarnational (MRI). An MRI is a test that shows the function and structural flow of the sermon: its organs, colors, form, structure, the inner workings of its impact, and the fluorescence of its message. It shows how God is always doing something surprising, contextual, and creative in the lives of all Jesus followers.

More and more I'm convinced that people have to be ready to hear something before they can really understand it. Some brain research backs up the Bible's claim that some people don't seem to like any ideas but their own.[41] That's why most of our preparation as preachers is not getting ready ourselves but "developing readiness" for people to hear what has been said, is being said, and echoes into eternity in the depths of their own souls. Rabbi and therapist Edwin H. Friedman (1932–96) used to say that people can't hear you unless they are turned toward you emotionally. If you are chasing them to give your message, they won't hear a word. You have to stop the pursuit so they can stop the escape. Then you can be heard.

But the homiletic "form" must take into account more than the "listening patterns" of the hearers; it must take into account the interactive patterns of the "participants." The major question of preaching is not "What do I say?" but "What do I want to happen?"[42] The organic sermon must pass the MRI test in order to be true to the blood of Jesus. The missional sermon issues a call for everyone in the body. The relational sermon connects the lives and stories of people with the Jesus story and with each other. The incarnational sermon allows for transduction to take place—for those engaged in relationship with the sermon to be radically and revelationally transformed by the life and person of Jesus.

3. EKG

The root of *animation* is *anima*: it's "alive." An EKG measures the amount of electrical activity in your sermon, the amount of energy and enthusiasm, but most of all the amount of exhilaration it will exude. To exhilarate is to delight and invigorate, to gladden. Does the sermon elicit joy and delight in the encounter with Jesus? John Wesley said we were created to be happy in God. Does your sermon pulse with the exhilarating presence of the Spirit? An organic sermon should touch people as if shivers of the Spirit's presence are kissing their cheeks and brushing their backs.

In Aristotle's *Poetics*, he identified *kathairein* ("catharsis") as the purging of emotions at the very crux or turning point of an encounter (especially in theater). Does your sermon create that crux or turning point in the lives of those who engage with it? A catharsis is a cleansing, a purifying, a healing, a releasing of emotions and a purging of fear, a moment when the metaphorical "turn" effects its most powerful and incarnational transduction. Can your sermon transport the space into a place where change happens in people's lives?

Someone once compared the preacher's task to that of a child operating a box crane in an arcade. The child tries to lift a treasure from a mound of trinkets and place the prize where it can be claimed before time runs out on the machine. Animations lift listeners from their immediate situations and transport them to another place where change can take place before their interest expires.

When that happens, the participant "suspends disbelief." J. R. R. Tolkien believed that Jesus' gospel of salvation could have the power of catharsis. He called it the moment of "eucatastrophe." In that moment, we see in a brief vision that there is more to this life than the ordinary world experiences. We see beyond our current life and recognize the alternative reality of the kingdom.[43] A great sermon has the power of catharsis.

Finally, the organic sermon must be a galvanizing force in the lives of the body of Christ. To galvanize is to stimulate, to shock to awareness, to arouse to action, and to make aware of Jesus' presence surrounding and protecting us from "rusting" in our faith. An organic architect must graft a sermon with the galvanizing energy of incarnation, innovation, and imagination. What a preacher hopes to attain and what sermon participants long for is the same: help in seeing Jesus' salvation message as a catharsis to living a sent life, and help to grasp hold of the reality of the kingdom of God.

Chapter 8

Blood Bank: Narrative and Metaphor = Narraphor

> The world is God's picture book.
> —Helmut Thielicke

IN THE BEGINNING WAS THE NARRAPHOR

The gospel of John begins, "In the beginning was the *Logos*." The *Logos* is a narraphor—a powerful and pregnant metaphor, image, and story all wrapped up in a single "Word." And a word is never just a word. Especially not the Word of God.

The "Word" is not skeletal bones but is clothed in flesh and blood. Words are living symbols that pass on truth in their organic breathings as narraphors. Hebrew literature is especially rich in hidden meanings and metaphors. The language itself is image rich and identity strewn. And in the Hebrew Scriptures, an entire covenant theology is created within the story-circle of the garden.

The testament of Hebrew religion is not just a garden-variety faith but a faith seeded in the Word of Yahweh, held fast in the roots of the Trees of Knowledge and Life, intertwined intricately and infinitely in a covenant relationship that binds all humanity—and all narraphors—together in Holy Writ. Hebrew narraphors breathe Yahweh like air, and they color Hebrew identity like the very creation story itself. If we look at the book of Genesis, we see indeed that in the beginning was a beautiful image created from that Word (or words) of "creation."

The very first words of the Bible, "In the beginning God created," tell us that God's (or the Word's) first and foremost act was as Creator of "heavens and the earth." The descriptions that follow are a series of images that describe God's brilliant work of creation. Like an artwork, God formed and breathed life, created textures and distinctions between land and sea, colored the world with perceptions, shaped man from clay, created bonds and boundaries and lineages, and invested and attached a judgment value to this piece of art: "It was very good."

God's transcendent truth, beauty, and goodness are inherent in the creation story. From the very onset, Scripture posits a narraphoric aesthetic. God painted a picture of a garden, Eden, which was in perfect harmony with the Divine, and a portrait of humanity as an *imago Dei* of the Creator. The essence of the "garden" is the divine-human relationship with all of creation. To be human is to engage in the creative process within the world under the supervision of a loving and merciful God. To read and speak the Scriptures is to see them as a creative and interwoven series of narraphors, a garden of meaning and identity waiting to be seeded, dug into, turned over, cultivated, played in, reaped, and reseeded.

The Bible is a story that interconnects these narraphors from testament to testament, from alpha to omega. The opening passage in John, although perhaps the most quoted one, is not the only link to the creation story. But Jesus' whole life and ministry are linked integrally and intrinsically narraphor to narraphor. Let's take a look for a moment at our earliest creation story, Genesis 2:

Lab Practicum
A SEMIOTIC CREATION STORY

FINDING THE NARRAPHORS

On the day the heavens and earth were created, there were no plants or vegetation to cover the earth. The fields were barren and empty, because the Eternal God had not sent the rains to nourish the soil or anyone to tend it. In those days, a mist rose up from the ground to blanket the earth, and its vapors irrigated the land. One day the Eternal God scooped dirt out of the ground, sculpted it into the shape we call human, breathed the breath that gives life into the nostrils of the human, and the human became a living soul....

The Eternal God planted a garden in the east in Eden—a place of utter delight—and placed the man whom He had sculpted there. In this garden, He made the ground pregnant with life, bursting forth with nourishing food and luxuriant beauty. He created trees, and in the center of this garden of delights stood the tree of life and the tree of the knowledge of good and evil.

A river flowed from Eden to irrigate the garden, and from there it separated into four smaller rivers. The first, the Pishon, flows around the land of Havilah—a rich land plentiful in gold of premium quality, bdellium, and onyx stones. The second, the Gihon, flows around the entire land of Cush. The third, the Tigris, flows east of Assyria, and the fourth is the Euphrates.

The Eternal God placed the newly made man in the garden of Eden in order to [conserve and conceive it]. God [gave certain instructions to] the man regarding life in the garden.

God: Eat freely from any and all trees in the garden. I only require that you abstain from eating the fruit of one tree—the tree of the knowledge of good and evil. Beware: the day you eat the fruit of this tree, you will certainly die.

After God gives the human this directive, God realizes something is missing.

It is not good for the man to be alone, so I will create a companion [savior] for him, a perfectly suited partner [to save him from his loneliness].

So out of the same ground the human was made from, the Eternal God sculpted every sort of animal and every kind of bird that flies up in the sky. Then God brought them to the human and gave him the authority to name each creature as he saw fit: whatever he decided to call it, that became its name. Thus the human chose names for domesticated animals, birds, and wild beasts. But none of these creatures was a right and proper partner for Adam [adama—"made from earth"].

The authority to name something is unique to humanity. To name is to share [as a subcreator] in God's creative act.

So the Eternal God put Adam into a deep sleep, removed a rib from his side, and closed the flesh around the opening. He formed a woman from the rib taken out of the man and presented her to him.

> **Adam:** At last, a suitable companion, a perfect partner.
>   Bone from my bones.
> Flesh from my flesh.
>   I will call this one "woman" as an eternal reminder
>   that she was taken out of man.[1]

In the passage above, which is the oldest of the two creation stories, we see a first image of God as an artist using the medium of clay to fashion a human being (genderless—merely *adama*) out of the earth. Humans don't come "into" the earth; we come "out of" the earth. At this point, humankind is still golem. Not until God breathes the divine spirit into *adama* is a soul born. (We see this same relational image at Pentecost in the Gospels when the Lord breathes life and power and authority into Jesus' bride, the church). God and humans exist in symbiotic relationship ("Follow me!"). God places the humans in a holy garden to be nourished in an intimate relationship with the Creator. (Jesus is the divine Gardener.) This relationship is nourished by the streams of living water that run through it.

The garden is an image or metaphor for the relationship itself—the ground continually nourished by water and inhabited by God who walks in it (to be in relationship with God is to walk with God, for Jesus said, "I am the way and the truth and the life,"[2] and "Whoever wants to be my disciple must ... take up their cross daily and follow me"[3]). In essence he directs the humans to "conserve and conceive." This is the heart of the first image of the covenant. Not to preserve but to conserve—to keep the garden identity ("Remember his holy covenant";[4] "Love the Lord your God with all your heart and with all your soul and with all your mind"[5]), and to conceive new creation within it—to perpetuate it, seed it, allow it to flower and flourish ("Be fruitful and increase in number; multiply on the earth and increase upon it";[6] "Go spread the gospel to the whole world"[7]), to care for it and be in relationship with it (the *halakah*).

In Hebrew theology, the seed itself is the Word of Yahweh; the soil is the layers of understanding of God's Word (the Torah). The garden environment is the ecosystem of relationships between Yahweh and humanity, the perfect covenant, and its blooms of food and beauty are the fruits of that relationship ("Bear much fruit"[8]). Eternal life is ensured ("I am the gate"[9]). As long as the Tree of the Knowledge of Good and Evil (that which separates) is not digested, God and humanity exist in a companionship relationship.

Yet God realizes that relationship with his own kind is missing for Adam. So yet more relationships are born: beasts of the field, birds of the air, domesticated animals. But they do not save him from his loneliness (the Hebrew word that we translate as "partner" is best translated "savior"—used only again for Jesus). But Adam is given reign to name them. At last, God slices open Adam's side, and a new entity is born, of the same body and blood (the water and blood spilled on the cross that births the church, the bride of Christ). This is the eternal reminder that the woman was taken out of Adam (the body of the church incarnated with the resurrected and living Spirit of Christ with and within us).

As this covenant relationship was formed, so Jesus reestablishes it yet again. (He tells those who have faith, "You will be with me in paradise,"[10] which best translates "garden.") The Bible is a storybook of interweaving narraphors that begin and end with a covenant story of God. Jesus, the Last Adam, is the fulfillment of the Hebrew Scriptures, and the Gospels are the narraphors of that messianic fulfillment. Our narraphors are our reality. The Scriptures are a "picture book" of our lives. These pictures form the way we see ourselves and our relationships to the world, God, and each other. This is why preachers must be imagesmiths, masters of narraphor.

Jesus was a Hebrew gardener, a teacher of husbandry truths. God sent his Son into the world to a particular people in order to draw all the world to himself. Jesus is steeped in the narraphors of the Hebrew Scriptures and represents himself as the fulfillment of the greatest covenantal narraphor of all—the Word made flesh. Out of this rich tradition of garden narraphors, Jesus brings us the most potent communication style in all of history: parables. Parables are narraphors that turn lives back to God, form disciples that will carry on the faith, build communities of shalom, and plant love in every heart.

Semiotic preaching lifts the veil of the Jesus narraphors. Semiotic preaching casts seed into the world to carry on the stories of the faith, the incarnated identity of Jesus, the images that form our discipleship and our vision of God and each other—the seeds that are the stem cells of Christianity.

STEM CELLS AND MUSTARD SEEDS

A stem cell is a master cell of the human body. It has the ability to grow into any of the body's more than two hundred cell types. Stem cells are of the same lineage and retain the familial ability to divide throughout life. Unlike maturing cells, which are destined to their fate, stem cells can renew themselves and create new cells of any kind. Bone marrow stem cells, for example, are the most primitive but primal cells in the body. From them all the various types of blood cells are descended.

If Jesus were here today, stem cells might be his "mustard seed" metaphor. The mustard seed in Jesus' day was every bit as contentious as the stem cell is today. But the mustard seed for Jesus carried the identity of the gospel in its core. It spread like wildfire without regard to command or control. Far unlike our Enlightenment-inspired gardens of Versailles or highly stylized Dutch gardens, mustard was a weed. It was most like a thistle or a dandelion but even more rambunctious. Once it hit the ground, it spread and took root deeply and pervasively. But for Jesus the metaphor powerfully conveyed how a weed could turn a whole world into a field of dreams. A weed could seed the faith like nothing else, and it bore an eternal life in its ability to perpetuate easily and indefinitely.

Should stem cells be used to heal human life? Should mustard weeds be used to perpetuate the gospel? These are not the arguments of this text. But narraphors are the stem cells, the mustard seeds of the faith. They are identity-making, disciple-forming, covenant-cutting, relationship-building, lineage-bridging, kingdom-coming images that embed the gospel story within hearts and minds, bodies and souls of communities.

*   *   *

"Did you know that images have the power to possess those who see them?"
—*Rubem Alves, Brazilian theologian*[11]

*   *   *

Narraphors are the blood cells of all blood cells. The blood of all blood is the blood of Jesus. Your blood bank must be a well-stocked reservoir of identity, a perpetrator of the stem cells of the faith. As Jesus knew so well, a metaphor has the power to change the world.

I NEVER MET-A-PHOR I DIDN'T LIKE

Some people say a businessperson will do anything for money, a politician will do anything for a vote, and a journalist will do anything for a story.

Well, a preacher will do anything for a metaphor. Preachers are metaphor maniacs.

If good communication is less "tell" than "show," then the preacher is an architect of images, an "imagesmith" even more than a "wordsmith."[12] All of homiletics is based on a fundamental law of the universe, a spiritual law of gravity, if you will. Spiritual gravity says humans are made to be in relationship with God and they will not work correctly until they are in relationship with God. To trust the story is to trust spiritual gravity to pull things together, to draw the heart toward God, to aggregate humanity into relationship. Even when matter "thinks" it has broken free from gravity's influence, it is only temporarily misled. Eventually the reality of gravity will take over.

*   *   *

"Images think."
—*Father William Lynch*[13]

*   *   *

Choose your metaphors carefully because they chart the course of your future. Part of what it means for the Bible to be "inspired" is that you can trust its metaphors. If you choose Jesus' mustard seed metaphor and delve deep into its roots, you can trust that the metaphor will seed the hearts and minds of your listeners, that it will germinate there and work miracles within. The genuine sign of greatness in a sermon is one slow-burn image — a deep image, not a penultimate point or superficial analogy.

What is a metaphor?

Metaphor is another name for veer, for swerve, for indirect interaction, for "telling it slant." Metaphors involve two different realities that are forced together to form a new reality, with the metaphor itself a frame that connects the conjoined meanings into a revelatory focus.

But there is one key feature of the metaphor that is both the source of its creativity and of its frustration, its magnetism, and its distancing. The interactions of frame and focus make metaphors fuzzy. In other words, even though a metaphor is easy to pick up, not everyone will get it, and those who do will be left wanting more. Like the Arians in the fourth century, who had no sense of metaphor — they believed that Jesus was literally begotten by the Father and could not comprehend the "begotten" metaphor — they will push back on metaphorical preaching. A mark of "primitive" cultures, as French ethnologist Lucien Lévy-Bruhl (1857–1939) told us long ago, is that they don't know what a metaphor is.[14] The problem with primitive faith is that it doesn't know what a metaphor is or is theologically allergic to the nonliteral. From the start, Christianity was fighting on two fronts: Jewish literalism and Gnostic symbolism. Semiotic preaching still fights on the same two fronts, beating back both as misguided.

In his verse preface to *Pilgrim's Progress* (1678), one of the great classics of Christian literature, John Bunyan deals with the anti-metaphorical bias of Puritanism. "Metaphors make us blind," he says in a theological joke on other activities that are said to do the same. But Bunyan says it is God who makes metaphors. And God has strewn those metaphors throughout the Bible. "By Metaphors I speak," Bunyan writes. By metaphors all preachers speak, even when we don't want (like Bunyan) to admit it.

★ ★ ★

"A screwdriver is for screws. When you pry open a paint
can with it, you have committed a metaphor, which is the
second use of things.... All we do is metaphorical."
—*James Richardson, Princeton poet*[15]

★ ★ ★

Berkeley cognitive linguistics professor George Lakoff and British neuro-scientist Mark Johnson, in their theory of metaphor, or what they call "imaginative rationality," explain that "one kind of reality is not just understood, but is actually experienced in terms of another."[16] In this way, something that cannot be known completely through direct inherence can be known at least partially through indirect interaction. Through metaphor, interaction becomes a means of understanding, even a revelatory experience.

By making us look at life in new ways, metaphors are powerful mediums of metanoia, eliciting repentance, a turning back to God. Metanoia is an experience of dynamic spiritual change that creates a new reality. As we saw in our section on organic architecture (chapter 7), a preacher "reframes" something not to make it more understandable but to make it inspirational and transformational, to heighten access to truth. Metaphor facilitates incarnational interactions—transductions—that can radically change the way reality, or the divine, is perceived and experienced in life.

Homiletician David Buttrick, who also profited from Lakoff's theory of metaphor, astutely says that "preachers who wish to transform human lives will have to grasp the sheer power of metaphorical language. With metaphors, we can rename the world for faith."[17] Other homileticians, such as Eduard Riegert, Warren Wiersbe, Paul Scott Wilson, and Richard Lischer, have encouraged preachers to focus on metaphors as the roots of dynamic preaching.[18] However, homileticians have primarily seen the metaphor as a means of communication between an active preacher and passive congregation. Semiotic preaching uses metaphor in combination with story as a narraphoric conduit for the interactive experience of the risen Christ, who alone can bring true metanoia.

Cultures are symbol systems. The current culture is expressing its spirituality through images and metaphors, symbols and stories—not words. In the new consciousness, words often get in the way of the truth. Twenty-first-century people hear and learn differently than most churches communicate. People today build their world on metaphoric narratives. That's why the ultimate in power is not to sit in the corner office. The ultimate in power is the right to choose your metaphors and stories. There is so much "spin" in the recording/reporting of "newsworthy" events that even word-worshiping Guttenbergers eventually suffer from motion sickness and look for another way to get information.

Preachers must go from being wordsmiths to imagesmiths that play off verbal and visual against each other, that help people snag the right images to live by and die for in a world where metaphors go whizzing by in all directions. The preacher's business is to wrap stories around images with the language of our culture.

"If you want people to think differently," Buckminster Fuller used to say, "don't tell them how to think; give them a tool."[19] The best tool is a metaphor. At least Thomas Aquinas thought so. He taught that in holy teaching the use of metaphors is indispensable.[20] He said that metaphors help us dive more deeply into the true literal level of the text. "When Scripture speaks of the arm of God, the literal sense is not that he has a physical limb, but that he has what it signifies, namely, the power of doing and making. This example brings out how nothing false can underlie the literal sense of Scripture."[21] By using metaphors in your preaching, you teach people to trust their lives to the Story, to trust not mere factual knowledge but narrative truth, to trust not scientific proofs but faith in a mustard seed.

★ ★ ★

"Preaching is helping people hear from God."
—Kenton C. Anderson's "nutshell definition of preaching"[22]

★ ★ ★

I can't say it enough: metaphor is metamorphosis. Change your metaphor and you change your world. Change your metaphor and you change your body. Change your metaphor and you change your mind. Everyone has the choice of what metaphors to build life around. Thankfully, the Bible offers a rich treasury of metaphors to draw on. When you imagine and image differently, you act differently. As you think in your heart—or as you connect your left brain to your right brain—Jesus taught, so you are. By using the art of metaphor, Jesus rearranges the molecules in your body. Metaphor is metamorphosis that becomes morphological.

The Willie Nelson of homileticians, Baptist preacher Carlyle Marney, used to complain that preachers learn to preach in Greek when they ought to preach in Hebrew. By that he meant that Greek is the language of words; Hebrew is the language of images. Jesus was a Jewish preacher, not a Greek preacher. He majored in images and stories, not in ideas, syllogisms, and logic. When we preachers learn to bleed, we need to steep ourselves in the Hebrew bloodline of the Bible.

But a word of caution: we can also face the possibility of metaphorical malpractice in giving blood. We can mangle minds and shrink souls with a metaphor. Preachers hold lives in their hands. Images can heal or images can kill. Narraphors are some of the most powerful forces in the universe. When you step out to preach the gospel, you take the preacher's version of the Hippocratic Oath—"Do no harm"—and you pray the Covenantal Prayer—"Not my power but yours." Never forget that you—and the narraphors you choose—are in the business of saving lives, not marketing lives or manipulating lives. Metaphors must always be motivated by the heart of Jesus, always mediated through the Spirit of God.

BE AN ARCHITECT OF IMAGES

Before delving into how to make a narraphor, we must first look at the power of images. Images are mirrors of metaphors. They allow us to look into the mirror expecting to see one thing but find something else reflected back. The image itself provokes our faculties into a kind of shock, after which our mind then seeks to "refocus" and "reframe" on multiple levels and with multiple capacities (particularly right-brain ones) what is reflected back. An image reflecting from a metaphor is more than just an image. It is a new reality that changes what we thought we knew into something we now know differently.

Metaphor has nothing to do with the literal but everything to do with the physical. It is bathed in body and livingness and has everything to do with how we understand the world and the world beyond. For example, poet and literary theorist Howard Nemerov (1920–91) suggests this metaphor—*a purple finch is a swallow dipped in raspberry juice.*[23] Now, he does not mean this literally, nor that it is something we should try out. Rather, he is suggesting a relationship between two images. The first image, a purple finch, is altered by a new image suggested, a swallow dipped in raspberry juice. When we hear this, we picture this second image, gaining a deeper sensation of what a swallow dipped in raspberry juice might look, smell, sound, feel, and taste like. We now experience the purple finch's whole body, in surround sound and living color. By using metaphor, we have taken a mirror image and have raised it to holographic reality. Not to mention our sense of purple has been expanded and vivified. Not to mention our sense of finch has been given "otherness." In swerving we have made the familiar strange.

*   *   *

"If we want to change someone's life from non-Christian to Christian, from dying to living, from despairing to hoping, from anxious to certain, from corrupted to whole, we must change the images—the imaginations of the heart."
—Elizabeth Achtemeier (1926–2002), Hebrew scholar[24]

*   *   *

A mirror is a metaphor in itself as well as a function of metaphor. The mirror can help us understand how metaphor works. A mirror can show us a truth that we want to avoid seeing. And a mirror is above all a metaphor of trust. Take the story of *The Picture of Dorian Gray* by Oscar Wilde, in which the portrait takes on a life of its own, mirroring the character's inner transformation with blatant truths that Dorian would rather not see. Jesus frequently used images in his metaphors like this to point to searing truths. In fact, the prophet Nathan did this very thing in showing King David his sins through the art of metaphor. Only after hearing the story and having the mirror turned to his own face, only after seeing his own image appear in the mirror, did a surprised King David realize and repent of his sin.

We see what we want to see. People are conditioned to see in prepared lenses, through conditioned eyeglasses. Images mirror contrasting alterations to those settled frameworks. New images disturb the status quo and can even create new realities—but only if those contrasting images are in relationship, which distinguishes an image from a metaphor. A metaphor is an image changer.

This is the kernel of truth in all of therapy. Change cannot happen without relationship. And relationship does not happen without trust. If a person will not enter into relationship with the therapist, the therapist cannot change the images of that person. And neither can the preacher. In this sense, trust and faith are the only true change agents of the homiletic event. But for the participant, the faith is in Jesus.

Blood Bank: Narrative and Metaphor = Narraphor

The metaphorical reframing of images empowers metanoia at the moment the participant enters into an experienced relationship with Christ through the conduit of the narraphor and entrusts his or her life to the Christ of that experience. In this sense, the semiotic sermon creates an uninhabited place into which people can enter uninhibited, a new reality wherein current reality is suspended and a new reality is dreamed into which they take trust steps forward. If those trust steps are taken, the movement of the metaphor is revolutionizing. Jesus was the master of metaphor, the maestro of narraphor. But his identity as Messiah, the only Son of God, is what changes everything. Without entering into a trust relationship with the divine, we are left seeing only our own realities. This is why Jesus' parables were meant not to provide clarity but to draw people into a trust relationship. Only his inner circle received the gift of explanation. But those "enfaithed" with trust could be healed with a mere touch of his robe (the metaphor of wings). Jesus told the bleeding woman who reached out in faith, "Your faith has healed you."[25]

Identity is at the heart of the metaphor, as it was with the stem cell and the mustard seed. We learn our place in the larger human story through the telling of our own story. Individuation comes through participation, though linking our story with the Jesus story. The identity of Jesus is at the heart of transduction. The image and identity of Jesus as Healer, Redeemer, and risen Lord therefore must be at the heart of any semiotic sermon.

⋆   ⋆   ⋆

> **"The meaning of a message is the change**
> **which it produces in the image."**
> —*Kenneth E. Boulding*[26]

⋆   ⋆   ⋆

Images are identity makers, not just identity markers. The images we hold of ourselves and others come from the way we image them or "imagine" them to be. As Madison Avenue would say, "Perception is reality." To cultivate image making, however, we need to tap into our right brains, our imaginations. Philosopher of education Douglas Sloan defines imagination as "the inner capacity for the making of images." The image is of central importance in all knowing and doing. Whenever we want to integrate and interpret the world, whenever we seek to infuse action with vitality and purpose, we draw upon images.[27]

But it's even more primal than that. The image is of prime importance in our being as well as our "knowing and doing." You don't "get" a body so much as you construct your body. Our stories and our metaphors shape our biology and body. Metaphors create morphology. Our metaphors alter our body's molecules and microbes. And they affect the way our bodies feel. As early as 1954, Carl Jung was intuiting the healing powers of metaphors: it is "not only possible but fairly probable, even, that psyche and matter are two different aspects of one and the same thing."[28] As a psychologist, Jung already knew the biochemical impact of images on the body. Bad images, destructive metaphors, cause us harm in a multitude of ways. They can quite literally make us physically ill. Jesus taught the relationship of mind, spirit, and body, but few have followed his lead (John Wesley was one prominent exception). Semiotic preachers then, as Jesus modeled, are first and foremost "healers." Our images and metaphors, our stories and songs not only define the way we see life in its manifold relationships; they also embody the way we act within those relationships.

The more experiential the image, the more effectual the embodiment. The greater the embodiment, the greater the change not only of heart but of living out the gospel in a world we are to be "in" but not "of." Essentially, our trust in Jesus' narraphors create for us a cloak of protection and a DNA of inoculation. We become encased and infused with Jesus' identity and provoked in ways that urge us to seed that gospel everywhere in the way our relationships are newly "imagined."

Words from a text cannot do that. Susceptibility to text is very different from susceptibility to story and image. In the case of text, your access depends on your level of literacy. In the case of visual media, there is no mediation between mind and vision. Our level of "imagacy" is more intimate than our literacy because it is the way humans dream, think, and feel. It is immediate, more direct, more in-your-face—and thus more spontaneous.[29] This can be one of the problems as well as the joys with image-dominated culture: the more we look, the less we see. Our culture, remember, is a forest of metaphors and symbols. Media today can create alternative realities that can be more attractive than our own reality. People can "lose touch" with reality just as much or more within the visual messages of culture (up to 3,500 daily bombardments) than within the time they hear your sermon. As Darrell Jodock reminds us, "The images on the screen are often more real to people than the lives they live."[30] This puts a huge responsibility on the preacher to be aware of these counterimages and to know how to make Christ images even more powerful. As preachers, we need to ask what images are worth seeing and worth lifting up. Hence there is a need for expertise in image management and image statements, for revealing good images and Christ images.

Blood Bank: Narrative and Metaphor = Narraphor

Yale biblical scholar Paul S. Minear (1906–2007) was one of the first biblical scholars to see that the ecclesiology of the early church amounted basically to the uplifting of various images (body, bride, vineyard, flock, household, servant, plus ninety others) to prod the church to assume certain missions and identities.[31] As we saw in the beginning of our chapter, the Ur-metaphors of the Bible, the stem cells of the gospel, the mustard seeds of our faith, begin and end with covenant theology: (1) identity and (2) reproduction. Every sermon needs to be in some form a "condensation, an enfoldment, of a tradition that begins with Genesis."[32] And like those stem cells and seeds, the images themselves must both be infused with the identity and image of Jesus and proliferated through every sermon.

*   *   *

"Happy is the preacher who realizes in himself all the symbols which apply to that office."
—*Humbert of Romans, French Dominican friar*[33]

*   *   *

Imagethinking works best in repetition. Advertisers know that it takes seven to ten "hits" to make a visual impression. Images are more like energies than objects, more like an organic tree than an inanimate substance. They are infused with incarnational livingness and with resurrection life. If something is alive, it reproduces. A live image will repeat and reproduce. Memory is the reproduction of images as well. And reproduction is recreation. Most people don't remember lectures and propositions, but they will always remember an image. Homiletician Ronald E. Sleeth used to critique his students' sermons with metaphors: "Your sermon had about as much structure as a mitten full of warm tapioca"; "Your sermon had about as much tact as a Sherman tank in a bed full of pansies"; "Your sermon reminded me of a baked apple. It just sat down on you." Sleeth's students never forgot those images. If you want people to remember your sermon, give them a mustard seed.

The sum total of your spiritual universe is a "metaphorical landscape."[34] A sermon builds narraphors by traveling this metaphorical landscape. This is what Jesus did: as he invited people "on the way" and into discipleship, he altered people's metaphorical landscape and in so doing generated new ways of living and thinking and feeling.

Metaphor is not just something we use for communicating; metaphor is how we think and reason and how we make sense of our world. Our actions are congruent with our metaphors.[35] Metaphors create a culture. And biblical metaphors create a biblical culture, or a scriptural landscape of the soul. Scriptural holiness is having the image of relationship with Christ in every walk of life. As a preacher, you need to be a landscaper of the garden of Hebrew narraphors, and be, as Jesus was, a *tekton* (architect) of images. Be a potter. Good images are not just ethereal and metaphysical. Good images embody. Make your images images of embodiment and earth. Create images that your congregation can hold, touch, encounter, take with them when they leave. Be an architect of icons.

IMAGES AS ICONS

The Reformation church suffered from an acute case of iconophobia. John Calvin rightly warned that "the human mind is a perpetual forge of idols," which is why he banned any use of visual imagery in the conveyance of divine truth. But Calvin failed to see that the printed word could be as much of an idol as any icon or image. Remnants of this bias against the visual and the iconographic can still be found in many Western churches.

Yet our culture is awash in icons. Every "celebrity" is some kind of an icon at least, idol at worst. Schools, sports teams, and corporations identify themselves by icons. Celia Lury calls images "thinking with things."[36] The problem is that images aren't packets of things, they're pockets of energies, or what I call "thingies," that have sacramental power. Our preaching needs to become more "thingy" as we sacramentalize the material. While we must not worship any "thing," people need many "thingies" if they're going to worship.

The virtual nature of so much of our culture is making us hungry for more tactile, more iconic, more multisensory experiences. We have also learned from neuroscientists that in terms of neural activity, only our lips and our feet command more of our brain's attention than our hands. When you hold something in your hands, your brain stands at attention.

*   *   *

"I remember what has happened in my life through moments that I remember visually."
—*Dorothea Lange, photojournalist*

*   *   *

A pastor walked by the sanctuary one day and saw a young woman kneeling at the altar and clutching the cross, clinging to it. The pastor didn't disturb her but waited until she was done. Then he said, "I'm the pastor here. Is there anything I can do to help?"

"No. My parents just separated. I didn't know what to do, but something told me that if only I could touch the cross and hold it for a moment, I would feel better. And I do. Thank you for having that cross here for me to hold on to."

If you tell this story, at the end of your sermon, take the cross off the altar and invite people to come down and hold the cross. Couples can take hold of either arm as they hold on to one another.

There's natural resistance to the "thingification" of worship. Didn't Jesus say, "You cannot serve both God and mammon"?[37] Do our "things" get in the way of the divine? Jesus' word for "mammon" literally means "money." Not materiality, but money. The incarnation is God's way of affirming our "thingyness." We ourselves are "thingies," or as Aquinas would have it, "gift-things." And the literal bodily resurrection of Jesus affirms the fact that some form of "thingyness" will accompany us into eternity.

Thingies can be identity icons—identity markers that bind us as a community and remind us of our covenants. These icons can be manifested in clothes, symbols, sculptures, insignias, art, rituals, artifacts, pictures, or gestures. All are icons that embody identity.

The early church had the fish as its icon. The anagram of the ichthys in the early Greek-speaking community stood for *Iesous, Christos, Theou Yios, Soter* (Jesus Christ, of God Son, Savior). When one Christian would meet another person he or she suspected was a Christian, that person would draw half the fish symbol in the dirt. If the person completed the other half, it revealed his or her identity as a brother or sister in the faith. For our ancestors, the fish was both a metaphor and an icon of the faith, an embodied image.

Another early icon was the ostrich egg. The eggs would be decorated and hung in the church as an orienting symbol to point people to Christ. I have an ostrich egg hanging in my study right above where I write.

Icons capture all five senses. An icon is as much about a song you can't stop hearing as it is a picture you can't stop envisioning. Mervyn Nicholson talks about "seeing with the mind's eye, hearing with the mind's ear, tasting with the mind's tongue, touching with the mind's fingers, and smelling with the mind's nose."[38] An icon is an incarnational bridge that connects the spiritual and the physical, reminding us that the incarnated Christ lives within the body of the church, that his identity lives on within each of its faith communities.

The centerpiece of Christian theology is iconography—the incarnation. The Orthodox Church has preserved in its purest form the power of iconic identity, ritual, and sacrament. Good liturgy is embodied image in action, as any trip to a monastery will reveal. I will never forget the exhilaration of using all of my senses when attending Trappist services at the Abbey of the Genesee in Piffard, New York: processions with cross and candles, icons, incense, chanting, silence, dancelike movement. I loved evensong because of the darkness and candles. Worship with the monks was less of a "we talk and you listen" and more of a "we dance, sing, sit in silence, listen, pray together in God's presence—and we do that together, because in doing so, we are intentionally more attentive to God's presence and our sensibilities are honed so we can see, hear, and feel God's presence in the world around us."

★   ★   ★

> **"People forget what you say, they forget what you did, but
> they never forget how they felt when they were with you."**
> —*Maya Angelou*[39]

★   ★   ★

Gil Bailie, the president of the Cornerstone Forum, believes it is the role of artists to turn idols into icons. Bailie says:

> [I recollect] the marvelous moment in Dante where he says that the glory of Paradise is too difficult to be described, and he uses a metaphor: "The folds of heaven's draperies are too bright." If you can't show the shadow, you can't show the folds in the draperies, because there's no contrast. This is the challenge the artist faces: the ineffable mystery surrounds us, but we experience it sacramentally, through material reality, through the earth and through experience with other people, through physicality. It seems to me that artists are the technicians of sacramental sensibility. Their job is to transfigure the senses, to move us from idols to icons.[40]

Orthodox worship is a celebration of the transfiguring power of symbols. The process of being carried deeper is not actually a symbolic process but a form of substantive process, because if a symbol goes beyond itself, it moves from shadow to substance.[41] The icon is not simply decorative, inspirational, or educational. Most importantly, it signifies the presence and participation of the signified reality. The icon is a window that links heaven and earth. Like a sacrament, the icon is an outward and visible sign of an inward and spiritual work of grace: (1) it conveys (transformative intercession); (2) it bears (presence bearing as a form of prophetic declaration); (3) it points (it acts as a witness and testament); (4) it manifests (which is an expression of symbolic reification).[42] In short, an icon is theology in image.

For this reason, icons are never signed. They are not meant to be works of art for art's sake or to be lavished with attention to an artist. Rather, the icon's creator, as well as the icon itself, are vessels of meaning and vehicles for the divine. Image icons, for a community of faith, are like the grails that hold the blood of Jesus. They enable us to experience the transformation of the Holy Spirit within us by serving as tactile and tangible connectors between community and Christ.

But there is a fine line between icon and idol. Most of our cultural icons turn into idols. They become our first priority, our obsessions, our objects of worship. Icons on the other hand are not priorities unto themselves. Icons of the faith, including image icons, point to Christ. They are signs but point to the reality of the incarnation within the body of Christ. Zwingli protested icons vehemently, saying the money spent on icons should be given instead to the poor. But it wasn't just the money that was the issue for many Reformers. Iconoclasts were not prohibitors of images but breakers of images. Iconoclasts believed strongly in images. They feared their power so much that they took to vandalizing them.

Semiotic preaching uses metaphors as icons. The vehicle of the narraphor is an EPIC experience of grace and a means of creating a new identity in Christ by establishing an image that becomes an internalized icon for Christ: "I will ... write [my covenant] on their hearts."[43] Like someone collecting icons, a semiotic preacher must be in the business of collecting metaphors.

BE A METAPHOR COLLECTOR

Cognitive scientist Andrew Ortony outlined three properties of metaphors: inexpressibility, vividness, and compactness.[44] These three features of metaphor give form to the inexpressible. By making use of everyday objects and relational aspects of life, they make the vague vivid, the unknown memorable. And they come in small packages that hide a huge amount of information.

Recent research reveals that the brain's ability to read print on a page is about one hundred bits per second, while the brain's ability to take in images is about a billion bits per second.[45] You do the math. Text/Picture = 100/1,000,000,000 = Picture=10,000,000 words. Or: A picture is worth 10 million words.

If a picture is worth 10 million words, then a metaphor is worth at least a thousand pictures. Metaphors magnify and reveal as they represent and embody revelatory experience. They "reframe" reality. We can think of our metaphor collection as a collection of portraits—images that we fit into frames. Metaphor making is a process of reframing images. George Lakoff defines frames as the "mental structures that shape the way we see the world. We reject new facts that don't fit into those structures. So to change behavior you have to change the frames."[46]

N. T. Wright explores the ways narratives and metaphors form narraphors when he says:

> Tell someone to do something, and you change their life for a day; tell someone a story and you change their life. Stories, in having this effect, function as complex metaphors. Metaphor consists in bringing two sets of ideas close together, close enough for a spark to jump but not too close, so that the spark in jumping, illuminates for a moment the whole area around, changing perceptions as it does so. Even so, the subversive story comes close enough to the story already believed by the hearer for the spark to jump between them; and nothing will ever be quite the same again.[47]

This culture speaks in narraphors—narratives merged with metaphors. Stories are metaphors writ large; metaphors are stories writ small. When we collect metaphors, we are compiling the frames by which people will experience truth. The type of frames used may depend on your culture, your participants, your Scripture, or your syntax. But frames, or metaphors, are windows for relationship, ways to connect powerfully in EPIC ways. Every masterful sermon has a master metaphor behind it. There is no metaphor so dusty and hackneyed that it can't be reframed into startling new life.

*　　*　　*

"All the fun's in how you say a thing."
—Robert Frost, poet laureate[48]

*　　*　　*

Metaphors are not propositions. Propositions are metaphors gone bad. A proposition is a metaphor in sheep's clothing. All attempts to relate truth take both propositional and metaphorical form. We hear the proposition, but we engage with the metaphor. Metaphors keep things moving. They are magnets for relationship. They create community. Metaphors are fungible with "fuzzy edges," which makes it easier for people to pick them up and share them. Some metaphors don't use words at all. These are "phatic" images, signals that maintain dialogue but have little or no intrinsic meaning. Stooped shoulders, bitten nails, chewed pens, a blushing face, a look of surprise—these are all nonverbal metaphors. But no matter which you choose, a metaphor is a power-packed vessel.

Blood Bank: Narrative and Metaphor = Narraphor

How can you be a miner for metaphors? Is there an art to being a collector of these rare and beautiful gems of incarnational and iconic power? Do you have to be a Gawain to seek the Holy Grail? Harvard developmental psychologist Howard Gardner has been one of the leading scholars of creativity in the world for the past three decades. After subjecting the greatest minds in history to scholarly scrutiny, he concludes that there is no genius to genius. Gardner demystifies the tradition of "geniuses" by identifying three common traits that characterize the minds of those who have revolutionized the ways we think and live and move and have our being. Gardner says that creative people, first, think in metaphors; second, mix metaphors to create new metaphors; and third, brainstorm to create and produce new ways of seeing.[49]

★   ★   ★

"Don't try to make your metaphors stand on all four."
—Old saying

★   ★   ★

As a preacher, you are a miner of metaphors, a collector of the gems and rocks that you will use to reframe reality. You are visualizers of God. Your mission is to help people visualize truth. For this you need to train yourself to think in metaphors. One of my daily devotional practices is to post on Facebook and Twitter. This is not a "break" in my day in which I let people know what I am doing. This is a theological exercise in which I ask the question, "What is God doing in my life and in the lives of others around me today?" The discipline of social media helps me to think metaphorically about the world and to practice the art of reframing.

Mixing metaphors is a process of looking for contrasting, even paradoxical, ways for framing by flouting convention and crossing frames of reference. For example, Olivier Messiaen saw the "colors" of a tone; Picasso saw numbers as patterns and images (0 was an eye; 2 was a folded pigeon wing). The apostle Paul couldn't write without mixing his metaphors.[50] Jesus did story stacking (Matt. 13; 25; Luke 15).

How can you find new frames? Go spelunking into new caves. Chase rabbits into new fields. Walk where the sidewalk ends. Practice the spiritual discipline of "randomness" to make sure your brain keeps fresh and looking at things in new ways.[51] Randomization forces us to see perspectives that we would not normally choose and helps a preacher resist the thought molds of the day. Brainstorming is the art of scanning various disciplines, experiences, and travels, and synthesizing these into "custom-made" frames. The best metaphors are customized, not the prefabricated ones found on the shelves of the corner store.

Sooner or later, every metaphor breaks down. You can only travel with a metaphor so far in one direction. When you push it further than it wants to go, the metaphor becomes dangerous.

What is more, metaphors can be taken in a different direction than the one you're headed. Once you throw your metaphor onto the field for everyone to handle, anything can happen. As a semiotic preacher, you need to be prepared to "play ball" no matter which way the sermon starts going.

I'll never forget speaking at the Southern Synod of the Dutch Reformed Church in South Africa, where I made a presentation on an understanding of disciples as "pneumanauts" and discipleship training as "pneumanautics." I started to explore the biblical metaphor of the wind and asked for help from those attending the conference. After a couple of comments and questions, a distinguished older gentleman rose rather decorously. I later found out everyone knew him as a respected medical doctor who was the head deacon in the church that hosted the event. His comment was in perfect English. When the wind blows through the church, he noted, and the church is narrow, it makes a weird sound. From his view, the narrower the church gets and the stronger the wind blows, the more the church can be heard fighting the Spirit, and the sound the church makes when it's fighting the Spirit sounds like the church is farting. He then sat down.

Most of all, be ready to counteract bad images. The power of images should not be underestimated. Whole nations and communities have been wiped out in the pursuit of bad metaphors. People's lives have been ruined by one bad image. People have lost their faith due to a bad image of God. Always be on your toes to come up with new frames for bad images. Sometimes, you will find yourself spending more time brainstorming how to reframe bad images as coming up with new ones.

*   *   *

"Anything can be made to look bad
or good by being redescribed."
—*Richard Rorty, philosopher*[52]

*   *   *

Here is an example of the use of bad images: The Hutu imputed to the minority Tutsi a dehumanized image of horns to portray them as wicked by their very nature. Some Rwandans came to believe that people classified as

Blood Bank: Narrative and Metaphor = Narraphor

Tutsi actually had horns on their head and professed to see them. Just before hundreds of thousands of them were killed by the Hutu, the Tutsi underwent metaphor surgery by their killers. A similar process went on during Hitler's regime. Scientists and professors taught students that there were biological and physiological flaws in the genetic makeup of Jews, which conditioned the German people to see Jews as less than human.

Some metaphors can appear to be good images, but like a slow cancer, they eat away at the life of the body. Here are some examples of "killer metaphors" of the church that kill from the inside out, or problematic metaphors that do almost as much harm as good:

1. *Harbor.* The image of your church as a "harbor" or a "refuge" may just be the number one metaphor that is killing the church today. Does your church see itself as a retreat from the world? Or as a vanguard of God's dream in mission to the world?

2. *Family.* Does your church see itself as a "home for the people of God" versus a *koinonia* (community of disciples)? In a family setting, people need to feel "held," to be "held" in the arms of the family, the church, the community. The missional "touch" is quite different from being "held." It is being compelled, "covered" (as in, "I've got your back covered") in order to take risks in the world. The family is supposed to be a family; a church is supposed to be a church. A good missional church will be made up of many healthy families, with the recognition that every healthy family has its unique dysfunctions.

3. *Hospital.* Tired metaphors deserve a rest, even to be put to rest. There's no tireder metaphor for the church than this one: "The church is not a museum for saints but a hospital for sinners." Even "hospitals" now want to be known as "wellness centers," not hospital dormitories of the diseased and dying. Is your church just a place that treats people who are sick? Or also a place that helps people stay well and not get sick?

4. *Center.* A journey to the "center" is a journey away from the margins, the periphery, the edges. In other words, a journey toward the center is a journey away from Jesus and where Jesus is to be found: not at the "centers" of privilege and power but at the margins of the community. So much of "centering" language focuses on the self rather than on Christ. When you're always trying to operate out of the "center," you start thinking you *are* the center.

5. *Excellence.* The church is not a performance-based, goal-oriented place for achievement but a community of needy people who gather in humility and humanity to be real and authentic.[53] The pursuit of excellence has led us down the path of goal seeking rather than God pleasing.

169

6. *Best practices.* Ray Kurzweil argues that the next eighty-eight years could see the equivalent of the last ten thousand years' worth of change.[54] The fixation on "best practices" always keeps us behind and copying. The world is changing so fast that what works today won't work tomorrow.

What triumphs today will be defeated tomorrow.

*   *   *

"Victory is a poor adviser, and nations tend
to slip on the blood they have shed."
—*Wolfgang Schivelbusch*[55]

*   *   *

7. *Lifeboat.* The church as a "lifeboat," an image that derives in part from the third-century African lawyer Cyprian, who defined the church as the "ark of salvation," has given rise to what New Zealand theologian Alan Jamieson calls "lifeboat theology." Using this lifeboat image of salvation, certain premises naturally follow:

1. There is a clear division between those in the lifeboat and those in the water, so there is a clear division between the saved and the unsaved, the lost and the saviors.
2. God is seen as being at work in the boat and not at work in the ocean, where the devil is most often seen at work.
3. The basis on which someone is on the saved list is clearly seen. Using the lifeboat image, it is determined by whether or not you are in the boat.
4. The image provides an intrinsic motivation for helping people get out of the water and into the boat. Christian people who care for others, especially their own loved ones, are strongly motivated to ensure they make it into the lifeboat. The image also carries an inherent sense of guilt for those on the boat who are not otherwise motivated to help sea dwellers into the boat.[56]

The connections we make, the ways we use metaphors to create narraphors of hope, will be revealed in a community's readiness for ministry and mission.

NETWORKS AND PATCHWORKS
The creative edge of framing images rests in finding the patterns of coherence that lie behind seemingly disconnected variables. Metaphors bridge realities

and invite people to step in faith across to the other side. Sometimes those bridges are slowly crossed; other times a person may be catapulted to the other side in a wind of revelation.

★　★　★

"Metaphor is the language that conveys the indivisibility of visible and invisible, of seen and unseen, of heaven and earth."
—*Eugene Peterson*[57]

★　★　★

The best metaphors are like tidal waves, lifting someone up and out of where they are, and before they can get their bearings; they find themselves gripping the rails of the other side. This is the nature of conversion. Images are not simply visages but venues of relationships—with self, world, each other, Christ. The more dynamic the imagethinking and the more trusted the journey with the new metaphor, the more solid the ground of that new reality.

The most fertile metaphors are those that juxtapose the unlikely, fuse the oppositional or unusual. I think here of Comte de Lautréamont's observation about the beauty of the unexpected encounter of an umbrella and a sewing machine.[58] The more dissimilar things are to each other, the greater the magic of the light that radiates from their contact and kenning.[59] This method of pairing is not a twenty-first-century discovery. In early literature, the art of pairing opposites and connecting unusual images was called a "kenning."[60] Freud called this same process "associative chains." But twenty-first-century advertisers have perfected this art of translating ideas into images and abstractions into sensory "imaginariums." You need only to look at Super Bowl ads to see some of the most amazing stories built around jarring metaphors without words. One of my favorites was the 2011 ad for Volkswagen in which a child was juxtaposed to Darth Vader, juxtaposed to a VW Passat. What may seem like strange pairings can become a very powerful message.

Images are like networks. They generate identities. Preachers are in the identity business and the generativity business. Seek metaphors that do both of these—that interconnect relationships between images and realities, that interconnect relationships between Christ and body. This cruciform net is your ichthys. Like the mustard seed, images both carry identity and generate reproductive imagethinking. When a metaphor releases its reframing energy, it will generate indefinitely, like a stem cell, within the soul. It will, in a sense, seed itself within, making connections to contexts, other images, other experiences, other stories within the life of each person. Images are the "thoughts of the heart" and powerful provokers of emotion.

★ ★ ★

"There seems then to be something which is better said with metaphor than without, which goes straighter to the mark by going crooked, and hits its aim exactly by flying at tangents."
—Austin Farrer (1904–68), twentieth-century Anglican theologian[61]

★ ★ ★

While the process of seeking out unusual and diverse connections must be unending, preachers must also make sure these metaphors serve the contexts of the lives with which they've been entrusted. For example, the line in Song of Songs 4:1 — "Your hair is like a flock of goats descending from the hills of Gilead" — may not be one you want to use for a twenty-first-century woman.

Sometimes, too, you can outfit a metaphor with too many accessories, so many that the metaphor itself gets lost and can't see where it's going. At other times, the metaphors can simply get out of hand and a bit outlandish. Here, for example, is a sermon title from the seventeenth century: "Some Biscuits Baked in the Oven of Charity, Carefully Conserved for the Chickens of the Church, the Sparrows of the Spirit, and the Sweet Swallows of Salvation."[62] There is such a thing as metaphorical overkill.

Often metaphors can become outdated. For example, this nineteenth-century metaphor — "He is a featherless parrot with more beak than brain" — while still wonderful, has little resonance today because the word *parrot* has lost its currency as someone who copies, someone who repeats whatever he hears.

Building a good metaphor can be like creating a patchwork quilt. You take seemingly unconnected images and sew them together, thereby creating a unique and revealing pattern. Soon the story generated by one set of patches will create more stories that generate more patches until you have an entire quilt of interconnected stories. Or as W. B. Yeats defined a successful poem, it is one in which "sound, color, and form are in a musical relation, a beautiful relation to one another."[63]

WHERE YOU USED TO THINK POINTS, THINK METAPHOR

One can be persuaded by George Lakoff and Mark Johnson's argument that "the conceptual systems of cultures and religions are metaphorical in nature"[64] without taking it as far as they do when they contend, "Truth is always relative to a conceptual system that is defined in large part by metaphor."[65] From a historical perspective, however, they are right that "the most fundamental values in a culture will be coherent with the metaphorical structure of the most fundamental concepts in the culture."[66] Or in the words of Argentinian poet and essayist Jorge Luis Borges (1899–1986), "Perhaps universal history is the history of the diverse intonation of a few metaphors."[67]

*　*　*

"The development of civilizations is
essentially a progression of metaphors."
—E. L. Doctorow[68]

*　*　*

Metaphors define reality. If you start to doubt it, look no further than how we talk. Copernicus died centuries ago. Yet we still say, "Look at what a beautiful sunrise" or "The stars come out at night." Wizard of Oz author L. Frank Baum knew the importance and power of images and metaphor: "And for you, Scarecrow, a diploma!" "For you, Lion, a badge of courage!" "For you, Tin Man, a heart!"

Our perceptions of the world, ourselves, each other, and God are dependent on what metaphors we trust and hold. Our metaphors carry with them our values and visions. They influence the way we think, feel, and experience the world. Metaphors are not merely language; they embody all aspects of the human experience.

Each of us, without even realizing it, lives a rich metaphorical life. But not all of our metaphors are good ones. Some are not bad but aren't good enough to allow us to live abundantly and fully. Jesus gave us narraphors that will help us enter into a faith relationship of fullness with him. Preaching helps people lean into and live those narraphors.

How do we cultivate good metaphors? How do we enable people to experience the narraphors of Jesus in ways that transform their lives into a new kingdom reality? We must re-create the narraphors of Jesus in ways that stun, surprise, and switch on lives. This requires an understanding of the EPIC nature of metaphors. We also must incarnate biblical narraphors within the cultures in which we live and preach. Finally, we need to understand the nature and power of the "metaphorical turn," or what I will call "metaphor-induced metanoia." And we need to know how to build our metaphors into narraphors—superstories and metanarratives that speak to the lives and hearts of people, win their trust, and catapult them into new realities, dreams, and images of redemption and resurrection hope.

Metaphor is not persuasion. Metaphor is not assent to an equation or a proposition. Metaphors appeal to the whole-greater-than-the-sum-of-its-parts person, to the emotions as well as to reason.[69] Metaphors change lives, not because they make sense but precisely because they don't. Jesus used parables to call people into a relationship within which he could then teach his followers to live in different ways. Jesus "reframed" reality, reframed the Scriptures, reframed Judaism, and went beyond John the Baptist's first step of repentance. Jesus called for a person's whole being to be in relationship with him.

The metaphorical act is an act of metamorphosis. For some this metamorphosis is a process that takes some time, but Jesus himself modeled the willing investment of time in remolding, reshaping, and reframing old wineskins into new.

And with each "metaphorical turn," the kaleidoscope shifts to reveal new realities of truth. One parable was enough to shock some former God followers into "turning back" to God. But for others, even Jesus' inner circle, turn upon turn upon turn was required until at last the morphing would come. Some would never get it. That's why, to those who don't know Christ, the gospel sounds like foolishness.[70]

Morphing is a whole body transformation. It is metabolic, metaphoric, and metamorphic. As the process of metamorphosis is different for each person, so must the metaphoric stages of preaching also be a journey. In a sense, semiotic preaching is a lifelong journey on the "disciple ship," with all of its storms and stops, upheavals and downturns, tidal waves and lighthouses. Each sermon is another hoisting of the sails, steering of the vessel, on that "disciple ship."

THE METAPHORICAL TURN AND SUPERMETAPHORS

A metaphorical "turn" is a twist, a transfiguration, an unveiling so momentous and shocking that it shifts something from or into view. When it happens, it appears so obvious that we wonder why we hadn't seen it that way before. Biblical scholars have always spoken of the "spell and shock" function of parables. However, many have not understood that this is precisely the function of the metaphor.

The metaphorical turn goes far beyond a mere "hook." A hook draws you in, gains your attention and interest, keeps you "on the line." But a hook won't change your life. Advertisers are in the business of luring you with an image of something ideal, massaging your soul until you desire things you don't need. Preachers are surgeons of the soul, replacing one image with another so that you can be healed by the blood and power of Jesus.

A metaphorical "turn" is not a dangling carrot, but a diamond carat that suddenly shines from a new kingdom reality, from an unexpected angle of truth, leading to change of life and livingness. The Jesus metaphorical turn does not offer a product; it opens to the reality of eternal life. To be part of this kind of transformation is the awe-someness of preaching. And the responsibility that goes along with it should feel awesome.

Not everyone will get your metaphors. Some people didn't get Jesus' metaphors: the learned orthodox Jew Nicodemus didn't get the "born again" metaphor; the Samaritan woman at the well didn't get the "living water" metaphor. A metaphor estranges the familiar, and some people shut down the strange and shutter the stranger. But when the moment is embraced, reality folds, twists, and turns, and the incarnational presence of Jesus enters into personal experience, amazing transformations—and transincarnation—can happen.

A metaphor by its very nature lifts language into experience and then further into the wild blue yonder of beyond. Preaching makes metaphor a participatory event, a shared reality, a communal experience as well as an individual experience. In a sense, it is living a dream of a better reality now, not just described, but felt, sensed, experienced, tasted. At the very moment someone participates in that reality, he or she enters the "twister."

Think again of the story *The Wizard of Oz*, which Judy Garland made famous. Dorothy knocks her head and falls into a dream at the moment a powerful twister begins turning her known reality around. When she "wakes," she steps into another world, another reality. At the moment the house thuds to the ground, she notices something different. Everything is in living color, everything has changed. But she trusts "the story" enough to step into it and journey with it.

The "spell and shock," the "twist" that catapulted her mind and soul from one reality to the next, is the essence of the "metaphorical turn." Remember, not until the end of the story does Dorothy realize she has been at "home" all the time. But her home and her homeland perspective have changed forever. This is the metaphorical turn at its best. When the metaphorical "twister" carries us into a new place, every one of us dreams of new realities and imagines new possibilities of living a Jesus life.

Supermetaphors carry the most powerful "twist and turn" potential. They are powerful twisters in stories that catapult us head over feet into incarnational spaces of immense amplitude and plenitude, even into "conversions." Our faith is thrown across the precipice, and before we even realized we were traveling there, we found ourselves gripping the other side. Supermetaphors are born when an EPIC metaphor meets a scriptural/real life narrative and the two go out to play together.

METAPHOR AS EPIC EXPERIENCE AND EVENT

Your metaphors are only as powerful as they are received. Every metaphor is an experience, a vertebral venture. In preaching, metaphors mediate experiences of Christ. Preachers can't choose whether to use metaphor. Metaphor is the word way we have of talking about a God who is greater than we can imagine or think. The way beyond the rational is the metaphorical.

★　　★　　★

"[Christ] is the image of the invisible God."
—*Apostle Paul*[71]

★　　★　　★

But the key to the use of metaphor is the "is/is not" tension. Every metaphor is a bipolar extremist. A metaphor is true ... and false. To say with the psalmist, "The Lord is my shepherd," is to say something both true ("the King of Love my shepherd is") and not true (God is not a shepherd, and we are neither sheep nor dogs). Literalize the metaphor and you lose the metaphor. Of course, some metaphors are easier to literalize than others.

Every image must be broken, or it becomes idolatrous. But once an image is broken, pick up those broken shards carefully. The edges of broken images are sharp: they cut; they draw blood. They also cut both ways. When bad images are ingested, they quickly get digested and become part of the person experiencing them. This is the problem with violent images. They become part of you, and they begin to define your identity. Our visual memory is very durable: "That's why we're much more likely to forget a name than a face, and why we remember months later that a certain quote appeared on the upper-left-hand corner of a page even if we've forgotten the wording of the quote itself."[72] A metaphor that arrests you with its gripping realism, whether good or bad, elicits almost a primal reaction that is experienced bodily — mentally, spiritually, emotionally, sensually.[73]

Because a metaphor is an interactive, relational experience, our understanding of the "meaning" of a metaphor must likewise be revised.

Blood Bank: Narrative and Metaphor = Narraphor

Metaphorical "meaning" is not a conceptual construct. The meaning comes from the mind's hospitality to the image, which stirs the imagination. And if it's in your imagination, it's in your heart, head, hands, and liver. This mental image becomes enacted, thereby becoming an image of other things. As Mervyn Nicholson likes to put it, what begins as a picture becomes a lens.[74]

Every metaphor is EPIC. Even body expressions (gestures, movements) and nonverbal sounds (grunts, coughs) can be metaphors. When you preach, make those assembled hear the hoofbeats of the four horsemen, see and smell the lilies in the field. Metaphors will allow them to experience those things not just in ordinary ways but in new ways. Metaphors engender curiosity, joy, humor, suspense, surprise, laughter, shock, relief. They have the power to compel. They have the power to heal.

*   *   *

"Metaphor is the dreamwork of language."
—Donald Davidson[75]

*   *   *

Experience is not only sensory, however. Not only emotional. Inspired intuition (in the Scriptures this comes in prophetic dreams, angelic messengers, etc.) allows us to tap into deep reservoirs of trust that allow us to bond with the metaphors. This bonding allows for the very nature of revelatory experience. Intuition allows us to enter into a vulnerable place where God's Spirit can move and motivate our spirit.

I will never forget the funeral for Stanley Grenz, who died unexpectedly in 2005. Just before his wife, Edna Grenz, rose triumphantly from her seat and came forward to direct the choir and congregation in the concluding song, Handel's "Hallelujah Chorus," Dr. Bruce Milne challenged everyone present to look one last time at the table directly under the pulpit. There we would find, he said, not a dead body but a cornucopia of artifacts memorializing the many roles—husband, father, pastor, theologian, professor, musician, storyteller, bridge builder—of the one we had gathered from across North America to honor: a trumpet, a guitar, twenty authored books, a Mickey Mouse tie, a teddy bear tie, favorite CDs and DVDS.

But spread across the table, Dr. Milne insisted, there was something else. If you looked very carefully, he insisted, you could see a sword, the "sword of truth," not brandished to slay opponents in theological sword crossings but wielded in true "cross-sword" fashion to lay open the hidden heart and heal the wounded soul. The cross-sword of truth Stanley J. Grenz had so honorably carried for fifty-five years had now been laid down. And it was ready to be picked up. In a world and church raging with sword-crossings, would someone present take up the cross-sword?

No one person came physically to the table to take up the sword. But Handel's "Hallelujah Chorus" became an altar call led by Stan's widow. Every person present came forward in some sense to carry forward Stan Grenz's legacy.

Our thingy-stuffed homes are semiotic jungles. When someone asks about an item that is rich in story and dense with meaning, we often say, "Well, that's a conversation piece." In displaying at his funeral some of Grenz's "things," Dr. Milne provided mourners with a conversation piece. Points lined up like soldiers or a barricade are often conversation stoppers. But thingies can be conversation starters, icons that channel meaning.[76] Points are often conversation potholes; thingies can be conversation launch-pads—and balms in Gilead like those that helped bring peace to me as I was mourning my friend Stan.

Metaphors are not only EPIC in an individual way, but also in a communal way. Without shared metaphors, there are no shared streets, no shared neighborhoods, no shared society.[77] Without shared metaphors, there are no changed lives, no changed churches.

A POETIC FOR PREACHING

Building your preaching with metaphors is a poetic practice as well as a theological one. It is a *haemopoietic*, if you will—a practice of blood forming using the stem cells of the faith. The Greek word means literally "to make blood." In a sense, when we exegete the images of Scripture, the narraphors of Jesus, we are taking the "stem cells" of Christ and creating from them new kinds of cells—new metaphors that carry the covenant in their core, carry the blood of Jesus to the body—each one good, true, beautiful. The biblical passage must control the metaphor. The haemopoietic, or blood-building poetic, is a creative and aesthetic act, generating "garden" truth.

*　　*　　*

"When artists give form to revelation, their art
can advance, deepen, and potentially transform
the consciousness of their community."
—*Alex Grey*[78]

*　　*　　*

178

Blood Bank: Narrative and Metaphor = Narraphor

The art of blood building with metaphors is also a divine act. Every metaphor must be spirit breathed and must serve as a revelatory medium for the incarnational power and presence of Christ. In this sense, the preacher is a subcreator of the divine Artist. Preachers are semioticians by nature. They must have ears and eyes for the revelatory signs of God. They must be "mediating eyewitnesses." That is the role of an artist, according to Gil Bailie: "To be a Christian is to believe in mediation, and to believe that this mystery must come through bread and wine and music and incense and architecture and visual art. The task that comes to the artist is to be an eyewitness on behalf of people who don't have your vantage point, to use that God-given insight for others."[79] In imagesmithed worship, the sermon becomes a whole worship experience, and every participant becomes a subcreator.

$$\star \quad \star \quad \star$$

"The greatest thing by far is to be a master of metaphor."
—Aristotle

"Significant images render insights beyond speech, beyond the kind of meaning speech defines."
—Joseph Campbell[80]

$$\star \quad \star \quad \star$$

Remember, too, as an artist, what you create, you set free. Once you frame an image into a metaphor or reframe an existing metaphor, let it run free. Let its colors and textures run from the frame to color and texturize the lives it touches. Be a master improvisationist. Allow people to hold your metaphors, to feel their grit and power in the palms of their hands. Let them peel away layers of meaning until their lives are touched. Let them mix their stories into each handful of clay until their lives emerge in patterns and colors and each life is spun into a new creation. Allow your metaphors to fold, unfold, and enfold people's lives with the narraphors of truth. Every preacher is a potter. Every preacher is an artist of life. Every pot is a beautiful *imago Dei* of wholeness and humanness formed in relationship with the hands and mind of Christ.

Lab Practicum
THE GOSPEL GRAIL: CREATING HAEMOPOIETIC VESSELS THAT CARRY THE BLOOD OF JESUS

1. *Find and touch the image.* Dwell in the Word until it becomes a dwelling for your soul. Unleash your creativity and intuition until you see and feel the biblical narraphors.

2. *Trust the image.* Connect it to other images in Scripture — to the covenant, to Jesus. Discover how it manifests itself within the stories of both testaments. Submit yourself to its authority. Honor it. Respect it. Stand under it so you might understand it.

3. *Embody the image.* Enter into relationship to it yourself. Don't just see it, but hear it, taste it, smell it, feel it. Experience it with your senses. Allow it to live and breathe. Allow it to speak.

4. *Texturize and contextualize the image.* See how it fits into its stories and cultural contexts. Explore how it can fit into other contexts if at all. Experiment with how it can be crafted, molded, shaped, contoured, embodied, turned. Try to make a sculpture from it.

5. *Keep the image moist.* Don't let it harden or get brittle, but keep it fresh. Moisturize it most of all with prayer and the living waters of faith. Fashion vessels of truth and beauty and goodness from it. Fold into it the colors of diversity and the vividness of livingness. Turn it on the Potter's wheel, and mold it with your hands into a sacramental vessel.

6. *Twist the image.* Twisting makes the familiar strange and new. Veering its path gives it freshness and power. Turn it inside out like a sock. Give it a different reality. Twist it hard and unexpectedly so that it surprises and stuns with revelation and beauty. Allow it the movement and freedom to keep on twisting even as it speaks.

7. *Spin the image into life and let it go.* Allow it to gyrate lives and coil them to Christ. Don't just put a finished pot into someone's hands. But hold their hands to the wheel, and allow them to spin their lives into it. Allow them to be a potter too.

STORYTELLING IN NARRAPHOR

Once you have tapped your blood bank for your best haemopoietic images, you must create movable art. Preachers are not mere sculptors but motion picture directors. As I said in chapter 1, every sermon is a "movable feast." Metaphors are most powerful when embodied within narrative. Remember your stem cells: identity and reproduction. Remember that style and meaning are one in an image.

If a metaphor is your holodeck, then a narraphor platforms that holodeck into a moving picture of life. Take blood cells and make the blood of Jesus flow organically through the body in every part of life. Take the stories of Jesus and animate the lives of others with them. Each narraphor contains both the identity and generativity of Jesus into lives that will carry its seed to others. The gospel is viral.

Narraphors, like parables, are both centripetal and centrifugal. They seek to draw persons inside the experience, to introduce to them a new reality and invite them to take on a new identity in Christ, all the while sending them out in discipleship with a renewed sense of mission.

President Reagan spent a significant amount of time watching movies. At the White House family theater, he watched almost a movie a week. At Camp David alone, he saw some 350 feature films. Who knows how many other movies he saw in the private screening rooms of friends? Reagan's storytelling skills came as much from what he encountered on screen as what he encountered in real life.

The power to change the world belongs to the storytellers. The world is story shaped. The stories we tell shape the world we live in. So we had better tell the right stories — the good, the true, the beautiful. Christians, have we no story of our own to tell?

The twenty-first century will be a search for identity. Humans find identity in stories that tell us who we are. Story is what touches people. In some of the most beautiful words ever written about story and the Scriptures, poet Luci Shaw references her friend and colleague Eugene Peterson when she says this:

> Story is the primary way in which the revelation of God is given to us. The Holy Spirit's literary genre of choice is story. The biblical story comprises other literary forms — sermons and genealogies, prayers and letters, poems and proverbs — but story carries them all in its capacious and organically intricate plot. Moses told stories; Jesus told stories; the four Gospel writers presented their good news in the form of stories. And the Holy Spirit weaves all this storytelling into the vast and holy literary architecture that reveals

God to us as Father, Son, and Holy Spirit in the way that he chooses to make himself known. Story. To get this revelation right, we enter the story.[81]

Peterson himself is equally eloquent about story, not doctrine, as "the gospel way":

Somewhere along the way, most of us pick up bad habits of extracting from the Bible what we pretentiously call "spiritual principles" or "moral guidelines" or "theological truths" and then corseting ourselves in them in order to force a godly shape on our lives. That's a mighty uncomfortable way to go about improving our condition. And it's not the gospel way. Story is the gospel way. Story isn't imposed on our lives; it invites us into its life. As we enter and imaginatively participate, we find ourselves in a more spacious, freer, and more coherent world. We didn't know all this was going on! We had never noticed all this significance! Story brings us into more reality, not less, expands horizons, sharpens both sight and insight. Story is the primary means we have for learning what the world is, and what it means to be a human being in it. No wonder from the time we acquire the rudiments of language, we demand stories.[82]

Jesus is not a statement but a Story; Jesus is not an idea, but the Source Image; Jesus is not a proposition but a Person who invites us to follow him in narraphors. By placing ourselves in the Jesus story, first through visualization then by volition, we experience his story and discover his identity.[83] We cannot keep alive the memory of Jesus without images because memory is nothing but the reproduction of images. If something is alive, it will reproduce. If something does not reproduce, it is dead.

★   ★   ★

> **"There is more to heaven and earth, Horatio,
> than is dreamt of in your philosophy."**
> —*William Shakespeare, Hamlet's famous insistence to his friend*[84]

★   ★   ★

Stories are organic entities, force fields of holiness. Stories sherpa their participant on life's journey. But these journeys are more like a mountain prayer walk than a marathon run. Like the mustard seeds from which they germinate, biblical narraphors come with meaning tucked inside. Biblical narraphors radiate from the center. I remember one time when I was visiting London, I decided one beautiful morning to take a walk "around the block." Seven hours later, I eventually found my way back. European cities are not formed in the US style of grids, but in circles, radiating from a central high point, usually by a river. The oldest part of the city is the highest point, usually bejeweled with cobblestone paths and the oldest, most magnificent "ur-buildings": the town hall and the church. As the city grew and the years went by, the town was formed in circles around the mound. Streets radiate outward from the crown "icons" of the town.

Mary Douglas describes ancient literature as being written in precisely this way in her book *Thinking in Circles* (2012). She describes the art of storytelling in ancient literature, including in the Bible, as "ring composition," a technique that places the meaning in the middle, framed by beginning and ending in parallel. To read linearly, for Douglas, is to misinterpret the text. Stories are a series of metaphors and folds, like Russian nesting dolls. The largest opens in the middle to reveal a smaller doll, which opens in the middle to reveal yet a smaller doll, and so on. According to Douglas, this makes meaning not linear, one-directional, individual, solitary, but makes meaning communal, relational, interdependent, interrelational.

Biblical stories are reverberating metaphors. A core "stem cell" is mediated out into concentric circles of truth (metaphors within metaphors).[85] Each circle is a symmetrical unveiling—a kind of prismatic storytelling—in which the end always references the beginning, coming in and going out with a "turning point" in between. "Storytelling is the byproduct of imagethinking."[86]

Think again about our mustard seed. The seed in which identity is held grows into a tree with branches that spread out in every direction in order to shade and bear fruit that will reseed the stories to others. *Node* is a term used to refer to a special place in the branch or stem of a plant from which a new branch can grow, somewhat like a bud. Stories have nodes. They are creatively charged moments of unfoldment. A node in a poem contains the whole poem within itself.[87] It is a primal kernel or source seed that sprouts.

Narrative is the product of the proliferating rhythm of the illustration that produces one image out of another image in sequence, each being an unfoldment of what has gone before it, as well as the seed or prior form of what follows. Imagethinking does not work according to the "association of ideas," as it is called. It works by an unfoldment by which one image comes out of another.[88]

A parable is a "narrative metaphor,"[89] or what we are calling a "narraphor." The metaphors of truth revealed in the biblical narratives are unfolding narratives—narratives that proliferate from a covenant identity and interconnect in branches and leaves throughout the First and Second Testaments. The parable is one of these branches. It contains within it the covenantal seed. It then grows into a fruit-bearing branch that reproduces as it flowers.

★ ★ ★

**"The images we spin inwardly become
the reality we spin out."**
—*Maureen Murdock*[90]

★ ★ ★

One of the greatest teachers of Judaism in history, Moses Maimonides (1135–1204), believed that Solomon's proverb "A word fitly spoken is like apples of gold in settings (*maskiyyoth*) of silver"[91] was about parables:

> The term *maskiyyoth* denotes filigree traceries; I mean to say traceries in which there are apertures with very small eyelets, like the handiwork of silversmiths. They are so called because a glance penetrates through them.... The sage accordingly said that a saying uttered with a view to two meanings is like an apple of gold overlaid with silver filigree-work having very small holes. Now see how marvelously this dictum descries a well-constructed parable. For he says that in a saying that has two meanings—he means an external and an internal one—the external meaning ought to be as beautiful as silver, while its internal meaning ought to be more beautiful than the external one, the former being in comparison to the latter as gold is to silver. Its external meaning also ought to contain in it something that indicates to someone considering it what is to be found in its internal meaning, as happens in the case of an apple of gold overlaid with silver filigree—work having very small holes. When looked at from a distance or with imperfect attention, it is deemed to be an apple of silver; but when a keen-sighted observer looks at it with full attention, its interior becomes clear to him and he knows that it is of gold. The parables of the prophets, peace be on them, are similar. Their external meaning contains wisdom that is useful in many respects, among which is the welfare of human societies, as is shown by the external meaning of Proverbs and of similar sayings. Their internal meaning, on the other hand, contains wisdom that is useful for beliefs concerned with the truth as it is.[92]

In the Jewish literary tradition, there are two parts to a parable: the *mashal* or the telling of the story, and the *nimshal*, the explanation or application of the parable. While parables can be exegeted (images/metaphors) using the fourfold method already illuminated in chapter 6 on bicameral preaching and then built into an organic architecture, when we start brainstorming with our central images/metaphors, in order to decide how to present our narraphors, how do we do that?

Jesus used the ancient and highly evolved Jewish teaching technique (Matthew employed this in his gospel rampantly), the *mashal* and *nimshal* method, to change lives not only with the story itself, but by using the story to draw people into a discipleship relationship with him. Jesus' stories were designed not only to reveal truth but to invite relationship. When Jesus spoke to the crowds and masses, he spoke only in "parables." This meant he spoke only the *mashal*; he gave only the story, not the *nimshal*, or explanation. The *nimshal* he reserved only for his inner circle of disciples. Meaning is not *explained* but *revealed* to those of faith and in relationship. The method was designed to create a reciprocal teaching relationship between Master and student.[93] To obtain the full truth required a discipling relationship. If Jesus had told everyone everything right out, there would be no need for relationship. There is a price to discipleship, and an affiliated reward: the mysteries of the kingdom. The parable is a call—a call into relationship with the Source of all secret wisdom.[94]

Narraphors, like parables, establish relationship. They establish intimacy with Christ so that Christ can "open our eyes to reveal the meanings of the Scriptures." Remember the *darash*? The *sod*? In order to access the *darash* and the *sod*, you need to be in communion with the Creator. Jesus' parables or narraphors demanded participation and personal decisions from people. A follower could not just be a listener but had to be a participant. Every narraphor is a call to discipleship!

PREACHING FROM THE BLOOD BANK

Semiotic preaching majors in relationship and discipleship building. It celebrates gifts of visual evocation and multisensory narrative. Edmund Steimle and his colleagues describe three overlapping stories in preaching: the Bible's story, the preacher's story, and the congregation's story.[95] It is important we understand the "Bible's story" as the Jesus story. Narraphor is thick incarnation.

The blood bank is your garden. It is your primal source, your stem-cell bank, and your mustard seed. Preaching from the blood bank means going back to the Ur-story, re-creating the story with seed intact, contextualizing the story to live in another place, another garden, another dream. Every dream resurrects life.

What dreams are to sleeping, play is to waking. Semiotic preachers get people to "play" with images and metaphors. They call people into the *paradeiso*.

Chapter 9

Blood-Enriching Nutrients: Style and Twist

Style is as much under the words as in the words.
It is as much the soul as it is the flesh of the work.
Style is life! It is the very blood of thought!

— Gustave Flaubert

STYLEBOOKS, *Stylistics for Dummies, Rules of Good Rhetoric, Writing with Flair, Principles of Good Grammar, Style and Flourish, Elements of Style*—you won't find traditional conversations about "style" here. Not because the Puritans were right about their estimation of "style" as "sinful" unless it aroused in the hearer a sense of his or her sinfulness. But because the Puritans were right about Christians needing their own distinctive style that sets them apart, a homiletics with attitude, a sermon that isn't "without form and void" but that has a "Jesus style" that reflects and resonates with the "style" of our cultural moment.

What was considered good "style" for the rhetorical sermon included the following:

1. How to be grammatically efficient and write cleverly.
2. How to organize and put forth good arguments.
3. How to cajole and convince—the art of persuasion.
4. How to compose and illustrate good thoughts.
5. How to turn doctrines into three points.
6. How to be clear and concise.
7. How to construct "well-tempered sentences."

All of this is irrelevant or subrelevant in the semiotic sermon.[1] When you're exegeting metaphors, you don't read word for word but metaphor by metaphor. The semiotic sermon seeks to design a participatory experience, a conversion conversation, an immersion into an alternate reality, a Christ consciousness where there is fullness of joy. It appeals to the whole brain and is as much sensory based as logic driven, as much emotionally charged as it is intellectually chiseled.

The semiotic sermon seeks a "style" that above all provokes the heart and lures it into love. Rhetoric is the public addresses of the mind: it argues people into belief in the words and principles of Jesus that ensure right living. The semiotic sermon opens the soul to the resurrection reality of Jesus and a right relationship with God through the assurance of Christ's saving grace, which ushers in a life of unending alleluias.

This chapter, then, is not so much about "style" as about the "stylus" preachers use to sear the identity of Christ into the soul. With our unique "style," we give blood in many ways and many places to many peoples and cultures. In short, our style is the manner in which we save lives.

Metaphors are our stem cells. But each person's stem cells come tailored. A "style" is not a relevant trend or a rhetorical flourish. A style is the function that tailors the transcendent, the form by which we employ and embody biblical metaphors, the manner in which we make the familiar strange. That's why style *is* substance. A style is what makes the metaphorical twist and turn possible. A style is a stylus. It creates a groove and leaves an impression. It can write, even tattoo the name of Jesus on people's hearts. Or in more biological terms, style imbibes and imbeds with the nutrients that seal our identity with the blood of Christ. Style also gives the sacramental strength that builds antibodies into our blood that can fight off sin and resist the viral powers of evil. Style makes both identity visible and incarnation viable. In the semiotic sermon, style cannot be separated from the blood substance of the Jesus story. Style does not organize or arrange stem cells. It only reveals and magnifies those stem cells, fusing them into our own identity. There is no separation of form and content, style and substance. Style is merely the form and fashion in which we choose to "give blood." Just as the sacrament of Communion and the blood of Jesus become one as we partake, the conduit of the sermon must reveal the content. As one and the same, style does not just reveal but transducts and incarnates the substance.

Followers of Jesus should be able to "touch" the blood of Jesus, feel his presence coursing through their lives, feel his heart beating in their own hearts. When you give blood in preaching, you don't pump it into bags and containers, but straight into the veins of needy receivers. Preaching connects vein to vein, allowing the life of Jesus that flows through you to connect and course through the entire body of Christ. In the semiotic sermon, EPICly delivered, text and context are indivisibly bound with both stem-cell and blood giving.

*   *   *

**"When we see a natural style, we are astonished
and charmed; for we expected to see an
author, and we find a person."**
—*Blaise Pascal*

*   *   *

Every culture is a complex adaptive system of networks and narraphors. Within that semiotic universe, text and context are woven as warp and weft of a single tapestry. God designed the Scriptures to serve both an original purpose and a present purpose. These are not separate. The discipline of historical context is integral to the integrity of transmitting the text today.[2] No text exists in isolation from other texts or from the overarching biblical message. Semiotic exegesis discerns how any text functions in the wider biblical context. Some meanings we discern by taking out our exegetical magnifying glasses. Others we pick out by examining a text with a theological fish-eye lens, as Bryan Chapell puts it.[3] The best expositors use both lenses, knowing that a magnifying glass can unravel mysteries in a raindrop but fail to detect a storm gathering on the horizon.[4] A narraphoric or semiotic styl(us) must write the story of Jesus in searing passion into people's hearts. To do that, we must use that stylus to interconnect the roads that lead from the Scriptures to the intersections within and between people's lives. The Mozart of homileticians, Charles Haddon Spurgeon, told a young preacher:

> Don't you know, young man, that from every town and village and every hamlet in England, wherever it may be, there is a road to London?... So from every text in Scripture there is a road to the metropolis of the Scriptures, this is, Christ. And my dear brother, your business is, when you get to the text, to say, "Now what is the road to Christ?" And then preach a sermon, running along the road towards the great metropolis—Christ.... I have never yet found a text that had not got a road to Christ in it, and if ever I do find one ... I will go over hedge and ditch but I would get at my Master, for the sermon cannot do any good unless there is a savor of Christ in it.[5]

Yet at the same time, we must "write" the story of Jesus and etch a Jesus identity into people's hearts in a variety of ways and using a variety of types of stylus. The stylus we use must be one that will work for the place and the people in which one preaches. What was innovative about a quill pen in the eighteenth century was passé in the twentieth century with the invention of the ballpoint pen. Today few people study "handwriting" anymore, since even kindergartners learn typing skills and use touch screens in their classrooms. Our style must be adaptable, changeable, and capable of transporting the message of the gospel to every generation. When asked at a White House dinner what he had done to get invited, Miles Davis replied, "Well, I've changed music five or six times." How many times have you changed your preaching style? Do you think you can go through your entire ministry with the same preaching style you started with? Style is part of substance in much the same way context is part of text. Style erupts from an unchangeable truth (stem cell) that connects with changing times. The best way to reach the new world is not with a "new story" but with the old, old story made new.

Just as stem cells can be used to grow and regrow various organs, a semiotic style can be used in various ways and in various bodies of Christ differently. Yet no matter how these are incarnated, the blood of Jesus cannot be mutated, left out, or watered down. In Corinth, Paul drew on Gnostic preaching styles to convey his concepts and reframe his thoughts. Yet he was clear that Jesus' way, truth, and life are not defined by gnosis.[6] Paul's message was somewhat different to each congregation and in every place he went. And yet the truth was the same: Jesus is Lord. Jay Adams notes that "if you preach a sermon that would be acceptable to the members of a Jewish synagogue or to a Unitarian congregation, there is something radically wrong with it. Preaching, when truly Christian, is distinctive.... Jesus Christ must be at the heart of every sermon you preach."[7]

"STYLISTIC" INGREDIENTS

Preparing your stylus to autograph the story of Jesus into the hearts of the body requires the infusion of several "stylistic" ingredients: accessibility, imagination, energy, rhythm and gesture, experience and impact, timing, nourishment, and revelational/incarnational potential (the lifting of the sermon to the Jesus power!), as in blood type ABO^Ω.

ACCESSIBILITY

Every sermon must be made accessible to worshipers. Semiotic homiletics wields the incarnational power of cultural compliance and/or compatibility. A sermon is like pizza dough. Every baker can form it into his or her own personal pizza. To do that, the baker must engage with it, handle it, and stretch it, just as a preacher must do with a sermon. And every sermon, no matter what the flavors of one's life, will always taste like the bread of

Jesus. Accessibility is the way your stylus can create a Jesus identity in each person—an identity of an unchanging Savior within the story of an ever-changing life, the imperishable in the midst of all that passes away.

IMAGINATION

For left-brain rhetorical masterpieces, the art of persuasion is without doubt the most coveted gift of the written and spoken Word. In the art of semiotic sermon giving and image exegesis, however, persuasion is passé. Imagination is paramount. Without a lived-in look and experience, *persuasion* is merely a kind word for manipulation. To "persuade" as imaginal event with "style" is not to convince someone of a set of points and postulates, but to enable someone's mind and heart to be metaphorically "turned" (the best translation of the Greek *metanoia*) to the reality of the gospel—to dream a new reality and to be thrust into it experientially.

The stylus-tic sermon must be creative and imaginative, allowing people to use their whole brains in ways they may not be able to in any other context. The semiotic sermon imagines new and alternative realities. It imagines a better place, a different paradigm, an astonishing possibility. To imagine things other than as they are is the essence of hope. It is also the stuff of revolution. Every preacher of the gospel is a revolutionary, and every sermon is a revolutionary act. Martin Luther King Jr.'s "I Have a Dream" speech was revolutionary because it allowed people to see a reality radically different from the tormented one in which they lived—not only see it, but believe any curse cast in cement could be crushed by love.

Creativity can be much more life-altering than persuasion. Creativity draws not only from the head but from the heart and encourages people to touch the robe of Jesus in new and life-changing ways and to trust with a faith that floods the imagination.

But in order for "soul surgery" to be complete, the sermon must use that imaginative power and emotional resonance to "reframe" people's images of God, themselves, and others. Reframing creates fresh images of a new life with Christ. As God changes their hearts, their minds and hearts undergo a reframing of existence that positions them on the sea of change. Imagination is the pivot stone of the semiotic stylus. In a sense, the imaginal art of "reframing" allows people to lift their current anchor and to throw it into the future, allowing Jesus to lead them into new and strange waters, past "There Be Monsters" warnings and with the land of milk and honey already in sight.

The semiotic stylus writes the Jesus story into the life of every individual and into every Christ-body community. This is the art of metanoia. Stylus-tic "persuasion" is not argument, not a handbook with the answers in the back, but a reframing of one's heart and mind to find Jesus within the story of one's life, and to see the beauty and excitement of a life changed by God from the old self on the old way, to the old self on the new way, to the new self on the new way.

*　　*　　*

My eyes are dry, my faith is old,
My heart is hard, my prayers are cold.
And I know how I ought to be,
Alive to You and dead to me.
Oh, what can be done, for an old heart like mine?
Soften it up with oil and wine.
The oil is You, Your Spirit of love.
Please wash me anew in the wine of Your blood.
—*Keith Green*[8]

"Big art is a process of elimination.... Do your hardest work outside the picture and let your audience take away something to think about."
—*Frederic Remington, painter/sculptor/illustrator of the West*

*　　*　　*

ENERGY

Matter is the creation of energy. Without energy, nothing matters. No stylus moves without a mover who forces something out of nothing. Energy is the disruption of the status quo with design. A style without energy is stylustically useless. The bud must be opened to let out the rose. Energy is the motion of (e)motion, the two thrusts of transformation.

On-your-feet preaching is as nimble and "fleet-footed" as it is "surefooted." In the ongoing process of self-creation, sermons that set people on fire are open to the Spirit's invasion of the body of Christ in combustible and movable ways that are "in the moment."[9] Homiletic resiliency is a new requirement of preaching in a world that requires the ability to adapt to constantly changing conditions.

But the key component of "timing" is knowing when to quit, when sufficient energy is expended. A troubled English vicar asked a farmhand why he came to church only when the assistant preached. "Well, sir," said the laborer, "young Mr. Smith, he says, 'In conclusion,' and he do conclude. But you say, 'Lastly,' and you do last."[10]

An unenthusiastic sermon provides neither nourishment nor energy. For the blood of Jesus to enrich and enrapture, it must be delivered with earnestness, not lifelessness. "Blood-earnestness" is a phrase often used to describe the preaching of people as diverse as Jonathan Edwards and Thomas Chalmers.[11] The energy of passion involves incorporating elements of rhythm, gesture, music, and emotion. A purely rational sermon, devoid of spirit, appeals only to the mind. To enter the heart, you need to appeal to the emotions. True thralldom (or what the Greeks called *thauma*, "a sense of wonder") makes the mind reel and the blood run and leaves the hearer with tremors the rest of the week.

★   ★   ★

"Unless someone like you cares a whole awful lot,
nothing is going to get better, it's not."
—*Dr. Seuss, immortal closing lines of* The Lorax[12]

★   ★   ★

RHYTHM AND GESTURE
Semiotic sermons give sound and rhythm to word and narraphor. The black church more than any other tradition has mastered the magic musical mix of energy coupled with rhythm and gesture. The essence of African preaching is "*nommo* and *kuntu*" (word and rhythm). For the black church, preaching is an "oral and gestural activity,"[13] an "animated conversation"[14] in the guise of a "celebration" that rapper Q-Tip calls a "vivrant thing."[15] The Louis Armstrong of homileticians, Henry Mitchell, labels black preaching an "embodied hermeneutic."

"Soul energy" is the phrase that comes out of the black church to describe the phenomenon of preaching. The John Coltrane of homileticians, Samuel DeWitt Proctor, was a master at "style switching": at the end of the sermon, he would transition from discursive to rhythmic, prose to poetry. Some preachers like Charles Adams even continued the poetry in a whole-body gestural "hoop." African-American preaching excels at first capturing the head then enrapturing the heart.

EXPERIENCE AND IMPACT
Thomas Long articulates well the experiential base of a sermon:

> Texts are not packages containing ideas; they are means of communication. When we ourselves ask what a text means, we are not searching for the idea of the text. We are trying to discover its total impact upon a reader—and everything about a text works together to create that impact. We may casually speak of the form and the content of a text as if they were two separate

realities, but if content is used as a synonym for meaning, the form must be seen as a vital part of the content.[16]

Southern Baptist nineteenth-century homiletician John Albert Broadus said, "If there is no summons, there is no sermon."[17] The experiential and participatory act of living the gospel in "real-time" requires story sharing, or what our ancestors called "testimony time." You can't share stories without participation. A summons will be only as powerful as the eyes and ears of your participants.

TIMING

As we saw in chapter 8, "Blood Bank," Jesus was master of the "twist." Each story or parable began with an ordinary circumstance and then, just as the listeners thought the ending would be obvious, Jesus would give the story a semiotic "turn," and the surprise jolt would shift their perspective and empower their rise to a totally new life.

But the secret to the semiotic turn, as any storyteller will tell you, is "timing." You cannot "turn" what you have not first tuned in and turned on. And good timing depends on that attunement, not on your own prior syncings. Read the signs. To be a preacher means not only to be a semiotician of the Scriptures but a semiotician of the spirits of people. Style requires eyes and ears—and not just theirs. Some preachers never get to "turn" anything. They've spent too much time massaging their metaphor.

If you have a powerful story but you run out of time to tell it, you've only summoned people to a roast preacher lunch. Without timing, you may be giving people a whiff of freshly baked bread without the experience of eating it. You may be drawing them into the Jesus story but stopping just short of the blood transfusion that will stay with them when they leave. In the art of stylus-tics, timing is everything.

NOURISHMENT

When Jesus said to Peter, "Feed my sheep," he didn't mean fast-food fries and bottled soda. The Bread of Life sometimes takes a while to form and bake within the life of a follower. If a sermon is to be life sustaining and disciple making, it needs to serve up house food that is garden fresh, homegrown, nutrient rich, and organically local.

The body is Christ's presence in the world. Like any garden, it needs to be fed and watered, or in our sense, nourished with the bread and blood of Jesus. For a sermon to provoke revelatory and incarnational change within the person and the body, it must lift the spirits and not flatten them. The George Gershwin of homileticians, and popular Methodist preacher, Clovis G. Chappell (1882–1972), who never used a poem he hadn't memorized, liked to say, "No one has a right so to preach as to send his hearers away on flat tires. Every discouraging sermon is a wicked sermon." If your congregation is wilting, you need to check your food supply.

REVELATIONAL/INCARNATIONAL POTENTIAL
Radio preacher pioneer Donald Grey Barnhouse (1894–1960), the Rachmaninoff of homileticians, described the sermon's revelatory capacity in terms of the metaphor of nourishment:

> Have you ever held a progressive dinner with a group of friends? You go to one person's house and have appetizers. Then you go to someone else's house for the salad. Then you go somewhere else for the main course. You work your way around until you've eaten the whole meal. Well, that's the sort of process the Bible went through, only we call it "progressive revelation." Over time, God slowly unveiled the truth of His Word.[18]

The full unveiling came in Jesus the Christ, which is why all Scripture points to him.[19] The semiotic sermon is a pointer par excellence, reframing the context with narraphors and opening the lines for revelation and incarnation. But even the One to whom we point, the Point of every point, who is a person and not a point, said that there would be fuller unveilings of himself. This is why *revelation* is less a word describing divine action than a word about divine activity.[20] No sermon is ever finished. A sermon is not a product but a conduit. Giving blood opens veins to allow God's grace and mercy to move in due course, or more accurately, in divine course.

God does the rest. Only God changes hearts. Only Jesus saves. The sermon is a means, not an end. And every preacher should be careful not to get lost in the means when we have on our side the one who is the Beginning and the End.

LAB TEST FOR GOOD STYLUS-TICS—FMRI
Just as we had an MRI lab test for organic architecture (missional, relational, and incarnational), we also have a lab test for good stylus-tics: the functional MRI, the fMRI, a function for magnetism, resonance, and imaging—the key nutrients for infusing accessibility, imagination, energy, rhythm and gesture, experience and impact, timing, nourishment, and revelational/incarnational potential into the bloodstream of the worship experience.

The fMRI is in essence a test for a person's or a congregation's "change potential." When God writes the Name above all names on the human heart, the recipient experiences the transincarnational power of metanoia. Good stylus-tics is knowing the right tools for open heart surgery. The fMRI takes a look at the key nutrients that help people to submit themselves to the risen Christ and to bind the blood of Christ securely to the soul.

What is an fMRI? It's the stylus guide for the semiotic sermon: magnetic, resonance, imaging. In recent decades, "change studies" have become so sophisticated in their methodologies that they have achieved almost scientific status. We now know there are three key ingredients for lasting, transformative change: the *magnetism* of a big dream, the *resonance* of emotional engagement, and the use of *imaging* to reframe the present to fit it for the future.[21] The fMRI is a *function* for engraving a Jesus identity on the heart. The three fMRI ingredients of style that will enable your sermon to effect lasting change are (1) to encourage the raw inspiration of magnetic dreams, (2) to cultivate the intense commitment and emotional engagement that comes from resonant hope, and (3) to provoke the creativity that comes from reframing images.

MAGNETIC

What gets you up to greet the midnight hour? What keeps you awake to burn the midnight oil? What gets you to take a breathtaking gamble on the future?

Man-on-the-moon dreams. Not half measures or puny, pint-sized visions but amphetamine ambitions, great expectations, heroic imaginations of operatic sweep, swing-for-the-fence endeavors. The only way life change happens is when humans imagine a different world, when they dream soul-sized dreams that nurture the human spirit. The primary challenge of the church in a Google world is to live a magnetic faith in a demagnetized world.

Contrary to almost everything we've been taught about how to get people to change, "radical, sweeping, comprehensive changes are often easier for people than small, incremental ones."[22] The discovery of the *M* in the fMRI comes to the world of change studies from the medical community. Dean Ornish has researched why two-thirds of patients prescribed one of the wonder-working statin drugs stop taking them within one year. The reason is that statins "Roto-Rooter" the veins silently and without visible changes. "Small changes in life (popping a pill)—especially changes that don't show visible effects—are harder to sustain than big changes that require lifestyle alterations."[23]

This need for big dreams does not minimize the importance of small steps and small-scale victories. In fact, other research has shown that the bigger the dream, the bigger the need for "short-term wins"[24] that keep people feeling the radical nature of the changes taking place and open them to risk. But small steps won't move us very far in the right direction if the system hasn't changed and been reframed. Small steps will not be taken without the encompassing "big picture" and extreme dream.

Where did Michelangelo get the energy to paint a thirty-meter ceiling virtually single-handedly for four years? He wrote home in July 1512, three months before the ceiling's completion, "I work harder than any man who ever lived." Michelangelo had an acute sense of life's brevity. To one apprentice, he signed a sketch with these words, "Draw, Antonio, draw, Antonio, draw and don't waste time."[25]

Daniel Burnham was the architect whose planning was primarily responsible for the rebuilding of Chicago after the great fire. These are Burnham's thoughts, present in the aftermath of the Chicago fire of 1871, not present enough in the aftermath of our cultural tsunamis and hurricanes and floods: "Make no little plans; they have no magic to stir men's blood.... Make big plans; aim high in hope and work."[26] Preachers must release in people's imagination the next big thing, the next big idea, the next big dream.

We are deeply ambivalent about ambition. One moment we criticize a kid with the words, "He's got no ambition"; the next moment we criticize another kid with these words: "He's ambitious, you know." Or we use that powerful metaphor "vaulting ambition," by which we mean a "vaulting ambition which o'erleaps itself."[27] In fact, at one point Paul warns a rebellious church to "make it your ambition to have no ambition."[28]

* * *

"Whatever you can do, or dream you can, begin it. Boldness has genius, power, and magic in it. Begin it now!"
—Attributed to German playwright-philosopher
Johann Wolfgang von Goethe

* * *

But rightly understood, it's not our ambitiousness that is going to ruin us. It's our lack of ambition. Life gets quickly miniaturized, and the "smallness" that was in Zacchaeus—"a small man" refers to more than just his height—starts miniaturizing and mediocritizing us. To the smallness in each of us—small of spirit, small of dreams, small of hope—the gospel shouts, "Come down and grow up! Reach full stature!" At what point do our ambitions stretch no further than Hummer houses in the suburbs? At what point do Christians settle for ordinary, run-of-the-mill lives? At what point do preachers settle for ordinary, run-of-the-mill sermons? At what point do "converts" become lumpen laity that settle for ordinary, run-of-the-mill churches?

Absence of ambition spawns a life of anxiety. The word *anxiety* comes from the Latin word *angustia*, which means "narrowness." It's the narrowness of our expectations, our confining God to narrow categories and hamstringing the Holy Spirit, that issues in anxiety. When anxiety rules the church, the church will never pass up an opportunity to pass up an opportunity. Hope and shalom swell along the riverbanks where maximum dreams flow.

Bursting our narrow banks and letting the river flow is an exercise in what Alan Kreider calls "bunking."[29] It is easy for us to do "debunking," or criticizing other preachers for such things as out-of-date hair, odd notions, or off-key singing. But the major task of semiotic homiletics is to "bunk"—to climb out on a limb and offer this Google world "the big bunk," the big picture, to make connections between the past and future that combine to form a present framework for understanding and analysis. The big bunk, the grand metanarrative, is an intoxicating brew of past and present and future that is as arousing as Ammonite wine.

What is your greatest desire and dream? Is it for the advancement of your own personal kingdom? Or is it for the kingdom of God? If preachers are ambitious for God's glory, the church will embody a rich aspirational life. The world will gravitate to aspirational places and artisanal communities that paint on a big canvas pictures of a better future for their locale and for the globe, clear in general no matter how cloudy in detail.

Semiotic preachers must become big-picture artists. This defense of big, magnetic, mesmeric dreams is not a defense of the megachurch. Just as big pictures look best in small rooms, so big dreams often hang best in small spaces. But all places where the "Amen" or "So be it!" comes to mean "Make it so!" have a role in the filling in of the big picture.

M research that documents the power of a galvanizing dream really should not surprise Christians. The very definition of metanoia ("repentance") is an about-face, a radical turning and re-turning of one's life toward God. Metanoia is more than an inward turning, it's a paradigm shift, a turning to get "on the way," toward the truth, in the life. If your church is not "on the way" it's "in the way" of truth and life.

The dream is bigger than the "survival" of a church. The story is more than the church's story. Why was your church created in the first place? A dream of "balancing the budget" isn't doing "great things for God." Even a multiracial church is not a big enough "I can do all things" dream. Why not the bigger leap forward of bettering your community and joining Jesus in saving the world?

Jesus creates good desires, true dreams, and beautiful hopes amid the prevailing cynicism and despair. "Hope that is seen is no hope at all. Who hopes for what they already have?"[30] In teaching us that reality can be the daughter of dreams, and by laying out God's dream for a new heaven and a new earth—a vision of the kingdom of God—Jesus made us eschatologically motivated. Because we expect confirmation of the Bible's truth claims in the future, preachers should not get entangled in tiresome debates about doctrinal details or political platforms. The Christian thrives and ripens on dreams, and the most magnetic dream ever presented is God's dream of "Thy kingdom come, thy will be done on earth, as it is in heaven." To give a stylustically powerful sermon, you have to move people to dream up, to "dream big," to dream a Jesus dream.

RESONANCE

The *R* in the fMRI reminds us that the gatekeeper to change is not rational thought so much as emotional response. The resonances of emotionally engaging experiences override rational communication every time. The heart wins out. People do not so much come to the emotions via the intellect; they come to the intellect via the emotions. It is the blur of emotion that clarifies the blinding light of reason.

★　　★　　★

"We are standing on whales, fishing for minnows."
—*Old Polynesian expression*

"The soul would have no rainbow had the eyes no tears."
—*J. V. Cheney*

★　　★　　★

If the magnetism of the big dream does not resonate emotionally, it will fall flat. The moral imagination requires an emotional as well as intellectual resonance and response.

As we have seen, a "head first" Gutenberg world dismissed emotions in favor of the intellect. But the greatest communicators in history have been those who had the ability to turn thoughts into emotions that move peoples and nations. Good scholars have the power of concentrating into a single image or phrase a world of intense thought. Good poets have the power of concentrating into a single image or phrase a world of intense feeling.

Blood-Enriching Nutrients: Style and Twist

Great preachers have a power of concentrating into a single image or story an intense world of thought and feeling.

*   *   *

"I would rather feel compunction than know its definition."
—*Thomas á Kempis, The Imitation of Christ*

*   *   *

In spite of modernity's attempts to deodorize the slime of feeling from every source, alternative voices from the world of the arts and literature—like this one from D. H. Lawrence in 1913—insisted that beauty, truth, and goodness could not be defined rationally, only experienced emotionally: "My great religion is a belief in the blood, the flesh, as being wiser than the intellect. We can go wrong in our minds. But what our blood feels and believes and says, is always true."[31] People need integrated, emotionally engaging experiences. No one wants to live a flat life, a life without senses, a life that does not resonate. The decline of "rationalist religion" is one of the characteristic features of a TGIF[32] world. With the loss of faith in the power of reason comes openness to the emotions and to the suprarational. Homiletics is no longer helping people cross some rational threshold that panders to our need to calibrate, manipulate, fabricate, magnate. We preach in a culture that approaches life feelingly, senses things feelingly; and the last thing anyone native to TGIF culture wants is an unfeeling faith.

People want to live and love "by heart." And they know that the "heart has reasons that reason knows not of."[33] The discovery that John Wesley was unsettled as a boy by the attentions of a poltergeist would have scandalized Gutenbergers, but it charms Googlers.

In fact, the operation known as "heart bypass" may be a fitting metaphor for one of the key troubles of a Gutenberg world. When you bypass the heart, there is no end of trouble. A primary cause of heart attacks may be the lack of attack hearts—lives trained in deep, hard, attack thinking but suppressed in wide, compassionate, attack feelings that can take on the challenges of life.

For those Gutenbergers whose lives have been spent burrowing in rational furrows and learning to flex logical muscles, all this talk about "emotional intelligence" and "feeling level" and "thinking-feeling" sounds like worthless drivel. To be sure, faith is not emancipation from thought. Sermons that dull the mind quell the emotions. While we must never lose touch with our feelings, we must not always give in to them either. We must be open to the very real possibility that our emotional state may be weird or wonky, since each one of us carries certain cargo that occupies too much space in our emotional life; each of us carries stories of emotional derailments. Every heart has emotional alimony to pay.

No one can make the choice to change for you. No one can make the choice to change but you. But to choose change is as much an emotional as it is an intellectual decision. If a sermon doesn't "move" you, you won't move. As Jonathan Swift liked to put it, "it is useless to attempt to reason a man out of a thing he was never reasoned into."[34]

To move people to the future, sermons must unleash the emotional power of Christianity that is part of its genetic code. Christians brought a whole new set of emotions and ethics to Roman life. In fact, Christianity greatly increased people's capacity for genuine emotional response.

*　　*　　*

"If you're going to be convincing, brother, you've gotta be convinced."
—*Willa Dorsey, gospel singer*

"No tears in the writer, no tears in the reader."
—*Robert Frost*

*　　*　　*

The gospel doesn't give us many windows into Jesus' personal life. We don't know about Jesus' physical appearance, his social demeanor, or his intellectual life. But we do have lots of windows into his emotional life. His emotional side is explored and expressed on nearly every page of Scripture, and one thing is clear: Jesus was about as far from being Stoic as one could get. Jesus was fully himself, completely authentic. He did little to hide his emotions, to partition off his emotions, or to restrict the full range of emotions at play in his life: from wrath to wrangle, scorn to sneer, rage to rant, passion to compassion, sorrow to smile.[35]

The fMRI requires emotional persuasion and especially an emotional closure that can "mark" the choice of change. Billy Graham was right: for change to be lasting, there needs to be a "moment of decision," or more precisely, "moments of decision," and such imprinting moments require emotional appeals and closure. For change to last, there needs to be emotional markers, memory that gets imprinted not so much by emotional highs but by emotional heights.

If I were to do an essay on "How Seminaries Lost Their Way," one of the longest sections would be on the de-emotionalization of homiletics. Preachers are taught to be masters of analytical, critical thought. Preachers are not taught to grow their "emotional intelligence" or to be adept at emotional persuasion, neither of which is taught in seminary at all. Only critical, disciplined, logical argument is taught. Seminaries don't have a problem with preaching that employs the force of reason, but they do have a problem ("that's manipulative") with preaching that employs the force of emotion. No wonder Gutenberg sermons remembered the head but forgot the heart. Manipulation is using emotions and reason to get people to do things for your benefit. Motivation is using emotion and reason to get people to do things for their benefit or the greater benefit of the gospel.

★　　★　　★

"Instruction may make men learned,
but feeling makes them wise."
—*Bernard of Clairvaux*

★　　★　　★

To reach a Google world, rather than being afraid of strong feelings in preachers, we ought to pursue strong feeling and learn approaches that touch the emotions as much as they deepen understanding. This is where the *R* and the *I* connect, since images appeal to and expand our emotional heritage.

IMAGING

The difficulty of change and the power of inertia are reflected in an alarming statistic. Even when patients know their very life hangs in the balance (after a heart attack, stroke, cancer) unless they make lifestyle changes, the odds are nine to one against that change happening, whether it be stopping drinking or smoking or gambling or overeating or whatever.

There are at least two reasons for this. One is the pressure of family systems to keep people in the status quo. Rabbi Edwin Friedman claimed to spend only 10 percent of his time helping patients to change and 90 percent of his time helping people who had changed resist the pressure of family members to go back to the old patterns.

The second problem in effecting change is less learning new behaviors than it is letting go of old ones. Cognitive scientists like George Lakoff, Mark Johnson, and others have proven that to overcome the inertia of old patterns we need new "frames," new "mental pictures" or metaphors that can redefine and reinvent how we perceive reality. To change how we live, we have to change the frames, or "reframe" our images. Just as you need to "format" your disk, you need to "format" your brain. And that's what metaphors with style do: reformat.

As befits a book culture, Gutenbergers learned how to parse and exegete words. In fact, images were seen as shallow, without intellectual content, and dangerous. The secure and stable "fixed meaning" of words contrasts sharply with the openness of visual images and metaphors.

In a Google world, the primary cultural currency is image and metaphor. Biologically as well as socially, metaphors are primary and primal. The natural language of the brain is metaphor, which explains why creative children register more dream activity than noncreative ones. Indeed, revelation reaches us in the form of images: these images take form in us from the Word and are incubated in the mind and soul into more complete images that comprise narratives and songs and words.

When you rearrange images in people's minds, when you change frames, you are doing brain surgery. Jesus is without peer in history for "reframing," for shaking people out of old habits and seeing the world afresh in new terms. Jesus' whole ministry can be seen as metaphor surgery—which is soul surgery—replacing one way of looking at God and the world with new mental models. "You have heard that it was said.... But I tell you ..." was one of Jesus' favorite segues. What came next? A new frame, which often was an unsettling, upsetting image that was designed to shake things up (e.g., Matt. 10:34). And we wonder why rabbinic Judaism and the Jesus movement parted company.

The major war going on in the world today is "iconoclash": a war of images. Philosopher Nelson Goodman says that images are more than "world mirroring." They are ways of "worldmaking." You want to change people? Give them a new metaphor. You want to change a church? Reframe your church by giving it new metaphors. A Gutenberger church is concerned about people having a "Christian worldview." A church incarnating the gospel in a Google world is more concerned about narrative identity than "worldview." We all think narratively, which is where we form our worldviews anyway.

The ultimate "proof" is this: who tells the better story? Who conceives the better metaphors? Give someone a task, and you change his life—for a day. Give someone a metaphor that wraps a story, and you change his life—for a lifetime. To change behavior, we must change the frames, and it is images that do the "framing."

This is why an increasing number of churches are using artists and poets as image consultants and "imagesmiths." I even know of one church that has a "metaphorist" as part of the pastoral team.

So powerful are "pictures" that W. J. T. Mitchell (professor of art history at the University of Chicago) treats images as living things—"image-as-organism"—that have a life of their own and make demands on us. In fact, Mitchell says that the question is less one of "What do pictures mean?" than "What do pictures want?" and "What do we want from pictures?" If images are potentially much more redemptive than words, they can also be much more destructive. Many of our current metaphors of the church are preventing the church from being the church. I call these soul-jacking metaphors that steal the soul of the church "killer metaphors."

If a couple hundred thousand people die a year from medical error (iatrogenic illnesses), thousands of churches die each year from an ecclesial form of iatrogenic illness: bad metaphors, bad frames. In chapter 8, I said that the number one metaphor that is killing the church is "harbor" or "refuge." Does your church see itself as a retreat from the world, or as a vanguard of God's dream for the world? Or what about the church as a place where you are "fed" and your needs are met? If the church exists to spoon-feed people, you will spend all your time dealing with complaints about "bad food." When preacher M. G. Johnson hears people say "I go to church to be fed," he usually tells them, "Then you'll end up a junk food junkie!"

It is important to remember three things about metaphors. First, every metaphor breaks down. There comes a time when to push a metaphor any further is to falsify the truth. Second, metaphors do not exist apart from communal relationships. They are by nature interactive and thus need to be contextualized and homegrown in native soil. Third, not everything is a metaphor. Some things are not metaphorical. God does not conform to our images. Jesus' death and resurrection were not metaphorical then, and they are not metaphorical now. The fact that Jesus wants to live his resurrection life in you and me is not some satisfying metaphor. It is the hard essence of gospel truth.

It has been said that there are two kinds of people in this world: those who build dams and those who build bridges. If we strive not to build a dam church but a bridge church, we must learn to preach with an fMRI style: magnetic, resonant, imagining.

Each component of the fMRI is a feedback loop to the other. For example, emotional engagement feeds back into images, which then enable the magnetism of the big dream to shine. And the more images we create, the better our emotional life and the higher up our relationships. A love letter that describes the beloved as a "giant pigeon crapping on your heart"[36] may be factual and accurate, but it will not inspire marriage.

But even when we build fMRI bridges to this Google world, even when we deploy M and R and I to their fullest degree, we still lack one thing: only God can truly change the human heart.

Chapter 10

Blood and Guts: Passion

A sermon should be as fresh as a spring rain and as passionate as a first kiss.

—Eric Baker

WHAT ARE YOU PASSIONATE ABOUT? Are you more passionate about your favorite restaurant, your rival sports team, your chicken cacciatore, or your child's soccer game than the sermon you give on Sunday morning? If you are not passionate about your sermon, why should anyone else be? If you find yourself yawning while preparing it, or even while delivering it (which I once experienced), it's likely that you won't create an atmosphere of excitement in those hearing it. Your passion for the gospel needs to be the guiding force not only in your life but in the worship you enable for others.

It's easy to do well when you are doing what you love. The actor Harold Norman was killed in 1947 during an especially dramatic sword fight in the last scene of *Macbeth*. Although a tragic loss to the stage community, what a way to go: dying doing what you've dedicated your life to doing. The truth is, each time you give blood, as your sermon takes off on its own with the updraft of resurrection power, you "die" a little. The sermon is blood in the body and love on the wing.

Homiletics is a blood-and-guts reality. But it must be a bird that flies, not one lying motionless on the ground. Not all sermons soar like eagles. But when a sermon feels and smells like roadkill, you are in serious trouble. Charles Spurgeon used to say, "A dull minister creates a dull audience. You cannot expect the office-bearers and the members of the church to travel by steam if their chosen pastor still drives the old broad-wheeled wagon."[1]

If sermons are to stir up gifts of godliness within the body, they must manifest the passions of quality and depth. No one but an infant enjoys swimming in a pool only one foot deep, nor in water that is muddy or frigid. No one is passionate about prime rib that chews like leather. No one is passionate about a novel with cardboard characters and dialogue that smacks of a bad infomercial. No one will be passionate about Jesus if you bow before the Scriptures as superficially as you curtsy on stage or offer up a taste of truth that has all the texture of duck liver.

You can take it to the bank: a philosophical treatise will get you snores; a scold or reprimand will get you a week of chores as you clean up the mess you've made. "Speak when you are angry," Laurence J. Peter has warned, "and you will make the best speech you'll ever regret." Only a passion-filled experience of Christ is worth your people's time and attention.

        ★   ★   ★

"I have owed to them in hours of weariness, sensations sweet,
Felt in the blood, and felt along the heart."
—*William Wordsworth*

        ★   ★   ★

How can you ensure that your sermon has passion, quality, and depth? First, speak to the senses—the ear, the eye, the nose, and all the rest. Too much preaching has aimed to help people "understand" the gospel; too little preaching aims to lift up Christ in the context of community. Too little preaching is hearts on fire, and too much preaching is heads in the sand.

Paul tells the church at Rome, "I am eager to come to you in Rome, too, to preach the Good News."[2] The word "eager" or "ready" is the Greek *prothumos*, which carries the notion of being literally on fire! Paul burned inside to preach the gospel. He had a passion to save lives in the name of Jesus.

"Is not my word like fire," declares the Lord to Jeremiah, "and like a hammer that breaks a rock in pieces?"[3] The symbol of the Holy Spirit is fire. Preaching is playing with fire. Preachers don't build fake fireplaces or make-believe campfires. Preachers are those who are willing to run into burning buildings to save lives, who will risk their lives for the sake of the gospel. A life dedicated to risk management is not the preaching life.

Preachers with passion have not just a flare for fire and blood-and-guts realism. They also sound an urgent voice. William Randolph Hearst, who had heard and observed some of the greatest orators in US history, was asked to name the most eloquent speaker he had ever heard. He replied, "A slave, sir.

She was a mother, and her rostrum was the auction-block."[4] A desperation, an urgency, a quickening call to awaken has characterized the best sermons in history. John Wesley, Jonathan Edwards, George Whitefield, Charles G. Finney, Dwight L. Moody, Billy Sunday, Aimee Semple McPherson, and Billy Graham didn't serve up Jesus like a turkey on a platter. They were firebrands who called attention to the Spirit of Christ moving and flaming live before people's eyes. They kindled fires by getting people to see the warning lights, smell the smoke, feel the heat. Marked urgency issues in memorable unction. The Columbian Dominicans have a saying: "Five minutes for the people, five minutes for the walls, and everything else is for the Devil." As any firefighter will testify, you meet fire with fire.

⋆　　⋆　　⋆

"Everyone will be salted with fire."
—Jesus[5]

⋆　　⋆　　⋆

Preaching is holding in one hand the visible world, holding in the other hand the invisible world, then clapping hands until the thunder rolls, the seas roar, the lightning strikes, the heavens cheer, and "glory crowns the mercy seat."[6] "Thunderbox" is what preachers used to call the place where they filed their old sermons. Preaching worthy of the "thunderbox"—preaching that pulls down the thunder and lightning—isn't all sweetness and light.

Too many preachers feel that to make their sermons popular, they have to make them honeyed and sunny. Now, I love chocolate. I don't know about you, but if I ate several pounds of it in a sitting each week, I'd not only be sick of chocolate, but I'd probably have poor nutrition, bad bones, diabetes, and bad teeth to boot. That's no way to treat a "body." Too many of our churches are "diabetic." And our sugary sermons have taken the place of the fire of Spirit-filled flesh.

A quality sermon is "meat on the bones" of a hungry congregation. And grade-A sirloin takes a fiery hot grill. While you don't want to toast your congregation, you don't need to sugarcoat the gospel to entice them to eat. When John F. Kennedy started the Peace Corps, the first ad they ran to entice young people to sign up was one of the greatest ads in history. I'll never forget it. Will you? The commercial opened with a scene in an underdeveloped country. An American in his midtwenties walked behind a plow that was being pulled by an ox. As you watched him till the parched earth, an announcer began talking off camera. What he said went something like this: "If you've just graduated from college and you're looking for a job half-way around the world where you can work in 120-degree heat, sleep on a dirt floor, risk getting malaria, get paid $1.25 an hour, and feel better about yourself than you ever thought possible, have we got a job for you!"[7]

Every pastor needs a Peace Corps speech—a signed-sealed-delivered call to conversion that seals the wax on the decision to choose a life of faith. We have forgotten to our detriment the warning of nineteenth-century Southern Baptist homiletician John Albert Broadus: "If there is no summons, there is no sermon."[8]

Preaching is not just fiery, not just nutritious; it is creative and presented in a way that makes you want to taste it. If passion is the fire, then creativity is the kindling. But remember: your fuel will burn only so long in a single sitting. There is nothing worse than a sermon that outlasts its fire. The humorist Mark Twain had many friends who were clergy and campaigned for shorter sermons than the one-hour or longer discourses he was used to. During a talk at Andover Theological Seminary, Twain said that he went to church in Hartford to hear the address of the Reverend Samuel Hawley, a missionary who was doing wonderful work in the slums of New York City. Here is the way Twain tells it:

> He gave us many instances of the heroism and devotion of the poor. I remember he said, when a man with millions gives, we make a great deal of noise: but it is noise in the wrong place, for it is the widow's mite that counts. Well, Hawley worked me up to a great pitch. I could hardly wait for him to get through. I had four hundred dollars in my pocket. I wanted to give that and borrow more to give. I looked around at my friends, and I could see greenbacks in every eye. But instead of passing the plate then, Hawley kept on talking and talking, and as he talked it got hotter and hotter, and I got sleepier and sleepier. My enthusiasm went down, down, down ... a hundred dollars at a clip ... until finally when the plate did come around, I stole ten cents out of it. It all goes to show how a little thing like this can lead to crime.[9]

In the past, various devices have been used to keep worshipers alert. Revivalistic preachers have thumped and roared. Thumping and roaring does usually keep people awake, but it tends to awaken them only to the fact that the speaker is thumping and roaring. All the ingenious devices we employ to keep people's attention do just that. They keep people's attention. They may do nothing to promote creativity. They keep us awake; they do not by any means necessarily awaken us to a new and sanctified life.

A bad sermon creates bad blood. And a sick and tired body. Sermons need not just more meat on their bones and blood in their veins. Preachers need creative ways to animate those "dry bones" into a life-affirming dance of joy.

★　　★　　★

"Thy soul must overflow, if thou
Another's soul would reach,
It needs the overflow of heart
To give the lips full speech."
—*Charles H. Spurgeon*[10]

★　　★　　★

Haddon Robinson once said, "I have come closer to being bored out of the Christian faith than being reasoned out of it. I think we underestimate the deadly gas of boredom. It is not only the death of communication, but the death of life and hope."[11] A passion for people means cultivating not just a creative voice but an authentic voice.

In the movie *The King's Speech*, the king has a stuttering problem that inhibits his ability to speak with authority and to creatively communicate his passion for the people of Great Britain. His voice coach encourages him to "find his own voice." Sometimes finding our own voice means losing our fear of taking up the call to preach. It is hard to be passionate about preaching if you are running from your call. In our story of Jonah in chapter 6, we saw how hard Jonah tried to run from his call to speak to the people of Nineveh. He found it hard to be authentic in his passion for mercy because he didn't feel it himself. To "take on the authority" that Jesus invests in us as preachers of the gospel, we must feel the passion for Jesus in ourselves and be willing to take up the cross, to answer the call, to "take authority." You can't be a passionate preacher without the burning of the gospel in your own heart. John Wesley knew this better than anyone. Wesley's entire mission and ministry changed after his Aldersgate experience, when he felt his heart "strangely warmed," by Jesus' saving grace. To come into our own as a preacher, we must first let Jesus come into our own hearts. When we speak with an authentic voice, we speak with the voice of Jesus. And there is nothing more passionate than Jesus' voice.

Rick Shrout, a Facebook friend of mine, tells a story of a friend named Kurt who ministers to street people. Kurt once had a horrific stuttering problem. Years ago he was a guest speaker at a church, and when he got up to preach, he couldn't get a word out of his mouth. The pastor had to get up and take over at that point. After the service, a man came forward wanting to speak with the pastor. Essentially, he said he was touched by Kurt's desire to share about God even though he found it hard to speak. This man wanted to know the same God that Kurt so wanted to share about. There is sometimes more ways of communicating authentically than being eloquent of tongue—being eloquent in love with God, for starters.

Taking authority does not mean merely sounding authoritarian. Authentic preaching starts with learning who we are as a called prophet, preacher, and blood-letter of the gospel, and allowing Jesus to send us out in power and grace. Too much preaching tells people how they can do things differently to receive God's favor and blessings. Too little preaching is honest and authentic about the "dirty little secret of Christianity": there is *nothing* you can do to win God's approval. It's all the grace and mercy of God—unmerited grace and unmatched mercy. If that isn't something to be passionate about, I don't know what else there is.

Chapter 11

Blood-Pumping EPICtivities: Pumping Up Preaching with Apps

> Don't say, "The old lady screamed."
> Bring her on, and let her scream.
> — Mark Twain

MY FAVORITE WAY OF EPIC[1] PREACHING? I don't always get to do it (and don't make an issue if I can't), but when I'm invited to preach somewhere, one of my first questions is, "Do you have a live Web feed?" If the answer is yes, I then ask the second question: "Can you find me a dancing partner?"

In this type of EPICtivity, I stand in the middle of the congregation with my Bible open to a text that is also featured on one of the two (or three) screens up front. Together the congregation and I exegete the leading image(s) of the text. The second screen, however, is totally under the creative promptings of my VJ (video jockey), my dancing partner. Preferably, this is a person who has grown up on Google. While the people and I are more and more immersing ourselves in the Word, my dancing partner is searching the Web for images that are tossed up through our interactions. These images are flashed up on that second screen as contributions to and animations of our conversation. The energy that flows from these multilayered connections and colorful metaphors can only be described as "divine."

That said, not everyone will get it. As far as I know, back in the mid-1990s I preached what some are calling the first web-based sermon with a live (but very slow) Web feed. It took place at the Kentucky Pastors' School for the

United Methodist Church. When the organizers sent me the "evaluations," I was drawn to one in particular. The pastor had written: "Sweet was a total waste of time. Left the pulpit and tried to talk to us while using the Internet. Got nothing out of it."

But EPIC preachers, take heart. There were many who said the same of Jesus, that they did not get him. As I said earlier, this twenty-first-century world has revolutionized our standards of excellence: no longer is the quality of the performance the standard; instead, it's the quality of the participation. Good "apps" can increase the interaction, which gets the blood pumping through people's veins and sends your message straight to the heart. Apps can take the fMRI style of your sermon and lift it into living color and surround sound. Apps are "style enhancers" and "blood pumpers," the adrenaline that "ups" the experience into full throttle. For some, apps work like magnifiers and hearing aids—allowing the gospel to impact the heart with increased power and magnitude. For a visual world that dreams in metaphors, apps are the holograms of those dreams—up close and personal.

Apps appeal to our creative side, our emotional side, our visual and auditory side, our sensory and embodied self. And they allow us to experience in ways that go beyond words. In some cases, they are transcendent of words. Reinhold Niebuhr said that on Christmas, he preferred to go to a church where there was no sermon, only music, art, and drama. "Words just aren't up to it," said Niebuhr.[2]

Apps are nothing new. In the *Divine Comedy*, Dante's journey with Virgil through Hell and Purgatory is a fast sermon with visual aids and sound effects. But the types of apps we have access to have changed quite a bit. Googlers not only want to "experience" apps. They want to engage with them, participate in them, help create them. *Koinonia*, the Greek word for community, is arguably best translated as "participation."[3] If you want to pump up your preaching with apps, you need to treat your congregation as a coproducer of your sermons. Preaching is no longer soliloquy or dictation but conversation and dialogue.

Today our world is defined (or rather, increasingly undefined) by networking, fiber optics, Internet, intranets, Web. We think no longer in linears but in interlacings. Simple 1–2–3 has become a beauty of complexity. And our minds have moved from thinking in ordered diagrams and hierarchical building blocks to the intricacies of fractals, motherboards, and string theory.

We no longer want to be mere receivers; we want to be creators. We not only want to listen; we want to contribute. We need to think in cable communications instead of chain-link communications. Cables interlace with an ensemble of fibers (stories and images, etc.) and encompass a multitude of diverse colors, directions, interlacings, and connections. Chains link single points and go in only one direction. But our lives are increasingly intertextual. And the intertextual power of multimedia can be our biggest asset. With intertextual and multisensory apps, we can link visuals, aurals, and textual forms with each other and with other kinds of experiences.

Worship is an action word: worship is active; it does things. But our worship needs to do more than "do things" with words. Homiletics professor Paul Scott Wilson argues that by means of the sermon, "a relationship with God is begun and maintained, not just a relationship with ideas about God," but a real relationship.[4] Pamela Moeller insists on the mystery and freedom of God's presence in worship: "But who can say how and when God will offer the divine self? God floods us with God's love in a full-bodied manner—engaging all our senses, faculties, emotions, being, in discovering what it means to be embraced in God's arms and participate in the Body of Christ."[5] In worship, we not only learn about God, we also encounter God.

In literary criticism, there is a school of interpretation based on "reader response"; in a sense, this is what is missing in homiletics texts: how the preacher and congregation work together to create the sermon using interplay and interaction. In the semiotic sermon, you cannot escape interplay. It is there whether you want it to be or not. Metaphors are by definition experiential, interactive, and relational. EPIC preaching is at its best when it turns images into props and when those props become interactive icons that people can take home with them. Jesus was a master at this. In the story of the trap set for him by the Pharisees, the tribute to Caesar, Jesus makes the Pharisees produce a coin with Caesar's image stamped on it. In their producing the coin, Jesus springs the trap on them. They have already proven that they are willing to employ and deploy an idol, a graven image, which was specifically forbidden by the Jewish law. The both/and answer ("Give back to Caesar what is Caesar's, and to God what is God's"[6]) typifies the metaphor's multivalence: both sides could feel that Jesus was supporting them even as he told them both that they were asking the wrong question, and pointed them instead in the right direction.

EPICtivities move participants from knowing God with our left brain to knowing God with our whole brain; from faith formation through catechism to faith formation through proverbs, metaphors, music, images, imagination, and dance; from teaching through disquisition to teaching through narration by artists, mentors, coaches, and ministers. "I pretty much preach one-point sermons," says the Miles Davis of homileticians, Louie Giglio, a popular speaker on college campuses. "My goal is to give them one image to take away with them that will help them live out their lives the rest of the week. It's all about story, about inviting people into God's story, about telling about others who are joining God's story. People aren't hungry for information—they hunger to know that there is a God who loves them."[7]

The perception congregants have of pastors will change as the pastor's role shifts from spiritual example to fellow traveler. "I think of it as all of us going into a cave together and sharing what we've discovered with our pickaxes," said Julie Pennington-Russell, pastor of Calvary Baptist Church in Waco, Texas. "It's not like where you tie a Scripture to a chair and beat it with a rubber hose for 20 minutes to see what you can get out of it."[8] When pastors and congregants are engaged in the journey of following Jesus together, the sermon becomes more and more a naturally shared experience and a mutual creative endeavor.

The semiotic and EPIC sermon is a natural habitat for apps. In a way, the sermon is a landscape with mountains and valleys, echoes and sounds, visual intensity and sensory richness. Participatory worship becomes not just a landscape but a storyscape, a mediascape, a bodyscape, a visualscape—an alternate reality where liturgy can become ecstasy. Today we are limited only by our creativity. Whether music, dance, or arts, in the new epistemology, people celebrate experience, learn by participation more than presentation, process information visually, and they want to engage all their senses.[9]

A good VJ can be the best app you have in designing an EPIC experience and bringing your narraphors to life. Instead of citing a book or quotation, what about interacting with an author who is live? Get her on the phone. Skype him on the screen.

Music has always been a known blood pumper and warmer in the worship experience. Music cuts out all middlemen and communicates directly to the soul. Even Jesus knew this. After he finished the meal known as the Last Supper, he and his disciples sang a hymn. At the brook, just before entering the garden to pray, again they sang. Jesus could not explain to his followers the mysterious road he was heading down, a road to salvation for the world, so they sang a song. Music provides the conduit that so often takes us into God's presence, with words or without words. And that reminds me of words I so often repeat: *Good music will carry a bad sermon a long way!*

Today we don't have to limit our apps to music or video. We have a multitude of sensory experiences at our fingertips. We must only be sure that our apps are pumping up our sermon and not detracting from it.

In 1998 the youth minister at Livingway Christian Fellowship Church International in Jacksonville, Florida, tried to use the power of image: he wanted to embody the fact that sin was like Russian roulette: using drugs, doing wrong was like carrying a loaded gun that would catch up to you. So Melvyn Nurse stood in the pulpit in front of 250 kids and their parents, as well as his wife and four daughters, opened a .357 caliber pistol, inserted a blank, spun the cylinder, closed it, put the gun to his head, and pulled the trigger. The blank exploded and shattered his skull.[10] There is always a point where apps can go too far. As a sermon builder, you need to choose carefully what apps will increase your blood supply and which may be just a set of gaudy beads on a beautiful vase.

Lab Practicum
PACEMAKERS, BLOOD PUMPERS, AND NARRAPHOR BOOSTERS

Apps and EPICtivities are "add-ins" and "add-ons" that make your semiotic and narraphoric sermon EPIC. They complement the sermon and allow it to morph from event to experience. They assist as karaoke handles and interactive portals that allow people to participate in the experience. They appeal mostly to the right brain, the creative, relational, and connective mind. They elicit emotional and engaged responses.

EPICtivities above all must serve the narraphors and stories that you are introducing. They add an element of surprise and move the story forward. In a sense, they create a 3-D reality for your narraphor that can be sensually experienced. They are always supporting the narraphor and identity of the Jesus story but are never the story itself.

What kinds of apps can get people's blood pumping and get them to participate in the Jesus story? You are limited only by your (and their) creativity. Jesus will do the rest.

How do you create an EPIC sermon? Let's bring, for example, the story of the murder of John the Baptist into the lab. Take a look at Mark 6:17–29 (NRSV):

Herod himself had sent men who arrested John, bound him, and put him in prison on account of Herodias, his brother Philip's wife, because Herod had married her. For John had been telling Herod, "It is not lawful for you to have your brother's wife." And Herodias had a grudge against him, and wanted to kill him. But she could not, for Herod feared John, knowing that he was a righteous and holy man, and he protected him. When he heard him, he was greatly perplexed; and yet he liked to listen to him. But an opportunity came when Herod on his birthday gave a banquet for his courtiers and officers and for the leaders of Galilee. When the daughter of Herodias came in and danced, she pleased Herod and his guests; and the king said to the girl, "Ask me for whatever you wish, and I will give it." And he solemnly swore to her, "Whatever you ask me, I will give you, even half of my kingdom." She went out and said to her mother, "What should I ask for?" She replied, "The head of John the baptizer." Immediately she rushed back to the king and requested, "I want you to give me at once the head of John the Baptist on a platter." The king was deeply grieved; yet out of regard for his oaths and for the guests, he did not want to refuse her. Immediately the king sent a soldier of the guard with orders to bring John's head. He went and beheaded him in the prison, brought his head on a platter, and gave it to the girl. Then the girl gave it to her mother. When his disciples heard about it, they came and took his body, and laid it in a tomb.

Of course, before you can decide on EPICtivities, you need to exegete your narraphors. What images in the text will you use for your semiotic sermon? What narraphors will you build on? What kind of organic architecture will support your narraphors?

When we look at the text in Mark for standout images that cry out for exegesis, we find images of Word or words (telling, listened, swore, oaths) and body (danced, head). We also find metaphors of righteous and holy (which brings up related images or metaphors of covenant, promise, Word, kingdom, lawful, Jewish, God) as opposed to secular kingdom and law metaphors (courtiers, officers, guests, soldier, guard, king, orders, oaths, kingdom, leaders, Galilee, birthday, banquet, and platter). Additionally, we have bodily metaphors (head, dance, body, beheaded) as opposed to mind/Jewish/Word metaphors (head, telling, righteous, holy, lawful, baptizer—which brings up issues of repentance, message, turning). The physicality of turning in dance—here a sensual and seductive act—is set against the spirituality of "turning back or around toward God," an act of repentance and discipline. We also see the act of protection (what is hidden or doesn't appear, imprisoned) being pitted against the act of regard (here meaning appearances) and what is displayed (dance, banquet, platter).

We have Herod (male) in contrast to John (male) and the women (Herodias and daughter). What does John represent for Herod? Jewishness, heavenly kingdom, and spirituality—God's sovereignty and the prophetic voice. The women represent his carnal desires (of all his appetites), power, worldly kingdom, the sovereignty of the king, his oaths and their requests, and the importance of his appearances. Likewise, the warmth, mercy, and love of God is symbolized in the call for spiritual metanoia (turning and changing one's heart) and in the covenantal relationship between God and the *imago Dei*. These are pitted against the grudge (the immovable, vengeful, cold, oath-demanding, controlling) act of "ravenous revenge," which begins with a physically violent act and concludes with an equally appalling display of carnal violence to the body, decked out as a hideous abomination of humanness and creation (distorted image of the Creator).

Of the images and metaphors within the passage, the head and platter stand out as central to the story. The beheading of John and the placing of the head onto the platter (in addition to the dance) clearly stand out as the most prominent of the visual images. Just check the history of Christian art if you don't believe me (Masaccio, Donatello, Caravaggio, Bellini, Botacelli). The acts of dancing, beheading, and displaying convey the most active of verbal imagery. Therefore, in order to exegete the images, we need to know more about the metaphors of the head, the severing of the head, the dance, the platter (called a charger), and how these both interrelate and relate to other submetaphors. Let's probe deeper:

WOMEN

Herodias's influence over this whole scene is inferred by her daughter's eagerness to find out what she should request of Herod. Herodias states succinctly what she wants: "the head of John the baptizer." The dancing daughter outdoes her mother with a flair for the theatrical. With a kind of teenage slasher-movie delight in the gruesome and grisly, the young girl demands John's head be brought to her "on a platter."

Herod's response is to be "deeply grieved" (*perilypos*). This term is used only one other time by Mark—to describe Jesus' own spiritual state as he prayed in the Garden of Gethsemane (14:34). It is truly a wrenching sorrow, a personal agony, that Herod experiences. Yet the weight of Herod's social status among the elites gathered as witnesses and the self-importance of his royal oath are heavier than his heart. Despite all of Herodias's plots and ploys, it is Herod himself who ultimately gives the order for John's beheading. The parallel to Pilate's bowing to the shouts of the crowd to crucify Jesus is evident. Likewise, not unlike crucifixion, beheading was a form of execution designed to dishonor and belittle the reputation of the one being executed. Finally, even as Jesus' body would later be claimed by Joseph of Arimathea, John's disciples claim John's corpse and "lay it in a tomb."

HEAD AND BEHEADING
The head is the part of the body that houses the mind, and in the Jewish/Hebrew tradition, this is also the seat of the heart or spirit. From the head comes the voice. In John's case, the prophetic voice and voice of God's authority is the disembodied "voice calling in the wilderness" with the message to "repent" and turn to God. John's voice is the Jewish voice and clearly influences Herod, who as a leader, often felt pulled toward Jewish law. The head is the eyes of God as well, and the witness to unlawfulness. They are the testimony to what is and isn't a "righteous" image of God. The head symbolizes the thoughts and sovereignty of Jewish law and Jewish identity and John's control over Herod. The beheading then is the cutting off of that control, identity, dilemma, indecision, and loyalty to the Jewish law and to God. It is the severing of relational ties between Herod and Jewishness, Jewish law, and Yahweh's authority and sovereignty.

As a vessel of prophecy, John's severed head is made into a "vessel" for the women's revenge and a communal "gift" in service to the women and their own agenda of "moral" or in this case "immoral" code. A beheading is not just an annihilation of physicality but a severing of the thoughts and influence of a life that represents an opposing force in the life of Herod and in the eyes of Herodias and her daughter (a dancing puppet but a lethal one). The head becomes a trophy to the women's authority and their "turning" of Herod to their own attentions and to the "law" of their own secular kingdom. In the beheading, John's holiness is defiled, and he who was so unconcerned with appearances is made to be the center of all superficiality and the image of ridicule. In a farce of Yahweh's "cutting of the covenant," Herod literally severs off "half of his kingdom" (his Jewish spiritual kingdom) in favor of his physical kingdom. In his oath to the women (witnessed by his guests), the cutting off of John's head mimics the cutting of the covenant in a way that separates/severs Herod from the covenant with God in the ultimate sin of blood spilling (note Cain). And in this, God's Word is nullified and held in contempt. The beheading exercises dominion and exerts status. In sum, John's head placed on the "platter" becomes a hideous communion.

PLATTER

The platter represents everything carnal, displayed, opulent, and manipulative. The platter is as violent a metaphor as the sword that severed John's head. It is the "image" of sin deliberately and haughtily displayed. The guests are bade to "feast" their eyes on the "enemy" of the court who would challenge the secular order and the manipulative and incestuous agendas of those in "power." The platter represents the oath and promise, the loyalty to the secular kingdom and all it represents, as opposed to the chalice of the communion bowl or the tablets of the law. The king's banquet is a lavish affair, and the attention is all on carnal and sensual desires—food, drink, women, bravado. It is a world of appearances and "image," a mirror for narcissism. The women demand that all eyes be on them. The head on the platter demands that all eyes see the reduction of Jewish law and John's prophetic voice to silenced absurdity. The head on the platter is treated as decorative and trivialized as decor (like a fruit garnish or a dressed pig). In doing so, John's prophecy is rendered useless, absurd, mere bauble. And his prophetic voice is silenced, mummified, severed. Additionally, Jewish law itself is ravaged, made fun of, trivialized, and the "eyes" of witness frozen and nonaccusing.

This large ornamental platter, or charger, was the type used for decor in the center of a large banquet table. The heads of the tribes of Israel used similar platters to present their offerings at the dedication of the tabernacle.[11] Such plates were also used to display the "spoils" of war. Herod's party could therefore be seen as a victory banquet and

John's head (Jewish authority) as the spoils. The platter and its opulent authority attest that the ruler of Galilee is "above the law." It attests also to the status of the women and to the superficiality of this kingdom. William Congreve could identify with this situation when he wrote, "Heaven has no rage like love to hatred turned / Nor hell a fury like a woman scorned."[12]

What is "holy" has been defiled. What is carnal has been made an idol. The golden or silver platter is the "golden calf" of the banquet.

In a sense, the violence committed is done just as much to Herod as to John. In the act of beheading and public display of the head on the platter, Herod's authority serves that of the women's carnal demands—he becomes subservient to the women, and he serves up their request by "cutting off" his own covenantal life from God. Herod essentially "severs" his spiritual self (head) from his carnal and bodily desires. Herod himself is essentially "devoured" by the lusts of these women and overtaken by his own weakness. In a sense, to bear the weighty platter as a gift is a heavy burden. And in choosing his sovereignty, Herod has essentially lost it. John's questioning whether Herod had the spiritual authority to be "king of the Jews" becomes a question of whether he can be a king of anything.

THE DANCE

In a strange irony, Herod ends up "dancing" to the tune of Herodias and her daughter in this twisted tale. He succumbs to peer pressure in which his head (and John's) is sublimated to the body and his spirit is trodden under by the carnal desires of the dancing body of Herodias's daughter (who is attributed historically the name Salome, although her name doesn't appear here in the gospel text). The attention given to the dancing girl, the seductive twists and turns of sin, take precedence over the "turning to God" proclaimed by John in the story. The dance of the story is the story itself: the dance of death versus the dance of life. The interactions of the characters display a macabre dance, as the story plays out to its surreal end.

TAKEAWAYS

How does your faith pan out when your head is on the platter? What does this story say about Herod? About your life as well? If Herod had not listened to Salome (and Herodias), perhaps his head would have been "on the chopping block." As it was, John's appeared on the platter.

We all experience peer pressure to perform, show bravado, parade pride, and look good in front of our peers, especially when we are in positions of power or status. But the question of who is really in "charge" is answered by the one carrying the "charge."

A "charge" to keep may be the oath that defines your life. What defines your life? Who is in charge of your life? What is on your "charger" reveals who you are in the eyes of God and in the eyes of others. Your platter is your own face, your offering to God of the way you will live your life, and to whom you will pledge your charge. Will you sacrifice another to save "face" with the world? Or will you risk your own neck and "save" yourself for God? Will you place your own life at risk—stick out your own neck—for the sake of the gospel and show the face of grace and mercy to the world?

As I said above, a charger is a decorative centerpiece that holds decor, fruit, or other foods. The fruit is a gift to the guests, just as the offering plate or sacrificial plate is a gift on the altar to God. What do you bring to the altar to please God? Or do you please your peers instead? What fruit will you bear as a witness to your face, your image—the fruit of God's image or the fruit of sin and selfishness? By his decision, Herod took what was holy in the sight of God and created of it a twisted and vile image of an idol. The prophet who was Herod's spiritual icon—and Herod's relationship with him—now lay severed for all to see. The dance of meaningful life has become a dance of macabre death for Herod, the king who has lost face with God and the Jewish people. Herod had a choice: to face the music with Herodias and turn his life around in a different direction or to dance to her tune. Herodias knew it would not take much—the threat of not bringing him to her bed—to bring Herod to his knees. This is a story about power, pressure, temptations, and loyalties. It is a story about manipulation and appearances, sacrifice and choices.

What does your platter reveal about you? Whom do you "serve"? Do your gifts please God or others? Does your fruit nourish or horrify? When you "serve up" the fruits of evil, they are a twisted and grotesque, an inedible abomination of God's beautiful creation. When you serve the Lord, it may be without a silver platter. There may be no "worldly" success, applause, or praise. But when you keep your head in the right place, you will dance the *perichoresis* (circle dance) with God in beauty that is unmatched and peerlessly exquisite. What does it mean that God's majesty is peerless?

APPLICATION

Now that you have exegeted your images, how will you build your sermon? What primary story lines and metaphors will you focus on? What narraphors will you choose to build on? What experience or application to the congregation's lives do you want them to take with them when they leave? How can they experience Christ within this story? How can you help people relate it to their own experiences and bring this story and theirs into a transductive participatory event with Jesus? What stories or metaphors in their own lives can help them connect with this narraphoric event? And how? How can your apps help you do that? What will your organic architecture look like? Will it pass the test of MRI? Will your style pass the test of fMRI? What kinds of apps can pump up your semiotic sermon so that it connects with people on multiple levels and in a variety of ways and in surround sound? Can you hear the voice of Jesus within it?

Once you can answer these questions, you can move on to look at what might make your sermon an EPIC experience that people can tap into, connect with, participate in, see the image of Jesus within. Let's take a look at some ways you might do that.

PUMPING UP THE SERMON WITH APPS

Once you have exegeted your text, built your organic architecture, and decided on your style, you can choose apps that will further bring out the images and metaphors in your narraphor. Below are some of the types of apps (among many others) that you might consider to EPICize your semiotic sermon:

- drama/theater
- drawings
- liturgical dance
- music
- placards
- poetry
- posters
- puppets
- quizzes/questions
- storytelling
- Twitter feed
- visuals

Visuals on a screen, on a bulletin, or used as placards or inserts can lend additional color to your images and metaphors. The image on the left is *Salomé reçoit la tête de saint Jean-Baptiste* by Bernardino Luini (1480). The image on the right is *Salome Carrying the Head of John the Baptist on a Platter* by Gustave Moreau (1876). In addition to these images, you can also tell the story of John the Baptist through images on a screen or by using images of the dance.

Drama or theater is another way of creating an experience of the event of this narraphor. For example, Oscar Wilde wrote a one-act tragedy in 1863 in French called *Salome*, which dramatized the story, adding its own twist to the ending. You could act out a play such as the one Wilde wrote, or you could write your own dramatic rendering of the story. You could also choose to have congregants play participating roles in acting out or reading the various character roles in the drama. *Puppets* are another way to dramatize or narrate an event. Puppets can be used simply to dialogue about an event or to ask and answer questions about the dilemmas the event brings up. *Props* may be used as worship display, in drama, or simply as items to show when telling or narrating the story. These may include anything from candles to a platter to rope to a sword. Having a prop, such as the platter, even as a display will lend a real-life feel to the story, and people will be able to identify and "touch" the story in real and palpable ways. You could invite some of your people to bring their favorite platters to church and put them on display.

From opera to hip-hop, *music* can lend a magnificent effect in bringing your narraphors to living color and surround sound. Although some composers have actually created songs about the story itself, music can be used as sound effects, or songs can be chosen that relate to the feelings evoked, such as mourning, violence, seduction, fanfare, and so forth. Music can assist with drama too in elevating the emotional experience. In worship, music can bring out the theological underpinnings of the story. Hymn choices or psalms can frequently complement narraphoric stories. For example, a song of lament, such as "God Weeps" (TFWS 2048), can serve as a powerful emotional response to John's death, whereas a Hebrew dancing song, such as "Clap Your Hands," accompanied with tambourine and lyre, might be used for Salome's dance. Hymns such as "By Water and Spirit" can underpin the baptismal theology. Additionally, sound effects and mood music may contribute to the dramatic rendering of the narrative.

YouTube can be a powerful way to show small clips either of the narrative, of music, of dialogue, or of dancing. YouTube videos are easy to create (at least for your kids!) and easy to put up on the screen. They are accessible and can be rendered as real-life or cartoon/animation. Additionally, other types of animations, cartoons, drawn figures, or avatars may be used to depict characters in the event.

Liturgical dance is another way of rendering the narrative — either part of it or all of it. Creative participants may be willing and able to join in with dances as well as simply watching them.

Mime and *motion* are another way to experience the event without full-blown dance choreography. The following link depicts the "Dance of the Seven Veils" thought to have been the one that Salome danced for Herod: http://www.youtube.com/watch?v=S1qHsZBqg8w&feature=related.

Poetry and creative *liturgy* can be additional ways to express the story and metaphors of the John the Baptist story. They can be read aloud or with special effects. You can also have congregants write their own. Sometimes a powerful story (either in words or music) is one you create yourself; other times, you can re-create a story in terms of your own life. For example:

MY LIFE AND MY FAITH

In my life, I have been baptized by _____ at _____.

Two images of my baptism are _____ and _____.

Sometimes I have been tempted by _____ and have turned
away from God's voice.

Liturgies can be used in participative ways to affirm faith or to confess sin. They can be used additionally as powerful statements of repentance or redemption. They can be narratives themselves of the "voices" of the story. Creative liturgies can be put to music, used in YouTube videos, or put on placards. They can be dramatized or characterized. They can be call and response.

Poetry and liturgy can be in many forms and used in many ways—even in images alone. And you can invite people to put those poems and liturgy to music. Additionally, you can use poems from well-known authors as supplements to the text. Thomas Merton wrote two well-known poems about the death of John the Baptist. Kahlil Gibran wrote a poem about John the Baptist speaking from the experience of his prison cell.

Twitter feeds can invite responses or questions about the story and about the stories of others. Other types of feeds can open the congregation to participation by commenting on the story or by creating the story in other ways and relating it to contemporary issues and lives. Well-thought-out questions, interactive drawings, games, or quizzes can add thought-provoking extras to the experiential event.

These are only a sampling of apps you can use to enhance your semiotic sermon. What other types of apps would you use? You are only as limited as your creativity and the creativity of your participants. Who knows what apps will be available in the next five years?

Chapter 12

Blood Thinners:
The Role of Humor

Humor is mankind's great blessing.
—Mark Twain

TO OUR PERIL, we take the fire out of hell, the gold out of heaven, the blood out of the altar, the divine out of the human, the saint out of the sinner, and the humor out of holiness. A preacher has a gleam in the eye, flutter in the voice, fever in the blood, magpie in the mind, ants in the pants, and hyenas in the belly.

Too many sermons suffer from a surfeit of seriousness. The medical community has long known the value of laughter in healing. Humor lowers blood pressure, boosts the immune system, decreases stress hormone production, and unleashes the flow of beta endorphins, the chemicals that leave us feeling euphoric. Humor stabilizes the heart and lifts the spirit. For many it literally "thins" the blood and makes for a lighter, easier walk through life's hardest moments.

For the Lord's "body," humor is not just a blood thinner but a lifesaver. The link between body and mind is inexplicable but palpable, no less the body of Christ. Jesus knew this and encouraged people to laugh and celebrate with friends and community. He also knew that humor could lighten the blow for people when smacked in the face with reality. And sometimes he knew he needed to give his body of disciples and others a reality check. As Jewish humorist Ted Roberts would say, "If you get someone laughing, you can punch them in the mouth without splitting their lip." Quips Jesus made, such as comparing the difficulty of a rich person entering the kingdom of God to a camel entering the eye of a city gateway ("needle"),[1] were designed to strike a strong point but

226

with a gentle blow. Jesus' saying, "When you give to the needy, do not announce it with trumpets,"[2] would not have led to stomach-rolling gales of laughter, but it would have made people laugh. "Don't have others singing your praises; don't blow your own horn" might have translated instead something like this in contemporary terms: "When you write a generous check out and put it into the offering plate, don't have the organist play the theme from *Rocky*!" A message like this can allow people to look at their own faults, to laugh at themselves, and to be able to feel accepted even in the throes of their own worst character flaws.[3]

Within congregations, humor breaks anxiety and increases approachability.[4] Humor is a savvy teacher. It allows for the preacher to dare to speak truths that may otherwise sting but to enable people to respond by laughing at themselves. Humor introduces the maverick into the mainstream. It increases intimacy and sharing within the faith community. A hearty chortle at one's own faults can create an atmosphere of shared awkwardness or bares a mutual weakness.

Like apps, however, humor must be used carefully to enhance the worship experience and not to derail it. The line between offensive and efficacious is often precarious and depends on context. Jokes that pertain to sensitive issues, such as race, gender, and illness, may injure rather than tickle. Your humor should be therefore provocative and penetrating but never pretentious or belittling.[5] It should enhance faith and call attention to your narraphors in a creative way but not be used as a substitute for substance. The humor of false modesty, which friend Teri Hyrkas calls "worm theology," may seem ingratiating, but self-deprecation easily becomes self-glorification masking as self-deprecation.

*   *   *

**"Humor is a prelude to faith, and laughter
is the beginning of prayer."**
—*Reinhold Niebuhr[6]*

**"It is easy to be heavy; hard to be light. Satan
fell by the force of gravity.... Angels can fly
because they take themselves lightly."**
—*G. K. Chesterton[7]*

*   *   *

Life is punishing. When people are anxious, they resist taking in new information. Humor relaxes the mind and opens the heart. In the same way that a drowning person will put a stranglehold on their rescuer's neck or thrash around, making it more difficult to be saved, stress can prevent a person from

227

relaxing enough to hear the good news and to feel the joy of God's healing presence. Humor is like a life preserver—a floating device that allows someone to calm down and start thinking again. You can't swim if you are thrashing. You can't hear the rousing voice of Jesus if your mind is swept up in the "white noise" of an anxiety attack. Laughter breaks the bonds of anxiety and allows people to revel in gospel joy. It is hard to lift up Christ while you're crowned by a frown. It's hard to dance with the Spirit when you're beaten down by despair. Throughout history, laughter has allowed people to momentarily disconnect from the weights that drag them down and to reconnect with themselves and the relationships that give them courage, hope, relief, and breath. This "intimacy of sharing" becomes the "blood thinner" that allows love to flow easily through the body of Christ—even to the outermost limbs and limits.

★   ★   ★

"If you can laugh at it, you can survive it."
—Bill Cosby

"Humor is not a mood but a way of looking at the world."
—Ludwig Wittgenstein[8]

★   ★   ★

The church has not always seen the advantages of humor as a companion to faith. William McKendree, an early Methodist circuit rider, wrote in his diary on September 13, 1790, "O how unbecoming for a Christian, especially a preacher, to laugh. O Lord, give me more grace, more holiness of heart and purity of intention."[9] In 1876 literary critic, mountaineer, and one-time ordained minister Leslie Stephen wrote that "a fashion has sprung up of late regarding the sense of humour as one of the cardinal virtues."[10] In the 1890s, Victorians had so banished laughter from faith that they could not even imagine that Jesus laughed. "Get serious" was the message equated with religion. Laughter was associated with the superficial, the shallow, the foolish. Preaching texts were designed to wipe smiles from sermons more than to create them.

It is estimated that about 5 percent of the Christian population still today are not just humorless but are opposed to humor.[11] The Palestrina of homileticians, John Piper, disdains humor in the pulpit still.[12] God's kingdom is serious business, he says, reflecting Sirach 21:2 (a book that didn't make it into the Hebrew canon): "Only a fool raises his voice in laughter."

True homiletics is not hackwork, but it is humorous.[13] A sense of humor is a homiletic requirement to ward off evil and temptation. Why? The devil

Blood Thinners: The Role of Humor

never laughs. The thirst for mirth increases with the aridness of life's turmoils. But most find it hard to muster the laughter that can release them from their sorrow. Perhaps part of homiletics training should be showing preachers how to "load the gospel gun and shoot it," not always with bullet points but with squirts of mirth that pierce the veins of an ailing but willing congregation. In Egypt, if someone has a good sense of humor, they are said to be "light blooded." Preachers need to lighten up in order to lift up. Preaching needs to become lighter, funnier, more unpredictable, and more emotional.

Humor is the hallmark of a homiletics of joy. "Come and share your master's happiness!"[14] is an invitation to lightness and laughter. The "angelic doctor," Thomas Aquinas, the Pavarotti of homileticians, who preached almost every day, even when he was teaching, believed that the joyless and jokeless were morally unsound. As a professor, he was known as "the happy teacher." Meister Eckhart said as well, "Now I shall say what I never said before. God enjoys himself. His own enjoyment is such that it includes his enjoyment of all creatures."[15] For Eckhart laughter was at the heart of the Trinity and the periochoretic dance: "The Father laughs at the Son and the Son at the Father, and the laughing brings forth pleasure, and the pleasure brings forth joy, and the joy brings forth love."[16] And love is at the center of holiness. Anne Lamott calls the humor she finds in everyday life—which abounds in her novels, essays and memoirs—"carbonated holiness."[17] John Wesley, the founder of Methodism, said that we can only find true happiness in God: "Happiness is holiness." When we are attuned to the Spirit, we are filled with joy.

*　*　*

"Great faith requires a great sense of humor!"
—*John H. Armstrong*[18]

"If you are going to tell people the truth, you had better make them laugh or they will kill you."
—*Oscar Wilde*

*　*　*

Humor, however, can be misused in the pulpit as well. Humor as a kick-start to a sermon, especially if it seems contrived, can be something that ticks off more than kicks off. Humor that is fake, too dry, inauthentic, or disconnected from your message can come across as manipulation—or, worse, can have the effect of disconnecting you from your congregation. Worst of all, it can cause distrust. That's why self-effacing humor is the best remedy at times for building bridges from preacher to pew.

The Jerome Kern of homileticians, Johnny Ed Matheson, tells the story of going to dinner at a restaurant with his wife. During dessert, a gentleman came up to his table smiling and said, "Aren't you Dr. Matheson, the pastor of Frazer Memorial Church?"

"Yes, I am," said Johnny Ed. "Tell me who you are."

"Well, I do what you do. I'm an anesthesiologist."

While laughter is the most authentic voice of faith, it must be rendered responsibly and faithfully. French physician Laurent Joubert set forth in his sixteenth-century *Treatise on Laughter* the best advice of all: "A remark is funny only if the author does not laugh [and] it does not seem prepared."[19]

Maltese physician and creatologist Edward de Bono crowns a sense of humor as the highest form of intelligence. "Humor is by far the most significant activity of the human brain."[20] Humor is also the hair trigger for creative thought, connectional interaction, and metacommunication. Humor is by definition interactive. Shared laughter is a social gesture. Why do people remember humor so well? Interactivity increases retention.[21] Laughter helps learning. Studies have shown that a comic anecdote helps children remember; even chortling improves memory.[22]

Here are a few of the communication benefits that flow from humor—

- humbles the speaker.
- provides a safety valve.
- enables one to approach taboo topics.
- builds group cohesion and fosters community.
- connects speaker and audience and bridges distances between the two.
- provides an interactive instant.

Laughter lessens the blows from evil's slaughter and speeds up recovery time from life's bruises and battles. Humor above all allow the preacher's narraphors increased access to the soul. Humor can be used to exchange entrenched metaphors that damage the soul with new ones that provide fresh hope and daring dreams.

A. R. Radcliffe-Brown sees humor as a form of "permitted disrespect";[23] others see it as enforced disequilibrium. Humor makes a congregation walk the plank and jump into places where it does not really wish to go. Sometimes humor can allow the preacher to force people to look into the mirror, to face into the future, to push beyond their comfort zone. But humor only works if it provokes involuntary reactions. If humor is forced, it will feel false. Holy humor dares to push the envelope by disrupting and upending assumptions, throwing the hearer off balance, and surprising through irony and paradox.

Blood Thinners: The Role of Humor

Blood thinners are load lighteners and stroke preventers. They are metaphor reframers.

Where to find good humor? Look around you. Preachers themselves prove God is humor. After all God chose you and me to preach the gospel.

Interactives

1. Take the following questionnaire to determine if you are left- or right-brain dominant. Discuss how your answer affects your sermon building. If you are left-brain dominant, how might you increase your right-brain functioning in order to increase your creativity, relationality, and communicative ability as a sermon builder? How might increasing your right-brain intuitive side affect your faith? Your semiotic awareness? Your effectiveness as an EPIC and trans-ductive preacher?

   http://www.intelliscript.net/test_area/questionnaire/questionnaire.cgi

2. Take this right/left brain visual test. Does this test agree with the first? Do you have the ability to focus one or the other side of your brain at will? What would be the advantage of that facility?

   *http://www.dailytelegraph.com.au/news/weird/the-right
   -brain-vs-left-brain/story-e6frev20 – 1111114577583*

3. Discuss how the church can or should shift toward a right-brain focus in order to reach a new kind of twenty-first-century world. How can you build your sermons to create EPIC experiences?[24]

4. Watch this video clip of Jill Bolte Taylor's "Stroke of Insight." What are the implications of Taylor's suggestion that using our right brains more effectively may make us more compassionate and empathetic people? What kinds of spiritual disciplines may encourage right-brain functionality? How can we encourage pastors and church leaders to take a step "to the right" in order to be the church in a twenty-first-century world?

   *http://www.ted.com/talks/lang/en/jill_bolte
   _taylor_s_powerful_stroke_of_insight.html*

5. Why do you think Jesus chose to use story and metaphor so strongly in his teaching and preaching? Can you name three to five parables Jesus used and what metaphors and/or images he chose to use within them? What connections can you make between these

stories and current twenty-first-century culture and the everyday problems people face today? How would a left- or right-brain "reading" of these parables change their meaning? Their impact?

6. In the November 2011 issue of *Scientific American*, Keith Oatley notes in an article about storytelling that stories and images, especially fiction, have the power to change personality, influence people, and make people more compassionate and empathetic. Stories also increase one's social skills. Discuss three to five reasons why you think this might be so. How can the church use storytelling more effectively? How can you build your sermons more effectively using narraphor, story, and images? What is the advantage of EPIC delivery to the narraphoric sermon? How can a semiotic reading of the Bible rather than a splice and dice reading of individual verses change the way we understand Scripture?

http://www.scientificamerican.com/article.cfm?id=in-the-minds-of-others

7. Scientists say children laugh approximately four hundred times per day, while adults laugh only 15 times per day.[25] What do you feel are the advantages of laughter in everyday life? Can you name two or three times in the Bible when Jesus employed humor? Why and how do you think it would be an advantage to use humor in your preaching?

8. What kinds of "EPICtivities" have worked well in your ministry? Why are hands-on rituals important in experiencing Christ within the church body?

9. Watch this talk on changing educational paradigms. How do you feel this paradigm shift impacts the church? How can preachers adapt to a new paradigm? How can the church instill a Jesus identity while engaging people to become active and committed disciples?

www.youtube.com/watch?v=zDZFcDGpL4U

10. Find five to seven uses of the metaphor of hair in the Bible. Compare the stories and images, the ways the metaphor is used, and in what contexts. How can you exegete this image to create your own sermonic narraphor?

11. Think about these questions regarding communication:

    - How will people learn in the future?
    - What are the right questions when deciding on a style of communication?
    - How will we tell the story?
    - Where is the "pulpit"?
    - Do we have to assume that speaking is the only way of communicating or the primary way of communicating or the most effective way of communicating?
    - Can content and delivery be independent of culture?
    - When we force applications, do we rob people of the ability to be creative in their own situations?

12. Humor is contextual. Read the following jokes. In what context might you use these in one of your sermons? In what context would it be a mistake?

    "I'm very pleased to be here. Let's face it, at my age I'm very pleased to be anywhere." — George Burns

    "At my age, flowers scare me." — George Burns

    "Youth would be an ideal state if it came a little later in life." — Herbert Henry Asquith

    "I don't feel old — I don't feel anything until noon. Then it's time for my nap." — Bob Hope

    "Another good thing about being poor is that when you are seventy your children will not have you declared legally insane in order to gain control of your estate." — Woody Allen

13. Humbert of Romans collected scriptural symbols for the preacher.[26] Choose five of the following and exegete the images. How do these images apply to preaching? What messages do they hold? What theology do they embed?

    "the Lord's mouth"
    "angels"
    "the eyes and teeth and neck and breasts of the church"
    "heaven"
    "stars"
    "doors of heaven"

"clouds"

"snow"

"thunder"

"precious stones"

"mountains"

"fountains"

"eagles"

"cocks"

"ravens"

"dogs"

"horses"

"oxen"

"standard bearers of the army of the king of heaven"

"the messengers of that Ahasuerus who is our joy"

"the strong men of David"

"the officers of the true Solomon"

"bricklayers"

"watchmen of the house of Israel"

14. I'll give you the image; you give me the person or people it's associated with (see the note for the answers).[27] How many others can
you add?

a. rainbow

b. milk and honey — Promised Land

c. bulrushes — rod and plagues

d. pillar of fire by night, cloud by day

e. rebuilt wall

f. uncut long hair

g. big fish and withered gourd

h. prostitute wife

i. marred clay pot

j. lions' den

k. fiery furnace

l. sewing needle

m. sycamore tree

n. wild honey and locusts

o. coat of many colors

15. Think about the metaphor of the mirror. What does a mirror suggest to you? In *Snow White*, the mirror is an image of truth sounded through voice in contrast to the image the queen chooses to see. Many of our images of life are like that. We "see" and "hear" what we are conditioned and trained to see and hear. And even though we sometimes look something in the face that is different, still we see the same thing. This is the frustration Jesus must have had trying to get his disciples to see differently from what their upbringing, their laws, their culture, and their traditions trained them to see. Jesus used metaphors to create a shock effect through images. How can you apply the metaphor of the "mirror" and "image" to the church? What examples can you give?

16. Images define lives. Sometimes people see in their mirrors of themselves the images of their brokenness rather than the images of themselves as God sees them—as children of God. We also reflect these mirror images on others. How can we alter "bad" images and present "new" and "fresh" images of our relationship to God through metaphor? Give an example of how you can or have done this.

17. Canada decided to get down and dirty with their antismoking campaign. They featured full-color snaps of diseased body parts on tobacco products. Teenagers loved the gross-out and made the pictures collectors' items.

    Minnesota's Thomas Lake Elementary School has as its logo a mean-looking tiger. School officials, worried about images of violence, decided to tank the tiger and introduce a new school logo: school supplies. That's right: a picture of pens, pencils, and a ruler.

    After reading the above descriptions, describe how each cultural "icon" embeds an identity. What is the identity of each? How is it manifested?

18. Paul's image of the body in 1 Corinthians 12 was a brilliant choice of metaphor. This may not be the metaphor you want to use for your people. Can you think of another metaphor that conveys a similar message?

19. Try suggesting a sermon notebook in which congregants can keep notes for future reference as well as to help them concentrate, absorb content, and retain what they have heard. What metaphors

did they record? What stories and images stuck with them the most?

20. How come people never remember sermons? How many sermons can you remember? Drew theologian Wesley Ariarajah contends people aren't supposed to remember sermons. Rather, he says, sermons are like water that waters the plants. You don't remember the water. You look for the flowers that grow because of the water.

    What do you think? Do you agree with Professor Ariarajah or not? Will people invest their time in something that is not memorable?

21. See who can talk the longest stretch without lapsing into metaphor.

22. In many ways, the typological reading, or in its extreme, the allegorical reading, is the most sophisticated left-brained reading of the text. Here is Jerome's allegorical take on the favorite Psalm 42:1, "As the deer pants for streams of water, so my soul pants for you, my God."

    > Quaintly, he maintains the imperviousness of deer to snake-bites. They never succumb to them, but they do, if bitten, feel raging thirst. There's hidden ecclesiology here. The deer is the Church: it cannot be killed by the ancient Serpent. Its children may be bitten, though, and if bitten will only long more for "flowing streams," the springs that slake their thirst. Which are? Jerome, citing Jeremiah 2:13; Baruch 3:12; and John 4:13, concludes surprisingly: "From the testimony of these texts, it is established beyond doubt that the three well-springs of the Church are the mystery of the Trinity," the Father, the Son, the Holy Spirit (Homily 92).[28]

    How does this reading contribute to the meaning of the text? What does it miss?

Part 4

"AB+" GOING LIVE

Blood Supply:
Incarnation and Culture

The tools of one generation are useless for the next.

—Virginia Woolf

IF THE OPERATING SYSTEM OF CHRISTIANITY is missional, relational, and incarnational (MRI),[1] the incarnational component is the last component to be considered. If you are on planet Earth, if you are in the world, you are "in" a zip code. You can get off of it for a little bit—longer if you're Michael Jordan or Julius Erving or Vince Carter or Nate Robinson or LeBron James—but your removal from your zip code doesn't last long. An incarnational faith lives in its Zeitgeist and zip code.

What regulates the blood supply and releases an ongoing talent pool for the church is the Great Commission, the original mission statement of the church: "Go and make disciples of all nations...."[2] If we want to make disciples of all cultures, we need to know the culture to which we're sent. Part of our "sentness" is to a time and place. Like Paul, preachers are under appointment to a local context that exists in living, local color. We communicate in specific not generic cultures. Every sermon is a summons to faith that needs to resonate in a familiar but often "foreign" land.

The great missiologist D. T. Niles gave us a parable of "the seed and the flowerpot" in which he compared the gospel to a seed, which when sown in Palestine, grows up into a plant called Palestinian Christianity. When sown in Roman soil, it germinates into Roman Christianity. When sown in Appalachian soil, the seed grows into Appalachian (or mountain) Christianity.

Preachers must break the flowerpot and sow seed organically in the native soil to which we are "sent." Thus Christ can be found in our own ground, born in our own time and clime.[3] Semiotic preaching breaks all premolded flowerpots (especially the "modern" ones) and sets the seed in native soil. That means Christ will flower and flourish in people who instantly "access" information 24/7, think and dream in pictures, hunger for experience and relationships, and yearn to connect on emotional and spiritual levels with a present and accessible God.

★ ★ ★

> **"We must all preach to our age, but woe to us if it is our age we preach, and only hold up the mirror to our time."**
> —*P. T. Forsyth*[4]

★ ★ ★

Too many preachers are still struggling to hand people apps and blueprints and equations when people need the next brick to build their bridges over troubled waters. "Amazing Grace" was initially titled "Faith's Review and Expectation." Which title resonates more? Not so long ago, some of the most powerful sermons in every preacher's repertoire were those "Tell-Mother-I'll-Be-There" sermons. No longer are these tear-jerkers, but those who tell them are seen as jerks. Canadian church consultant and coach (and one of the smartest people I know) Thomas G. Bandy laments how "preaching is going on inside the established church instead of outside in the mission field."[5]

Today people spend two to three hours watching a movie and enjoy every minute of it. Years ago we used to spend two to three hours listening to a sermon and enjoyed every minute of it. Now the digital clocks come out after the first ten minutes. That's called a revolution in consciousness.[6]

It is not easy to preach a good sermon. In fact, it is one of the hardest things imaginable. You have every political stripe out there. Every theological stripe. Every economic stripe. You have people who'd rather not be there and will do all they can not to be there. Why make it harder than it actually is by speaking a language no one can understand?

In a world when people are bombarded by multisensory stimuli;
in a world where a cup of coffee is an expression of identity;
in a world where community is found in urban camp meetings with old-fashioned tents and paper signs that protest the depersonalization of institutions and claim to be part of the 99 percent;
in a world where relationships are cultivated online but people will spend big bucks to buy local and shop locally grown;

in a world where film and story *are* reality TV;

in a world where Country Time Lemonade contains no lemon, yet
Pledge Furniture Polish is "made with real lemons";[7]

in a world of "please touch" touch phones and touch pads where "every-one has a voice" —

In that world . . . we expect people to sit down in straight rows on hard seats and give undivided attention while we take them for a ride on some apocalyptic express or enable sleeper service during our hot-under-the-collar Aesopian moralisms and ramblings about the 1, 2, 3s of this or that?[8] What are we thinking?

Established institutions and command-control hierarchies are holding on to power as tightly as they can and are as entrenched in the ground as the wire-draped telephone daggers with which we refuse to stop stabbing the earth. Credentialed mountains of authority have toppled into the sea of accessible information opened by social media. Yet many of our churches hold on to controls and command a Pharisaic sense of righteousness with a death grip that may be the last gesture of their demise.

Often denominational establishments support preaching that does not challenge the status quo or liberate people for ministry. Preaching has been in the service of "protecting the memories" rather than in the service of "presencing" the risen Christ and the mission of the kingdom. In turning in upon themselves, churches seek sanctuary in the past rather than following Christ in the unfamiliar present and into the frontier future.

Many also seek the "sanctuary" of universalism or the "sanctuary" of ecumenism or the "sanctuary" of political correctness to avoid going "out" into the evangelistic mission field to resonate the voice of Christ to the world. When our churches become ashamed or embarrassed to utter the name of Jesus and no longer believe that Christ's saving grace is good news worth sharing, the Christian mission has already died within its walls. Our sanctuaries have become our tombs.

*   *   *

**"We thought we were the children of Abraham but
discovered we were merely the children of Descartes."**
—*Craig Loscalzo*[9]

*   *   *

And yet we live in a culture that yearns to experience resurrection! We preach not to seek bodies in seats who will put money in plates to hold up buildings and their memories after they've been patted on the head. We preach to a culture where people are looking not for a place to park but for a person to embrace. To become a follower of Jesus offers an identity in a multicultural world, a sense of direction in a sea of messages and images, and hope in a world of pain, uncertainty, and confusion. Preaching must recalibrate, recirculate and recelebrate the stories of the body and blood of Jesus for a world that is hungry for real life and resurrection promise.

Google culture is ripe for a great awakening. Preaching must stir the blood so that revival will happen in the body. Otherwise Christianity will continue its melt into secularized oblivion in the West. The Clemmer Group, a North American network of personal improvement experts, says that we are already in the midst of a spiritual awakening. According to another ten-year study, there is a "new" paradigm for living among about 44 million Americans who are heavily invested and involved in spiritual consciousness but not in church or synagogue or mosque.[10]

Our preaching moment arrives at a time when it's not just the concept of sin that is foreign territory. Whether it's conversations about the Bible, truth, morality, heaven and hell, providence, or Jesus, Christians find themselves on a mission field in a foreign land. What is worse, Christians have all too often succumbed to culture instead of celebrating Jesus within culture, culture's subliminal messages silently and surreptitiously sapping our identity from our very bones. While we have locked up Jesus tightly in our sanctuaries, the world is starving for the Bread of Life.

*　*　*

"Human beings are never united with each other except through tears and wounds."
— *George Bataille, French anthropologist*[11]

*　*　*

As semiotic preachers, we need to pay attention to the signs not only in Scripture but in the mission field we're in. Preaching must take some responsibility for the fact that Christianity is declining on our watch in western, denominational churches, even as people are becoming culturally more spirit hungry and faith inclined.

When Claude Petri changed his allegiance from France to England, he inconveniently demanded an eight-pint transfusion in an effort to replace his French blood with that of his adopted country.[12] In a sense, the church needs a blood transfusion from the culture of Gutenberg to the culture of Google. Preaching is the source of that blood supply.

*   *   *

"People have changed address ... and unless we work out where they are, we will fail to communicate with them."
—*Peter Corney, Australian Anglican minister*[13]

*   *   *

The John Coltrane of homileticians, Samuel DeWitt Proctor, liked to instruct his preaching students to "make it portable." The sermon must be "portable"—and by this he meant that it ought to address the big issues of human existence, the hungers of the heart that are the same for someone in San Diego or San Paulo.[14] Implicit in Proctor's "portable" imperative was the need for preaching to be "potable"—preaching must present the living water in forms that are indigenous and healthy to its context. The world deserves a portable, potable homiletics.

The best sermons are not in the lab but go readily from lab into life. They are the sermons that address the crux of the human dilemma and "cascade grace"[15] into all of human existence. Second Testament writers made a distinction between preaching and teaching. Preaching was proclaiming the gospel to the non-Christian world. Teaching involved such things as ethical instruction, exposition of theological doctrine, and apologetics for the church or those interested but not yet convinced.[16] "The cross," sings Paul Simon, "is in the ballpark."[17] In our preaching, it is our mission to take the blood supply out to the masses, to the culture, to those who need it most. If you are to preach your sermon to a bloodthirsty world, you must incarnate Christ within the culture in which you live. Preachers weave the language of the cultic into a tissue of reality, hinting at the veiled truths beyond all cultures. It is easy to lose sight of the congregation. It is even easier to lose sight of the culture of the congregation.

Chapter 14

Blood Transfusions: Infusing Creativity

WEED KILLER IS nothing other than superfertilizer. It causes weeds to get so hyped up they die from hard work. Put down the right measure of that superfertilizer known as manure (or, more politely, "organic compost") and plants will thrive. Dump a truckload of manure on the plants and they will die. There comes a time when the prep work comes to an end, and it's time to craft the sermon with the "right measure" of fertilizer.

No matter how much you "prepare" and "build" your sermon, the time will come when you must let it sprout wings and fly. The best wings are the wings of the Holy Spirit. "Without blood" describes every attempt to preach without the Spirit.

Semiotic preaching is "out of control" and "off the wall." It allows for the spark of creativity to ignite the movement of the Holy Spirit. Transfusions of the Spirit's fire and breath will take it from there, baptizing with tongues and blowing tones all its own.

The modern mind-set has trouble with these three words: "trust the Spirit." It has learned to "trust the plan," to "trust the process," to "trust the formula." But "trust the Spirit" gives the hearer heebie-jeebies. Why? To "trust the Spirit" is to dance in circles that move, more than to think in ordered triangles with three stationary sides that ring when struck.

In the seventh century, Greek theologian John of Damascus developed most fully the metaphor of the Trinity as *perichoresis.*[1] *Perichoresis* means literally "circle dance." *Choros* in ancient Greek referred to a round dance used at banquets and festive occasions. The verb form *choreuo* meant to dance in a round dance. The prefix *peri* (Greek for "round about" or "all around") emphasized the circularity of the holy dance envisioned by John. A perichoretic image of the Trinity is that of the three persons of God in constant movement in a circle that implies intimacy, equality, and unity — yet distinction, relationship, and love.

Theologian Shirley Guthrie portrays the perichoresis as a kind of "choreography" (Gk. *choros-graphy*) similar to a ballet. "Father, Son, and Holy Spirit are like three dancers holding hands, dancing around together in harmonious, joyful freedom."[2] Guthrie writes, "The oneness of God is not the oneness of a distinct, self-contained individual; it is the unity of a community of persons who love each other and live together in harmony."[3]

To "trust the Spirit" is not first an intellectual response but an emotional and spiritual response. People in pews can believe in the historical Jesus intellectually without trusting Jesus as the Lord of their lives. Knowing Jesus is the Savior of the world is not the same as knowing Jesus as your Savior. Trusting the Spirit is personal. And every sermon must be a "personal" experience of gospel grace.

The more EPIC the sermon and the more creative the participation, the less you stifle and straitjacket the Spirit. EPIC preaching is a "movable feast," an aesthetic experience of God's life in motion within human lives. Once we attempt to "nail down" the gospel into tight, neat categories and confined liturgies, or once we turn the sermon into a planned performance or one-act play, we have duct-taped the Spirit's voice and have vaulted it safely under our stone walls.[4]

★   ★   ★

"The intellect must not ... be supplied with wings, but rather hung with weights, to keep it from leaping and flying."
—Francis Bacon (1561 – 1626), pioneer scientist

★   ★   ★

Some have critiqued extemporaneous preaching as a lack of exactness and diffuseness. I prefer Hannah Arendt's encouragement to train "one's imagination to go visiting."[5] And perhaps also to open the door to Jesus' knock so that he can visit and enter within us.

What frightens us so much about the freedom of the Holy Spirit? The Holy Spirit is not predictable. Christ's presence resists definition even as the Holy Spirit reveals the meanings and mysteries of God. Where the Holy Spirit is moving, worship is no longer a "safe zone." It is however a SAVING ZONE.

Chapter 15

Blood Donors:
Congregational Interplay

> You are to be taken, blest, broken and distributed, that the work of the
> Incarnation may go forward.
>
> —Augustine[1]

ON AUGUST 31, 2012, the chief engineer of the US economy, Ben Ber-
nanke, confessed his learning curve. At a Jackson Hole, Wyoming, conference, he admitted that the economic climate was so chaotic, so unprecedented,
so unpredictable that the Federal Reserve was making it up as it went along.
He called this "the process of learning by doing."[2]

Chaos and paradox are the defining features of life in the twenty-first
century.[3] Any notion that the way we've done preaching in the past is a formula for success, not death, is delusional. The secret to great communication
in the future is not your ability to persuade but your ability to help people
open themselves to the Spirit and your facility using tools for interaction. The
key to connecting with a Google culture is to move from pulpit-centric command-and-control homiletics to people-centric conduct-and-unwrap homiletics marked by a new kind of collaborative trust between preacher and people.[4]

A great deal of our worship habits have to do with control: hence command-
and-control preaching. The preacher was the controller: of the space, what was
said and when, the order, the flow, the timing, the outcomes. Parishioners
had very little influence over the course of the service and almost no influence within the sermonic space. When I first started out in ministry myself,
I used to demand total control over the worship service, even when carried
out by other persons (staff or lay). Though the "harmony" of the service may

have been "tighter," I've since learned that turning folks loose with narraphors and allowing them creative freedom has made for some very powerful services where the liturgists or musicians or worship leaders were able to develop the narraphor in a way that I totally missed or was unable to express. I've come to the conclusion that the Holy Spirit writes better harmony than I do!

"Conduct-and-unwrap" homiletics—I choose these two words carefully as a replacement for "command-and-control" homiletics. The transductive preacher is more of a symphonic conductor than a solo performer. This does not mean any diminishment of virtuosity. In many ways, "conduct" requires more strength and confidence than "command," since the preacher's personality is always in play, with attendant weaknesses and strengths more visible than ever. But the very nature of the preaching enterprise is now a communal affair.

The word "unwrap" comes from the story of Jesus raising Lazarus. Jesus said to Lazarus, "Come out!" but he said to his disciples, "Unwrap him."[5] Jesus will not do for us what we can do for ourselves. Only Jesus can raise the dead. Hence, "Come out!" But it is our task to unwind and unbind each other for ministry. Hence, "Unwrap him." It is up to us to unwrap the stories and images that are boxed inside our people and to release the sermons within them.

Preaching now requires a reveling in paradox—a constant melding of structure and spontaneity, failure and success. Preaching is the dance of preparation and improvisation, standing and shuffling, firm footage and roundtable, top-down and bottom-up-ness, hierarchy and free form, storytelling and story catching, formulation and nimbleness, a skeletal grid and a fleshy adaptability, a confident mastery of material and an openness to learning from anyone—anywhere, anytime, a set trajectory, and the trench ability to adjust on the fly.

*   *   *

"The tale is not beautiful if nothing is added to it."
—*Tuscan proverb*

*   *   *

This form of conduct-and-unwrap interactivity is not a delayed, suggestion-box approach of "Please send me your sermon ideas." Nor is it turning spectator into spectacles. Nor is it the current definition of "active engagement" as different modes of hearing—listening to what the preacher is saying, to what God is saying—or even as moments of silence for meditation and contemplation. Conduct-and-unwrap preaching is a real-time, face-to-face rhythmic resonance that soars on a shared consciousness of surfing the Spirit together.

In his classic text with Louis Palter titled *If It Ain't Broke ... Break It* (1991),

Robert J. Kriegel gives us "Surf's Up," a chapter in which he explores "The 7 Surfer's Rules" for riding the waves of change. I want to adopt and adapt his "Surfer's Rules" for preaching that surfs the Spirit and rides the waves and winds of participation. I call these moments of high interaction with the congregation "going live."

"Going live" is not one person giving a presentation, but a symphonic creation of communal participation orchestrated by the preacher. More *Table Talk (Tischreden)* than "pulpit prince," more "people's court" than pulpit pyrotechnics, more discussing than dispensing, more rhythmic interaction than one-way downloads, more open mic than proprietary soapbox, open-source preaching is a time of living dangerously. If to live by faith is to go through life walking on water, the preaching life is to "go live" walking on air.

DISCOVERING THE ABANDON OF FAITH

Preaching needs to rediscover the abandon of faith. Sometimes you leap wingless into the unknown then surf the unpredictable winds of the Spirit. Other times you are shoved, only to discover under you the breath of God—"underneath are the everlasting arms."[6] Once you go live, it's hard to go back or go dark.

Preaching needs to rediscover its origins in the kinetic East. The word *homiletics* is based on a Greek verb meaning "to converse." The Greek word often translated "preaching" in the New Testament is *dialogizomai*, which means to have a dialogue or conversation between people. When Paul "kept on talking until midnight" in Ephesus[7] and young Eutychus fell to his death, it wasn't that Paul bored him to death with a monotonous monologue. Rather, Paul was convening a time of questions and answers, which involved everyone and kept them interested.[8] In this type of preaching, the participants have a chance to drive the teaching by their own questions and steepen their learning curve. In the words of Wolfgang Simson: "The style is kinetic: the topic of discussion literally moves around the table from person to person, and everyone is involved. After such deliberation, a consensus is built, collective opinion emerges, and corporate action can follow.... The participatory and kinetic model is most effective in changing opinions and values and therefore in changing people."[9]

When we read, "Jesus spoke to them about the kingdom of God" (Luke 9:11), the verb for "spoke" (*lalein*) is not an authoritative discourse or someone lecturing. *Lalein* implies conversation, interaction, hearing out questions, and respect for others' opinions. In a Jesus "speech," there is a conversational tone where everyone has a say. In a Jesus "talk," there is discussion, chat, even at times chatter (as birds "chatter"). The Jewish manner of "preaching" was sitting together in a group where the "teacher" shared the historical or expository "teaching" with the group, and everyone felt free to jump into the "teaching."[10] Long before sermons became a recital or a recitation, sermons were a vibrant reciprocation.

1. PASSION RULES

Bill Cosby dropped out of Temple University in his junior year to devote every ounce of energy to train himself to be a comedian. "Anyone can dabble," he confessed, "but once you've made that commitment, then your blood has that particular thing in it, and it's very hard for people to stop you."[11]

When the fire of the Holy Spirit burns in our hearts, and our "blood has that particular thing in it" about the narraphor, we are fired up about what we sense God wants to do with this story and image. "Going live" means our passion is contagious and inspires ways to invite participation of the flock in the unfolding of the narraphor. No preacher can be hot in his heart and cold in his preaching. No preacher can be sweet in her spirit and sour in her mouth. Preaching is less about the state of the sermon than the state of the preacher.

Preaching is the craft of evoking incarnational experiences of the transcendent. The issue of preaching is not getting something said; it is not even getting something heard; it is getting something experienced as a community that can transform lives for God and the gospel.

* * *

"The thread of your speech comes alive through the very joy we take in what we are speaking about."
—*Augustine*[12]

* * *

You are not preaching to "inform" people of what and whom they should believe. You are preaching to embolden and empower people to take the necessary steps toward an incarnation of Christ in their lives. Whether you use apps, arts, litanies, or liturgies, your task is to make sure these serve to infuse the "blood [that] has that particular thing in it" into the body that is the church.

2. NO DARE, NO FLAIR

To go live means to dare to take steps based on questions, like, What new things am I trying? What limits am I pushing? What risks am I taking? Sometimes called "the Billy Graham of India," E. Stanley Jones reinvented "retreats" for Indian culture starting in the 1920s. He called them "ashrams" ("forest retreats"), as a way of indigenizing the Christian faith among people of different religions and tribes. Every ashram began with a set ritual, which featured an invitation for those present to open their hearts and tell their stories. Only after hearing the hopes and dreams of those present did Jones say anything. He preached to their hearts and yoked his passions to their stories. He approached each ashram with a prepared heart, not a planned presentation.

The strongest force in the church should not be the status quo but the Holy Spirit. My favorite Pharisee is Gamaliel, who gives us the theological grounding that makes it possible to ride this "no dare, no flair" wave: "If this idea of theirs or its execution is of human origin, it will collapse; but if it is from God, you will never be able to stop their design and you risk finding yourselves at war with God."[13] We can dare something great for God and dare to preach differently for God because God *will* be God. Our preaching can go where we dare not let it go because it is not our will that is to be done but God's.

3. EXPECT TO WIPE OUT

Just because the most wonderful pirouette is sometimes followed by the most embarrassing pratfall doesn't mean you stop dancing.

It's hard for us to accept big wipeouts, but sometimes it's even harder for us to embrace little wipeouts.

David Brainerd attended Yale when the school became upended by the preaching of George Whitefield, James Davenport, and others. The faculty brought in Jonathan Edwards in an attempt to douse the revival fires, but he just threw fuel on the flames. In a moment of adolescent righteousness, Brainerd referred to a professor there (Chauncey Whittelsey) as someone who "has no more grace than this chair." Because of this comment, the president of Yale expelled him in 1742. Though Brainerd tried repeatedly to be reinstated and finish his degree, he failed. That failure led to him becoming perhaps the eighteenth century's most famous missionary.

There is no sin in trying and failing. But there is salvation. It's time for the church to make failure possible in the same way companies like 3M, Rubbermaid, and Proctor & Gamble introduce new products each year fully expecting that a significant percentage of them will fail. In interactive preaching, some things work and some don't. But what fizzles and falls flat doesn't make you look bad. By showing that you are authentic and real, your duds and thuds make you look better, not worse. Your very failures enable you to fly. Plus, what you think are failures may be meat-on-the-bones for someone else.

$\star$ $\quad$ $\star$ $\quad$ $\star$

"To sum up, my friends: when you meet for
worship, each of you contributes."
—*Apostle Paul*[14]

$\star$ $\quad$ $\star$ $\quad$ $\star$

But don't be stupid about it. I like the preacher who had an idea for Pentecost Sunday. He gave each person who entered the church a helium balloon on a string. He asked the congregation to let go of their balloons at any point in the service in which they felt touched by the Spirit or moved by God through his preaching or their singing. At one point, a single balloon went up. During the last hymn, two more were released. When the benediction was uttered, the vast majority were still clinging to their balloons.

To go live is to look at failure not as something negative but positive. In fact, we want certain things to fail, to break, for example, eggs — with a shell hard enough not to break but soft enough for the baby beak to break through. Everything in nature is designed to have its breaking point. Even the atom. The challenge for preachers is the same as that for architects: to design sermons open to breaking, and to turn breaking points into break dancing.[15]

4. NEVER TURN YOUR BACK ON THE OCEAN

To step forth in faith is by definition to step over the line. Sometimes it's the leap of faith; other times it's the high jump of faith. But faith means to stick your neck out, to face the chaos, the uncertainty, and the unknown. As preachers, you will be hit by wave after wave of unpredictables and serendipities.

As any fund-raiser will tell you, the first rule of development is "Never refuse a donation." As any comedian will tell you, this is the first rule of improv: "Never refuse a line." Never turn your back on a wave. Never refuse a story or metaphor. Take the line and go somewhere with it. Even go fishing with that line if you have to. Cast it out there as bait for someone else. But the one unpardonable sin is to rebuke or refuse a line.

The God moment is when the right word, the right narraphor, "knows" the right place and the right time.

In this anything-can-happen-and-probably-will template, you will always be violating the lawyerly dictum that says never to ask a question you don't already know the answer to. I will never forget a children's sermon at Trinity United Methodist Church in Lansing, Michigan. One of the pastors at the time, Cindi Green, asked the neatly assembled children, "What do you want to be when you grow up?" All hands went up. As she pointed to each child, the answers came flooding forth: "Teacher," "Police officer," "Coach," "Builder." A cute little girl with blond braids raised her hand and stood up when it was her turn: "A vampire," she announced proudly.

Be forewarned: in conduct-and-unwrap preaching, the best lines and biggest laughs may not be yours. Sometimes you will play the role of the "straight man" as you hand the applause and glory to another. Be prepared to platform people who are more insightful and entertaining than you are. Sometimes the best laughs will not come from your wit and wisdom but from a congregant's mouth. Sometimes you will be surprised into new thoughts and will find yourself in the shoes of John Newton (1725–1807), Anglican clergyman and hymn writer. Newton thought he was at his best as a preacher "when an idea suddenly caught his attention when he was in full flow, in the middle of a sermon, and he allowed his thoughts and words to move with the inspiration."[16]

Always draft in your mind or on your iPad your expected closing. But like any river, in the course of your sermon you may find your community has contributed new tributaries, new sediment, and new coordinates to the direction and shape of the narraphor. Be fast on your feet to thrust aside your draft and trust the story as the Spirit rustles up another ending.

5. KEEP LOOKING "OUTSIDE"

The best preacher is not the ultimate "insider" or the penultimate "outsider." The best preacher is the insider's outsider. Can you take in new facts, confront new realities, and not be scared voiceless or immobilized? Can you unwrap the inside story of outsiders? Can you trust others, even outsiders, to give "inside" information and insight?

Preachers can be divided into two groups: the skulls and the lobsters.

First, the skulls. At a certain point early in life, the skull gets as big as it's going to get. The skull freezes in the form it's in for the rest of its life. There are preachers who cease being learners and instead become learned. Skull preachers learn one preaching style, and they stick with it for the remainder of their preaching life, doing the same thing over and over while trying to get better at it.

Second, the lobsters. In spite of their hard shells, lobsters—or what those who fish for them call "bugs"[17]—keep growing for their entire lives. How is a lobster able to grow bigger when its shell is so hard? How do crustaceans mature? The lobster sheds its shell at regular intervals, about twenty-five times in its first five years alone. When its body begins to feel cramped inside the shell, the lobster unzips itself from the tight carapace in order to grow a more spacious one. It looks for a reasonably safe spot to hide while the hard shell comes off and the pink membrane just inside forms the basis of the new shell. But no matter where a lobster digs in the sand and mud to find a protected den for this "molting" process, it is vulnerable. Without its protective shell, it can get tossed against a coral reef or eaten by a fish. In other words, a lobster must risk its life in order to grow.

Is your shell too tight? It may keep you safe, but it won't let you grow. When lobster preachers feel stifled in their shells, they shed them, embrace what is "outside" despite the dangers, and prepare themselves for new and better adventures.

These new and better adventures in preaching will come when we stop thinking *line*, and start thinking *field* and *future*. Line thinking is sequential and consecutive and linear. Field thinking is simultaneous and concurrent and nonlinear. How can the human brain process forty thoughts every second? It has 100 billion neurons that make 100 trillion connections. You can never only do one thing as you love God with your whole mind, heart, and soul.

While the narraphoric sermon itself is EPIC and meant to engage, there are things you can do to increase the level of interactivity and interplay with your congregation. By creating a "playing field" within your worship space, you can make your sermon more dialogic, more conversational.[18] Challenge your people with this: "You're all preachers. How do we capture the messages in this room?" Approach your sanctuary as a smart room: "You're a smart room. How do we capture the wisdom of this room?"

Lobster preaching doesn't profess lines but processes fields—not fields of combat but fields of conversation that face the future where God is found. Our word *profess* comes from *profer*, which comes from Latin *pro-ferre*—to carry forward. The Greek *prophetes* means "one who speaks beforehand" or, more accurately, "the one who speaks *for*" or "the one who carries *forward*." "For" what and "forward" where? For the future and forward to the God who comes to us from the future, revealing the Christ who is always ahead of us.

✶　　✶　　✶

"Hope has two beautiful daughters: Anger and Courage. Anger at the way things are and Courage to ensure they don't stay the way they are."
—*Augustine*

✶　　✶　　✶

One of the biggest things we have to learn in all aspects of the church's teaching ministry is that the modern world thought that a sales presentation was a learning experience. If God could deign to share responsibility for creation right from the start in a deliberate trusteeship with humans, even with all the risks that such a trusteeship implies, then what is holding preachers back from lobster preaching that shares responsibility for a sermon?

6. MOVE BEFORE IT MOVES YOU

Once you have immersed your sermon missionally within the inhabited culture—now that your participants are open to the movings of the Spirit within it—you can begin to move with the movements of your people's stories so that participants become part of the experience and not mere spectators of a performance.

Keep moving. You may be one step away ... one hop to the holy. One step away from an explosion of energy. Take that one step. Keep moving. The outcome of each move affects the overall experience.

Keep listening. Every person present has something to teach the body and a narraphor to unwrap. As Ralph Waldo Emerson said long ago, "In every man there is something wherein I may learn of him, and in that I am his pupil."[19] "Disciple" or "learner" is Matthew's favorite word for a follower of Jesus.[20] Preaching enrolls people in the Jesus School, which is peer-to-peer learning. Jesus even promised us a divine teacher; he said, "The Holy Spirit ... will teach you all things."[21]

Listen and learn: listen to your participants' fears, hopes, and concerns. A rich interactive experience goes beyond "hearing them out." It goes beyond passive "listening" (which can go in one ear and out the other) to active listening, which requires concentration and attention and moving alongside the one who is speaking. Don't harass but harness the insights and energy of those present. As you draw them out, you begin to piece together a communal "quilt" in which each person can claim a patch and part, with a pattern sometimes arbitrarily imposed, other times artfully generated.

What the body needs more than anything else is not storybooks but story people. Every person is a story wrapped in skin. To be human is to own, and to live out of, a store of stories. Everyone lives multistoried lives. As the old country song put it, "We live in a two-story house. She's got her story, and I've got mine." Your mission as a preacher is to help people to live well-storied lives and to tell a bigger story with your life than the story of yourself. Your story is too small if it only tells your personal story.

Our role as preachers is to give the Jesus story *provenance*, a French word that literally means "to come from." The Jesus story wants "to come from" your own story, as the stories of your people document the Jesus story; to provide authentication as you make the Jesus story your story. Just as provenance (story) can double or triple the value of an antique, artifact, or gemstone, the scriptural provenance of a story can enhance it immeasurably.

7. NEVER SURF ALONE

Authors only write a book when a book wants to be written—unlike preachers, for whom a Sunday is always coming. The only way we can live under the lash of this every seventh-day date with destiny is in the company of the community. We are all in this together.

The congregation is an essential part of the sermon composition, not just in the sense that each person gets the feeling that the sermon "hits" them but that the sermon belongs to them. The real content of a sermon is not the information but the interaction. This is the "value" of preaching. Its true content is interaction. Above all else, worship is a pattern of interaction that is open to strangers.

The congregation is more key to the preaching craft than the preacher, and the need to exegete the congregation is more pressing than ever. There are times when people must cease being participants and start being observers, but when in the role of spectator, they need to have ringside seats.

EPIC PREACHING[22]

The key to preaching that transducts is to turn worship activity into worship EPICtivity. Worship should be participatory not passive. We must ask more of the congregation than to sit still and listen. We breed passivity when we plunge people into darkened sanctuaries and enfold them into padded seats. But even without all of the cocooning, many of our worship services can be "attended" without so much as moving a muscle or saying a word. At most, people might stand and sit a few times, sing a few songs, perhaps recite a bit of liturgy. But the bulk of the time, they are silent and motionless.

The EPIC sermon, by contrast, is an interactive experience. You don't *attend* worship; you *attend* a concert. You *participate* in worship. You *contribute* to worship. Yet we count attendance, not participation.

    ★   ★   ★

"[In black preaching], the preaching moment is a moment of communal participation. We are really all in this together.
—*David L. Blow Sr. and Frank A. Thomas*[23]

    ★   ★   ★

Semiotic preaching cultivates not a passive audience issuing consensual nods but a playing field of participants with spontaneous voices and movements. Preaching in a sense is more "blood sport" than chess match. As in any field sport, there are guidelines and markers. But during "play," the ball can move around spontaneously and be touched by any number of hands in the course of the action.

In an EPIC sermon, what is begun by you and continued by another can be carried forward by yet another hand and voice. Your narraphors and stories can be intermeshed, continued, extended, and morphed to the lives and needs of participants. In early days, preachers engaged in something called "field preaching." Not confined to a specific region or sanctuary, preachers would travel about and preach to great multitudes in open fields. There were no assigned seats, no limits to who could attend, no class barriers, and no "etiquette" of traditions. Preaching was spontaneous, off-the-cuff, and powerfully mesmerizing. This was the way Jesus preached to crowds and multitudes, the way John Wesley spoke to the masses, and the way each Great Awakening was carried out. Yet field preaching had more to do with the leveling of the playing field than with the field itself. You can create a "field" within any space or sanctuary. If you want congregational interplay, you need to create a "*playing* field." How do you create field worship? You begin by paying attention to your space as the playground of the Spirit.

Photographs of empty churches meant to showcase architecture fail to show the beauty of what it means to have "worship space." Historically, great cathedrals were built simply to exemplify architectural theology or to exhibit theories of sacred form and geometry. But they didn't show the beauty of what really makes up a church — its people. Empty churches are like dry bones. To be a viable worship space, a church needs to be filled with people. Without the "clothing" of people and priest or pastor, the space is nude or bare. Whatever your worship space, it must serve the purposes of fostering relationships and experiences.

What designs help build the best relationships among the people? What kinds of spaces are best suited to "playing fields" for the Lord? Space needs both rest and movement. And there has been in the past an invisible line separating pulpit and pew.

Once you have created your playing field or playground, you need to engage in play. In an EPIC and interactive sermon, the ball never stays in your own court. The semiotic sermon is a "live-action" sermon. Preacher and congregation are involved in an open-ended experience.

Everyone is a "player." Medieval artists had a way of painting themselves frequently into pictures of the crucifixion. There in the crowd would be the artist or recognizable townspeople, the mayor, the king, the bishop, sometimes even the pope. The artists understood that somehow this draws everyone in and that in some way we are all there. That's what good preaching does. It draws everyone into the picture so that all are "drawn in." To paraphrase Michel Foucault's thesis, "The reader writes the text." One might argue that it's the listener who preaches the sermon—or at least copreaches with the preacher and many others. But no matter what, the "playing field" is leveled. The person in the pulpit must connect with the person in the street if the shivers of the Spirit's presence are to kiss the cheeks and brush the backs of those present.

A live-action sermon is filled with participatory discourse: conversation, dialogue, interaction, fill-in-the-blanks, talk-back, callback—and sometimes silence. The ball cannot be passed when someone is always bouncing it. If you never stop talking, your congregants won't be a part of what you are trying to share. Sometimes good preaching also means good listening.

* * *

**"Listening looks easy, but it's not simple.
Every head is a world."**
—*Cuban proverb*

* * *

The same letters that make up the word *listen* make up *silent*. Silence can be an important part of your sermon—a musical "rest" in a way, in which you allow other voices to take part in the piece. To be a "listening presence" can be a powerful reminder that all voices are important in God's ears. The gift of listening is the greatest gift you can give anyone. When you play in the field, you occasionally need to pause to let other players have the ball. Preaching a narraphoric sermon is a team sport. Exercise soulful, prayerful, dialogical, relational listening, and you will give your parishioners greater opportunity to participate in the sermonic experience.[24]

A poster shows a little girl at the beach looking toward the ocean. The words beneath the picture read: "The polite part of speaking with God is waiting long enough to listen." Sometimes the playing field isn't only about other voices speaking. Sometimes all of the "players" need to be silent and listen for God's voice too. Tim Tebow made big news praying on the football field. No moment of silence ever said so much or made so much "noise" about faith in the sports world today!

If listening hones our inner ear, then speaking hones our voice. Each of us needs to "find our own voice"—our identity as a follower of Jesus, individually and in community. The field is a wonderful place to lay out the stories of the body—shared stories of sacred experience, each voice different, each experience different, and meshing into the tapestry of the whole, interacting and interweaving to make a "field of dreams." Beautiful art is made of textures. What is most beautiful is not what is all of one color or all of one brushstroke. But the individualities, the "voices" within the piece, its diversity and difference, are what makes it not the same but a unified symphony of songs. Voices are the textures of a semiotic sermon.

The arts of conversation and dialogue play out in the field in ways that allow for those voices to take on identity, to each embody the story of Jesus within another individual story or strand; and then all are woven together in still another communal story of the lives of faith. The voices of the playing field are those of story catching, story sharing, and story building. "The conversation of mankind is the meeting place of various modes of imagining. The image of this meeting place is not an inquiry or argument, but a conversation."[25] English political theorist Michael Oakeshott (1901–90) names "poetry" this kind of "dialogue in pictures": "the activity of making images of a certain kind and moving about among them in a manner appropriate to their character." The "conversation" of the body on the playing field need not be limited to words. "Painting, sculpting, acting, dancing, singing, literary and musical composition are different kinds of poetic activity."[26]

★   ★   ★

"When you come together, each one has a song, has a lesson, has a revelation, has a tongue, has an interpretation. Let all these things be done for the strengthening of the church."
— *1 Corinthians 14:26* NET

★   ★   ★

First-century Christians shared their stories within community, and early churches were places of symbols and aesthetics. People jumped for joy. They sang and danced the Psalms. They shared an identity-making metaphor of the *ichthys* (fish). They cultivated the silence of "the secret" of the Trinity among the faithful. They wrote gospels, and they painted icons. They spoke in tongues, and they told stories. The "conversations" were the shared experiences of Jesus and his resurrection life. Through these "conversations," the stories of Jesus meshed with their own stories, and they built an identity as Christ-ians: those following the way, truth, and life of the Messiah Jesus.

All followers in God's field of dreams have a double calling: a ministry and a mission. Their time in the sermonic playing field and their conversations with each other will prepare them to go out into the fields of the world in mission, with their identity in Christ intact and embedded within their lives.

Semiotic preaching requires a new theory of congregation. The issue is not how you become a better preacher, but how your people become better participants, a better congregation. The congregation is now an essential part of the sermon composition. The real content of the sermon is not the information but the interaction. A participative or interactive homiletic is based on the priesthood-of-all-believers commitment that the whole community is called to collaborate in the ministry of the word. The preposition *with* must replace *for* in everything we do. We don't do anything *for* people. Everything we do must be done *with* people, including preaching.

The Story of Aaron's Rod

The rod as metaphor is a powerful one for walking and talking the way, truth, and life of Jesus. In field preaching, the rod can mark the identity of individual, family, community, and chosen of God. From Old Testament times forward to Jesus' day, the rod was a family symbol and keepsake. It would typically have the family symbol engraved on it and would be passed down from generation to generation. Each rod would represent the social status, financial prosperity, and authority of the family it belonged to. The rod was also a branch used for walking and symbolized the way we walk our faith with God. Each rod would be unique. And then each customized rod would be placed communally in the tabernacle of meeting before the ark of the testimony.

Aaron's rod was a key symbol. The blooming rod symbolizes the ministry of each of us. And each of us is chosen by God in a unique way. Each of us has a unique voice and a unique walk with God, and yet all of us have a place within the community of faith. God's wish for all of us is to become "living rods" of faith, to bring forth buds and bear fruit, not to remain a dead piece of wood but to be a green branch, fresh in faith going forward into the world as a follower of Christ.

But what does *participation* mean? What is it to converse on the practice field? What is the difference between *dialogue* and *diatribe*?

In the past, churches embraced participation in the forms of repetition, call and response liturgies, hymn singing, and unison prayers. Today participation can include Twitter feeds, congregational drama, "roundtabling" and other sorts of more risk-taking participatory play. In a narraphor-based sermon, the participation creates an alternate reality. The hearers participate in that reality. Interactive homiletics is filled with out-of-control moments and elements of surprise, times of improvisation and creation. A participation homiletics contains an element of the aesthetic. It creates a sense of living in the story of Jesus within our twenty-first-century culture.

*   *   *

"Readers [of the Bible] are not asked to understand,
to extract meaning. Understanding is never
at issue. We are asked to take part.... We have
read not to understand but to participate."
—*Gabriel Josipovici*[27]

*   *   *

For dialogic and conversant participation to take place in the "field," you need to develop an intimacy between preacher and congregation. John Stott stressed the need for "partnership" between preacher and people in determining what needs should be addressed by the preacher without abnegating prophetic responsibility.[28] The sermon is most participatory as "controls" decrease. The preacher serves as a sort of coach, but the congregational responses and interjections create the energy of the event. In an interactive sermon, one doesn't just hear an occasional "Amen" or "Have mercy!" but responses include facial expressions, swaying bodies, nodding heads, raised hands, foot tapping, shouting, tears, and hand clapping, among others. During the Great Awakenings, participatory responses characterized both black and white preaching. What happened to the white church? And why did the black church continue such responses? How can you infuse a sense of interactivity back into your twenty-first-century "awakening" churches?

Anything you can do to make your preaching more interactive and participatory is welcome in the twenty-first-century narraphoric sermon. You can (1) leave the pulpit and play from the center, (2) give voice to your people, (3) let people finish your sentences, (4) have them help exegete metaphors, (5) have them answer questions, and (6) have them add to stories in an updating of the old "testimony time." Whatever you do, a transfusion of interaction is like a transfusion of blood. Blood donors have a stake in the sermon, and their hearts will find new blood for ministry and mission through their experience.

Jonathan Edwards called the church to be open to what he called "the surprising work of God."[28] When all are involved in worship, all practicing their ministry and mission on and in the field, anything can happen. And will.

Chapter 16

Blood Drives: The Closure of Altar/Alter Calls

> Final thoughts are so, you know, final. Let's call them closing words.
> — Craig Armstrong

HOW DO YOU "CLOSE" A SERMON? How do you "bring it home to Jesus"? How do you conduct "altar" calls and life-"altering" transductions that make every sermon a blood drive?

For me, bringing the experience "home," landing the plane, is the hardest part of the preaching craft. Have you ever crash-landed a sermon, slid off the runway, or brought your sermon skidding in too far from the terminal? In any case, Wayne Brouwer is right that "nobody will remember the flight if the plane crashes rather than lands. When a message lands well, people know they've come home to the Kingdom of God."[1]

In some ways, your takeoff at the beginning of the sermon will prepare people for an effective landing later. But if you build them up and lift them into the air and then drop them hastily into a sea of confusion or boredom—or worse, put them to sleep so that they miss the landing altogether—you have not come to that point of transduction that will turn people's hearts to a new place.

One of the worst things a preacher can do? It's not to preach sermons of electrifying mediocrity. It's to give people the sense that their worship experience has been hijacked—hijacked by politics, by personal agendas, by individual druthers, by private vendettas. Bringing a plane in for a landing

263

should leave people with the feeling that their lives have been forever altered by the experience of flying on the wings of the dove in the dawning light of the heavens.

I love the story of Lisa Derman, a holocaust survivor from Poland who was fourteen when the Nazis invaded her town. She died while telling her story at the 2002 Illinois Storytelling Festival. The closing words of her storytelling were these: "Please remember this story and tell it to others, because I don't know how long I will be here." Then she sat down, handed the microphone to her husband Aron, and died.[2] I'm not suggesting that you need that startling an ending to induce altered souls. But there is no closing triumph without "vavoom."

Worse than dying unexpectedly in the act of preaching is the slow and agonizing "death" that many preachers bestow on the most creative sermon, suffering it to breathe in gasps in its final moments. One might call this the "slow torture closure." The seemingly endless sermon "fakes them out" with closing words and then leaps back up into the air for a last circle around the hangar, while the people wait expectantly and more and more impatiently in hopes of the sermon's final words.

Then there is the sermon that levels the "death blow," leaving people bludgeoned by guilt and dazed by a graceless nosedive into the landing strip. Still another is the "candyland flight" in which listeners never feel the takeoff or the landing and emerge from the plane feeling as if they haven't gone anywhere. And finally, we have the sermon whose wheels refuse to come down, and people are forced to eject from the plane still in flight and parachute to the ground on their own. I could go on and on, but you get the picture. Or rather, the narraphor.

Not every sermon needs an actual "altar call" in order to be "altering." A multiplicity of ways are available to guide your congregation into their transductive moments. You could end with a song that sings your sermon—an earworm that bores its way into mind and heart to the point that people are still whistling it on Wednesday.

You could end by allowing people to think through a dilemma about their own lives. Or let them "finish" the story on their own. An alive sermon is an unfinished sermon, for everything alive is unfinished, and everything dead is finished.

You could end with a sacramental service. You could end with something joyful, such as congregational dance, chant, or shouts. Every worship service is a resurrection celebration. Whatever you do, always end by lifting up Christ.

Blood Drives: The Closure of Altar/Alter Calls

Some sermons go out with praise, some with meditation, some with joy, some in silence. Some close with testimonies, some with altar calls, some with healing, some with anointing with oil, some with prayer and laying on of hands. But the most successful landings of EPIC sermons are hands-on and sensory in some way. You need to give people something to "take with them" from their experience—a "stone of remembrance" or memento or some physical keepsake from their flight. As we have already seen, in a culture that digitizes everything, people need "thingies," and sermons need to find ways to sacramentalize the material. Faith and touch go together. People remember most what they touch with their hands, feel with their fingers, see with their eyes, smell with their noses. Jesus' ministry was filled with "touch." Altar calls and heart alterations go together. Whether by foot washing, serving of bread and wine, candle lighting, or any host of interactive and participatory hands-on experiences, a preacher of semiotic sermons needs to try to think of creative ways to bring people into hands-on rituals at the end that leave people with thingies that memorialize the experience.

For example, your "altaring" could be the story of an altar Moses built: "And Moses built an altar and called the name of it, 'The LORD is my banner' [*Yahweh-nissi*]. He said, 'A hand upon the banner of the LORD!' "3

In the ancient world, when a person put his hand on the banner that belonged to a king or general, it was a sign of loyalty and commitment. It meant he was willing to march under that flag, to give his loyalty to that banner, and even to risk his life in faithfulness to that person. Will we step forward and stretch out our hands and touch the banner of the Lord? Or are we flying our own banners?

One of my upcoming books is called *Rock, Paper, Scissors*. In it I talk about the concept of sin in terms of the way that Jesus, the Rock, breaks the power of sin (scissors) and renews our story in witness to him (paper). If I were to preach this as a semiotic sermon, I might close by walking people through the hand motions for paper, scissors, and rock—the motion of rock breaking scissors and the restoration of paper. What more powerful way for people to embody the message than to use their hands to play it out with each other? They may not remember my every word. But they will no doubt remember the gestures and the motions and the meanings attached.

No matter what your ending, what kind of way you choose to close, remember that only Jesus can incarnate. Your job is to create the scaffolding for an experience of God, trusting the Holy Spirit to take it from there.

Chapter 17

Blood Vessels: Sacramentality

The Church makes the Eucharist and the Eucharist makes the church.
—Adage of Pseudo-Jerome[1]

FOR THE LAST FIVE HUNDRED YEARS, there has been an uneasy relationship between Word and sacrament, Protestants stressing the first to the detriment of the second, Catholics stressing the second to the detriment of the first. In semiotic preaching, which makes the communication of the Word as much liturgical as exegetical, Word and sacrament kiss and make up.

A vessel is a conduit for liquid, or in the sacrament of Holy Communion, a cup for the "blood" of Jesus. Every preaching moment is a drop of blood. Every act of giving blood has a sacramental element within it. Giving blood is a salving, saving transduction of the body.

For most of Christian history, the blood of Christ, celebrated daily in the sacrament, was the centerpiece of religious life. It was the sacrament of wine and bread, more than any other signifier or symbol, that caused sons and daughters to prophesy, youth to see visions, elders to dream dreams.[2]

We enter the sacred through ritual process. To live outside ritual is to live outside of spirituality. Preaching is a ritual act, and rituals make us simultaneously think and feel. Ritual memorability comes from reason bonded with emotion. At the same time, rituals help us experience one thing in terms of another.

We live in a world that is as ritually starved as it is ritually out of phase. The word *ritual* is at the heart of "spi*ritual*ity." There are rituals of repetition and rituals of variation. Some rituals are a bouillabaisse of both. Rituals provide people with security from glorying in repetition, and they provide people with adventure from chancing in variance. Whether a ritual of variation or repetition, every ritual should give people something to see, something to hear, something to touch, something to taste, and something to smell.[3] Rituals do important theological work as they perform their sacramental duties. They provide symbolic carriers like authority, participation, transcendence, and immanence for deep theological debates.

The sweet spot of the sacraments is not just the summit of faith in Christ but the very source of faith's vitality. Would God call what we do worship? How can we worship God in spirit and in truth without images and sounds and smells and tastes and touches? Publisher Robin Baird-Smith once asked Scottish novelist Muriel Spark (1918–2006) if he could accompany her to Mass. Spark agreed but warned that she always arrived after the sermon. She could not bear the drivel from the pulpit.[4] Preaching at the Lord's Supper must invite the participants to taste the fruitiness of the vine; to hear the crunch of the bread; to feel its crumbliness on the tongue. Preaching at baptism must help participants feel, whether literally or figuratively, the water wash over them as the winds of the Spirit surround them.

Preachers have become laborers of points rather than painters of pictures and tells of stories, just the opposite of Jesus. Metaphor is at the heart of sacramentality. The whole fabric of sacramental interconnections is held together through metaphor. Some metaphors don't use words. There are verbal metaphors, nonverbal metaphors, and body expressions: gestures, movements, stooped shoulders, sagging mouths, bitten nails, chewed pens, blushing faces. The sacraments are sacred moments for nonverbal metaphors and body expressions, arms that guide the baptized in and out of the water, fingers that care for the bread, hands that cradle the vessel.

God sealed the Abrahamic covenant with a traditional contractual ceremony[6] and with a foreshadowing sign of blood.[7] There are three witnesses to Jesus on earth: the water, the blood, and the Spirit[8]—water for washing, blood for drinking, Spirit for resurrecting.

Anselm of Canterbury (1033–1109) is given the honor of being the first to identify the wound in Jesus' side as the connection to the wounded heart within. His phrase *"Non per dolorem sed per amorem in doloribus"* means "We were not saved through suffering but through love in suffering."

Sacraments are inherently both deeply personal and highly communal. When Jesus' side was pierced as he hung on the cross, "blood and water" issued from the wound.[9] Just as the first Adam's side birthed his relational partner and he was "saved" from a solitary existence, so the second Adam's piercing was a birthing of his spiritual partner and bride, the church.[10] The church is not only Spirit breathed but blood born. Love is its contagion.

Lab Practicum
RE-MEMBERING THE SACRED

There is nothing more irrelevant than the pursuit of relevance. To make the sacraments more EPIC, preachers must be less trend spotters and more spelunkers, those who can rummage around in the past, poke a stick in the attic of Christianity, and discover long-forgotten artifacts and apps, rites and images, fragments of antiquity that you forgot you had, and then creatively use your finds, combining and reshuffling them in new combinations to offer Christ and deepen discipleship for the people in your care. Following are four examples.

1. You can build your sermon around the Hebrew word for "know" (*yada*), which means more than "knowledge" or "knowing about something." To "know" in Hebrew means to be in intimate relationship with someone, as God "knew" Adam and Adam "knew" Eve. The opposite of "knowing God" is not ignorance but rebellion. After you have established what it means to truly "know," challenge each recipient of the bread (or wine) to say two words after they receive the bread and hear the words "The body of Christ broken for you": "I know."

2. You can recount the ancient tradition of the "five holy wounds of Jesus," which in its original form was the two wounded hands, two wounded feet, and wounded side. Or you could redefine the five wounds to encompass all of Jesus' suffering: wounded head (crown of thorns), wounded back (from flagellation), wounded hands, wounded feet, and wounded side. Each one of these wounds could symbolize a different brokenness of the human species.[5] After you explore the cost of the cross, ask your congregation to consider looking you in the eye as they receive the cup, and after they hear you say, "The blood of Christ shed for you," say in response, "And I will live my life for him."

3. Make a centerpiece on the altar of a tower of bread. Big loaves of different kinds of bread stacked on top of each other, loaves of bread from as many continents around the world as are accessible: Greek pita bread, Swedish limpa bread, Jewish challah bread, French bread, German pumpernickel bread, Russian rye bread, Egyptian flatbread, Colombian corn bread, Mexican tortillas, Welsh fruit bread, Serbian

soda bread, African monkey bread, Italian focaccia, Southern hush puppies, Canadian hardtack, Indian naan, English muffin bread, Japanese rice bread, Chilean sopaipilla, and others. Talk about the meaning of the Great Commission, emphasizing that Jesus wants to be incarnated in every culture. You might even want to have different people say in the bread languages, "This is my body, broken for you," and then write out the phrase on a sign where everyone can see it. Then ask the people to come forward to receive the bread from whatever culture they will promise to learn more about and pray for every day for a month. Ask them also to kneel with the bread in their hands and pray for that people group before consuming the bread.

4. One of the largest Christian churches in the world is in Surabaya, Indonesia. I was there to preach at a service where Pastor Alex Tanuseputra served Communion to more than ten thousand people. The ushers brought the bread forward; then Pastor Alex took a host from the ciborium, bowed his head, and held it aloft as the ushers distributed the bread to all the congregation. He did the same with the Communion cups. This simply EPIC act of holding up the elements with heads bowed long enough to take it in unison is an experience I will never forget.

★ ★ ★

"When I compose, I cook with water, and when I conduct, I cook with fire."
—*Pierre Boulez*[11]

★ ★ ★

When we envision a dying Jesus with water and blood pouring from his side, we are witnessing the birthing moment for the sacramental life of the church—both eucharistic and baptismal birthings. In the dying of Christ, the church is born. Just as a woman issues blood and water in birthing a child, the church is born of a labor of love. Jesus was wounded by the Roman soldier at the pleura, which is where Eve was ushered out of Adam's side.

From the blood of sacrifice surges the water of life. In Jesus' promise that the Spirit would flow from his heart[12] to quench the thirsts of the soul and rebirth the world, we have stumbled upon the hidden stream and shrouded secret. Out of the broken heart of Father and Son comes the Holy Spirit.[13] Out of the blood comes the water of life, the spring of paradise reopened; Isaiah's water in the desert discovered;[14] Ezekiel's river pouring out of the temple, making even the Dead Sea fresh;[15] Zechariah's fountain in Jerusalem flowing full and free.[16]

British novelist and mythographer Marina Warner contends, "Blood is the vital fluid, the mystical ink of Christianity, in which the martyrs and many saints sign their professions of faith."[17] When preachers give blood, they tap a vein running back to the cross and the incarnation. As the bride of Christ, the church depends on the blood of Christ for its identity and sustenance.

The blood that stains the church is the blood that sanctifies the church. It is the blood that refuses to let the church become another social organization, another club, another charity, another self-help group. Terry Tekyl, friend and nationally known prayer evangelist, released a book titled *The Presence Based Church.* What I call the *divine intersection,* Tekyl calls *presence-based.* Tekyl shifts the church's focus from seeking more people to seeking more of God.[18] If the church is to be the church that Christ intended, then it must find its identity in the sacramental union with Jesus. As bride of the Savior, the church binds with Christ irrevocably and embodies the love of Christ to the world in his name. The church becomes a sacramental means of grace to the world.

The church has both blood rituals and water rituals. The blood and water that births the church not only symbolizes its Holy Communion with Christ in covenantal bond, but also its process of cleansing and rebirthing that initiates members of the covenant in baptism. Christ's baptism is not just an incarnational presence (baptism of water) but also a bestowal of Pentecostal power (baptism by fire). Our water sacrament has elements of both.

Yet we have weakened our baptismal sacraments in the church. In the Gutenberg world, we replaced the visual with the verbal. Our ancestors led those receiving baptism into rivers and baptisteries where they could drown. When infants were baptized, the priest literally dunked the babies into the water so that they were entirely submerged. Our baptismal fonts are so weak and shallow they barely function as birdbaths.

True semiotic worship embodies the sacramental in its very essence. A preacher is someone who gives you the body and blood of Christ. In the communion of body and blood, bread and wine, Jesus takes us as we are and tells us we are his body and blood, for his grace makes us so.

The Scriptures are a declaration of love, a love letter straight from God's heart, written in red, the primary color of a Christian.

Chapter 18

Blood Chills and Thrills: Impact and Delivery

A sermon on the page is like a figure in a wax museum. The form stands there, but the flash of the eye, the language of the face, the sweep of the hand, the range of the voice, the life and breath are missing. Sermons are never preached in cold blood.

—Haddon Robinson[1]

NO SERMON LIVES UNTIL IT IS SET FREE. A score is not music. A score must be played and notes put in motion for there to be music. But how that score is played determines whether the music lives or dies.

In cold blood, there is only rational engagement. Only when the blood gets "heated" are there chills and thrills. Sermons read from a manuscript make for cold-blooded preaching. Scottish Presbyterian Thomas Chalmers (1780–1847) and Cardinal John Henry Newman (1801–90) always read their manuscripts completely, hardly lifting their eyes from the paper. But that was another culture. Most sermons don't read well. Thomas Long even contends that a "written sermon" is a contradiction in terms. Preaching that sends chills down and thrills up the spines of a twenty-first-century congregation needs incarnational gooseflesh. You can have the best words on paper or even the best thoughts in your head, but if your delivery is disconnected from your people, even the best sermon will fall and hit the ground with an uneventful thud.

The Duke Ellington of homileticians, Bishop Kenneth Ulmer of Faithful Central Bible Church in Inglewood, California, credits Gardner C. Taylor with changing his ministry forever by insisting on the difference between a sermon and a message. "A sermon might well originate with the sermonizer. A message suggests that there is a prior claim and that the messenger is but a conduit. It does not originate with him or her. He or she is a conductor."[2] When we bleed the song of the Lord of Life, we are all only conductors in the grand symphony of creation, choreographers of the victory dance of the risen Christ. The number one law of homiletics, according to Al Fasol, is this: Great preaching "maximizes the message and minimizes the messenger."[3]

★   ★   ★

"No one of himself can preach the grace of God. One can only stand aside and let it shine; the dart of light comes out of the body of light, and the sharp point of the dart which touches and pierces us is called the grace of God."
—*Austin Farrer*[4]

★   ★   ★

A sermon's impact, then, is the stunning realization of grace erupting from a pierced heart. When Christ enters into the delivery, every participant becomes a bleeding heart for the gospel.

The transmission must be good, but so must the reception. There is no great sermon without a great congregation. The congregation must be in a receptive place. A preacher can fail people, but the reverse is also true. The Irving Berlin of homileticians, Brett Blair of sermons.com, says of his days when he was pastor of a United Methodist church, "I never knew what to expect from my sermons when I was preaching. Sometimes, you think you bombed and people will come up and say it was moving. Then another time, when you think you did great, all you will hear is crickets." People fail preachers when they only listen for confirmation that the world and the Bible are exactly how they already see them. As a preacher, all you can do is give your best and then let the Spirit do the rest.

Preaching is like a journey. Preachers are guides who show the way. But for congregants—and preachers too, when they are feeling the Spirit moving—the experience of the uncharted journey is a wondrous adventure. As the trail unfolds, preachers will want to see that people arrive at destinations that they discover on their own with the help of their encounter with Christ. Preachers get the blood flow stirred up. But Christ circulates the blood to the heart. Only Christ makes the heart beat.

Yet there are some "helps" you as a preacher can provide to ensure at least that people are "paying attention" and are ripe for an encounter with the divine. Each preacher will need to customize his or her own helps, or what I call homiletic calisthenics. Here are the homiletic calisthenics I go through before going out to meet my Maker every week. My own personal homiletic calisthenic I call ZIP, which is an acronym for three body-mind-spirit push-ups.

Z is for *zipper*. I have heard too many stories of preachers who didn't check their zipper (or blouse) not to start with this little exercise. The focus on personal appearance is a reminder to use good body language. Be aware of your kinesthetics—posture, gestures, facial expressions.

Then comes *I*, which stands for *image*. There are three parts to image: tongue, teeth, and eyes. Tongue-twister exercises (my standards are "three short sword sheaths"; "lovely lemon liniment"; "sea shells by the seashore") get your mouth moist and your tongue under control. Project your voice to fill the entire space. Breathe for optimal speech. Cultivate your fullest, richest voice. Depending on your content, alter your pitch, your volume, and your rate, and dot all of it with occasional pauses. Think of your sermon as a song. Make it sing.

"Teeth" reminds me to check for food particles (in my case, poppy seeds, since I'm always eating poppy seed bagels). One of the more embarrassing moments in my ministry was preaching on television with black diamonds sparkling in my teeth whenever I smiled.

"Eye" reminds me to eye myself in the mirror to make sure all the other body parts are put together and arranged properly. It reminds me, too, that eye contact needs to be made with each person as often as I can. Ideally, keep eye contact with your participants 100 percent of the time.

The *P* in ZIP is the most important. It stands for *prayer* and puts the acronym ZIP literally to work. Reciting Psalm 51:10, I pray to be zippered in a "right spirit" as I speak (NRSV). I also pray to zipper my own thoughts and desires, and to zip myself in the promise of this verse from Deuteronomy 18:18: "I will put my words in [your] mouth. [You] will tell them everything I command [you]."

I also pray that my message will become for my people an embodied prayer. And not just mine, but a "Lord's prayer" that we all offer with our lives not just our lips. Remember that the greatest impact will be not your performance but their participation. Above all, know that your greatest delivery is the delivery of a relationship, enabling a divine encounter with the person of Jesus Christ.[5]

Interactives

1. If you were asked to preach in an Asian church, how would your sermon be different than the way you would imagine it within your own congregation? How would you alter your "blood supply" to incarnate your sermon within the culture in which you find yourself? How might it be different if in a Hispanic church? On a college campus? In a prison?

2. Can you think of a time when you altered your preaching as the Spirit moved you? What happened? How did it alter your message? How was it received?

3. An example of interactive preaching might be this: "If you could invite any biblical character to be with us here this morning, who would it be and what would you ask him or her?" Play out this exercise with a partner or a group in your "lab." What was your response to this question within your group? What happened when the entire group began speaking?

4. Language itself is metaphorical to the point that Friedrich Nietzsche argued, "What therefore is truth? A mobile army of metaphors, metonymies, anthropomorphisms, in short a sum of human relations which become poetically and rhetorically intensified, metamorphosed, adorned, and after long usage seem to a nation fixed, canonic and binding; truths are illusions of which one has forgotten that they *are* illusions; worn-out metaphors which have become powerless to affect the senses; coins with their images effaced and now no longer of account as coins but merely as metal."[6] In what ways is Nietzsche right? In what ways is he wrong?

5. Colin S. Smith contends that the challenge of preaching to this culture is this: "In the past ... preachers have been able to assume the basic building blocks of a Christian worldview.... You could take texts like John 3:16; Romans 5:8; and Isaiah 53:4–6 and hang them on the line of a Judeo-Christian worldview. The problem in trying to reach postmodern people is that there is no clothesline. So when we try to hang our texts, they fall to the ground in a messy heap....

The great challenge before the preacher is to put up the clothes-line."[7] What do you think? Do you agree with this challenge of the clothesline?

6. In the medieval world, there was less speculation on "how many angels could dance on the head of a pin" than on "how many drops of blood did Christ shed in the passion?" Estimates ranged from 28,000 to 547,000.[8] Discuss what it might mean for even an atheist like Christopher Marlowe (1564–93) in *Doctor Faustus* (1589) to say, "See, see, where Christ's blood streams in the firmament a drop would save me, half a drop!"

7. Annie Dillard tells her writing students to approach a blank sheet of paper as if they were dying and their audience consisted solely of terminal patients. "What would you begin writing if you knew you would die soon? What could you say to a dying person that would not enrage by its triviality?"[9] In what ways is this good advice for preachers as well? How does it not apply?

8. To what extent is preaching a "package deal"? Some studies contend that words convey only 7 percent of our message, tone of voice conveys 38 percent, and body language constitutes 55 percent of our communication.[10] Does this seem extreme? How would you define "the total package"? Is preaching a whole-body art form? How can you make it so?

9. In the African-American song-speech tradition of preaching, there is "tuning" and "whooping." The former is the singing of words; the latter is the saying of words. Henry Mitchell defines whooping as "the use of a musical tone or chant in preaching" as the preacher, usually toward the end of a sermon, moves from speech to song.[11] Have you ever been a part of a worship experience that included "tuning" or "whooping"? If so, tell the story of "embodied preaching" as you've been a part of it.

10. Every preacher needs a homiletic hit parade. What are some of your best sermons?

11. New Zealand novelist Janet Frame (1924–2004) compared writing a novel to "not merely going on a shopping expedition across the border to an unreal land: it is hours and years spent in the factories, the streets, the cathedrals of the imagination, learning the unique functioning of Mirror City, its skies and space, its own planetary

system, without stopping to think that one may become homeless in the world, and bankrupt, abandoned by the Envoy."[12] Why not the same for a preacher crafting a sermon? What metaphor would you use to describe your craft?

12. A Sunday school teacher asked the children just before she dismissed them to go to church, "And why is it necessary to be quiet in church?" Annie replied, "Because people are sleeping." After having slept through a sermon, the poet Carl Sandburg was asked how he could offer an opinion on the sermon. "Sleep is an opinion," Sandburg replied.[13] If Jesus were boring, could he have saved the world? How would you ensure a sermon doesn't evoke merely doze?

13. Evaluate this assessment of current homiletics from the late Calvin Miller: "Preaching is a polygamist with ugly consorts. Preaching is so married to liturgy, architecture, and popular detente that it spends all its energy in running from wife to wife. It doesn't try to set things right, only to keep from getting things wrong. Sermons are often so dead that dying denominations seem the perfect place to deliver them."[14]

14. In a midrash on Genesis 17:9–13, it is revealed that Turnus Rufus, the Roman governor of Palestine in the early second century, asked the great Talmudic sage Rabbi Akiba this question: "If God dislikes a man having a foreskin, why did he create him with one?" Rabbi Akiba replied that God has created an incomplete world in order that human beings should have a role in bringing the world to perfection.

God gives us a mission to accomplish, not to complete. Moses' mission was accomplished but not completed. Otherwise, why Joshua? "It is not thy duty to complete the work but neither art thou free to desist from it."[15]

What does it mean that God has given you a sermon to do, not to complete? And how do you know when you're done?

Part 5

"AB-" DEALING
WITH NEGATIVES

Chapter 19

Blood Clots:
Preacher's Block

WHAT KIND OF A RELIGIOUS TRADITION begins with a surgical procedure? What kind of a profession of faith begins with body alteration? An incarnational one, that's what.

The centerpiece of Christianity is a divine-human exchange that is expressed in the doctrine of the incarnation: God became one of us. The triune God was birthed as a flesh-and-blood human — once definitively, but with new incarnations of that one possible and powerful in every human being. The role of preaching is pivotal in linking the divine and the human in that sacramental story of the God of a billion incarnations, only one of which exhausts the capacitance of God.

Even the most careful lab can prepare a batch of "bad blood." But every precaution is taken to make sure that bad blood goes no further than the lab. What makes something a life-giver can also make it a dealer in death.

Preaching is a life-and-death exchange — more blood sport than chess game. Before you gift blood to others, your blood must be true and your heart in the right place. To be sure, ever since Augustine fought the Donatists, it has been settled: the sacraments as channels of God's grace are effectual irrespective of the giver's personal holiness. We are but vessels, blood vessels that deliver not our own blood but royal blood, the blood of Christ. But there are viruses that can infiltrate the blood supply and spoil your message's impact.

Let's say you have learned the skills to craft your preaching in the semiotic

and narraphoric manner outlined in this book. You have thought about how
to offer up the Jesus story in an EPIC way. What can go wrong?

The following chapters will take you through some of the things that
can go wrong: (1) preacher's block, (2) congregant criticism, (3) bruising
your congregants, (4) the nervous preacher, (5) false props and bad leads,
and (6) dealing with heresies.

★   ★   ★

"I'm just the postman, I deliver the songs."
—*Bob Dylan[1]*

★   ★   ★

First, let's look at the peril we know as preacher's block, the blood clot of
our preaching. Before you even say a word, you can experience a blood clot—
an episode of blockage, a period of time when your creative juices just won't
flow. Sometimes these blockages will occur when you start to think and pray
about your message or read through your Scriptures. Other times they may
occur when you are in the midst of preaching.

Either way, you may be overwhelmed by too many thoughts about the
text, too many pastoral issues, or too much fire-hosing of your creativity that
past week by both friends and enemies. Or the passage may initially, for one
reason or another, leave you cold and wanting for a creative direction.[2] In
literary circles, the Russian word for "writer's block" is *izgoy*, which means
literally a person with a flaw or crack that makes it impossible for them to
perform their role.

How do you turn your flaws into fulcrums for creativity? How do your
cracks become channels of light that enable you to shine, not just leak light?
What to do?

Above all, blood clots need blood thinners. Sometimes a well-timed bit of
humor can come from yourself, while you regather your thought. Sometimes
your block simply stems from too hasty and too thick a reading of the text. It
may take thinning out the text, reading it slowly a dozen times or more, before it
breaks open and begins speaking to you. Advertisers claim it takes seven "hits" to
embed a desired message into the mind of the average person. We are inundated
with thousands of those messages every day. Take the time to read the Scriptures
at least seven times in various ways until you feel the revelational reverb of Jesus'
voice ringing in your ears and the touch of his robe in your hands.

Remember: early Christians heard the Scriptures read. Silent reading in
general, much less the silent reading of the Bible, is a recent innovation. Julius

Caesar admired anyone who could read while talking to others—in other words, who could read silently. The Greeks and Romans had to read aloud, and as late as the Middle Ages, people who could read still read aloud. St. Patrick prayed a hundred and fifty psalms a day out loud.[3] The connection between the audio and the visual was broken by print. The Bible is best read out loud, with feeling, and with others. The Gospels are truth with a story line and sound track. They were meant to be read aloud in liturgical settings and church gatherings.

In the South Korean Tong movement led by Dr. Byoungo Zoh, Christians are being taught to read the Bible out loud in their personal and family devotions. I will never forget talking to some kids who described what it was like to awaken in the morning to the sound of their father reading the Bible.

Another blood thinner is to use the ideas outlined in the part 3 blood-building chapters. Simplify the text by finding the singularities of the story—the driving images, the backstories, the undersongs. Contemplate the ways those singularities work out—and play out—in everyday life.

*   *   *

"'Veni, vedi, velcro'—I came, I saw, I stuck around."
—*Steve Sjogren, master church planter*

*   *   *

Another blood thinner comes from the Roman Catholic process of naming saints. For every saint nominated, there is created a "God's advocate" arguing for sainthood. But at the same time, there is also created a devil's advocate who makes the case why this person should not be canonized. For every idea you have as to how best to tell the story, you can create positive and negative advocates for that idea that fight with each other, and the "sparks are often beaten forth by the flints striking together," as the Puritans used to put it.

Sometimes you may need to immerse yourself more in scholarly sources like commentaries and dictionaries. Or search the Web to jar forth ideas and jump-start your imagination. At times it helps to Google using the image search bar. What kinds of images are associated with the words from the Scripture passages? These pump primings can stimulate your creativity and get your brain networking more organically.

Sometimes a disciplined process of simply highlighting key words and images in the texts will lubricate the connections between the biblical drama and the current dramas of your congregational context. Everyone can train his or her brain to become more adept at creative thinking.

My preferred antidote to preacher's block is what I call "reimaginative reason" or what Jorge Luis Borges called "reasoned imagination," which he deemed the essential skill of any storyteller: reimagine and reincarnate the biblical story in contemporary settings. Make the story into a movie, not just one that takes place in the time it was written, but one that takes place today. Then imagine the story set to music or in conversation and dialogue. Visualize the dialogue. Imagine the feelings or the characters. Imagine yourself as the various speakers, or as someone "in the crowd." What would you be thinking, feeling? What narraphors parallel with other biblical stories, or within other witnesses? What cultural icons are hinted at within those narraphors?

*   *   *

"An effective leader making the rounds asks one,
and only one, question: *Got any good stories?*
Stories are the 'red meat' that animates our 'reasoning
process'; [that] give us 'permission' to act; [that]
are photographs of who we aspire to be; [that] cause
emotional response; [that] connect; [and that] are us.
—*Tom Peters, best-selling author and business consultant*[4]

*   *   *

Smell the story and "realize it" with all your senses. How can you help your people come alive to this story?[5] What problems and issues in your congregants' lives resonate with the biblical narraphors? Television news programs label an interview "Live" to inform the viewers that it is really taking place at that moment. Which images are live in the culture, and which are not?

Automakers build futuristic "concept cars" that never see production but are intended to test the company's innovation and design sensibility. What are your "concept sermons" that never reach the ears of your people but are designed to push the edges of your preaching and force you out of your ruts?

One of the ways to routinize the exercise of your imagination is through what the ancestors called "convocations" with other preachers. Regular associations with other preachers through lectionary groups or ministeriums, or by just maintaining good connections with colleagues, is a surefire way to jog your creative ideas. Learn from other preachers, let yourself be inspired by other preachers, but don't compare yourself to them or copy them.

You can also get ideas and make connections by subscribing to homiletic resources in print and online, as well as reading randomly in unfamiliar subject areas such as art, science, technology, and architecture. You don't get out of a preacher's block by keeping on doing what got you there. Do the unexpected. Prime your creativity. Liberate your imagination. Learn from great communicators like the Wesley brothers, who "plundered the Egyptians" and popularized the metaphors and motifs of the "high culture" of their day.[6] If T. S. Eliot is right that mature poets steal and improve on what they have stolen while immature poets merely imitate and deface, then Dick Watson is right: "Charles Wesley demonstrates his maturity on every page."

Finally, consider this: preacher's block every now and then may even be good for preachers. It gives us something to push against.

Chapter 20

Blood Feuds and Blood Baths: Handling Criticism

Judge not the preacher; for he is thy Judge.
If thou mislike him, thou conceiv'st him not.
God calleth preaching folly. Do not grudge
To pick out treasures from an earthen pot.
— George Herbert[1]

THE ANCIENTS BELIEVED it was possible to kill someone with a glance. Some of your parishioners still do. How do you handle killer looks and critics baying for blood?

After blood has been donated, its red cells are separated from the plasma. Parishioners do that as well. As soon as the blood of Christ has been donated, they start taking it apart.

There is no "privilege of the pulpit" that provides immunity to criticism. There are cough-free congregations—you can get no rise out of them on Sunday—but blood cries can be heard on Monday. There are congregations that are known for coughing up blood—constantly complaining, always negative. Some fight among themselves and attempt to triangulate the pastor within their feuds. Others blame the pastor for everything from poor finances to a bad hair day. Some criticize the pastor for trying to do too much, and others for not trying enough. In fact, in some congregations, criticizing the preacher is their favorite blood sport. Every preacher will know the smell of cooking goose. Every preacher will discover that a punch in the mouth really hurts. Every preacher will swallow hard to love those members who have mastered the art of being difficult.

284

Blood Feuds and Blood Baths: Handling Criticism

In *Huckleberry Finn*, Mark Twain portrays Ermeline Granger Ford as so sour that when she died, "with her disposition, she was having a better time in the graveyard." You can't please some people. If you seek to be a people pleaser instead of preaching to please God, you might as well mount your head on a dartboard and hand out darts. There are conductors who conduct for the orchestra (Toscanini) and conductors who conduct for the audience (Bernstein). There are preachers who preach for God, and preachers who preach for the people. These words from Jeremiah should be framed and displayed in every preacher's study, for there will be times when it will seem you are just "not getting through" and you will be tempted to "tickle ears":[2] "You shall speak all these words to them, but they will not listen to you; and you shall call to them, but they will not answer you."[3]

Some preachers believe that if they do all the "right things," the entire congregation will surely like them. These preachers are headed down the road to Burnout Junction. You will be criticized, and it can be argued, the more "right things" you do the more you will be criticized. Machiavelli was right about some things: hatred is gained as much by good works as by evil ones, as much by excellence as by mediocrity. Try to build bridges, and you will be shot at from both banks. Preaching is not about being "right" in the eyes of the congregation but "being righteous" in the eyes of God.

The first sermon at Pentecost given by Peter ("standing up with the Eleven"—never stand alone) includes a key phrase: "I can tell you confidently."[4] The Greek word is *parrhesia*, which appears everywhere in Acts after the day of Pentecost. We translate it as "boldness," and it comes from the political vocabulary of the Greek city-states, meaning "the freedom to say all." However, the freedom felt by the disciples had nothing to do with any constitutional provision, but with resurrection endowments from the Holy Spirit.

In the Johannine letters, *parrhesis* means "the confidence we have before God."[5] This is the kind of boldness preachers need. To exercise the "call" of preaching is to speak with holy boldness. But the exercise of *parrhesis* is not bloodless. Think of Peter and John before the Sanhedrin;[6] Paul in Damascus;[7] Paul and Barnabas in Antioch,[8] Iconium,[9] and Ephesus;[10] Paul before King Agrippa.[11] What follows "holy boldness" is seldom hammocks and lawn chairs, but harassings and harnessings. Possibly no preacher of the gospel in the history of Christianity has not had the word *heretic* spreading like an oil slick over his or her name. The last people from whom you will ever hear descants on the dignity of humanity and the goodness of the soul are the spouses of preachers.

Curators of correctitude abound in every congregation, people whose idea of letting their light shine is to illuminate the wrongs, failings, and mistakes of others, especially the preacher. Such people will flail at your failings without ceasing, and it will seem at times as if every Sunday a firing squad is ready to riddle your body with bullets.

Their behavior reminds me of the story of a Boy Scout troop out on a first-aid training exercise: two young scouts were sent into the woods to play the role of "victim."

"Lay out here and wait for us to come to give you first aid," was the instruction.

The troop found the first little boy, but they took so long to minister to him that the second little boy became discouraged. When the troop finally got to the place where he was supposed to be, they found a note that said: "I have bled to death and gone home."

After you've bled your best, some people will just go home and serve "roast preacher" for lunch.

The best way to handle the scourge of criticism? The theological answer is to keep your eyes fixed on Jesus. Be a God pleaser, not a people pleaser. No doubt, being "prophetic" can become an excuse for being a failure. But the worst failure is a power failure, not an applause failure.

There are also some practical techniques you can use, responses inspired by Jesus himself. Perhaps one of the most interesting and stunning retorts in history was given by Jesus in response to the question, "Are you king of the Jews?" His answer: "So you say."[12]

Sometimes the best answers to criticism are given in the fewest words: (1) "So you say"; (2) "Say more"; (3) "You may be right." These three phrases are powerful dart diffusers.

One of the best ways to diffuse leers and fleers is to acknowledge the critic's sneers. The words "So you say" acknowledge the criticism but do not necessarily grant it power.

A second, perhaps even better, response is to listen: "Say more." In "deep listening," the words "say more" invite the critic to speak his or her mind. When you invite someone to criticize you and show them you can listen to and learn from their criticism, the blow often softens immediately. You have brought the ball into your own court by inviting the critic's opinion and by showing you are open to hearing it. "Say more" diffuses the "oppositional" strength of the criticism. "Say more" also gives the "saying" person time to hang themselves. John Randolph of Roanoke, one of my favorite nineteenth-century Virginia orators, once said of Henry Clay, "He has cut his throat with his own tongue."

Third, "You may be right" may be the most powerful of all responses to criticism. It deflects the attack with a death dismissal. It also showcases the humility of one who boasts, like the apostle Paul, not in strength but in weakness.[13]

At times, Jesus didn't respond to criticism at all. At other times, he responded with parables or riddles, humor or irony. Jesus was not only an expert semiotician of the Scriptures and of his culture, but he was a phenomenal semiotician of people. He "read" his crowds, the people he encountered, and especially his critics. Jesus most often responded to criticism by citing Scripture, as he demonstrated when Jesus' greatest opposer threw the book at him in the wilderness. Jesus could not be dissuaded or detoured from his mission, and he beat back every brandishing of the Psalms with an artillery blast from Deuteronomic writings. To deal with criticism well is to listen well and learn from the criticism by searching your heart, but keeping your eyes all the while on Jesus.

How much of your preaching life will you misspend aiming too low and succeeding rather than aiming too high and failing? Failure is a mark of faithfulness. Besides, we all say silly things from time to time. We all do silly things from time to time. Some of your metaphors will fall flat on their faces or will bounce back and slap you in the face. Jesus was less concerned with his disciples failing than with them succeeding at what matters least. Preachers are not "talkers" but "witnesses," a word that comes from the Greek *martyreō*. When you speak the truth, you can expect to reap the consequences, especially when you speak the truth as if it had consequences.

✱   ✱   ✱

"Nero finally caught Paul, put him in prison and cut off his head. Now we call our dogs 'Nero' and our sons 'Paul.'"
—*Winkie Pratney*[14]

✱   ✱   ✱

But Jesus did give his disciples then and now a ritual to get us to quit quitting. I call it Jesus' sacrament of failure.[15] He warned us that we would not be received well everywhere we go. He assured us that sowing seeds was more important than success. Reaping the harvest was God's bailiwick, not our business. Preachers are sowers. Some seed falls on good ground, some on hard ground. If our message is not welcomed, we are to shake the dust off our feet. I have been in the midst of many sermons and have started the sacramental shuffle.

"AB-" Dealing with Negatives

Some of the greatest artists were severely criticized or discounted in their own times and by their own people and colleagues. German monarch Kaiser Wilhelm II informed composer Richard Strauss to his face that he was "one of the worst" to ever compose music. Novelist Franz Kafka received this letter from a reader named Dr. Wolff:

> Sir, you have made me unhappy. I purchased your *Metamorphosis* and gifted it to my cousin, but she could not make sense of the story. My cousin gave it to her mother; she could not explain it. Her mother gave it to another cousin, but she could not explain it either. And now they have written to me, the supposed doctor in the family. But I am at a loss. Sir! I spent months fighting the Russians in the trenches without batting an eyelash. I won't stand idle while my reputation among my cousins goes to the devil. Only you can come to my aid. You must, since you cooked up this stew in the first place. So tell me please what my cousin ought to think of the *Metamorphosis*.[16]

My favorite criticism, however, is a response of an Irish woman to a Roman Catholic archbishop's sermon on marriage: "'Twas a fine sermon the father gave this morning. I only wish I knew as little about the subject as he does."

★   ★   ★

"Those who judge a sermon will always find plenty to criticize; those who listen for divine wisdom may receive hints of it even from the mouth of a man so unwise as to claim that he speaks in the name of the Father, and of the Son, and of the Holy Ghost."
—*Austin Farrer (1904–68), Anglican theologian*[17]

★   ★   ★

Someone has calculated that 80 percent of the references to the poet John Milton were negative in his lifetime.[18] When Luther posted his Ninety-Five Theses and called for a debate, no one came. When the newly acceded King James I published his Bible in 1611 to stiff-arm the Puritans, it was considered a shameful compromise and failure. Thanks largely to William Wilberforce, on February 23, 1807, the vote to abolish the slave trade in the British West Indies was 283–16. But that lopsided vote doesn't tell the whole story. William Wilberforce spent twenty years lobbying in support of abolition. In the 1790s, he was slandered in the press, physically assaulted, subject to death threats. He was once challenged to a duel. During certain periods, he had to travel with a bodyguard. His spirit was almost broken many times. He even suffered a nervous breakdown.

Blood Feuds and Blood Baths: Handling Criticism

In the early nineteenth century, when Robert Fulton first showed off his new invention called the steamboat, skeptics were crowded on the bank yelling, "It'll never start. It'll never start." It did. In fact, it got going with a lot of clanking and groaning. As it made its way down the river, the skeptics were quiet.

For one minute.

Then they started shouting, "It'll never stop. It'll never stop."

Sometimes *kairos* may take years for the sequences to fall and the providences of the divine to play themselves out. Do not judge before its time, Paul admonished, as he lifted up a God whose clock keeps perfect time.[19] The quintessence of being a "successful preacher" may be seen more in the person of Moses peering from the distance at Mount Nebo than in the crowds who were getting their feet damp as they walked through the Jordan River into Canaan.[20]

Who wouldn't rather preach to the choir? But we're called to take on the greatest challenge any public speaker faces: change hearts and minds. Of course, preachers can't persuade anyone of anything. The Holy Spirit does the persuading. The preacher's job is to sow the seeds, enable an encounter with God, tell the Story and name the Name. The Holy Spirit does the rest. We can bring the chalice to the body, but we cannot make the body drink.

★   ★   ★

"Dogs bark at what they don't understand."
—Heraclitus

★   ★   ★

You will always have skeptics in your midst. But with Christ in front of you, beside you, and at your back, you will take your ministry wherever the Spirit leads you. You may never be "successful" by the world's standards. Since when did we come to judge how much a preacher is doing for the kingdom by the size of a salary or sanctuary, or by a statue in the guild? But if you are committed to "giving blood" in the name of Christ, you will always be blessed as a God pleaser. The more you fear God, the less you fear critics.

In fact, if there is any "trophy" to preaching, it may just be the scars we bear from the criticism and conflict and failure. Far from scars being something to be ashamed of, scars are our Oscars. Every preacher has them, and God gave us artists to be there to frame them. Some days we just need more artists around us than others.

"AB-" Dealing with Negatives

In his autobiography, the Richard Rodgers of homileticians, Norman Vincent Peale, tells about failing miserably in the pulpit one Sunday. When he confided his embarrassment to a colleague, this is the response he got: "Tell you what, Norman. When you are in the pulpit, just do the best you can. And when it's over, come down and forget it. The congregation will, and you might as well make it unanimous."[21]

Chapter 21

Blood Hematoma: Avoiding Bruising

> No one has a right so to preach as to send hearers away on flat tires.
> Every discouraging sermon is a wicked sermon.
>
> —Clovis Chappell

SOME PEOPLE CONFUSE AN "ANOINTING" with getting angry. The more "anointed" preachers get, some think, the angrier these preachers get.

I'm tired of angry, "Ain't it awful" sermons. Negative sermons attract negative people.

If your sermon nags, bludgeons, swipes, pressures, slashes, or beats down, you have not "given blood" but "spilled blood." Spilling blood may just be the worst "sin" of a preacher. If your congregation leaves worship bruised instead of blooming, you have not brought your people to the beauty of the resurrection garden but have left them cold in the tomb with nails still in their hands.

Preaching should be a lifting experience, not a limiting or lacerating one.

The narraphor of Jesus forgiving the adulteress woman is a good example of avoiding bruising. Jesus does not dismiss or negate the fact that the woman in the story has sinned. Yet he sends her off in the grace of forgiveness, telling her to turn (metanoia) back to God. The story crescendos to its crucial image: Jesus does not throw stones.

Preaching must never throw stones. Preaching points to the rock of salvation that breaks the power of sin and bestows the body with grace. That doesn't mean that preaching pats people on the head and tells them what good boys and girls they are. There are no unmixed motives. Everyone in the body (including the preacher) needs the grace of God in everything. But in the "blood and body" of Jesus, there is beauty not bruises, cleansing not stripping, saving not savaging.

This is no more the case than in the preaching of what I call "thin-ice" sermons—difficult stories, demanding truths, and emotionally charged subjects—messages that are uncomfortable to hear and hard to tell.[1] Such stories include, for example, divorce, suicide, rape, incest, racism, sexism, any of the seven deadly sins. The preacher who fails to address such subjects, while at the same time avoiding the scandalous or the sensational or the confessional, is guilty of dereliction of duty. But when you're on thin ice, you move laterally—like a skater who pushes sideways to go forward. The best thin-ice sermon takes the congregation by the scruff of its clichés, leads it down comfortably predictable paths, and then swerves sharply sideways.

Loren Niemi and Elizabeth Ellis have done stellar work on the telling of difficult stories. "Stories are as personal as fingerprints and as mutable as mercury. They are also potentially as toxic as mercury if the story is not understood by the teller—or is told to the wrong audience in the wrong context or for the wrong reason."[2] Niemi and Ellis argue for a three-legged stool for the telling of difficult stories. One leg is trust; the second leg is permission; the third leg is ownership.[3]

The leg of trust means that you can be counted on to get your people safely home, that they will not be abandoned to find their own way back.[4] You can take people into blurry, confusing, strange places where they think they are lost—but only if you bring them back with great certainty, confidence, and new enlightenment.

★   ★   ★

"The secret of a good sermon is to have a good beginning and a good ending and having the two as close together as possible."
—*George Burns*

★   ★   ★

The leg of permission means you need your listeners' permission to tell this story now, that everyone knows you have protected people's identity, that if you use someone's name, you have their permission.[5]

The leg of ownership means you have internalized the story to the point that you "own" the story, and if it's about you, you are willing for people to know this about you.[6] You might say that once you become a preacher, nothing bad can ever happen to you again. For the rest of your life, everything that happens to you is grist for the homiletic mill. It's all good material.

Preaching that releases depth charges, not stink bombs, will be careful about what is revealed about the preacher's personal life. It is one thing to confess your humanity; it is quite another to showcase and flaunt it. Make yourself look perfect, and people can't relate, because they can never achieve your perfection. Rip the scabs off your festering sores and let your wounds bleed in front of your people, and you risk losing your credibility and respect. Share the story of your struggles; confess your woundedness—but not the details of the darkness or your deepest secrets and regrets. Best of all, share how you are one of Jesus' "Duh!-ciples" just like everyone else.

Chapter 22

Blood Pressure:
The Nervous Preacher

> When one for the first time mounts the pulpit, no one would believe
> how very afraid one is! One sees so many heads down there! Even now
> when I am in the pulpit I look at no one but tell myself they are merely
> blocks of wood which stand there before me, and I speak the word of
> my God to them.
>
> —Martin Luther[1]

PREACHING HAS MUCH IN COMMON with tightrope walking and
bungee jumping. Some preachers have nerves of steel about the challenge.
Others tremble in their TOMS at the sight of a pulpit and even more so at
the thought of speaking without it!

I've seen preachers holding the sides of a pulpit in a death grip. Some
preachers eschew looking anyone in the eye, as though doing so may cause
them to drop dead from exposure. Some preachers' voices take off by themselves in quake and trill. Still others may find themselves utterly lost in the
midst of a sentence, unable to carry on.

At some time it happens to all preachers: pure panic from hypertension.

High blood pressure comes most often from anxiety. But it also comes
from being under constant attack. "Performance anxiety," participation
dread, fear of criticism, dealing with mistakes, fear of intimacy, to name
the most obvious, all can cause a preacher's pressure to rise. Squeamishness
is very personal.[2] These "limps"[3] and other insecurities can make taking on
the authority of one's calling in front of a large group of people an adventure
in monumental terror.

Blood Pressure: The Nervous Preacher

What's a nervous preacher to do? How do you lower your blood pressure so that your preaching becomes less an experience of emergency room trauma and more of a walk through the garden with God?

One way is to spend time before you give your sermon in prayer and meditation, either alone or with a prayer team. Charles Haddon Spurgeon was once asked about the secret of his ministry. After a moment's pause, he responded, "My people pray for me."[4]

Another help to relaxation is to trial run your sermon out loud so that you feel more secure and prepared. It also helps to think of your sermon more as a conversation and a participation than a "performance."

Another method is to think less about producing a successful sermon and more about telling a story that resonates in one person's heart. Let go of your control. Conceive your message not within a logic of control but within a logic of risk and trust. Worry less about whether you labor in vain than whether you let Jesus speak in and through you. Worry less about rewarding your "golden tonsils" with gold medals than about throwing out the golden fleece and trusting the Spirit to bring it home.

John Wesley believed that "happiness is holiness." But a preacher named Fearing defined happiness as the ability to preach like Wesley. One day Preacher Fearing said to Wesley, "If I could preach like you, I should be happy."

"Sir," said Mr. Wesley, "we are building God's temple. Go now, read the third chapter of Nehemiah, and learn that he who repaired the dung gate was counted of as much honour as he who touched the gate of the fountain. All did their bit; you and I can do no more."[5]

Preachers are disciples of Jesus just as every sheep in the fold. The more you see yourself as "one of the sheep," the less pressure you will put on yourself to be an "outstanding shepherd." Step down from the pedestal of "A+ Preacher" and tell the story of Jesus to the "little ones" around you.

Sometimes we need to "preach to ourselves." It's a spiritual practice preachers need to learn and even to teach to their congregations. Sometimes when we get discouraged and disheveled in spirit, we need to preach to our own hearts. Jeremiah did this when he said, "This I call to mind, and therefore I have hope."[6]

Chapter 23

Blood Doping and Bad Blood: False Props and Bad Leads

There comes a time when we must take the bull by the tail and face the situation.

—W. C. Fields

SOME OF MY APPALACHIAN ANCESTORS put it like this: "My sermon dribbled off of my lip, down my shirt, onto my shoes, and onto the floor." What happens when your blood just doesn't pump, and you can't get it to emerge from your vein in anything but a trickle? You can't squeeze blood from a finger if it isn't flowing—or from a vein if you haven't got the line in right.

Warren Wiersbe says, "Every sermon is not going to be a 'great' sermon. Every sermon should be your best sermon. But not every sermon is going to be the greatest sermon you've ever preached."[1] On the other hand, sometimes, things just go horribly wrong: "It had the wrong speaker, with the wrong message, in the wrong tone, at the wrong time, and even in the wrong language."

So, what do you do with bad sermons?

Sometimes you have to try another line or tap another vein or go in at an angle or from the underside. Sometimes you can salvage enough to keep on going. Other times you just have to start again.

Every preacher needs a hazardous waste bin, where some sermons should go that are just not worth sending to the blood bank. Poet Margaret Avison sends her bad poems to the archive at the University of Manitoba, which is where her writings are being kept "so people can see how very bad my writing sometimes is."[2] Preachers are human. And even the most gifted preacher has a bad sermon or two in the blood bin.

296

Yet you can look out for certain things that may cause your sermon to drizzle and fizzle instead of streaming a spray of grace with fire in the blood. Sometimes you multiply when you should subtract. Sometimes you need to infuse your mind with fresh food: get creative. Sometimes you have to let go and let Jesus do the talking.

DON'T MULTIPLY WHEN YOU SHOULD SUBTRACT

In the fourteenth century, William of Ockham, a Franciscan friar, warned against explanations that are more complicated than they need to be. Ockham's razor (or Occam's razor) is the principle that "entities must not be multiplied beyond necessity" (*entia non sunt multiplicanda praeter necessitate*). In other words, the simplest explanation is usually the correct one, when "simplest" is not defined by the time or number of words it takes to express the theory. The principle is often expressed in Latin as the *lex parsimoniae*—the law of parsimony, law of economy, or law of succinctness.[3]

What does Ockham's razor mean for a preacher? Keep it simple! Keep it out of the clouds and put it into the hands of the people where they can smell it, see it, feel it, touch it. The simple truth is always the best.

GET CREATIVE

Every now and then you will run up against a wicked sermon—where "wicked" does not mean "evil," but a sermon resistant to resolution and completion, as in "That's a wicked problem." Every now and then you will feel like you are not connecting. For example, listen to this exchange between an author and a critic:

"What's your opinion of my book?"
"It's worthless."
"I know, but I'd like to hear it anyway."

A wicked sermon can be an aid to stimulating creativity if you "blood dope" the wickedness. The practice of "blood doping" in track and field events means giving yourself injections of your own, previously taken, oxygenated blood just prior to an endurance event. There is a homiletic practice of "blood doping" that is good, not bad. Inject yourself with some of your own prior creativity. Delve into past sermons and notes, especially your personal "classics," those sermons so strong as to remain meaningful through all your transformations and recognizable and replicable in all your contexts.

Look for alternate ways to present old ideas and get the blood moving through your veins again. Spend some bonus time in prayer. Oxygenate your blood with deep breaths of the Holy Spirit.

If your sermon still isn't "making the cut," you can do one of two things. First, drop it into the bin, dig out one of your former sermons, and give one of them instead. But remember: no sermon should ever be given twice to the same group of people. Reuse a sermon only with a different group of people in a new setting. Old sermons may still be applicable if they're adaptable to your new context. Second, give the message anyway in all its "wickedness." The Claude Debussy of homileticians, Ralph Sockman (1889–1970), insisted that once a year a preacher should bring to the congregation a message so odd, so off-beat, so "wicked," that few will know what you're talking about, thereby reestablishing your reputation as a deep thinker.

*   *   *

"A difficulty is a light; an insuperable difficulty is a sun."
—Paul Valéry[4]

*   *   *

Last but not least, if your blood is especially anemic one day, or your creative juices run dry, you may need a total blood transfusion. Maybe your imagination has shrunk to "cubicle creativity" where the size of your ideas is directly proportional to the space in which you're stuck. If so, get out of doors. Get out of your carrel. Come apart (as Jesus did) to the mountains, the water, or the desert. Attend a conference, preferably about something other than preaching. Randomize your life with rituals that rout your routines.[5] Surround yourself with new experiences. "Plunder the Egyptians," as John Wesley put it.

Or, in my variation of that theme, plunder the blunders. Whenever you find a blunder in life, there is something theologically deep in that blunder to be plundered. For example, a woman wrote the following note to an insurance company: "Dear Sirs: I can no longer afford to pay monthly installments on my husband's life insurance, as he died last July." How many Christians have at their disposal the inexhaustible "riches of his glorious inheritance in his holy people,"[6] and have never gone to the bank?

Whatever you do, get creative—get out more; listen twice as much as you speak; don't surround yourself with like-minded people but with people who are very different from you. Examine yourself to determine the extent to which you are still curious, imaginative, questioning, and creative—or to see whether you've allowed yourself to become conforming, unimaginative, predictable, and uncomfortable with novelty.

LET JESUS DO THE TALKING

Scottish preacher James Denney once said, "No man can bear witness to Christ and himself at the same time. No woman can at once give the impression that she is clever and that Christ is mighty to save."[7] Preaching differs from public speaking precisely here: "My message and my preaching were not with wise and persuasive words, but with a demonstration of the Spirit's power, so that your faith might not rest on human wisdom, but on God's power."[8] The story of God resounds more powerfully than anything, even more powerfully than our pathetic stumblings.

The Mozart of homileticians, Victorian preacher Charles Haddon Spurgeon, struggled with depression all his life. In fact, his depression was so severe that in his later years he was absent from the pulpit nearly a third of the time. Yet when he did preach, the experience was life altering. Sometimes you just have to let Jesus do the talking.

Chapter 24

Blood Poisoning: Dealing with Heresies

> You poison the very air we breathe.
> —Letter from Leo Tolstoy, preacher of universal love,
> to his wife, Sophia[1]

HERESIES ARE VIRAL. Especially ones that dwell in our popular culture. "Jesus was married." "The resurrection didn't happen." "Jesus didn't really exist." "Jesus was really the name for an amanita muscaria mushroom cult." The list goes on and on.

Yet these are not the most difficult "heresies" to overcome. For the most part, the heresies that sound the most extreme are the easiest to debunk. It is the subtle ones that seep into the blood like a slow virus or a lethal bacteria and eat away faith from the inside out.

Some heresies are like a bad diet or a diet too rich for the blood. And sometimes we don't even realize they've poisoned us until they are deeply invested in our life stream. What are some of these stealthy bugs? What follows is a short discussion about some of the most potent blood poisons and how to get rid of them.

1. CHRISTIANITY WITHOUT A MESSIAH (WHO NEEDS JESUS?)

Today you can go into some churches and sit through an entire service and never hear the name of Jesus. The excessive focus on seeker sensitivity, easy ecumenism, empty diversity, political correctness, and cultural atheism have all surreptitiously been planting the seeds of anything goes—ism within our Christian sensibilities.[2] These "bugs" have the effect, however, of robbing

Christians of identity. Without Christ there is no Christ-ianity. Many people are afraid to "offend" others with their faith in Christ. I will never forget the shock of hearing one of my homiletic heroes, Ernest T. Campbell, argue, "The term 'God' can be unifying. The name 'Jesus' has proved to be divisive."[3] Yet the words of Jesus echo loud and clear:

> "Whoever is ashamed of me and my words, the Son of Man will be ashamed of them when he comes in his glory."[4]

> "If anyone is ashamed of me and my words in this adulterous and sinful generation, the Son of Man will be ashamed of them when he comes in his Father's glory with the holy angels."[5]

> Do not be ashamed about the testimony about our Lord or of me his prisoner. Rather, join with me in suffering for the gospel, by the power of God.[6]

To "take up your cross and follow Jesus" means not to be embarrassed to name the name of Jesus. Every sermon I've been able to construct, every thought I've come up with, every wild idea I've dug up, one day I will lay on the altar of eternity. And in the presence of Jesus, it will fade.

If we are to rid our congregations of the heresy of Jesus Deficit Disorder (JDD),[7] we need to do what our ancestors called "plead the blood"—preach the stories of Jesus. Truth fashions an existence for itself in Jesus, who incarnates the divine in everything he does.

2. CHRISTIANITY CAN BE AN INDIVIDUAL SPIRITUAL EXPERIENCE

In our culture, approximately 92 percent of people believe in God or a "higher power." Many are searching for a sense of the spiritual. The word *spirituality* has become the catchword of our culture for anything and everything that can be made into a "personal religion." You can order your brand of spirituality the same way you order your coffee or a personal pizza.

But spirituality without embodied expression in a religious community is not much more than inverted narcissism. Religion is embodied spirituality. And embodiments are not pretty. Social organization is good, but show me a pretty government. Healing is wonderful, but show me a pretty emergency room. Spirituality is essential, but show me a pretty church.

Spirituality today has become the Ashtoreth or Astarte of our societies. There is no such thing as "spiritless" spirituality. And one needs to be very careful what "spirits" one is worshiping. Christianity is neither individual nor merely spiritual. Christianity is the most relational religion in the world. It is a covenantal faith with its embodiment in Christ. To worship Christ is to engage in a communal act, to be in relationship with God, self, others, and the world, and to see the Holy Spirit as life giver and life sustainer. To make Christianity merely "spiritual" and not "religious" is to deny the person of Jesus himself. As preachers, we need to preach the incarnational presence of Christ to a body that embodies the life and blood of Jesus.

★   ★   ★

"Throw religion out of the door; it flies back by the window."
—*Jonathan Benthall*[8]

★   ★   ★

"Speaking the truth in love, we will grow to become in every respect the mature body of him who is the head, that is, Christ. From him the whole body, joined and held together by every supporting ligament, grows and builds itself up in love, as each part does its work."[9]

3. WORSHIPING IDOLS (MONEY, CHURCH, BUILDINGS, AND BIBLES)

We all have our golden calves. Our serpents on a stick. Dangling carrots. And many Christians worship more than just Christ Jesus. In fact, if most churches were to honestly examine their missions—not the ones written beautifully on paper but the real ones, the ones dearest to their time, finances, wants, and desires—people would find not Jesus at the center but some other golden calf instead. What does your church talk about around the conference table? Where do the bulk of your finances go? What comes first? For some even the Bible itself has taken the place of the person of Jesus Christ as the object of our worship.

Whenever we are worshiping objects instead of the "person" of Jesus, we are engaging in the heresy of the "golden calf." When your sermons are focused on allowing the blood of Jesus to change the hearts and lives of people, you move always closer to smashing the power of those idols. Is Jesus your first love?

4. GNOSTICISM (MATERIAL DOESN'T MATTER; THE BODY IS NOT GOOD)

In our culture, the need for touch and things that rebuke gnosticism is getting stronger and stronger. We live in an almost "touchless" culture. As isolated people, we hunger for touch. Whether due to political correctness, rules, fears, or neglect, we avoid touching each other. Yet Jesus understood the amazing power of touch to heal. A body that does not touch, that does not acknowledge its own substance, is a body that has negated itself.

In our worship, we need to bring back the power of touch. The beauty of the incarnation is that Jesus is both fully human and fully divine, not merely divine nor half and half, what J. K. Rowling might call a "mudblood." Jesus was a physical person like you and me, who experienced life with all the physical senses. The church has so demonized the body that few preachers ever preach from the Song of Songs. We need to keep the bug of gnosticism out of our churches so that people can go about the business of making relationships and touching the lives of others with their real hands.

> A woman was there who had been subject to bleeding for twelve years. She had suffered a great deal under the care of many doctors and had spent all she had, yet instead of getting better she grew worse. When she heard about Jesus, she came up behind him in the crowd and *touched* his cloak, because she thought, "If I just *touch* his clothes, I will be healed." Immediately her bleeding stopped and she felt in her body that she was freed from her suffering.
>
> At once Jesus realized that power had gone out from him. He turned around in the crowd and asked, "Who *touched* my clothes?"
>
> "You see the people crowding against you," his disciples answered, "and yet you can ask, 'Who *touched* me?'"
>
> But Jesus kept looking around to see who had done it. Then the woman, knowing what had happened to her, came and fell at his feet and, trembling with fear, told him the whole truth. He said to her, "Daughter, your faith has healed you. Go in peace and be freed from your suffering."[10]

5. BAALISM (IF WE INVOKE GOD, GOD WILL COME)

Contemporary worship, with its summoning of the spirits and its pleading with God to "come down" and "visit us" and show up, sounds more Baalistic than Christian. God is already there. It's not God who needs to show up for us; it's we who need to show up for God.

Many of our churches have what we call an "invocation." I have never liked this term. We may call on God, but we don't "invoke" God. We don't call down the deity. We don't demand God's presence. We make ourselves aware of God's presence that is already around us.

I prefer the term *in vocation*. We are all called "into vocation," to be servants of God in the world. God does not come at our command. We do not exist to be "pleased by God." Instead, we exist to be pleasing to God. God is not at our beck and call, programmed to answer our every want and need. As preachers, we need to be aware of the heresy of Baalism in our prayers, in our worship, and in our lives.

Why do you *call* me, *"Lord, Lord,"* and *do not* do what I say?[11]

6. PHARISAISM AND COVENANT BREAKING (RULES INSTEAD OF RELATIONSHIPS)

"We never did it that way before," has always been known as the "death sentence" of the church. When a church becomes obsessed with rules, values, and traditions that have little to do with Jesus and everything to do with personal preferences and control, you have descended into the familiar territory of "pharisaism." Tradition helps you worship, but you don't worship the tradition.

Jesus came to tell a different story—one in which love rules and overturns every table. One in which forgiveness and mercy trump rules and regulations. In Jesus' day, breaking of one's relational "walk with God" was considered a breech of covenant (a breech of relationship). For Jesus, faith and love are about how well you cultivate your relationships, not how well you live by the rules. Even take the Ten Commandments, Jesus says. If you remember the first, you have taken care of them all!

As a preacher, make *love* and relationships the core of your story of Jesus. Keep pharisaism from infiltrating your churches.

"Love the Lord your God with all your heart and with all your soul and with all your strength and with all your mind."[12]

"What goes into someone's mouth does not defile them, but what comes out of their mouth, that is what defiles them."[13]

7. FINGER-POINTING AND PROJECTION: THE GOD COMPLEX

Perhaps the greatest heresy of all is the one that pastors assume themselves, and many parishioners as well: the seat of God!

Whether in judging, controlling, acting self-righteousness, or imparting guilt, when humans assume the seat of God, truth takes a backseat. What are your personal agendas? We will take a closer look at this kind of blood lust in chapter 25 because it is such a prominent "heresy." In fact, ironically, it is the "heresy" Jesus was finally arrested for committing: saying that he was God!

When we take on the "power and authority" invested in us by Jesus, we become not our own voice, but Jesus' voice in and to the world. This is why the doctrine of the incarnation is so very important. To "imitate" Jesus is to assume we have the means and the power to take on the world and the facility to "interpret" what Jesus would do in any given situation. Not only does "imitation" give us the power to wield our own judgments, but it reduces the person of Jesus in the world today to mere imitative characteristics. Not imitation but *impartation* channels the power of the risen Christ who is here and present within the body today with the power and authority to heal and save.

Paul reminded us that Jesus lives in and through us and is wedded to the body of Christ, the church. This is the essence of semiotic preaching—to design an experience in which people can be transformed by the missional, relational, and incarnational power of Jesus the Christ, alive in the world through each one of us together. As a preacher, make sure you are allowing "room" for Jesus. Too many preachers do more "finger-pointing" than laying on of hands. The fingers you want to feel are God's—when he lays his hand on you and says, "With you I am well pleased."

> Then Jesus came to them and said, "All authority in heaven and on earth has been given to me. Therefore go and make disciples of all nations, baptizing them in the name of the Father and of the Son and of the Holy Spirit, and teaching them to obey everything I have commanded you. And surely I am with you always, to the very end of the age."[14]

Interactives

1. Share an exercise of naming saints: create a "God's advocate" and create a "devil's advocate" to argue why this person should *not* be canonized. What images or narraphors resulted from this exercise? How could you use this exercise as fodder for sermon building?

2. Practice your storytelling skills. Take turns choosing a Bible story and then telling it in a new and creative way. What skills do you notice that you need to be a good storyteller? Write them down in your notes and discuss them around the table. What can you do to make your storytelling more exciting and more creative?

3. Have another colleague or partner choose a random Bible passage for you. You do the same for your partner. Take a few minutes to read the passages well. Come up with two or three possible sermon topics based on the metaphors, images, and narraphors you see there. Share them with your group. What additional ideas did your group have that you missed?

4. Describe a time when you have dealt with criticism either among your congregation or directly as the pastor or ministry leader. How did you handle it? Describe the pros and cons of your reaction. What might you do differently in the future?

5. Sometimes people can grow up with "bad stories" that color their vision of God. How can you help someone to "rewrite" that story into one that reveals God's grace?

6. Have you ever felt the jitters when you were about to give your sermon? Construct a prayer to say before you speak that will put your sermon in the hands of Jesus.

7. The "four horsemen of the apocalypse of noncreativity" can impede your creative flow. Take a look at these common creativity killers:

   - criticism
   - a team of like
   - a team that only praises success
   - a team of me

   Discuss how each of these "killers" can cause you "bad blood" and poor delivery. How can you overcome them?

8. Read the following definition: *Cubicle or carrel creativity: The size of your ideas is directly proportional to the space you have in which to think; your creativity is limited by the box you find yourself in.* How does this definition relate to what you know about creative preaching? How can you "break out of your box" and experience "resurrection" preaching?

9. Our current culture is filled with modern-day heresies. What are three ways that you can fit your sermon to the contemporary culture while still keeping the main thing the main thing?

10. What are some of the heresies you find among your parishioners? What misunderstandings do they struggle with? What heresies fascinate them and why? How can you address them?

11. Think of a time when you have heard a preacher platforming a personal agenda. What was the agenda? How did it make you feel? Think about the Scriptures used to justify that agenda. Did it feel like a valid justification? Why or why not? Often when someone platforms a personal agenda, he or she has something—or much—to gain. What might your speaker have to gain by platforming this agenda?

12. Today some churches are attempting to compete with movie theaters, coffeehouses, amusement parks, lounges—anything to "please people" into coming to church. The rise of consumerism in churches that are expected to meet the needs of people is becoming commonplace in our culture. Sadly, the one thing churches have to offer that nothing in the culture has, many are not offering: a relationship with Jesus. In fact, many churches don't even seem to realize that they have something to offer that is the greatest "good news" of our lives! Discuss this dilemma among your group or colleagues. How can preachers disciple people to become better followers and better servants rather than catering to the needs of "fast-food" junkies?

Part 6

"O" HOMILETIC MISCELLANY

Chapter 25

Red-Blooded Realities: The Preacher's Humility and Humanity

BEFORE LEAVING THE LAB, let's look at a few other factors that can make your preaching more authentic, more powerful, and easier to digest. The following chapters have to do not with homiletic preparation or delivery but with the nature of the blood donor.

In a way, the fact that "preachers are humans too" allows the giving of blood in the first place. A preacher who is "above the sins of humanity," who cannot confess to or identify with the frailties of the human condition, has a blood type with no match for any human parishioner.

To give blood, you must be rich in the blood of Jesus and yet acutely aware of the limitations of your own lot. Preaching is an act of humble confidence: a sense of importance ("I can do all things.... With Christ you can do anything") and a sense of impotence ("Without Christ you can do nothing"). Humility is not "putting yourself down." Humility is receiving the great gifts and talents God has given you as "gifts." To reject the gift is to reject the Giver.

Some preachers think they're the only stick in God's matchbox. The truth is, God likes to light the altar fires with many kinds of sticks. Hence the apostle Paul's warning that "there must be no competition among you, no conceit; but everybody is to be self-effacing."[1] Preachers can learn by picking up tips from other sticks. The power of collaboration, connection, and nour-ishing relationships among the community of preachers warms the blood and makes us more bloodthirsty for the life of Christ in our veins.

No preacher would be wise in giving blood without knowing if that bloodgraft is saving lives. Frequent "blood testing" is a staple of the preacher's lab work. Periodically we must type it and test it and tender it to criticism[2] if we are to upgrade the transfusions that the Spirit can make happen in our zip code.

Slander is saying that someone said something he or she did not say. One doesn't want to slander the Spirit or the Scriptures. The toe-curling, blood-curdling truth is this: there aren't many vocations more dangerous than preaching. And preaching can be dangerous to preachers more than anyone. The moment preachers take upon themselves the burden of their own preachments rather than seeing themselves as vehicles of Christ's saving presence and healing power, they have not only lost the congregation but themselves even more.

Humbert of Romans, the thirteenth-century master of the Fifth Domini-can Order, preached arguably the best sermon on the sermon in the history of the church. In his *On the Formation of Preachers*, he argued that "by the Merit of their preaching people win many spiritual boons,"[3] not the least of which is the preacher's very own salvation. "She who makes others joyful will herself be made joyful; she who saves others will herself be saved; he who anoints others will himself be anointed."[4] For it is not apart from our preaching that preachers experience and enjoy God. It is precisely as a preacher.[5] So preach we do and preach we must. But when we do, it must be with the awareness of our humanity and in the demonstration of our humility.

★   ★   ★

"Then the disciples went forth and preached
everywhere, and the Lord worked with them."
—Mark 16:20

★   ★   ★

The Palestrina of homileticians, John Piper, says quite graphically: "Go to your study and look down at your pitiful manuscript, and you kneel down and cry, 'God, this is so weak! Who do I think I am? What audacity to think that in three hours my words will be the odor of death to death and the fragrance of life to life (2 Cor. 2:16).' My God, who is sufficient for these things!"[6] All preachers are insufficient. But Jesus is all-sufficient. Human blood is the blood of Adam, and "In Adam's fall / We sinned all," as the *New England Primer* (1784 edition) put it in its first *A* entry. Only Christ's blood is the balm in Gilead. We are the carriers of the salve, but Jesus is the salvation.

Your humility will keep you tied to Christ; your humanity will allow you to connect with your congregation. The most approachable preachers are those who see themselves as the human beings they are, not merely leading the flock, but joining the flock in following Jesus, needing just as much as anyone the touch of his robe, the healing in his wings.

★   ★   ★

"My grace is sufficient for you, for my power
is made perfect in [your] weakness."
—*2 Corinthians 12:9*

★   ★   ★

Preachers struggle with passages in the Bible as much if not more than their parishioners. They know they battle life's travails as much as their neighbors. They know they can't answer life's every question. They know enough to allow for the mystery of faith to infiltrate their own lives.

Haddon Robinson gave this Proverbs 15:1 response to someone angry at a sermon: "Thank you for writing. I'm sorry I offended you. I wanted to communicate a great truth of Scripture and failed to get that across to you. I'm sorry."[7] A preacher with deep humanity is less concerned with being right or upright than with the rightness of relationships and wearing the cloak of righteousness. A hot-blooded spirituality cannot live in a coldhearted preacher. To love your people, you must not stand above them but with them. You must come out of the lab and hold the hands of real people—heart to heart, blood to blood. When you do, Christ will work within those relationships to transform lives through you. Jesus is the interface of God. God came to earth to face off with us, face-to-face. If Christ can hold the hands of outcasts and sinners, so can you.

Lab Practicum
KOPI LUWAK

In 2012 I reworked a sermon I first gave a decade earlier. I was preaching at a gathering of twelve thousand Christians in Surabaya, Indonesia. Indonesia is the home of a very exclusive coffee called Kopi Luwak. Only a couple of thousand pounds of this coffee from Sumatra is sold on the world market every year. It's a coffee bean with a story.

Kopi Luwak is the most exquisite, exotic, and expensive coffee in the world. It costs from $150 to $300 a pound. It is the only coffee sold like a drug—by the ounce. *Kopi* is Indonesian for "coffee." *Luwak* is Indonesian for the name of how we get this coffee: from a civet cat, a nocturnal creature with big bug eyes. The civet is about the size of a fox and is the Juan Valdez of the animal kingdom. Its uncanny nose sniffs out only the most perfect coffee cherries to pick and eat. It comes out at night and patrols the coffee plantations on the island of Sumatra. It would rather starve than feast on a Kona coffee bean or a Blue Mountain coffee bean. It only picks the most exquisite coffee cherries, swallows them, digests them, and then excretes the beans. In the morning the locals harvest these beans—gathering the dung, picking out the beans, and washing them.

The most expensive, exclusive coffee in the world is found in the dung of an animal.

Isn't it amazing how God works! In nature you see this over and over again. What is honey, the nectar of nature? Bee dung. In Asian cultures Geishas spend days trying to look beautiful with a kind of white paint. Do you know what this white paint is that they put on their faces? Nightingale dung. What do mushrooms grow in? What makes them so succulent and tasty? Animal dung. Go to any fish market and ask for a sardine. They will laugh in your face. You see, there is no such thing as a sardine fish. Sardine is a name that we give to trash fish that they put together in a can. There is a halibut, and there is haddock and salmon, but no sardine. It doesn't exist. What makes perfumery like Chanel No 5 and Shalimar so exquisite and expensive? Whale waste known as ambergris, now worth $1,000 a pound, feces from a sperm whale.

My favorite way of expressing how God works to bring nature and theology together is the dove. The dove does not exist. It is a poetic name for a trash bird called a pigeon. The symbol of the Holy Spirit is a trash bird. We prettify it by calling it a dove, but really it is a pigeon. Isn't it amazing how God works! Jesus held up a mustard seed to show the nature of faith. The mustard seed for Jesus was very much like the Kopi Luwak coffee bean is today. A mustard seed was a "trash weed."

The whole gospel is based in the idea that what is born of "trash" becomes "treasure" through the grace of Jesus.

Where was Jesus born? Jesus comes to this earth and is born in a trash place of the planet called the city of Bethlehem, the city of David. And where was he born? In a stable. What goes on in a stable? More "dung." And so what were Jesus' first smells as he was born into this world? What were Jesus' last smells as he exited this world? Where was he crucified? A place called Golgatha, which was the garbage dump for the city of Jerusalem, a trash place.

In I Corinthians 1:25, we read: "Divine folly is wiser than human wisdom and divine weakness stronger than human strength." Preachers, consider your call. Few of you are people of wisdom, by any human standard. Few are powerful or highly born. Yet God chooses what is weak in this world to shame the strong. God has chosen things low and contemptible. Things that are not lofty or elevated, to overthrow existing orders. And so there is no place for human pride in the presence of God for you are in Christ Jesus by God's act. He is our righteousness, and in him we are consecrated and set free. And so, in the words of scripture, if you must boast, boast of the Lord."

The gospel is about the way in which what is most weak, what is most despised, what is most contemptible in your life, in this world, can become, through the power of the Holy Spirit, what is most beautiful, what is most radiant, and what can most be a blessing. You see, we have a topsy-turvy upside down, inside out gospel. Like you do to a sock, you turn it inside out, upside down, topsy-turvy. And that is what the values of the gospel do to the wisdom of this world. If you want to be first, you have to be willing to be last. In God's eyes, the first will be the last. Do you want to be strong? You have to be willing to be weak. Do you want to win? You have to be willing to lose. We have an upside down, topsy-turvy gospel that says whatever is the buried trash in your life, God can turn it into buried treasure. Whatever you think are the trashcans of your existence, God can turn them in to treasure chests.

The Hebrew word for hell was Sheol. Heaven was Shiloh. God can turn any Sheol into a Shiloh if you will only let the Spirit of God take that pain, that suffering, that ugliness, that which is contemptible in your life, and let the Spirit turn it upside down. I am thinking now of a composer named Ludwig von Beethoven. What is the worst thing that could happen to a composer? To become deaf. The last twelve years of Beethoven's life, he was deaf. Think of the pain, think of the agony. And yet, in these last twelve years, Beethoven composed four of his five greatest symphonies. You see, he allowed the compost of his suffering and his despair to become the humus out of which God's Spirit grew some of the most beautiful music that has ever been composed.

Treasure chests and trashcans. In 1823 there was a student at a British school, The Rugby School; his name was William Webb Ellis. He was playing soccer one day and he forgot through a mental lapse what game he was playing and instead of kicking the ball, he caught it. William Ellis caught the ball, ran to the goal, and all of a sudden, instead of hearing the crowds cheering he heard a mocking crowd, a laughing crowd. This student, William Ellis, at this British school called Rugby, was so humiliated and embarrassed, he took his own life. But someone at that school watched what William Ellis had done and said, "You know, that is not a bad idea, that is a whole different sport." The man used William's mistake to found a whole different sport, named it after the school that it started at, and it became known as rugby, the predecessor to football. But it did no good for William Ellis, because he could not trust that a trashcan could become a treasure chest.

The whole story of the Scriptures—go through it from beginning to end, from Genesis to the maps, and you will find over and over again, sisters and brothers—is this story of how God takes what is worst, least, contemptible, lowest, and does what is greatest, best, and strongest. This is the story of the gospel.

We have images for this over and over again in the Scriptures. We have an image for it on Ash Wednesday. What are ashes that we put on our forehead—ashes are burnt palms.

Perhaps the most powerful image that we have in all of the Scriptures is spitting. The worst thing that you could do to someone in the

Bible—specifically named in Numbers 12:14—was to spit on that person. It was the ultimate insult!

To spit on another human being, to curse somebody by spitting on them is still the lowest of the low. One of the stories that came out of the civil rights movement was about a third grader, and eight-year-old by the name of Thelma. She was the first student to integrate into the Mississippi public school system. When she came to school the first day, her mother put her in a cute little pink dress. She showed up at school and the teacher said, "Thelma, I want you to stand right there by your seat. You are not to sit yet." And so Thelma stood by her seat as the rest of the class marched in front of that seat and spat in her seat. An entire class of third graders. When they all went to their seats the teacher said to Thelma, "You can sit down now." And yet, what did Jesus do when he wanted to heal the blind? He spat, and he scooped out of the ground some earth. He used his spittle in that earth to make a healing compound and transformed a symbol of devastation into a symbol of hope. Transformed a symbol of cursing and insult into an activity of healing and redemption. Read your Bible, over and over. What does God do? God turns cursing into curing, turns belittling into blessing, turns burrs into spurs. The curse of being hanged on a tree was transformed into a symbol of forgiveness and salvation. This is the gospel in a coffee bean.

That which is the worst, the least, the last in your life God can turn around and make your greatest instrument for healing and for blessing. Moses was a murderer; he recycled his rage and hatred and became the greatest leader in Israel's history. Jacob was a thief and a rogue. He recycled his cunning and became the father of the nation. David was an adulterer. He recycled his passion and became the greatest of the kings. Peter was a boastful, swearing fisherman. He recycled his pride and became the rock upon which Christ built his church. Mary Magdalene recycled her love and became a saint. Zaccheus, a tax collector, recycled his miserliness and became a disciple of Jesus. Saul of Tarsus, a persecutor, a hater of Christians, recycled his hatred and became the greatest of the missionary theologians. Esther, a harem girl, recycled her sex appeal and saved the Jewish people from history's first Holocaust. Ruth was an idol worshipper. But she recycled her foreignness, and she became a progenitor of Jesus the Christ.

And what about you? What is the worst about you? What is least in you? What are the very dregs of your life? God wants to turn all of it around—inside out, upside down, topsy-turvy—and make you into a source of healing, wholeness, and redemption. Do you believe that God can turn your trash into treasure? Do you believe that God can transform your Sheols into Shilohs? Do you believe that God can take the worst out of your life and turn it into the best?

As preachers, what is your trash? What are your weaknesses? We feel so often that we only bless people with our strengths. And truly, you have been given gifts and strengths to use in your ministry. Those gifts have already been given to you by God. You already have them within you in order to bless others. Use them. Use them well. But know this. Where God will bless others the most in your preaching is in the places of your greatest weaknesses. You have been given natural gifts and strengths. But it is out of your weakness that God will create gifts of supernatural in you strength that will pull people from despair and cause healing in their midst.

Will you let God take what is most cursed in you and use it to bless others? Preachers, your humanity and your humility will make you a powerful force in the name of Jesus. Go out, and preach, because you must!

★   ★   ★

"The word of the LORD has brought me
insult and reproach all day long.
But if I say, 'I will not mention his word
or speak anymore in his name,'
his word is in my heart like a fire,
a fire shut up in my bones.
I am weary of holding it in;
indeed, I cannot."
—*Jeremiah 20:8–9*

★   ★   ★

Chapter 26

Blood Ties:
Learning from Peers
and Relationships
with Colleagues

If the life of a river depended only on the rain that falls within the
confines of its own banks, it would soon be dry.... Be grateful for
your tributaries.

—William Arthur Ward[1]

WE LIVE IN A NETWORKED WORLD. Preachers need to make the
net work for them. Learning from colleagues and leaning on peers means
more now than simply joining the local ministerium or sharing a meal with
a pastoral colleague. We now have multiple ways to connect, both online and
offline. Connect we must.

The earliest image of the Creator in the Bible is that of Divine Potter.[2]
The Bible begins with three images: dirt, then water, the combination of
which gets infused with breath. God molds humans from dirt moistened
with water and then breaths into them the soul of life. The Divine Potter
molds us as long as we make ourselves malleable to him. One of the most
important questions every preacher must answer is this: What keeps your
clay moist?

How do you keep learning, keep being discipled? The greatest mistake
pastors often make is to conclude or sublimate their own discipleship journey when they end a course of study or find themselves swamped with the

challenges of ministry. Often when pastors graduate seminary or become ordained, they cease to have mentors. Before that they may have been surrounded by support systems, learning environments, and connectional groups. Once in ministry, pastors find themselves dreadfully and surprisingly alone. This isolation can cause not only burnout of energy but burnout of spirit.

Relationships are life's greatest moisturizers. That's why every message should aim for "conversion." Biblical conversion is not a change of behavior or change of values but a change of direction, a change of relationship—a return to God as Lord of life. All true change comes out of that conversion, that change of relationship.

Our relationship with Christ and relationships with peers and colleagues moisturize our souls and moisten our lives so that the Master Potter can continue to shape us into the vessels we were designed to be. The most important task of the preacher is to be a fully formed disciple of Jesus. Just as a laser turns random photons into a coherent laser beam, so the presence of a "fully realized" and "fully connected" preacher can make one's mind, body, and spirit coherent and focused.

When Princess Diana's body was returned to England from Paris, no one knew, but she wore a borrowed dress from a friend, and she clutched in her hands a rosary from Mother Teresa and pictures of her boys, William and Harry. What amazing metaphors! At the end of her glamorous life, what mattered most, what was most personal, were the relationships that nurtured the princess's soul. What matters in the end is not fortune, not fame, not power, not prizes, but our relationships. What matters most is our relationship with God, with others, with self, and with creation, the four broken relationships Christ came to repair and redeem.[3]

*   *   *

"The only gift greater than the air you breathe is the hand you hold."
—*Old Irish toast*

*   *   *

To act independently of one another is inhuman. Relationship is the ultimate reality of the universe. "Individual" is a political category, not a biological entity. The greater the number and complexity of connections, the greater the wisdom of the organism and the stronger the body. In the words of Nikos Kazantzakis, a Greek writer and philosopher: "Only he has been freed from the inferno of his ego who feels deep pangs of hunger when a child of his race has nothing to eat, who feels his heart throbbing with joy when a man and a woman of his race embrace and kiss one another. All these are limbs of your larger, visible body. You suffer and rejoice, scattered to the ends of the earth in a thousand bodies, blood of your blood."[4]

What is a faith community? It is "togetherness in Christ," not just togetherness per se but blood of your blood of Christ's blood. Why are faith communities so rare? Because we try to build our communities on flesh not blood, on gifts not weaknesses, on strength not brokenness, on success not failure. The beauty of being a member of the body of Christ is that our membership keeps us humble and hungry—for deeper relationships.

Chapter 27

Blood Testing: Interpreting Effect and Response

> One who is full loathes honey from the comb,
> but to the hungry even what is bitter tastes sweet.
>
> —Proverbs 27:7

OUR PROBLEM IS NOT that God doesn't "show up" when we gather. Our problem is that we aren't committed to showing up to what God is doing with all the resources with which God has gifted us.

Good feedback comes from the well fed. And as we have seen, you can do things to ensure that you are delivering food to the body in appetizing ways. The secret recipe of good appetizers (you might even call it the pixie dust of all great communication) is a two-ingredient, lion-lamb formula: (1) own the room, which takes lionlike confidence; and (2) get people to relax with you and to be open to you, which takes lamblike humility.

To own the room, you need to look at people one at a time. Use your eyes to sweep the room. Own the space with your gaze. Let people feel your humble confidence so they can feel they are in good hands. There are two kinds of animals: predators and prey. Predators have their eyes in front of their head; prey have eyes on the side of their head. When your eyes aren't making contact with your people, it shows fear and timidity, the trepidations of the mouse, not the confidence of the lion.

You can elicit feedback after the sermon, of course. But that may be too late. How can you interpret the subtle feedback you are getting even in the midst of the sermon? Even while engaged within the sermon, and even with little interaction, you can get a sense of whether people are participating actively in the sermon's semiotics and whether the experience is EPIC enough. You can tell quickly whether your narraphors are connecting and the blood is getting through.

Blood Testing: Interpreting Effect and Response

Read the spirit of the room. The whole is greater than the sum of its parts. The combined spirits of those present give off a communal spirit that pervades the room. Is the spirit of the room light, heavy, excited, challenging, or something else? You first must preach to that spirit and break through its barriers before you can preach to the people. While you're preaching, some people in the room will be hot spots of energy and encouragement. Others will be dead spots, where the minds aren't communicating with the faces and you have no idea what the reception is. Others will be hostile zones where everything you say is being thrown back at you in scorn, mockery, and derision. I try not to visit a hostile zone without having made a pit stop at a hot spot. The most dangerous spirits to the preacher are the vampires, people who do nothing but sit there and suck every available ounce of energy out of you, whether out of love or hate. I try to stay away from vampires when I'm on feedback patrol.

Scan the room for demographics. If your narraphors don't seem to have traction, determine quickly the predominant age group of those present. Make a quick mathematical calculation of the average age in the congregation. Subtract that number from the current year and add twenty to determine if your people are is aware of the narraphors you're using and the names you're referencing. Be a semiotician of your people. Pay attention to their expressions, their body language, their reactions, their responses, their words, their input, their participation, their eyes.

Sometimes my sermons launch like dazzling fireworks; sometimes they drop like a damp firecracker. Like some fireworks, they fizzle dormant for a time, and just when I think they are duds, they explode when I least expect it. Quite parabolic! Sometimes even damp firecrackers can surprise us with a bang after we walk away. So don't be too quick to judge. Sometimes a look of confusion may be merely a look of contemplation. Sometimes a look of distress may be a look of transformation. It can be easy to confuse upright and uptight.

In giving blood, as in any ministry, there are pleasures of predictability and joys of surprises. As a preacher, you need to enjoy the predictability of knowing what will cause your congregation's blood to flow and yet reap the joys and surprises of Christ's amazing power to do the unexpected. Every great preacher needs both surprise and surmise.

Paul was at best a mediocre public speaker. Luke delicately tells of Paul's speaking ability as "Paul talked on and on."[1] But people felt his dedication, his passion, and his authenticity, and he was able to give blood with a power of witness and a gift of relevancy unprecedented in his time. When your narraphors give form to revelation, your preaching is no different from the apostle Paul's. Through you, Christ can transform the consciousness of your community.

Interactives

1. Contemplate the following passage from Jeremiah. How is the prophetic voice a key to understanding the humility and humanity of the preacher?

   > If I say, "I will not mention his word
   > or speak anymore in his name,"
   > his word is in my heart like a fire,
   > a fire shut up in my bones.
   > I am weary of holding it in;
   > indeed, I cannot.
   >
   > Jeremiah 20:9

2. I worry about preachers who know already why bad things happen or think they can treat hurt with words and pain with propositions. How does this relate to the humanity and humility of a preacher? How can "bad stories" affect the lives of people and their ability to trust in Christ? What can you do to ensure that you as a preacher are mindful of your humility and humanity when sharing the stories of Jesus?

3. How many peer and colleague relationships do you have in your life? How can you increase the connections you have with others in ministry?

4. Pastors need "safe places" where they can air frustrations, talk about personal issues, and get advice on confidential matters. Who are your "safe" people?

5. In my book *11*,[2] I describe the eleven important and vital relationships every person needs in his or her life. Talk about how special relationships have nurtured your own life. Who are those people for you?

6. Name three ways you can elicit constructive feedback from your congregation. How can you discern feedback from pie in your face? How can you use these responses to move forward in your ministry and in your sermon building?

Part 7

FROM LAB
TO LIFE

Chapter 28

Life Blood:
Food for the Body

SPENDING TIME IN THE LAB is important. It's fun to mix ingredients and concoct new creations. But as with any organic thing, there comes a time to set your creativity free to fly, to let your sermon live in and among the world, to allow God's Spirit to give it breath, to allow it to metamorphosis from something you have offered up to something Christ may embody and empower.

Every message is an offering, a gift, a tithe of your calling as a preacher and a prophet. Every sermon is a giving of blood, a sharing of a piece of your heart, a gift of your soul, a renewal of your commitment to the mission of the gospel. You renew your calling every time you step out of the lab and into real life, to midwife again and in yet another way the living and breathing Word of God.

We have talked here before about the sermonic space as a playing field or a practice space in which the body minsters in preparation for mission. The lab is like that too. The lab is your practice field, but the world is your "parish." Just as in a football game there is a time for practice and a time for play, a time for the huddle and a time to move down the field, so your sermon at some point must be ready to leave the lab and move out and onto the mission field. There you will "give and take" the blood of Christ. In so doing, the body is not only nourished by the body and blood of Jesus but infused with the love and life of the risen Lord. With every sermon you "give and take," you witness to the resurrection.

The church gives us blood brothers and sisters. The church is the resurrected body, Spirit-breathed with life, constantly re-membered to be the living presence of Christ in the world. And the sermon is its Holy Communion.

Preachers have Augustine to thank for fighting the Donatists. When Augustine prevailed, it was settled: the sacraments as channels of God's grace are effectual irrespective of the minister's personal holiness. We are all sinners; we are all disease carriers. But the blood of Jesus Christ gives us heightened immunity. A healthy immune system doesn't mean we don't get attacked or suffer setbacks, but we are less susceptible to giving in to the virus and less susceptible to passing it on.

We live in a world where the average person is exposed to at least three thousand "sermons" a day—almost all of these declaring the gospel is wrong. These messages can be pathogens to our faith, which makes preaching the gospel all the more important. Preaching builds up the immune system. The blood of Jesus is our vaccine to protect us from the forces that would take us down and threaten our everlasting life.

The greatest eucharistic sermon ever written? My vote goes to the one preached in Pusey House Chapel, Oxford, by Austin Farrer. It was titled "Consecrated Bread."[1]

Well, in a manner of speaking, the bread he took was his body. A sculptor might show you round his shop, and pointing out pieces of wood grained suitably for several purposes, might say, "That is a Churchill, and that's a Victory; that is a greyhound, and this is a leopard." They are the raw materials of these things; and the food we will eat is the raw material of our body; let us call it our body if we like, by anticipation, or by exaggeration. Yet the bread Jesus took was not his own loaf or roll that he would eat. It was the bread of grace, a loaf specially symbolical of the whole company's food: a loaf over which grace was said for them all, and of which everyone present must taste a crumb. It did not stand for the bread or body of any one person there present, it stood for the common food of them all. As St. Paul says, writing of this very matter, because the loaf is one, we many are one body, for we all partake of the one loaf. Since food becomes our body, eating from one loaf or from one dish becomes a sort of natural sacrament. As we build up our body from one stock, we feel ourselves tied together in one body corporate; we are members one of another. And to the Jew, this natural tie became a religious bond: the one loaf shared by all was consecrated through the thanksgiving, or grace-before-meat.

This, then, was the bread Jesus took, on the night before he suffered, the bread which was the body of them all; it was this he called his body. The body he took from Mary was no one's but his. From the moment of birth it ceased to be hers; and it was certainly no other man's or woman's. But the bread he took to be his body was the body of the company, of Peter, John, James, Matthew, and Thomas: so determined he was, that the effect of his incarnation should not be shut within the confines of his skin. He took their body, but he took it to be made his own, to be consecrated, divinized, Christed; through the oblation of a voluntary death and the power of a glorious resurrection.

Christ took it into his blessed hands and said it was his body. He took, and he takes. He takes what we are; he is not ashamed of us, does not discuss us. Peter might deny Christ, but Christ set his eyes on Peter, his eyes and his heart. He takes us and says we are his body; for his love will make us so.... He takes us: he loves us for what we are and loves us into what we must be; he takes us, incorporate with him through his death and resurrection, and gives us back ourselves, that is himself, in the communion of bread and wine.

The blood is blood, and it is inside the whole of the body: it is the only element common to all members and all organs. Without blood there is no life; in other words, life is in the blood.

Blood is the dynamic, mobile, and vital substance which flows through the whole body. It is the pilgrim inside the body. If it should cease flowing, the body would die. And the blood is not visible. When it starts to show, there is an injury. If blood is shed, it is life that is shed; if all the blood is shed, life is lost. The blood comes and goes to and from the heart. The heart is not visible either! If it were out in the open, it would mean death. In a mysterious way, the blood, the heart, and life are most intimately interrelated. It is essential for life that the blood and the heart should exist inside the body.... The last wound, the spear plunged into Jesus' side, is the open heart, and the pouring out of blood and water upon the church at the foot of the cross and upon the world is the final giving up of blood and spirit—the gift of life ... that is what prayer is: the blood of hate crucified the Lord and the Giver of Life, flowing through the inner body, giving life, movement, and warmth. And where there is warmth, there is energy and light. In the church there are persons who belong to this inner space.... There are disciples of Jesus in the church who have this calling. In secular terms they have been defined as monks, as the contemplatives.... The poor and the contemplative, those of the inner being (Romans 7:22), are those who move inside the body, return to the heart, and go out again, until one day the whole body is taken up into glory, when the heavens open and this same body, transformed into the city bride, has no other blood but that of the Lamb. Then the trees of life will bear fruit twelve times (Revelation 21:22).

Christ's blood is our lifeblood; our need for it is as fundamental as life itself. All preaching should seek to mainline truth, to establish a direct connection to and through Jesus' blood. Doing anything less is just to pose as religious folk. Every sermon is a holy grail. All preaching is sacramental food for the soul. Every sermon is a narraphor of the covenant between God and humanity. Go out and preach the gospel.

Chapter 29

Giving Blood: Salvation and Resurrection

ONE OF MY ALL-TIME FAVORITE football players is running back Herschel "Junior" Walker, who was inducted into the Football Hall of Fame in 1999. When he played for the Dallas Cowboys, he was persuaded to help out the Fort Worth Ballet Company by moving from breaking tackles and bowling over defenses against the backdrop of cheers and roars to pirouetting and spinning to the classical strains of Tchaikovsky. When an interviewer inquired about how hard the transition was, Walker replied, "When I dance, I have to use a completely different set of muscles."

Like the muscular Herschel Walker in his transition from gridiron to dance floor, preachers face challenges in the transition from Gutenberg to Google that require us to use old muscles in new ways and to develop new muscles that the old ways didn't require. This book is designed to give you tips for your workout.

But in order for preaching to change, it also must remain the same. What stays the same?

Giving blood.

Do you bleed over every sermon? Do you give blood through every sermon? Preaching is the discipline and craft of giving blood. With every sermon, preachers have it in their power to jumpstart the world. Preachers have an awesome calling: to be a vein for the blood that washes away the sins of the world, for the water that renews and redeems, for the fire that purifies and ignites. We have the amazing opportunity to be ventricles for the voice and vision of Jesus in the world, and to bleed his life to all people.

He bled for me. He bled for us. Can we bleed his love for others?

After a great sermon of giving blood, people will want to touch you. But it's not you they want to touch. It's the power in the blood that flowed from you during that sermon.

Our preaching ancestors told the old, old, story with all they were. When they lay me in the ground, this is what I want said of me: "He told the old, old story with all he was."

Interactives

1. Choose your favorite narraphor from the Bible. How does that narraphor provide food for the body? How will it sound the voice of mission to the world? How will it proclaim Christ's salvation and resurrection?

2. Listen to or read each other's sermons. Can you find evidence of the joy of the resurrection in them? Does the sermon leave you with hope?

3. David Barry Weber is a preacher, blogger, and Facebook friend. Here is one of his posts when one day the conversation turned to sermons:

> I hear least-common-denominator sermons so often: platitudes without substance, empty (but pretty) phrases without application. I want to hear sermons that tear the scabs off our ignored wounds and take Jesus off the cross and put him where the blood from those open wounds needs cleaning. I want to hear Cormac McCarthy quoted in a sermon more than I want to hear C. S. Lewis again (much as I love him!). I want to see the colors of God in projections of Hubble pics, rather than sweet pink-satin pictures of Gap-clad children on Easter morning. I want to stop hearing all the words — all the 50 billion words on Sunday and the 25 billion on Wednesday nights — about Jesus, and actually see Jesus doing something! I want all the useless, gimmee-gimmee sermons on "Christian TV" put on Betamax tapes and taken to the dump. The sweeter-sounding that one calorie is, the more frenzied, it seems, the feeding. OK, I've gotta sit down now.

> What parts of this post resonate? What parts don't?

4. Lawyers are now taught that the dark blue suit, white shirt, and red tie is what you wear when you want jurors to focus on you. When you are in a direct examination of your client or an expert, the proper outfit is softer earth tones. But the major ingredient in the new "power outfit" for trial lawyers is ... the *prop*.

> Trial lawyers are now being taught that some form of visualization is imperative. Even something as simple as taking out a jelly doughnut and showing the jury how the disks that separate the vertebrae in the spine are just like jelly doughnuts ... then crush

it and the jelly (nucleus) will ooze onto your tie (nerves) and ruin our outfit (life).[1]

What is the preacher's "power outfit"? Do you agree that the ultimate power now is the ability to choose the metaphors? What is your favorite "power outfit"?

5. Orchestras are experimenting with video and film to keep people coming to symphonic concerts. Check out video artist and sound architect Bill Viola's work for the Los Angeles Philharmonic's "Tristan Project." Do you have any stories to tell from personal experience in which high culture is trying to transition to a screen culture?

6. Colleague and friend Clifford E. McLain often comes down from the front, stands with his people for the pastoral prayer, announces to his congregation, "The person next to you loves you. Reach out and hold his or her hand," and then proceeds to offer the morning prayer. Can you think of other relational twists to use for preaching and worship?

Notes

ACKNOWLEDGMENTS

1. Jeanette Thomeson posted this quote on her Whitestone Publishing web page for January 2013.
2. Rom. 8:23.
3. 1 Cor. 9:16.
4. Thanks to colleague Eric Baker for helping me formulate this better.
5. Ernest Hemingway, *A Moveable Feast* (New York: Bantam, 1965), 75.
6. John Wesley, "What Is Man," in his *Sermons*, in *The Works of John Wesley*, ed. Albert C. Outler (Nashville: Abingdon, 1987), 4:20–21.
7. Eph. 6:19–20.

INTRODUCTION

1. Ex. 12:13.
2. Hear it at http://www.firstbaptistfortlauderdale.com/media.php?pageID=7.
3. Rutledge served for twenty-two years as a parish pastor and was one of the first women ordained in the Episcopal Church. See Fleming Rutledge, *Help My Unbelief* (Cambridge & Grand Rapids: Eerdmans, 2000), 142.
4. See, e.g., Bruce F. Kawin, *Horror and the Horror Film* (London: Anthem, 2012).
5. *True Blood* is a US television drama series. It premiered on HBO on September 7, 2008, and immediately became a hit.
6. The first line is from the 1899 Socialist hymn by James O'Connell, "The Red Flag," http://users.powernet.co.uk/hack/sleaze/red_flag.html, accessed July 8, 2004. The second line is from the 1878 gospel song by Elisha A. Hoffman, "Are You Washed in the Blood?," *Best Hymns: Selections from Over One Hundred of Our Best Hymn Writers*, ed. Elisha A. Hoffman (Chicago: Evangelical, 1894), 52.
7. Acts 2.
8. John 6:53–54.
9. Ex. 24:6–8.
10. Matt. 26:28 NKJV.
11. John 6:56.
12. Heb. 10:10.
13. Rev. 13:8.
14. Gen. 4:4.
15. Ex. 12:3.
16. Ex. 29:38–39.
17. Num. 28:3, 9, 13.
18. Isa. 53:7.
19. Acts 8:32; Acts 8:35 is where Jesus as the Lamb of God is made explicit.

335

20. John 1:29, 36.
21. Song of Songs 2:4
21. Tamayo Family Vineyards in California offers "Cana" wine. See http://www.tamayo-familyvineyards.com.

CHAPTER 1: UNDER THE MICROSCOPE: PREACHING IN A GOOGLE WORLD

1. Daniel Chandler, *Semiotics: The Basics* (London: Routledge, 2002).
2. Dietrich Bonhoeffer, *Letters and Papers from Prison*, ed. Eberhard Bethge (New York: Macmillan, 1971), 279.
3. The study results were published in Ed Stetzer and Thom S. Rainer, *Transformational Church: Creating a New Scoreboard for Congregations* (Nashville: B&H, 2010).
4. Elisha A. Hoffman, "Are You Washed in the Blood?," *Favorite Hymns of Praise* (Chicago: Tabernacle, 1967), 328 (first published 1878, public domain).
5. See Richard Jones, *Mosquito* (London: Reaktion, 2012), 8.
6. *Corporalis* is the Latin from which *corporal* comes, the white linen cloth on which the consecrated elements are placed during the Eucharist.
7. George Herbert, "The Agony," in his *The Temple: Sacred Poems and Private Ejaculations, Together with His Life*, 12th ed., corr. (London: printed by J. Barber for Jeffery Wales, 1703), 29.
8. Robert Schmuhl, ed., *Making Words Dance: Reflections on Red Smith, Journalism, and Writing* (Kansas City, MO: Andrews McMeel, 2010), ixx–xx.
9. I once heard Presbyterian preacher Howard Edington say that if you're truly preaching, you will shorten your life a little, because every time you preach, you die a little. In the same vein, Charles Haddon Spurgeon said, "I shall not detain you any longer, but express the hope that your chest, lungs, windpipe, larynx, and all your vocal organs may last till you have nothing more to say." Charles Haddon Spurgeon, "On the Voice," in his *Lectures to My Students: A Selection from Addresses Delivered to the Students of the Pastors' College, Metropolitan Tabernacle* (Grand Rapids: Baker, 1977), 1:135.
10. Quoted in Kelly Miller Smith, *Social Crisis Preaching*, Lyman Beecher Lectures, 1983 (Macon, GA: Mercer University Press, 1984), 12.
11. Peter Cosentino, *The Encyclopedia of Pottery Techniques: A Comprehensive Visual Guide to Traditional and Contemporary Techniques* (New York: Sterling, 2002).
12. Susan Greenfield, *Tomorrow's People: How 21st-Century Technology Is Changing the Way We Think and Feel* (London: Allen Lane, 2003), cover. The actual full quote is: "As we stand at the beginning of the twenty-first century, the human mind could be on the brink of a makeover even more cataclysmic than that which separates the attitudes of these earlier generations from our own new millennium view" (10).
13. See http://www.youtube.com/watch?v=iMLDaVSxOYU.
14. Seth Godin, *Permission Marketing: Turning Strangers into Friends and Friends into Customers* (New York: Simon and Schuster, 1999), 29.
15. Hillel ben David (Greg Killian), "Rules of Jewish Hermeneutics," http://www.betemunah.org/rules.html.
16. Matt. 13:13 MSG, my emphasis. For the role of "nudging" in communicating the gospel, see Leonard Sweet, *Nudge: Awakening Each Other to the God Who's Already There* (Colorado Springs: WaterBrook, 2010).
17. Louisa Twining notes that the pelican does not appear in Christian art before the Middle Ages. See her *Symbols and Emblems of Early and Mediaeval Christian Art* (London: John Murray, 1885), 186. William and George Audsley mention in particular the pelican "as an emblem of the Crucifixion, and as such, is depicted shedding its blood

for the good of its young," and also note that the "Fable of the Pelican" is depicted in an ancient stained-glass window in the Cathedral of Bourges. See William Audsley and George Audsley, *Handbook of Christian Symbolism* (London: Day & Son, 1865), 86, 88.

18. Konrad von Würzburg, *Die Goldene Schmiede*, ed. Edward Schröder, 2nd ed. (Göttingen: Vandenhoeck & Ruprecht, 1927), 19, line 470.

19. Dante Alighieri, *The Divine Comedy of Dante Alighieri*, Italian Text with a Translation in English Blank Verse and a Commentary by Courtney Langdon (Cambridge: Harvard University Press, 1921), 3:296 (Italian), 297 (English).

20. Thomas Aquinas, *"Adoro Te Devote, Latens Deitas," Collected Hymns, Sequences and Carols of John Mason Neal* (London: Hodder & Stoughton, 1914), 63.

21. Gertrude Grace Sill, *A Handbook of Symbols in Christian Art* (New York: Touchstone, 1975), 24–25.

22. Augustine, *Exposition on the Book of Psalms*, ed. A. Cleveland Coxe, in *Nicene and Post-Nicene Fathers*, 1st ser., vol. 8, ed. Philip Schaff (Peabody, MA: Hendrickson, 1955), 497. See also E. P. Evans, *Animal Symbolism in Ecclesiastical Architecture*, http://www.archive.org/stream/cu31924032663290/cu31924032663290_djvu.txt

23. For more on the *Physiologus*, see Michael J. Curley's introduction to his translation, *Physiologus* (Chicago: University of Chicago Press, 1979), ix–xlvii.

24. "All about Pelican in Her Piety," http://www.pelicaninherpiety.cc.uk/pelican.htm. For more on the history of the pelican in her piety, see "The Heraldic Pelican," in John Vinycomb, *Fictitious and Symbolic Creatures in Art, with Special Reference to Their Use in British Heraldry* (London: Chapman and Hall, 1906), 184–86. See also Evans, *Animal Symbolism*.

25. Patricia S. Klein, *Worship without Words: The Signs and Symbols of Our Faith* (Brewster, MA: Paraclete, 2000), 64.

26. For more on these references, see "Medieval Bestiary: Pelican," http://bestiary.ca/beasts/beast244.htm.

27. Sill, *Handbook of Symbols in Christian Art*, 24–25.

28. Ken Medema Music, http://kenmedema.com.

29. Ken Medema, "My Story," www.professionalspeakersnetwork.com/espeakers/8227/KenMedema.html.

30. The Fred Bock Music Companies: Ken Medema, http://www.fredbock.com/Promo.asp?page=261.

31. An Ebenezer moment reminds us of God's presence.

32. "Homiletics Interview: Ken Medema. From Worship Service to Gathering," *Homiletics Online*, www.homileticsonline.com/subscriber/interviews/medema.asp.

33. Ibid.

CHAPTER 2: BLOOD AND WATER: NARRAPHOR—THE ARS COMBINATORIA OF NARRATIVE AND METAPHOR

1. Jonathan Edwards, "Some Thoughts Concerning the Present Revival of Religion in New England," in his *The Great Awakening*, The Works of Jonathan Edwards, vol. 4, ed. C. C. Goen (New Haven, CT: Yale University Press, 1972), 397.

2. Ralph L. Lewis with Gregg Lewis, *Learning to Preach Like Jesus* (Westchester, IL: Crossway, 1989), 23.

3. The phrase is that of Michael Green in *Evangelism in the Early Church* (Grand Rapids: Eerdmans, 1970), 173. Anglican John Parfitt has written a book with that title: *Gossiping the Gospel: Exploring the Gospel Readings* (London: Athena, 2007).

4. Sara Maitland, *A Big Enough God: A Feminist's Search for a Joyful Theology* (New York: Holt, 1995), 7.

Notes

5. This may be an adaptation of his quote: "Some books are to be tasted, others to be swallowed, and some few to be chewed and digested." Francis Bacon, *The Essays: Or, Counsels Civil and Moral of Francis Bacon*, ed. Fred Allison Howe (Boston: D. C. Heath, 1908), 158.

6. Sally Lloyd-Jones, *The Jesus Storybook Bible: Every Story Whispers His Name* (Grand Rapids: Zondervan, 2007).

7. Philip Pullman, "Carnegie Medal Acceptance Speech," *Philip Pullman: His Dark Materials*, www.randomhouse.com/features/pullman/author/carnegie.php

8. Mark 4:34 NRSV.

9. This began with the 1980 publication of *Preaching the Story* by Edmund A. Steimle, Morris J. Niedenthal, and Charles Rice (Philadelphia: Fortress). David James Randolph's 1969 book, *The Renewal of Preaching* (Philadelphia: Fortress), was a lonely voice crying in the wilderness for the recognition of story as a hermeneutic principle and homiletic method. See Richard L. Eslinger, "Narrative and Imagery," in *Intersections: Post-critical Studies in Preaching*, ed. Richard L. Eslinger (Grand Rapids: Eerdmans, 1994), 65. Anyone who cut their homiletic teeth on the mastery of Henry Mitchell's teaching will never forget his claim: "The dullness of most mainline preaching is due to its being conceived of as argument rather than art—as syllogism rather than symbol. The preacher as inspired artist can easily compel attention to the most profound themes of the gospel, once they are made to live in narrative, picture, and poetry." Mitchell continued, "It has always been so." Henry H. Mitchell, "Preaching on the Patriarchs," in *Biblical Preaching: An Expositor's Treasury*, ed. James W. Cox (Philadelphia: Westminster, 1983), 37. Richard Eslinger has also argued convincingly that story is "the hermeneutical key to interpreting Scripture." See Richard L. Eslinger's quote in the chapter on "Charles Rice: Preaching as Story," in his *A New Hearing: Living in Homiletic Method* (Nashville: Abingdon, 1987), 20.

10. David Martin, *Christian Language in the Secular City* (Burlington, VT: Ashgate, 2002), 158.

11. Tom Lehrer, "Oedipus Rex" (1959), in *Songs and More Songs* by Tom Lehrer (Los Angeles: Rhino, 1997), 17.

12. This concept is discussed throughout Joseph A. Schumpeter, *Capitalism, Socialism, and Democracy* (New York: Harper, 1942; repr. New York: Routledge, 1994).

13. Paul Ricoeur, foreword to Louis Simon, *"My" Jesus: Meditations on Gospel Texts*, trans. Charles Courtney (Eugene, OR: Wipf and Stock, 2011), viii, x, xii. See also the references to metaphor in Marcus J. Borg and N. T. Wright, *The Meaning of Jesus: Two Visions* (San Francisco: HarperSanFrancisco, 1999).

14. Ricoeur, foreword to *"My" Jesus*, xii.

15. Anthony C. Thiselton, "Paul Ricoeur on Metaphor and Narrative: Possibility, Time, and Transformation," in his *New Horizons in Hermeneutics: The Theory and Practice of Transforming Biblical Reading* (Grand Rapids: Zondervan, 1992), 351, 355. John Donahue agrees that "Paul Ricoeur's description of parables as a combination of the metaphoric process with the narrative form is the most adequate way of talking about the parables as metaphors. John R. Donahue, *The Gospel in Parable: Metaphor, Narrative, and Theology in the Synoptic Gospels* (Philadelphia: Fortress, 1988), 10–11.

16. Luke 12:48. The phrase "With great power comes great responsibility" does not come from Spiderman, but from Voltaire.

17. John Bunyan, *Pilgrim's Progress*, "The Author's Apology for His Book."

18. Matt. 28:20.

19. Richard A. Jensen, *Telling the Story: Variety and Imagination in Preaching* (Minneapolis: Augsburg, 1980), 151.

Notes

CHAPTER 3: BLOOD WORK: MAKING NARRAPHORS EPIC

1. *The Fran Lebowitz Reader* (New York: Random House, 1994), 120.
2. Edward T. Hall, *The Silent Language* (New York: Anchor, 1973), 162.
3. For more on EPIC, see Leonard Sweet, *Post-Modern Pilgrims: First-Century Passion for the 21st-Century Church* (Nashville: B&H, 2000), and Leonard Sweet, *The Gospel according to Starbucks: Living with a Grande Passion* (Colorado Springs: WaterBrook, 2007). See also Leonard Sweet, *So Beautiful* (2009) 35–36; *Soul Tsunami*; (1999), 185–240; *Carpe Mañana* (2001), 133, and *A is for Abductive: The Language of the Emerging Church* (2003), 72–75, 111, 119–23, 152–55, 232–35.
4. Mark 12:37.
5. Gustav Flaubert described early Lutheran pastors as "intellectuals, close to the people." All too often theological education trains pastors in a faith different from their people and fails to build bridges between the two worlds.
6. Robert Burns, as quoted by John Ramsay, *The Complete Works of Robert Burns (Self-Interpreting)* (Philadelphia: Gebbie, 1886), 2:352.
7. Marie Ponsot, as quoted by Benjamin Ivry, "Louis and the Angels," *Spirituality & Health* 3 (Winter 2001): 8.
8. 1 Cor. 6:19–20.
9. Pamela Ann Moeller, *A Kinesthetic Homiletic: Embodying Gospel in Preaching* (Minneapolis: Fortress, 1993).
10. Ibid., 12.
11. Ibid., 82.
12. Any scholar who has done any research into churches that are "working" comes to the same conclusion: they are mediating experiences. See Donald E. Miller, *Reinventing American Protestantism: Christianity in the New Millennium* (Berkeley: University of California Press, 1997).
13. For a whole book on that word *with* and the need for "with-nesses," see my *11: Indispensable Relationships You Can't Be Without* (Colorado Springs: WaterBrook, 2012). Another work is Skye Jethani's *With: Reimagining the Way You Relate to God* (Nashville: Thomas Nelson, 2011).
14. Islam is growing in North America, particularly in urban and prison environments, because being Muslim has now become related to the "black experience." One reason Catholic and Orthodox churches have not experienced the same decline as Protestantism may be due to their continued ancient-future use of hands-on ritualistic experiences, such as sacred gestures, candle lighting, and the imposition of ashes.
15. Quoted in Sarah Lloyd-Hughes, *How to Be Brilliant at Public Speaking: Any Audience, Any Situation* (New York: Prentice Hall Life, 2011), 101.
16. John 4:24.
17. For a defense of appealing to the emotions as well as to the intellect, see Ian Pitt-Watson, *Preaching: A Kind of Folly* (Philadelphia: Westminster, 1976), 44–51.
18. "Confirmation," *The Armenian Church: Mother See of Holy Etchmiadzin*, http://www.armenianchurch.org/index.jsp?sid=1&id=116&pid=30&lng=en. A slightly altered version is quoted in Vigen Guroian, *Incarnate Love: Essays in Orthodox Ethics* (Notre Dame, IN: University of Notre Dame Press, 1987), 63–64.
19. With thanks to Ed Wicklein of Belen, New Mexico, for introducing me to this quote of the 1940s and 1950s.
20. Timothy Keller is the pastor of Redeemer Presbyterian Church, New York City, where I heard him say this at a worship service.
21. Ps. 34:8.
22. Matt. 13:10.

23. John 16:18.
24. Mother Teresa is famous for saying that it is a mistake to demand clarity of God. Loving God supersedes understanding God. How many of us have made knowledge of God an idol?
25. Lyndrey A. Niles, "Rhetorical Characteristics of Black Preaching," *Journal of Black Studies* 15 (September 1984), cited in David L. Blow Sr. and Frank A. Thomas, "I Wish I Had Somebody: The Rhetorical Devices of Black Preaching," *African American Pulpit* 5 (Summer 2002): 24.
26. F. David Peat, foreword to John David Ebert, *Twilight of the Clockwork God: Conversations on Science and Spirituality at the End of an Age* (Tulsa, OK: Council Oak, 1999), x–xi.
27. Mark 4:9 NRSV.
28. George Edgar Sweazey, *Preaching the Good News* (Englewood Cliffs, NJ: Prentice-Hall, 1976), 310.
29. Thomas G. Long, *The Witness of Preaching*, 2nd ed. (Louisville: Westminster John Knox, 2005), 226.
30. Ralph L. Lewis with Gregg Lewis, *Learning to Preach Like Jesus* (Westchester, IL: Crossway, 1989), 22.
31. John Donne, "Sermon No. 1: Second of My Prebend Sermons upon My Five Psalms," in *The Sermons of John Donne*, ed. Evelyn M. Simpson and George R. Potter (Berkeley: University of California Press, 1954), 7:65.
32. Barbara Brown Taylor, *The Preaching Life* (Cambridge, MA: Cowley, 1993), 39.
33. See, e.g., Howard G. Hendricks and William D. Hendricks, *Living by the Book* (Chicago: Moody, 1991), 182.
34. Source unknown.
35. Horace, as paraphrased by Richard Sennett, *The Corrosion of Character: The Personal Consequences of Work in the New Capitalism* (New York: W. W. Norton, 1998), 10.
36. As cited in Michael G. Moriarty, *The Perfect 10* (Grand Rapids: Zondervan, 2000), 132.
37. The first person to use this language of "orascript," I believe, was Clyde Fant.
38. As quoted in Dave Andrews, *Building a Better World: Developing Communities of Hope in Troubled Times* (New York: Crossroad, 1998), 38. Thanks to Shane Claiborne for pointing out the quote.
39. As Murray Frick so memorably phrases it in his book by that title, *Reach the Back Row: Creative Approaches for High-Impact Preaching* (Loveland, CO: Vital Ministry, 1999).
40. Eric Qualman, *Socialnomics: How Social Media Transforms the Way We Live and Do Business* (Hoboken, NJ: John Wiley & Sons, 2010).
41. David Abulafia, "Libels of Blood," *Times Literary Supplement*, March 2, 2007, 11–12.
42. Fleming Rutledge, *Help My Unbelief* (Grand Rapids: Eerdmans, 2000), 142.
43. Elizabeth Gilbert, *Eat, Pray, Love: One Woman's Search for Everything across Italy, India and Indonesia* (New York: Viking, 2006), 81.
44. George Bernard Shaw as quoted in *Apple Seeds* 18 (September 2002), http://www.appleseeds.org/Sept_02.htm.

CHAPTER 4: BLOOD STREAM: SCRIPTURES

1. A helpful elaboration of the symbiotic relationship between sermon and Scripture is found in Raquel A. St. Clair, "Prayerful Exegesis," *African American Pulpit* 5 (Summer 2002): 20–22.
2. Charles Spurgeon, "The Last Words of Christ on the Cross," in *Metropolitan Tabernacle Pulpit: Sermons Preached by C. H. Spurgeon* (1899; repr., Pasadena, TX: Pilgrim, 1977), 45:495.

3. Leander Keck, *The Bible in the Pulpit: The Renewal of Biblical Preaching* (Nashville: Abingdon, 1978), 36.
4. 1 Thess. 2:13.
5. Luke 4:21.
6. Luke 24:45.
7. As quoted in Edward F. Marquart, *Quest for Better Preaching* (Minneapolis: Augsburg, 1985), 83–84.
8. Charles Haddon Spurgeon, Sermon No. 1675, "Out of Egypt."
9. Cf. Rev. 2:7.
10. Isa. 40:3; Jer. 22:29; Mark 1:3; Luke 3:4.
11. See Lisa Miller, essay, "Special to CNN"; Belief blog: "How Technology Could Bring Down the Church," May 15, 2011: http://religion.blogs.cnn.com/2011/05/15/my-take-how-technology-could-bring-down-the-church/ (accessed Oct. 10, 2013).
12. David W. Henderson, *Culture Shift: Communicating God's Truth to Others*, foreword by Haddon Robinson (Grand Rapids: Baker, 1998), 141.
13. Martin Luther, "To Philip Melanchthon, Wartburg, August 1, 1521," in his *Letters I*, ed. and trans. Gottfried G. Krodel, vol. 48 of *Luther's Works*, ed. Helmut T. Lehmann (Philadelphia: Fortress Press, 1963), 281–82.
14. With two important exceptions: Acts 18–28 and Rev. 8–20.
15. First *Homiletics*, then *Preaching Plus*, now Sermons.com. I also started the first open-source preaching resource on the Web, which I called "wikiletics," and contributed to that for two years.
16. See the essay by George Lindbeck, "Barth and Textuality," *Theology Today* 43 (1986): 361–76. See also Neil B. Macdonald, *Karl Barth and the Strange New World with the Bible* (Carisle, UK: Paternoster, 2000).
17. John Calvin, *Institutes of the Christian Religion*, Library of Christian Classics, ed. John T. McNeill (Philadelphia: Westminster, 1960), 2:1018.
18. Wesley bluntly told him "he should either labour with his hands, or preach no more," but then offered to set him up in business. *The Journal of Charles Wesley* (Grand Rapids: Baker, 1980), 2:90.
19. *Fulfilled in Your Hearing: The Homily in the Sunday Assembly of the U.S. Conference of Catholic Bishops* (Washington, DC, 1982); see http://old.usccb.org/plm/fiyh.shtml.
20. Ibid. See chapter 1 for an early critique of the historical-critical method of approaching Scripture from a Roman Catholic perspective. Walter Vogels, *Reading and Preaching the Bible: A New Semiotic Approach* (Wilmington, DE: Michael Glazier, 1986).
21. John R. W. Stott, *Between Two Worlds: The Art of Preaching in the Twentieth Century* (Grand Rapids: Eerdmans, 1982), 125–26.
22. As cited in James A. Wallace, *Imaginal Preaching: An Archetypal Perspective* (New York: Paulist, 1995), 19.

CHAPTER 5: BLOOD TYPES AND BLOOD SCREENING: DEDUCTION, INDUCTION, ABDUCTION, AND TRANSDUCTION

1. For more on a style to fit the culture, see David Buttrick, "On Doing Homiletics Today," in *Intersections: Post-critical Studies in Preaching*, ed. Richard L. Eslinger (Grand Rapids: Eerdmans, 1994), 95.
2. See David L. Marshall, *Vico and the Transformation of Rhetoric in Early Modern Europe* (Cambridge: Cambridge University Press, 2012).
3. Ralph L. Lewis with Gregg Lewis, *Learning to Preach Like Jesus* (Westchester, IL: Crossway, 1989), 27.

4. Eugene Lowry, *The Homiletical Plot: The Sermon as Narrative Art Form,* expanded ed. (Louisville: Westminster John Knox, 2001), 28–87.

5. LeRoy E. Kennel, "Cultural Counterpointing: A Hermeneutical/Homiletical Crux," *Papers of the 35th Academy of Homiletics* (2000).

6. Supposed examples of Jesus' expository style: Jesus' expounding of Isa. 61:1–2 in the synagogue (Luke 4:16–21); Emmaus (Luke 24:27, 32, 44–49). Other examples: Stephen just before they stoned him (Acts 7:2–53); Philip (Acts 8:27–35).

7. C. Richard Wells, "Jesus Did Not Have a Website: A Fresh Look at Jesus the Preacher," paper presented at the 2002 Evangelical Homiletics Society; www.ehomi letics.com/papers/02/papers02.php. Wells is from Criswell College.

8. Peter L. Steinke, *Healthy Congregations: A Systems Approach* (Washington, DC: Alban Institute, 1996), 91.

9. Logic texts often treat abduction as "reasoning to the likeliest explanation" and categorize it as a type of induction. Umberto Eco identified four types of abduction: (1) overcoded abduction; (2) undercoded abduction; (3) creative abduction—as exemplified in Thomas Kuhn's "paradigm construction" of *The Structure of Scientific Revolutions* (Chicago: University of Chicago Press, 1962); and (4) meta-abduction. See Umberto Eco, "Horns, Hooves, and Insteps: Some Hypotheses on Three Types of Abduction," in *The Sign of Three: Dupin, Holmes, Peirce,* ed. Umberto Eco and Thomas A. Sebeok (Bloomington: Indiana University Press, 1988), 206–7.

10. Peirce, the founder of pragmatism, and the one who coined the term, later disowned his own creation because of those like William James who took it in directions he didn't like. Peirce believed that "in order to reason well ... it is absolutely necessary to possess ... such virtues as intellectual honesty and sincerity and real love of truth." C. S. Peirce, "Elements of Logic," in *Collected Papers of Charles Sanders Peirce,* ed. Charles Hartshorne, Paul Weiss, and Arthur Burks (Cambridge, MA: Belknap Press of Harvard University Press, 1965), 2:43 (vol. 2, para. 82). For Peirce, again in his words, "Truth" meant a judgment "that something is SO ... whether you, or I, or anybody, thinks it is so or not." Peirce, "The Objectivity of Truth," in "Elements of Logic," in Hartshorne, Weiss, and Burks, *Collected Papers,* 2:71 (vol. 2, para. 135). For an excellent chapter on Peirce, see "A Place for the Coin," in Crystal L. Downing, *Changing Signs of Truth: A Christian Introduction to the Semiotics of Communication* (Downers Grove, IL: InterVarsity, 2012), 198–220.

11. Edward T. Oakes, "Discovering the American Aristotle," *First Things* 38 (December 1993): 27.

12. Ibid.

13. Peter Ochs, "Charles Peirce's Unpragmatic Christianity: A Rabbinic Appraisal," *American Journal of Theology and Philosophy* 9 (January–May 1988): 41–73, 41.

14. Ibid., 41–73.

15. "With your eyes open, awake to what is about or within you, and open conversation with yourself, for such is all meditation." See Peirce's 1908 essay, "A Neglected Argument for the Reality of God," in his "Scientific Metaphysics" in Hartshorne, Weiss, and Burks, *Collected Papers,* vol. 6, para. 461.

16. "Notice the extraordinary room, at the outer reaches of inference and affectability, that Peirce gives to the free play of the imagination as a moment of inferential judgment: at the outer penumbrae of his logic we sense almost a dance of free association going on. As logic radiates outward in the energy of entailment, it becomes less rigid, less deductive, and more reliant on hunches, hypotheses, free associations, where the 'entailment' is now no longer one of hard necessity but comes from Musement's delight in weaving hypotheses. One of his more startling metaphors, in fact, for the universe is 'melted con-

tinuity,' and that melting almost seems to well up from within a universe that is itself teeming with life and activity." Oakes, "Discovering the American Aristotle," 24–33.

17. Max H. Fisch (Peirce's official biographer), Peirce Edition Project by Indiana University Press; John K. Sheriff, *Charles Peirce's Guess at the Riddle: Grounds for Human Significance* (Bloomington: Indiana University Press, 1994); Michael Raposa, *Peirce's Philosophy of Religion* (Bloomington: Indiana University Press, 1993); "Peirce Turns Out to Be a Philosopher in the Grand Style of Plato, Aristotle, Plotinus, Kant, Hegel, Whitehead, and a Few Others," Gordon Kaufman; Ochs, "Peirce, Pragmatism and the Logic of Scripture."

18. For the difference between the three, see Hartshorne, Weiss, and Burks, *Collected Papers*, 2:632, 641–44.

19. For an excellent interpretation of Peirce's abductive method, see Downing, *Changing Signs of Truth*, 228–34.

20. Peirce, quoted in Oakes, "Discovering the American Aristotle," 24–33.

21. Matt. 7:16, my paraphrase. NIV: "By their fruit you will recognize them."

22. Robert A. Traina is responsible for the formulation of the "triad."

23. Charles S. Pierce, *The Essential Pierce*, The Pierce Edition Project vol. 2 (Bloomington: Indiana University Press, 1994), 235.

24. A scholastic maxim from Aristotle, acknowledged by many philosophers.

25. There are two kinds of attractors. First, stable equilibrium attractors draw all trajectories of a system to a single point or periodic cycle. In other words, a stable attractor functions in regular, predictable patterns and is highly integrated and ordered. It serves as "a pattern of behavior into which a system ultimately settles in the absence of outside disturbances." An attractor is a potential state of behavior that is in process of actualization.

26. William A. Dyrness, *Poetic Theology: God and the Poetics of Everyday Life* (Grand Rapids: Eerdmans, 2010), 307.

27. Haddon Robinson, "What Is Expository Preaching?," in *Making a Difference in Preaching: Haddon Robinson on Biblical Preaching*, ed. Scott M. Gibson (Grand Rapids: Baker, 1999), 64.

28. Ibid.

29. Charles Koller gives the best metaphor for expository "points" in his analogy of structuring sermons to crafting arrows, as practiced by Native Americans: "He realized that his very survival might depend upon the excellence of his arrow. The shaft must therefore be absolutely straight, lest it wobble in flight; the point must be sharp enough to penetrate; the feathers must be in just the right amount to steady the arrow in flight, yet not to retard its flight or dull its thrust. Similarly, the sermon must have a clear thought running straight through the length of it, a sharp point at the end, and just enough 'feathers' to cope with the atmosphere through which it must pass on its way to the target." See James Braga, *How to Prepare Bible Messages*, rev. ed. (Sisters, OR: Multnomah, 1969, repr. 1981).

30. Mark Abbott, "Should Preaching Teach?," *Preaching* 14 (May/June 1999): 4–6.

31. For the ways in which emotions drive behavior and learning more than reason, see Daniel Goleman, *Emotional Intelligence* (New York: Bantam, 1995), 8–9. See also Daniel Goleman, *Working with Emotional Intelligence* (New York: Bantam, 1998). Emotion researcher Paul Ekman learned that people around the world have common facial expressions that convey emotional states. Even with language barriers, facial expressions can be "read" across cultures. See Paul Ekman, Wallace V. Friesen, and Phoebe Ellsworth, *Emotion in the Human Face: Guidelines for Research and an Integration of Findings* (New York: Pergamon, 1972), 166–67. The emotional mind is more powerful than the rational mind.

Notes

32. Walter J. Burghardt, SJ, *When Christ Meets Christ: Homilies on the Just Word* (New York: Paulist, 1993), 61.

33. "I do not mean ranting and raving. I do mean that our people should sense from our words and our faces, from our gestures and our whole posture, that we love this sinning, struggling community with a crucifying passion; that we agonize over our own sinfulness, our failure to be holier than we are; that we weep with the refugees whose tears water the way of Kurdistan; that we too are awfully vulnerable, must at times cry out, 'Lord, help my unbelief'; that our celibacy has not turned us into crotchety old bachelors but opens us warmly to all who need the touch of our hand; in a word, that we too share the dread-full human condition." Burghardt, *When Christ Meets Christ*, 61.

34. Harvey Cox, *Fire from Heaven: The Rise of Pentecostal Spirituality and the Reshaping of Religion in the Twenty-first Century* (Cambridge, MA: De Capo, 2001).

35. As cited by Daniel O'Leary, "And Did Those Feet . . . ," *The Tablet* (August 18, 2012), 8.

36. This has always been the Celtic way of evangelism.

37. Or as Leith Anderson puts it, "If you experience God, you will have the right teaching." Leith Anderson, *A Church for the 21st Century* (Minneapolis: Bethany House, 1992), 21.

38. Arguably the inductive means of preaching began with the publication of Fred Craddock's *As One with Authority: Essays on Inductive Preaching* (Nashville: Abingdon, 1971).

39. Timothy S. Warren, "Preaching the Cross to a Postmodern World," *Ministry* 72 (May 1999): 18–20, quote on 20.

40. For an excellent introduction to "The Inductive Method in Preaching," see Fred Craddock's essay by that title in Richard L. Eslinger, ed., *A New Hearing: Living Options in Homiletic Method* (Nashville: Abingdon, 1997), 95–132 (quote on 96). Eugene L. Lowry, *The Sermon: Dancing at the Edge of Mystery* (Nashville: Abingdon), is a good primer on inductive sermons.

41. Wayne Brouwer, "How to Land the Sermon," www.preaching.com/sermons/11567362/page–2/

42. The best treatment of "moves" and the need to shift from "points" is from Vanderbilt's homiletics professor David Buttrick, *Homiletic: Moves and Structures* (Philadelphia: Fortress, 1987), 23–79.

43. Eslinger, *A New Hearing*, 125.

44. Preparation and the presentation can each go either way and go together or opposite. I can start my study of the biblical text without knowing what I want the main thread of my sermon to be and discover it along the way but introduce it at the beginning of my sermon and support it deductively with the rest of the message. Conversely, I can start my study with the premise, find Scripture to support it, but deliver the message with suspense and gradually (and inductively) unveil the premise as I go.

45. Eugene Lowry, *The Homiletical Plot: The Sermon as Narrative Art Form* (Westminster: John Knox Press, 2000).

46. Thomas G. Long, *The Witness of Preaching* (Louisville: Westminster John Knox, 1989), 85.

47. As quoted in Joseph Brent, *Charles Sanders Peirce: A Life* (Bloomington: Indiana University Press, 1993), 72.

48. I found this in Louis Jacobs, *Jewish Preaching* (Middlesex, UK: Valletine Mitchell, 2004).

49. James E. Loder, *The Transforming Moment*, 2nd ed. (Colorado Springs: Helmers & Howard, 1989), 29.

50. Charles Sanders Peirce, "Three Types of Reasoning," in his "Pragmatism and Pragmaticism," in Hartshorne, Weiss, and Burks, *Collected Papers*, vol. 5, para. 171.

51. Peirce, "Critical Logic," in Hartshorne, Weiss, and Burks, *Collected Papers*, 2:387
(para. 643).

52. Peirce, "Critical Logic," 5:181. Also see 5:395ff., where Peirce uses a musical analogy
to describe what abduction is. "We never hear a melody. We only hear one tone or set
of tones at a time. Memory and anticipation must work together with the presently
heard tone. Thus in even so simple an act as listening to a melody the mind is called
to fill in creatively. In the case of extremely foreign or strange music, it is unable to
do this and the mind cannot even determine what the melody is though it hears all
the notes!" The words are those of William H. Davis, who downplays the distinctions
between induction and abduction in "Synthetic Knowledge as 'Abduction,'" *Southern
Journal of Philosophy* 8 (Spring 1970): 41, 37–43.

53. For more explication of the three different kinds of reasoning—induction, deduction, and abduction (or sometimes Peirce called it "retroduction")—see "'We Prag-
matists': Peirce and Rorty in Conversation," in Susan Haack, *Manifesto of a Passionate
Moderate: Unfashionable Essays* (Chicago: University of Chicago Press, 1998), 31–47.

54. "Biblical preaching is not getting the truth out of the Bible, but allowing people to
get into the Bible at the level of lived experience. The Bible is not God's proposition
book, it is God's storybook." John Robert McFarland, "The Illustration Is the Point,"
Christian Ministry (January–February, 1988): 21.

55. David Storey, *A Serious Man* (London: Jonathan Cape, 1998), 128.

56. Oakes, "Discovering the American Aristotle," 27. The differences in logical order
between deduction, induction, and abduction are outlined below by Robert B. Stew-
art, assistant professor of philosophy and theology, New Orleans Baptist Theological
Seminary, as presented to the Evangelical Homiletics Society, October 18, 2002, in
response to my paper:

    Deduction
    Rule: All A are B Rule: All beans from this bag are white.
    Case: C is A Case: These beans are from this bag.
    Result: Ergo C is B Result: Therefore these beans are white.

    Induction
    Case: C is A Case: These beans are from this bag.
    Result: C is B Result: These beans are white.
    Rule: Ergo all A are B Rule: All beans from this bag are white.

    Abduction
    Rule: All A are B Rule: All beans from this bag are white.
    Result: C is B Result: These beans are white.
    Case: Ergo C is A Case: Ergo these beans are from this bag.

57. Robert S. Corrington, *A Semiotic Theory of Theology and Philosophy* (Cambridge:
Cambridge University Press, 2000).

58. John Milbank, *The Word Made Strange: Theology, Language, Culture* (Oxford: Black-
well, 1997), 115n42.

59. *Summa Theologiae* II–II, q. 1, a. 2, ad. 2. "The Creed expresses the things of faith as
they are the term of the believer's act. Such an act does not have a proposition as its
term, but a reality, since just as with scientific knowledge so also with faith, the only
reason for formulating a proposition is that we may have knowledge about the real."
See Thomas Aquinas, *Faith* (2a, 2ae 1–7), vol. 31 of *Summa Theologiae*, trans T. C.
O'Brien (New York: McGraw-Hill, 1974), 13.

Notes

60. Martin Gardner, foreword to Roger Penrose, *The Emperor's New Mind: Concerning Computers, Minds, and the Laws of Physics* (New York: Oxford University Press, 1989), v.

61. Penrose, *Emperor's New Mind*, 421.

62. Ibid., 282.

63. As cited in Oakes, "Discovering the American Aristotle," 27.

64. As Henry J. LangKnecht points out in his "A Homiletics of Surprise," Homiletixeforum (Academy of Homiletics Journal).

65. Murray Frick, *Reach the Back Row: Creative Approaches for High Impact Preaching* (Loveland, CO: Vital Ministry, 1999).

66. So argues Michael Quicke about holistic learning in "Preaching to Listeners: Communicating with Contemporary Listerners," Papers of the 2002 Meetings of the Evangelical Homiletics Society.

67. "I do not embrace the notion that preaching should tell stories because the gospel is essentially a 'story.' The language of faith is a 'horizontal' narrativity, but it is also 'vertical' symbolic-reflective language that grasps symbols within the hermeneutic of a 'being-saved community.' Thus, I stress the notion of plotted mobility rather than narrativity." Buttrick, "On Doing Homiletics Today," 95n30.

68. Leslie Houlden, *The Strange Story of the Gospels: Finding Doctrine through Narrative* (London: SPCK, 2002), 2, 7–9.

69. Lowry, *The Sermon*, 1997.

70. David James Randolph, *The Renewal of Preaching in the 21st Century* (Minneapolis: Fortress, 1969; 30th anniversary ed., Babylon: Hanging Gardens, 1998).

71. Ibid. (Fortress, 1969), 24.

72. Ibid., 30.

73. Ibid., 127.

74. Ronald Allen argues that there are more than four biblical forms and "invites the preacher to rediscover the experience that gave rise to the text and to create a similar experience for the contemporary congregation." Ronald J. Allen, ed., *Patterns of Preaching: A Sermon Sampler* (St. Louis: Chalice, 1998), 37–38. See also Robert Stephen Reid, "Postmodernism and the Function of the New Homiletic in Post-Christendom Congregations," *Homiletic* 20 (1995): 1–13.

75. "Inductive approach" is also equated with the "new homiletic" and is most associated with Charles Rice, Henry Mitchell, Eugene Lowry, David Buttrick, and David James Randolph. See the article by Robert S. Reid, Jeffrey Bullock, and David Fleer, "Preaching as the Creation of an Experience: The Not-So-Rational Revolution of the New Homiletic," *Journal of Communication and Religion* 18 (1995): 1–9.

76. Two key works in the new homiletic, Fred Craddock's *As One without Authority: Essays on Inductive Preaching* and David Randolph's *The Renewal of Preaching*, moved from deductive rationalism and argument to inductive reasoning.

77. See John 1:14.

78. In one important sense, participation was rediscovered by the Protestant Reformers. Congregations were expected to give responses in the 1549 Prayer Book, which was designed to elicit explicit participation. That's what a "vernacular" liturgy meant. In the 1552 Prayer Book, the laity were encouraged to join daily in the offices of the morning and evening prayer, formerly the preserve of the clergy.

79. New York Times article, "Carlos Fuentes Turns to Theater,"; www.nytimes.com/1982/06/06/theater/carlos-fuentes-turns-to-theater.html

80. George Lakoff and Mark Johnson, *Metaphors We Live By* (Chicago: University of Chicago Press, 1980), 125.

81. Ronald J. Allen et al., *Listening to Listeners: Homiletical Case Studies* (St. Louis: Chalice, 2004).

82. Interview with Brian Eno, "Organic, Unfinished, and Addictive," *180/360/720 Communication and Business* (Sept. 28, 2010); www.180360720.no/index.php/archive/ organic-unfinished-and-addictive/.

83. "Everything about the setting said control: ushers parading in lockstep, people sitting straight in even rows, mood lights controlled by rheostat, pristine architecture." Carroll Saussy, *The Gift of Anger: A Call to Faithful Action* (Louisville: Westminster John Knox, 1995), x.

84. See Ps. 27:8 KJV.

85. Kirk Byron Jones, "An Interview with J. Alfred Smith Sr.," *African American Pulpit* (Winter 1998–99): 81–82.

86. Lam. 3:21.

87. John S. McClure, *The Roundtable Pulpit: Where Leadership and Preaching Meet* (Nashville: Abingdon, 1995), 7.

88. James Baldwin, "Down at the Cross: Letter from a Region in My Mind," in his *The Fire Next Time* (New York: Dial, 1963), 25–120.

89. Buttrick, "On Doing Homiletics Today," 95n30. For Bishop Willimon's critique of narrative preaching, see William Willimon, "Preaching: Entertainment or Exposition?" *Christian Century* (February 28, 1992), 204–6.

90. Robert Frost's 1931 Amherst College lecture titled "Education by Poetry," in *Selected Prose of Robert Frost*, ed. Hyde Cox and Edward Connery Lathem (New York: Holt, Rinehart and Winston, 1966), 37, 39.

91. As cited by Wayne V. McDill, *The Moment of Truth: A Guide to Effective Sermon Delivery* (Nashville: Broadman & Holman, 1999), 137.

92. Joel B. Green, "The (Re-)Turn to Narrative," in Joel B. Green and Michael Pasquarello III, *Narrative Reading, Narrative Preaching: Reuniting New Testament Interpretation and Proclamation* (Grand Rapids: Baker, 2003), 22–23.

CHAPTER 6: BLOOD FLOW: BICAMERAL PREACHING

1. For more on "Pay attention," see my *Nudge: Awakening Each Other to the God Who's Already There* (Colorado Springs: WaterBrook, 2010), esp. chap. 1.

2. Fred Craddock, *Preaching* (Nashville: Abingdon, 1985), 204.

3. Jill Bolte Taylor, TED Talk, "A Stroke of Insight," http://www.ted.com/talks/jill_ bolte_taylor_s_powerful_stroke_of_insight.html.

4. François Mauriac, foreword to Elie Wiesel, *Night*, trans. Stella Rodway (New York: Bantam, 1960), x–xi.

5. For an especially provocative treatment of the reason for the brain's hemispheres—at least provocative enough for Archbishop Rowan Williams of Canterbury to host a private seminar with the author—see Iain McGilchrist, *The Master and His Emissary: The Divided Brain and the Making of the Western World* (New Haven, CT: Yale University Press, 2009).

6. Eugene L. Lowry, *The Sermon: Dancing at the Edge of Mystery* (Nashville: Abingdon, 1997), 43.

7. Our propensity to address God in terms of concepts and theology rather than relationships is explored by Mark Filiatreau in his critique of J. I. Packer's *Knowing God*: "I realized [the book] was not about knowing God, but about knowing about God.... *Knowing God* struck me as a careful scriptural exegesis of God's attributes, of which I was already well versed." See Mark Filiatreau, "'Good News' or 'Old News,'" *Regeneration Quarterly* (Winter 1995): 15.

8. McGilchrist, *The Master and His Emissary*, 74.

Notes

9. Ibid., 93.
10. See ibid., pt. 2: "How the Brain Has Shaped Our World," 240–427. See also W. F. Bynum, "On the Right," *Times Literary Supplement* (April 2, 2010), 12.
11. Ibid., 386. The actual full quote is: "It is the Industrial Revolution which enabled the left hemisphere to make its most audacious assault yet on the world of the right hemisphere."
12. Martin Luther, *Martin Luther's Basic Theological Writings*, 3rd ed. (Minneapolis: Fortress, 2012), taken from his "Preface to the New Testament (1522, revised 1546)," 93–96.
13. The Pharisees were known for their starch eloquence, a rhetoric that could feel like the dreary drip of desultory declamations.
14. Matt. 13:10.
15. Luci Shaw, "Reversing Entropy," *Image* 41 (Winter 2003): 96.
16. Robin R. Meyers, *With Ears to Hear: Preaching as Self-Persuasion* (Cleveland: Pilgrim, 1993), 2–3.
17. Richard Florida, *The Rise of the Creative Class: And How It's Transforming Work, Leisure, Community and Everyday Life*, 2nd ed. (New York: Basic, 2012).
18. Kotsker Rebbe, quoted in Adin Steinsaltz, *On Being Free* (Northvale, NJ: Jason Aronson, 1995), 13.
19. Amos N. Wilder, *Early Christian Rhetoric: The Language of the Gospel* (Cambridge, MA: Harvard University Press, 1971), 72, 84.
20. C. H. Dodd, *Parables of the Kingdom* (London: Nisbett, 1936), 5; and see p. 16 for the interaction metaphor discussion.
21. John Dominic Crossan, *In Parables: The Challenge of the Historical Jesus* (New York: Harper & Row, 1973), 10–15, 17–22.
22. Wilder, *Early Christian Rhetoric*, 84.
23. Franz Kafka, *Parables and Paradoxes* (New York: Schocken, 1958), 10 (German text) and 11 (English text).
24. As quoted in Jan Phillips, *God Is at Eye Level: Photography as a Healing Art* (Wheaton, IL: Quest, 2000), 25.
25. "And when Jesus finished these sayings, the crowds were astonished at his teaching, for he taught them as a parabolist, rather than as a scribe." Philip Culbertson, "Reclaiming the Matthean Vineyard Parables," *Encounter* 49 (Autumn 1988): 257–74.
26. Aristotle, quoted in Herbert L. Kessler and David Nirenberg, eds., *Judaism and Christian Art: Authentic Anxieties from the Catacombs to Colonialism* (Philadelphia: University of Pennsylvania Press, 2011), 388. Socrates was the first to suggest that abstract language might be at base metaphorical, a hidden, extended metaphor, a position Giambattista Vico later underlined with his argument that all perception begins in metaphor and that metaphors make or break philosophy, science, and religion.
27. Structuralism got rid of this Cartesian debate between "trope" (figure of speech) and "schema" (figure of thought): metaphors can coexist on both the linguistic and conceptual levels. For more, see V. Sage, "Metaphor," in *Concise Encyclopedia of Language and Religion*, ed. John F. A. Sawyer and J. M. Y. Simpson (New York: Elsevier, 2001), 266–73.
28. It is hard for literal-minded people to hear this, since literalism takes umbrage at images and takes no stock in metaphors. Such literalism can be found on both ends of the theological spectrum. I had a curate from England protest my metaphors of walking, kneeling, and standing because they weren't "inclusive" and excluded people of disabilities. When I challenged her with this politically correct fundamentalism,

which would also forbid any metaphors of dancing, or most other active verbs (e.g., see, hear, touch, taste), she remained unpersuaded and hostile to any metaphors that would ever exclude anyone.

29. Denise Levertov, "On Belief in the Physical Resurrection of Jesus," in her *Sands of the Well* (New York: New Directions, 1996), 115.

30. Aristotle, *De Poetica*, trans. Ingram Bywater, in *The Works of Aristotle* (New York: Clarendon, 1924), 11:1457b.

31. Luke 24:45.

32. See chapter 8.

33. As quoted in Jaroslav Pelikan, *Christianity and Classical Culture: The Metamorphosis of Natural Theology in the Christian Encounter with Hellenism*, Gifford Lectures Series (New Haven, CT: Yale University Press, 1993), 284–85.

34. Matt. 20:16.

35. Matt. 6:24.

36. Deut. 32:2.

37. Eric Waaler, *The Shema and the First Commandment in First Corinthians* (Tübingen: Mohr Siebeck, 2008), http://books.google.com/books?id=bM4FVcJ1f3EC&pg=PA21 4&dq=shema+and+rain&hl=en&sa=X&ei=h7t_Ub7RBa_h4AP3jYDgDw&ved=0C DIQ6AEwAA#v=onepage&q=shema%20and%20rain&f=false.

38. See my *Viral: How Social Networking Is Poised to Ignite Revival* (Colorado Springs: WaterBrook, 2012).

39. G. Michael McCrossin, *Broken Rainbows: Growing Faith in a Changing World* (Kansas City, MO: Sheed & Ward, 1997), 104.

40. See Leonard Sweet and Frank Viola, *Jesus: A Theography* (Nashville: Thomas Nelson, 2012). For more of the "double ring," see Leonard Sweet, *SoulTsunami* (Grand Rapids: Zondervan, 2001); and Leonard Sweet, *Carpe Mañana* (Grand Rapids: Zondervan, 2001).

41. For more on the "Well-Curve," see Daniel Pink, "The Shape of Things to Come," *Wired* (May 2003), 27, 30; Sweet, *Carpe Mañana*.

42. Matt. 19:24. I love how Harold Fickett reframes Jesus' riddle: "It is easier for an elephant to do the backstroke in a teacup … it is easier for a goldfish to play a Bach cantata … it is easier for a semi-trailer truck to ricochet through a microchip." Harold Fickett, *Conversations with Jesus: Unexpected Answers to Contemporary Questions* (Colorado Springs: Pinon, 1999), 69–70.

43. Patricia Wilson-Kastner, *Imagery for Preaching* (Minneapolis: Fortress, 1989), 13.

44. Luke 14:26.

45. Matt. 23:27.

46. Bob Phillips, compiler, *Phillips' Book of Great Thoughts, Funny Sayings* (Wheaton, IL: Tyndale, 1993), 295.

47. W. H. Auden, "The Truest Poetry Is the Most Feigning," in W. H. Auden, *Collected Shorter Poems, 1927–1957* (New York: Random House, 1957), 316.

48. Matt. 16:18.

49. Matt. 5:45 ERV. For more on Jesus' use of poetry, see Stephen Andrew Missick, *Jesus the Poet: Christ's Words as Hebrew Poetry* (Los Angeles: CreateSpace, 2011).

50. Walter Brueggemann, *Finally Comes the Poet: Daring Speech for Proclamation* (Minneapolis: Fortress, 1989), 9. For more on the preacher as poet and imagesmith, see Heather Elkins, *Holy Stuff of Life: Stories, Poems and Prayers about Human Things* (Cleveland: Pilgrim, 2006). My favorite that I've used often in sermons is Elkins's "The Economics of Epiphany."

Notes

51. For Jesus asking the questions, see Mark 8:14–21, 27–30. Also see Conrad Gempf, *Jesus Asked: What He Wanted to Know* (Grand Rapids: Zondervan, 2003).
52. Mark 4:13–20.
53. Mark 7:17–23.
54 Mark 4:34.
55. Michael Polanyi, *Personal Knowledge: Towards a Post-Critical Philosophy* (Chicago: University of Chicago Press, 1958), 199.
56. Walter Brueggemann, *Finally Comes the Poet*, 109.
57. See chapter 3 for the meaning of EPIC.
58. Jean-Paul Sartre, *Nausea*, trans. Lloyd Alexander (New York: New Directions, 1964), 39.
59. Ibid., 250.
60. Jonah 4:2.
61. William Butler Yeats, "Byzantium."
62. Luke 24:45.
63. Geerhardus Vos, *Biblical Theology: Old and New Testament* (Grand Rapids: Eerdmans, 1948), 13.
64. Shakespeare, *As You Like It*, act 2, scene 1.

CHAPTER 7: BLOOD CELLS: ORGANIC ARCHITECTURE

1. Edmund Wilson, in "'Edmund Wilson': American Critic," by Colm Toibin, *New York Times Book Review* (Sept. 4, 2005): www.nytimes.com/2005/09/04/books/review/04TOIBIN.html?pagewanted=all.
2. "The Greek word for 'carpenter' in the Gospels actually stands for an underlying Aramaic term that is used metaphorically in the Talmud to denote a scholar." Stanley E. Porter, *Criteria for Authenticity in Historical Jesus Research* (Bloomsbury: T&T Clark, 2004), 81; see also Margaret Starbird, *Magdalene's Lost Legacy* (Rochester, VT: Bear & Co., 2003), 53: "In classical Greek, the primary (and original) meaning of *tekton* was carpenter or wood-worker, but depending on the writer and period, it could also mean mason, metal-worker, sculptor, or a craftsman in any art, e.g. *tektones sophoi* ('wise craftsman, craftsman of wisdom') to refer to poets."
3. Mark 4:34.
4. In the nineteenth century, adventure stories of young boys/men battling dragons and monsters were called "bloods." See Iain Mackintosh, *Architecture, Actor and Audience* (London: Routledge, 1993).
5. Keith Oatley, "Fiction Hones Social Skills," *Scientific American* (Nov. 20, 2011), 7–11 (www.scientificamerican.com/article.cfm?id=in-the-minds-of-others) emphasized the power of image, metaphor, and story within one's life, noting that they can influence people from within the deepest levels of their psyche.
6. See my "Apples/Oranges" chapter in my *Viral: How Social Networking Is Poised to Ignite Revival* (Colorado Springs: WaterBrook, 2012).
7. So argued Paul Ricoeur in *Interpretation Theory: Discourse and the Surplus of Meaning* (Fort Worth: Texas Christian University Press, 1976), 45–69.
8. Luke 10:16.
9. 1 Cor. 1:23; 2:2.
10. Charles Haddon Spurgeon, "Christ Precious to Believers" in his *Sermons* (New York: Funk & Wagnalls, 1857), 6:357.
11. See Matt. 13:5; Acts 28:27; Heb. 5:11 KJV.
12. Matt. 11:15; 13:9; 13:43; Mark 4:9; 4:23; Luke 8:8; 14:35; Rev 2:7; 3:22. See also Prov 20:12.

Notes

13. 1 Cor. 11:18–22.
14. Geoffrey Preston, *Faces of the Church: Meditation on a Mystery and Its Images* (Grand Rapids: Eerdmans, 1997), 6.
15. Thomas Aquinas was insistent about this terminology because we don't so much encounter the "risen Christ" as the "rising Christ."
16. Friedrich Nietzsche, as quoted in Bruce Sanguin, *The Emerging Church: A Model for Change and a Map for Renewal* (Incline Village, NV: Copperhouse, 2008), 43.
17. For the preacher as "custodian of metaphor," see James A. Wallace, *Imaginal Preaching: An Archetypal Perspective* (New York: Paulist, 1995), 19. Thomas Troeger has also recognized the role of the preacher as architect of images in *Creating Fresh Images for Preaching* (Valley Forge, PA: Judson, 1982), 30; and *Ten Strategies for Preaching in a MultiMedia Culture* (Nashville: Abingdon, 1996), chap. 3 on "playing with an image," 39–47. So, too, Walter Brueggemann in his *Finally Comes the Poet* (Philadelphia: Fortress, 1989). Wallace, who is heavily influenced by Carl Jung and James Hillman, is a little addled (to my mind) when he says "Rhetoric, the art of persuasion, has given way to poesis, the art of making or shaping with words. Images have attained at least a parity with concepts" (*Imaginal Preaching*, 8).
18. Walter Benjamin, *Illuminations: Essays and Reflections* (New York: Schocken, 1969).
19. Jesus used both in his kingdom parables. See Matthew 13:44, "The kingdom of heaven is like treasure hidden in a field"; and Matthew 13:46, "The kingdom of heaven is like a merchant looking for fine pearls."
20. See Bryan Chapell, *Christ-Centered Preaching: Redeeming the Expository Sermon* (Grand Rapids: Baker, 1994), 269.
21. For more on defamiliarization, see Leonard Sweet, *Nudge: Awakening Each Other to the God Who's Already There* (Colorado Springs: WaterBrook, 2010), chap. 6.
22. The Renaissance rediscovery of the Lucretian notion that all creativity comes from the swerve is the subject of Stephen Greenblatt's book *The Swerve: How the World Became Modern* (New York: W. W. Norton, 2012). For its application in literary circles, see Nicholas Royle's *Veering: A Theory of Literature* (Edinburgh: Edinburgh University Press, 2012).
23. Louis Jacobs, *Jewish Preaching* (Portland, OR: Vallentine Mitchell, 2004), 23–24.
24. See the work of Lawrence W. Barsalou at Emory University; e.g., "Grounded Cognition," *Annual Review of Psychology* (August 15, 2007), 617–45.
25. I introduce this concept in *AquaChurch: Essential Leadership Arts for Piloting Your Church in Today's Fluid Culture* (Loveland, CO: Group, 2004).
26. Aristotle, *Poetics*, ed. Anthony Kerry, Oxford World Classics (Oxford: Oxford University Press, 2013).
27. Chapell, *Christ-Centered Preaching*, 39.
28. G. Robert Jacks, *Just Say the Word! Writing for the Ear* (Grand Rapids: Eerdmans, 1996), 37.
29. Paul Ricoeur, *Figuring the Sacred: Religion, Narrative, and Imagination* (Minneapolis: Augsburg, 1995), 309.
30. David L. Larsen, *The Anatomy of Preaching: Identifying the Issues in Preaching Today* (Grand Rapids: Baker, 1989), 121.
31. Thomas G. Long, *The Witness of Preaching* (Louisville: Westminster John Knox, 1989), 161.
32. Fred Craddock, *Preaching* (Nashville: Abingdon, 1985), 204.
33. Ian Macpherson, *The Art of Illustrating Sermons* (Nashville: Abingdon, 1964), 40.
34. Archibald Thomas Robertson, *Word Pictures in the New Testament* (Nashville: Broadman, 1932), 5:18.

35. For these stats, see Larsen, *The Anatomy of Preaching*.
36. Mark 4:27ff.
37. The best book on organic discipleship with gardening as the organizing metaphor is Robert Dale, *Seeds for the Future: Growing Organic Leaders for Living Churches* (St. Louis: Chalice, 2005).
38. Long, *The Witness of Preaching*, 93.
39. Craddock, *Preaching*, 204.
40. John 12:32.
41. Proverbs 18:2: "Fools find no pleasure in understanding but delight in airing their own opinions."
42. This case has also been made by Thomas G. Long in *The Witness of Preaching*, 105.
43. George Aichele, *Sign, Text, Scripture. Semiotics and the Bible* (Sheffield, UK: Sheffield Academic Press, 1997), 106–7.

CHAPTER 8: BLOOD BANK: NARRATIVE AND METAPHOR = NARRAPHOR

1. Gen. 2:4–23 VOICE.
2. John 14:6.
3. Luke 9:23.
4. Luke 1:72.
5. Matt. 22:37.
6. Gen. 9:7.
7. Matt. 28:19.
8. John 15:5.
9. John 10:7.
10. Luke 23:43.
11. Rubem A. Alves, *The Poet, the Warrior, the Prophet* (Philadelphia: Trinity Press International, 1990), 39.
12. Rob Weber, *Visual Leadership: The Church Leader as ImageSmith* (Nashville: Abingdon, 2002), 14.
13. Father William Lynch warns that the "world of the imagination is compact with ideas, so compact indeed that they cannot be sorted out from the images." William Lynch, "Religion and the Literary Imagination," in *Religion and Literature: The Convergence of Approaches* (*JAAR* Thematic Studies 47, no. 2 [June 1979]: 335), as quoted in *Intersections: Post-Critical Studies in Preaching*, ed. Richard L. Eslinger (Grand Rapids: Eerdmans, 1994), xii.
14. In *How Natives Think* (New York: Knopf, 1925).
15. James Richardson, *Vectors: Aphorisms and Ten-Second Essays* (Keene, NY: Ausable, 2001), 83.
16. George Lakoff and Mark Johnson, *Metaphors We Live By* (Chicago: University of Chicago Press, 1980), 5, 235.
17. David Buttrick, *Homiletic Moves and Structures* (Philadelphia: Fortress, 1987), 123.
18. See Max Black, *Models and Metaphors: Studies in Language and Philosophy* (Ithaca, NY: Cornell University Press, 1962); Buttrick, *Homiletic*; Lakoff and Johnson, *Metaphors We Live By*; George Lakoff and Mark Turner, *More Than Cool Reason: A Field Guide to Poetic Metaphor* (Chicago: University of Chicago Press, 1989); Richard Lischer, "What Language Shall I Borrow? The Role of Metaphor in Proclamation," *Dialog* 26 (1987): 281–86; Sallie McFague, *Metaphorical Theology: Models of God in Religious Language* (Philadelphia: Fortress, 1982); Andrew Ortony, "Metaphor, Lan-

Notes

guage, and Thought," in Andrew Ortony, *Metaphor and Thought*, 2nd ed. (New York: Cambridge University Press, 1993); Eduard Riegert, *Imaginative Shock: Preaching and Metaphor* (Burlington, ON: Trinity, 1990); Warren Wiersbe, *Preaching and Teaching with Imagination: The Quest for Biblical Ministry* (Wheaton, IL: Victor, 1994); Paul Scott Wilson, *The Practice of Preaching* (Nashville: Abingdon, 1995).

19. As quoted in Diane Hanson, "The Use of Automated Clinical Documentation," www.himss.org/asp/ContentRedirector.asp?ContentID=30601, accessed July 1, 2004.

20. Thomas Aquinas, *Christian Theology* (IaI), vol. 1 of *Summa Theologiae*, trans. Thomas Gilby (New York: McGraw-Hill, 1964), 35.

21. Ibid., 41.

22. Kenton C. Anderson, *Preaching with Conviction: A Connecting with Postmodern Listeners* (Grand Rapids: Kregel, 2001), 45.

23. Example taken from "Mirror and Metaphor," Pacifica Graduate Institute, http://www.pacifica.edu/innercontent-m.aspx?id=3278.

24. Elizabeth Achtemeier, *Creative Preaching: Finding the Word* (Nashville: Abingdon, 1980), 24.

25. Matt. 9:22.

26. Kenneth E. Boulding, *The Image: Knowledge in Life and Society* (Ann Arbor: University of Michigan Press, 1956), 7.

27. Douglas Sloan, "Imagination, Education, and Our Postmodern Possibilities," *ReVision*, 15 (Fall 1992): 46. See also Boulding, *The Image*.

28. C. G. Jung, from "On the Nature of the Psyche," in *The Basic Writings of C. G. Jung*, ed. Violet Staub de Laszlo (New York: Modern Library, 1959), 85.

29. According to Brian Stonehill, late director of media studies at Pomona College (Claremont, CA), "The mediation of print means that people have achieved literacy in order to get at whatever's in the text. But when you deal with visual media, you've done away with the mediation of print and gone directly to something that any illiterate, any child, has access to." Quoted in Roger van Bakel, "Welcome to the Next Level of the Videogame Biz, Where If You Don't Grovel and Adopt Ratings, Some Senator Will Rip Your Head Off," *Wired* (November 1994), 123; or "[Rating: 4 Grenades]," http://www.wired.com/wired/archiv/2.11/ratings.html?pg=38topic=8topic_set=.

30. Darrell Jodock, *The Church's Bible: Its Contemporary Authority* (Minneapolis: Fortress, 1989), 73.

31. Ninety-six images of the church are included in Paul S. Minear's study *Images of the Church in the New Testament* (Philadelphia: Westminster, 1960).

32. Mervyn Nicholson, *13 Ways of Looking at Images: The Logic of Visualization in Literature and Society* (Beverly Hills, CA: Red Heifer, 2003), 48.

33. Humbert of Romans, "The Scriptural Symbols of the Preacher," in *Early Dominicans: Selected Writings*, ed. Simon Tugwell (New York: Paulist, 1982), 224–28.

34. James Lawley and Penny Tompkins, *Metaphors in Mind: Transformation through Symbolic Modeling* (Highgate, London: Developing Company, 2003), 17.

35. Brett P. Webb-Mitchell, *Christly Gestures: Learning to Be Members of the Body of Christ* (Grand Rapids: Eerdmans, 2003).

36. Celia Lury, "Thinking with Things," in *Brand.New*, ed. Jane Pavitt (Princeton, NJ: Princeton University Press, 2000), 178–79.

37. See Matt. 6:24; Luke 16:13 RSV.

38. Nicholson, *13 Ways of Looking at Images*, 14–15.

39. Angelou's quote is a version of the earlier Carl Buehner advice to preachers: "They may forget what you said, but they will never forget how you made them feel."

Notes

Cinthia's Inspirational Quotes Collection, "Words," http://www.freewebs.com/cinthia/quotes/inspirationquotesW.html, accessed July 18 2004.

40. Brian Volck, "A Conversation with Gil Bailie," *Image* 41 (Winter 2003): 63–77, 75.

41. Ibid.

42. Chrysostom MacDonnell, *The Sacraments in Orthodox Life*, "The Mysteries of the Kingdom," a paper quoted in www.christianforums.com/t1189461.

43. Jer. 31:33.

44. Andrew Ortony, "Why Metaphors Are Necessary and Not Just Nice," in *Educational Theory* 25 (1975): 45–53, referenced in Thomas G. Sticht, "Educational Uses of Metaphor," in *Metaphor and Thought*, ed. Andrew Ortony, 2nd ed. (New York: Cambridge University Press, 1993), 622. See also Andrew Ortony, "On the Nature and Value of Metaphor: A Reply to My Critics," *Education Theory* 26 (1976): 395–98.

45. Tex Sample reports on this research by Larry Smarr in his *The Spectacle of Worship in a Wired World: Electronic Culture and the Gathered People of God* (Nashville: Abingdon, 1998), 30.

46. Culture Care Technologies, "Case Study 18: Making Change," http://culturecare.org.hosting.domaindirect.com/cases/case018.htm, accessed February 16, 2006.

47. N. T. Wright, *The New Testament and the People of God*, Christian Origins and the Question of God vol. 1 (Minneapolis: Fortress, 1992), 31–43, 40.

48. Robert Frost, "The Mountain," in *North of Boston* (New York: Henry Holt, 1915), 29.

49. Howard Gardner, *Creating Minds: An Anatomy of Creativity* (New York: Basic Books, 1993). See also "Metaphorical Capacity," in Howard Gardner, *Frames of Mind: The Theory of Multiple Intelligences*, 2nd ed. (New York: Basic Books, 1993), 290–93.

50. N. T. Wright, *The Epistles of Paul to the Colossians and Philemon: An Introduction and Commentary* (Grand Rapids: Eerdmans, 1986), 83 passim.

51. For my randomizing rituals, see Leonard Sweet, *Nudge: Awakening Each Other to the God Who's Already There* (Colorado Springs: WaterBrook, 2010), 98.

52. Richard Rorty, *Contingency, Irony, and Solidarity* (Cambridge: Cambridge University Press, 1989), 73. Richard Rorty once wrote snidely about those whom philosophers call the "metaphysical prigs" who still claim "to be seeking the truth," "Well, I plead guilty as charged. I'm one of those 'prigs.'" See Richard Rorty, *Essays on Heidegger and Others* (Cambridge: Cambridge University Press, 1991), 86.

53. See Steve Sjogren, *The Perfectly Imperfect Church: Redefining the "Ideal" Church* (Loveland, CO: Group, 2002), 18.

54. Ray Kurzweil, *The Singularity Is Near: When Humans Transcend Biology* (New York: Penguin, 2006).

55. Wolfgang Schivelbusch, *The Culture of Defeat: On National Trauma, Mourning and Recovery* (New York: Metropolitan, 2003), 39.

56. Alan Jamieson, *Journeying in Faith: In and beyond the Tough Places* (London: SPCK, 2004), 120.

57. Eugene Peterson, *The Jesus Way: A Conversation on the Ways That Jesus Is the Way* (Grand Rapids: Eerdmans, 2007), 25.

58. *Comte de Lautréamont, Maldoror (Les Chants de Maldoror)*, trans. Guy Wernham (Mount Vernon, NY: Golden Eagle, 1943), 263. Lautréamont was a pseudonym for Isidor Ducasse, who died at age twenty-four in 1870 in Paris. He was born in Uruguay in 1846, but little else is known about him. See, e.g., Alex de Jonge, *Nightmare Culture: Lautréamont and "Les Chants de Maldoror"* (New York: St. Martin's, 1973); and Gaston Bachelard, *Lautréamont*, trans. Robert S. Dupree (Dallas: Dallas Institute of Humanities and Culture, 1986).

Notes

59. A kenning is a "kind of riddling poetic periphrasis in which a base word (which might at first sight seem inappropriate to the object finally denoted) is hauled into aptness by one or more determinates. To give a modern example: 'the ship of the desert' denotes a camel, even though a ship is exactly what one would not associate with a desert; the specific base word 'ship' stands for the generic 'vehicle,' and the determinant 'desert' imposes applicability." This process may liberate unexpected insights.

60. Gilles Fauconnier and Mark Turner give new thought to "kenning" in their book on "imagethinking," *The Way We Think: Conceptual Blending and the Mind's Hidden Complexities* (New York: Basic Books, 2002).

61. Austin Farrer, *Reflective Faith: Essays in Philosophical Theology* (London: SPCK, 1972), 25.

62. In Peter Cooper, *The Anglican Church: The Creature and Slave of the State* (London: Dolman, 1844), 82.

63. W. B. Yeats, "The Symbolism of Poetry," in his *Ideas of Good and Evil* (London: A. H. Bullen, 1914), 169.

64. Lakoff and Johnson, *Metaphors We Live By*, 40.

65. Ibid., 159.

66. Ibid., 22.

67. Jorge Luis Borges, *Other Inquisitions 1937–1952*, trans. Ruth L. C. Simms (Austin: University of Texas Press, 1965), 9.

68. E. L. Doctorow's earliest essay, "False Documents" (1977), in his *Poets and Presidents: Selected Essays, 1977–92* (New York: Papermac, 1994), 164.

69. Antonio Damasio's books *Descartes' Error: Emotion, Reason and the Human Brain* (New York: Putnam, 1994) and *The Feeling of What Happens: Body and Emotion in the Making of Consciousness* (New York: Harcourt, Brace, 1999) collapse the division between reason and passion, or cognition and emotion; the opposition of the two goes back to Aristotle. From a neurological standpoint, he argues, emotion is integral to the integrity of reasoning.

70. 1 Cor. 1:18.

71. Col. 1:15.

72. Steven Johnson, *Interface Cultures: How Technology Transforms the Way We Create and Communicate* (New York: HarperCollins, 1997), 12.

73. For a defense of appealing to the emotions as well as the intellect, see Ian Pitt-Watson, *Preaching: A Kind of Folly* (Philadelphia: Westminster, 1976), 44–51.

74. Nicholson, *13 Ways of Looking at Images*, 97.

75. Donald Davidson, "What Metaphors Mean," in *On Metaphor*, ed. Sheldon Sacks (Chicago: University of Chicago Press, 1979), 29.

76. See also Michaly Czikszentmihalyi and Eugene Rochberg-Halton, *The Meaning of Things* (New York: Cambridge University Press, 1981).

77. Nicholson, *13 Ways of Looking at Images*, 215.

78. Jan Phillips, *God Is at Eye Level: Photography as a Healing Art* (Wheaton, IL: Quest, 2000), 63.

79. Volck, "A Conversation with Gil Bailie," 63–77, 75.

80. Phillips, *God Is at Eye Level*, 63.

81. Eugene Peterson, *Leap Over a Wall: Earthy Spirituality for Everyday Christians* (San Francisco: HarperSanFrancisco, 1997), 3; Luci Shaw, "Reversing Entropy," *Image* 41 (Winter 2003): 91–101.

82. Peterson, *Leap Over a Wall*, 4.

83. Nicholson, *13 Ways of Looking at Images*, 20.
84. Shakespeare, *Hamlet*, Act 1, Scene 5, ll. 166–67.
85. See James Geary, *I Is an Other: The Secret Life of Metaphor* (New York: Harper Perennial, 2012); and Lakoff and Johnson, *Metaphors We Live By*.
86. Nicholson, *13 Ways of Looking at Images*, 155.
87. Ibid., 157.
88. Ibid.
89. Amos N. Wilder, *Early Christian Rhetoric: The Language of the Gospel* (Cambridge: Harvard University Press, 1971), 72, 84.
90. Maureen Murdock, *Spinning Inward* (Boston: Shambhala, 1987), ix.
91. Prov. 25:11 NKJV.
92. Moses Maimonides, *The Guide of the Perplexed*, trans. Shlomo Pines (Chicago: University of Chicago Press, 1963), 11–12.
93. See The Parable Discovery—Understanding the Parables of Jesus, www.theparable discovery.com, for further information on the discipleship relationship.
94. 1 Cor. 2:7.
95. Edmund A. Steimle, Morris J. Niedenthal, and Charles Rice, *Preaching the Story* (Philadelphia: Fortress, 1980).

CHAPTER 9: BLOOD-ENRICHING NUTRIENTS: STYLE AND TWIST

1. Some things are as helpful today as when they were first written, however. George Orwell's "Politics and the English Language" set out six rules that were adopted on the first page of the *Economist* style book: (1) Never use a metaphor, simile, or other figure of speech which you are used to seeing in print. (2) Never use a long word where a short one will do. (3) If it is possible to cut out a word, always cut it out. (4) Never use the passive where you can use the active. (5) Never use a foreign phrase, a scientific word, or a jargon word if you can think of an everyday English equivalent. (6) Break any of these rules sooner than say anything outright barbarous.
2. "Before one can determine the meaning of a text for today, one must know what the writer intended to convey to his original hearers/readers." Sidney Greidanus, *The Modern Preacher and the Ancient Text: Interpreting and Preaching Biblical Literature* (Grand Rapids: Eerdmans, 1988), 166.
3. See Bryan Chapell, *Christ-Centered Preaching: Redeeming the Expository Sermon* (Grand Rapids: Baker, 2005).
4. Bryan Chapell, *Christ-Centered Preaching: Redeeming the Expository Sermon* (Grand Rapids: Baker, 1994), 269.
5. Charles Haddon Spurgeon, "Christ Precious to Believers," in his *Sermons* (New York: Funk & Wagnalls, 1857), 6:357.
6. In 1 Cor. 2:6–16, for example.
7. Jay E. Adams, *Preaching with Purpose: A Comprehensive Textbook on Biblical Preaching* (Grand Rapids: Baker, 1982), 147.
8. Keith Green, "My Eyes Are Dry," lyric at http://www.lyricsfreak.com/k/keith+green/my+eyes+are+dry_20077346.html.
9. For an excellent book on this, see Fred R. Lybrand, *Preaching on Your Feet: Connecting God and the Audience in the Preachable Moment* (Nashville: B&H, 2008).
10. As quoted in Chapell, *Christ-Centered Preaching*, 252.
11. See John Piper, *The Supremacy of God in Preaching* (Grand Rapids: Baker, 1990), 50, quoting James W. Alexander, *Thoughts on Preaching* (Edinburgh: Banner of Truth, 1975 [orig. 1861]), 311.

12. Dr. Seuss, *The Lorax* (New York: Random House, 1971), 58.
13. James Henry Harris, *The Word Made Plain: The Power and Promise of Preaching* (Minneapolis: Fortress, 2004), 83.
14. Ibid.
15. As quoted in Harris, *The Word Made Plain*, 85.
16. Thomas G. Long, *The Witness of Preaching* (Louisville: Westminster John Knox, 1989).
17. John A. Broadus, *On the Preparation and Delivery of Sermons* (New York: Harper & Row, 1944), 210.
18. As referenced in Howard G. Hendricks and William D. Hendricks, *Living by the Book* (Chicago: Moody, 1991), 228.
19. For more on this, see Leonard Sweet and Frank Viola, *Jesus: A Theography* (Nashville: Thomas Nelson, 2012).
20. Geerhardus Vos, *Biblical Theology: Old and New Testament* (Grand Rapids: Eerdmans, 1948), 14.
21. See Leonard Sweet, in *Postmodern and Wesleyan? Exploring the Boundaries and Possibilities, with Responses by Leonard Sweet*, ed. Jay Richard Akkerman, Thomas J. Oord, and Brent D. Peterson (Kansas City, MO Beacon Hill, 2009), 93.
22. Ibid.
23. Ibid.
24. Ibid.
25. See Holland Cotter, "Artistic Mesche, Flexed for Medicis," *New York Times* (Feb, 1, 2008).
26. PBS, "Make No Little Plans," premiered Sept 2010; http://www.pbs.org/programs/make-no-little-plans/.
27. William Shakespeare, *Macbeth*, act 1, scene 7.
28. See 1 Thess. 4:11.
29. In Stuart Murray, *Post-Christendom* (Carlisle, UK: Paternoster, 2004), 1.
30. Rom. 8:24.
31. D. H. Lawrence, from a letter dated Jan 17, 1913: http://homepages.wmich.edu/~cooneys/poems/dhl.letters.html.
32. Recall that TGIF stands for Twitter, Google, Instagram, Facebook.
33. Blaise Pascal, http://quotationsbook.com/quote/46706/#sthash.RdJWb4y1.dpbs.
34. See www.goodreads.com/quotes/182840-it-is-useless-to-attempt-to-reason-a-man-out.
35. He got angry—with Satan and others. He was easily surprised—at the centurion's faith. He was exasperated—with the disciples over and over again. He was disappointed—in Peter. He was very empathetic—with the crowds who skipped meals to follow him. He could get very teary—and cried twice in public, once over a people and another time over a place. He could get joyful—"Why are you not dancing?" He could cry from anguish—"Why have you forsaken me?"
36. Lisa Kudrow as Phoebe in the pilot episode of *Friends*, 1994.

CHAPTER 10: BLOOD AND GUTS: PASSION

1. Charles Haddon Spurgeon, "Earnestness: Its Marring and Maintenance," in his *Lectures to My Students: A Selection from Addresses Delivered to the Students of The Pastors' College, Metropolitan Tabernacle* (Grand Rapids: Baker, 1977), 2:147.
2. Rom. 1:15 NLT.
3. Jer. 23:28.
4. In Robert Penn Warren, *The Legacy of the Civil War* (Lincoln: University of Nebraska Press, 1998), 88.

5. Mark 9:49.
6. That last phrase comes from hymn writer Hugh Stowell in verse 4 of "From Every Stormy Wind That Blows" (*The Methodist Hymnal: Official Hymnal of the Methodist Church* [Nashville: Methodist Publishing House], 232):

> Ah! there on eagle wings we soar,
> Where sin and sense molest no more,
> And heaven comes down our souls to greet
> And glory crowns the mercy seat.

Glory crowning the mercy seat is a biblical image found in Ex. 25:20 and Heb. 9:5.
7. As quoted in Bill Fromm, *The Ten Commandments of Business—and How to Break Them: Secrets for Improving Employee Morale, Enhancing Customer Service, Increasing Company Profits, While Having More Fun Than You Ever Thought You Could Have at Work* (New York: Putnam, 1991), 131.
8. John A. Broadus, *On the Preparation and Delivery of Sermons* (New York: Harper & Row, 1944), 210.
9. Mark Twain, *The Wit and Wisdom of Mark Twain*, ed. Alex Ayres (New York: Harper & Row, 1987), 209.
10. Spurgeon, "Earnestness: Its Marring and Maintenance," 2:147.
11. As quoted in David W. Henderson, *Culture Shift: Communicating God's Truth to Our Changing World* (Grand Rapids: Baker, 1998), 19.

CHAPTER 11: BLOOD-PUMPING EPICTIVITIES: PUMPING UP PREACHING WITH APPS

1. Refer to chapter 3 for the meaning of EPIC.
2. Reinhold Niebuhr, *Essays in Applied Christianity*, ed. D. C. Robertson (New York: Meridian Books, 1959), 29–33. My favorite Niebuhr work is his essay "A Christmas Service in Retrospect," which first appeared in the *Christian Century* in 1933 and was reprinted fifty years later.

> I went to church in the Cathedral on Christmas Day. It is one of the few days of the year on which I am able to attend church without preaching myself. On that day, although a free-church Protestant myself, I prefer a liturgical church with as little sermon as possible. It is not that I don't like to hear anyone but myself preach. I merely dislike most Christmas sermons. Only poets can do justice to the Christmas story, and there are not many poets in the pulpit. It is better therefore to be satisfied with the symbolic presentation of the poetry in hymn, anthem, and liturgy.... I suppose it is necessary and inevitable that the poetry of religion should be expressed in rational terms, but something is always lost in the rationalization. Dogma is rationally petrified poetry which destroys part of the truth embodied in the tale in the effort to put it in precise terms.

3. See 1 Cor. 10:16–17.
4. Paul Scott Wilson, *The Practice of Preaching* (Nashville: Abingdon, 1995), 23.
5. Pamela Moeller, "The Integrality of Homiletics/Liturgy: Overcoming False Dualities," *Papers of the 27th Academy of Homiletics* (Louisville: Academy of Homiletics, 1993), 71.
6. Luke 20:25.
7. Louie Giglio, "Church Leaders Wonder: Will Preaching Survive a Postmodern World?," www.baylor.edu/mediacommunications/news.php?action=story&story=21277.

Notes

8. Julie Pennington-Russell, formerly available at www.biblicalrecorder.org/cgi-bin/pf.pl.
9. See Tim Elmore, *Generation iY* (Atlanta: Poet Gardener, 2010); and Leonard Sweet, *Viral: How Social Networking Is Poised to Ignite Revival* (Colorado Springs: Water-Brook, 2012).
10. "Florida Minister Dies after Shooting in Sermon," www.nytimes.com/1998/10/03/us/national-news-briefs-florida-minister-dies-after-shooting-in-sermon.html
11. See Num. 7:13.
12. William Congreve, *The Mourning Bride*, act 3, scene 8 (1697).

CHAPTER 12: BLOOD THINNERS: THE ROLE OF HUMOR

1. See Matt. 19:24; Mark 10:25; Luke 18:25.
2. Matt. 6:2.
3. For humor in preaching, see especially James R. Barnette, "Humor in Preaching: The Contributions of Psychological and Sociological Research," PhD diss., Southern Baptist Theological Seminary, 1992. See also idem, "A Time to Laugh: Principles of Good Pulpit Humor," *Preaching* 11 (March–April 1996): 5–11.
4. Barnette, "Humor in Preaching." See also idem, "A Time to Laugh," 5–11.
5. For an example of humor that doesn't work, here is Jimmy Carter at a press conference: "I'm not going to say anything terribly important tonight, so you can all put away your crayons."
6. Reinhold Niebuhr, *The Essential Reinhold Niebuhr: Selected Essays and Addresses* (New Haven, CT: Yale University Press, 1986), 49.
7. G. K. Chesterton, *Orthodoxy*, in *The Collected Works of G. K. Chesterton*, vol. 1., ed. D. Dooley (San Francisco: Ignatius, 1995), 325, 326.
8. See www.brainyquote.com/quotes/quotes/l/ludwigwitt395439.html.
9. Quoted in Donald G. Mathews, *Religion in the Old South* (Chicago: University of Chicago Press, 1979), 63.
10. As quoted in Daniel Wickberg, *The Senses of Humor: Self and Laughter in Modern America* (Ithaca, NY: Cornell University Press, 1998), 84.
11. Academic discussions of humor are invariably humorless and often distinguish three kinds of theory: the incongruity theory (we are amused by the incongruous), the relief theory (humor is an expression of relief in difficult situations), and the superiority theory (we laugh to express our sense of superiority over others). F. H. Buckley's *The Morality of Laughter* (Ann Arbor: University of Michigan Press, 2004) argues the superiority thesis and presents the ridiculous thesis that humor is always an expression of a sense of superiority over someone else, whom he calls the "butt."
12. Mistaking seriousness for solemnity (in my view), Piper contends, "Laughter seems to have replaced repentance as the goal of many preachers. Laughter means people feel good. It means they like you. It means you have moved them. It means you have some measure of power. It seems to have all the marks of successful communication—if the depth of sin and the holiness of God and the danger of hell and need for broken hearts is left out of account." Piper says that there is not one joke in Jonathan Edwards's two thousand sermons. Not so. Piper also says that Jesus never told a joke. Not so. For Edwards and humor, see my "Sweetness and Light in Edwards and Franklin," in *Benjamin Franklin, Jonathan Edwards, and the Representation of American Culture*, ed. Barbara Oberg and Harry S. Stout (Oxford: Oxford University Press, 1993), 114–33.
13. Bernard Shaw insisted that "all genuine intellectual work is humorous." Quoted in *Times Literary Supplement* (December 18 and 25, 2009), 27.
14. Matt. 25:21.

15. Sermon 27: *"Nolite timere eos,"* in *Meister Eckhart: A Modern Translation*, trans. Raymond B. Blakney (New York: Harper & Brothers, 1941), 225.

16. Sermon 18: *"Scio hominem in Christo ante annos quatordecim,"* in Franz Pfeiffer, ed., *Meister Eckhart: Deutsche Mystiker des Mittelalters*, as quoted in Paul Murray, *The New Wine of Dominican Spirituality: A Drink Called Happiness* (New York: Burns & Oates, 2006), 63.

17. "Anne Lamott: The Habit of Practice," *Leadership* (August 6, 2011), www.faithand leadership.com/qa/anne-lamott-the-habit-practice.

18. John H. Armstrong, "What Great Work Does God Require of Us?" http://johnharm-strong.typepad.com/john_h_armstrong_/2010/04/what-great-work-does-god-require-of-us.html

19. Laurent Joubert, *A Treatise on Laughter* (Tuscaloosa: University of Alabama Press, 1980).

20. See www.brainyquote.com/quotes/quotes/e/edwarddebo383454.html.

21. Comedians use the term *callback* to describe a certain theme, phrase, or story line that is repeated in different forms throughout a stand-up performance and designed to facilitate interaction. The callback might appear in just one stand-up bit, or it might be used during multiple performances. When it works, the callback serves as a thread that tightens the sketch and makes it more memorable. Sometimes certain callbacks become "signatures" for a comedian — Jack Benny's love of money; Rodney Dangerfield's getting no respect; Joan Rivers's arguments with her husband, Edgar; Dave Letterman's Top Ten List; Jimmy Fallon's slow jam; Aziz Ansari's RAAAAAAAAndy with eight *A*s.

22. Charmaine Liebertz, "A Healthy Laugh," *Scientific American Mind* (November 2005), 90.

23. A. R. Radcliffe-Brown, *Structure and Function in Primitive Society* (London: Cohen and West, 1952), 90.

24. Daniel H. Pink, *A Whole New Mind: Why Right-Brainers Will Rule the Future* (New York: Penguin, 2006).

25. See http://www.funfactz.com/people-facts/children-laugh-about-400-times-day-while-422.html.

26. Humbert of Romans, "The Scriptural Symbols of the Preacher," in *Early Dominicans: Selected Writings*, ed. Simon Tugwell (New York: Paulist, 1982), 224–28.

27. a. Noah; b. Abraham; c. Moses; d. Israelites; e. Ezra; f. Samson; g. Jonah; h. Hosea; i. Jeremiah; j. Daniel; k. Shadrach, Meshach, and Abednego; l. Dorcas; m. Zacchaeus; n. John the Baptist; o. Joseph.

28. Hugh Gilbert, "I Was Thirsty and You Gave Me Something to Drink," *The Tablet* (August 14, 2010), 14.

CHAPTER 13: BLOOD SUPPLY: INCARNATION AND CULTURE

1. For more on this, see my *So Beautiful: Divine Design for Life and the Church* (Colorado Springs: WaterBrook, 2009).

2. Matt. 28:19–20.

3. As referenced in Mortimer Arias, "Contextualization in Evangelism: Towards an Incarnational Style," *Perkins Journal* 32 (Winter 1979): 3.

4. P. T. Forsyth, *Positive Preaching and the Modern Mind*, Lyman Beecher Lectures on Preaching, Yale University, 1907 (Cincinnati: Jennings and Graham, 1907), 8.

5. Thomas G. Bandy, "Seeker Sensitive Preaching," *NET Results* 24 (February–March 2003): 16–18, 32.

6. An excellent book on incarnational preaching is Graham Johnston's *Preaching to a Postmodern World: A Guide to Reaching Twenty-first Century Listeners* (Grand Rapids:

Baker, 2001). His chapter 2, "Postmodernity: Animal, Vegetable, or Mineral?," is one of the best short introductions to postmodern culture from the standpoint of evangelical Christianity.

7. Thx! Paula Champion Jones for pointing this out on my Facebook wall.
8. The late Calvin Miller puts it more pungently: "Preaching is a polygamist with ugly consorts. Preaching is so married to liturgy, architecture, and popular detente that it spends all its energy in running from wife to wife. It doesn't try to set things right, only to keep from getting things wrong. Sermons are often so dead that dying denominations seem the perfect place to deliver them." Calvin Miller, *Marketplace Preaching: How to Return the Sermon to Where It Belongs* (Grand Rapids: Baker, 1995), 19.
9. Craig Loscalzo, "Apologizing for God: Apologetic Preaching to a Postmodern World," *Review and Expositor* 93 (Summer 1996): 412.
10. Reported by Dow Jones & Company.
11. George Bataille, "The College of Sociology" (1938), as quoted in Marina Warner, *Signs and Wonders: Essays on Literature and Culture* (London: Chatto & Windus, 2003), 193.
12. Edward Marriott, *Claude and Madeleine: A Story of Love, War and Espionage* (New York: Picador, 2005).
13. Peter Corney, as quoted by Graham Johnston in *Preaching to a Postmodern World*, 16.
14. James Henry Harris, *The Word Made Plain: The Power and Promise of Preaching* (Minneapolis: Fortress, 2004), 34.
15. The phrase is that of Bandy in "Seeker Sensitive Preaching," 16–18, 32.
16. See C. H. Dodd, *Apostolic Preaching and Its Developments: Three Lectures* (Chicago: Willett, Clark, 1937), 1–2.
17. Paul Simon, as cited by film critic Jeffrey Overstreet in "Redeeming the Time: A Symposium," *Image* 42 (Spring–Summer 2004): 40.

CHAPTER 14: BLOOD TRANSFUSIONS: INFUSING CREATIVITY

1. For the importance of this metaphor, see George Cladis, *Leading the Team-Based Church: How Pastors and Church Staffs Can Grow Together into a Powerful Fellowship of Leaders* (San Francisco: Jossey-Bass, 1999), 5. Also Leonard Sweet, *I Am a Follower: The Way, Truth, and Life of Following Jesus* (Nashville: Thomas Nelson, 2012).
2. Shirley C. Guthrie, *Christian Doctrine*, rev. ed. (Louisville: Westminster John Knox, 1994), 91.
3. Ibid., 92.
4. Pamela Moeller insists on the mystery and freedom of God's presence in worship: "But who can say how and when God will offer the divine self? God floods us with God's love in a full-bodied manner—engaging all our senses, faculties, emotions, being, in discovering what it means to be embraced in God's arms and participate in the Body of Christ." Pamela Moeller, "The Integrality of Homiletics/Liturgy: Overcoming False Dualities," *Papers of the 27th Academy of Homiletics* (Louisville: Academy of Homiletics, 1993), 71.
5. Hannah Arendt, *On Revolution* (New York: Penguin, 2006), 43.

CHAPTER 15: BLOOD DONORS: CONGREGATIONAL INTERPLAY

1. Augustine, as quoted by Nicholas Henshall, "Take It to the Limit," *The Tablet* (November 3, 2012), 16.
2. Peter Coy, "Life at 0%," *Bloomberg Businessweek* (October 11, 2012), 190. Coy is economics editor for *Bloomberg Businessweek*.
3. For chaos as the defining feature of the current business climate, see Robert Safian, "Secrets of the Flux Leader," *Fast Company* (November 2012), 98.

Notes

4. Presbyterian minister Craig Douglas Erickson's 1989 book, *Participating in Worship*, is a classic of sorts. The volume holds this distinction not only because of its useful blend of practical theology and pastoral sensitivity, but also because it has long been one of the only books squarely addressing the subject of participation in worship.
5. John 11:43–44.
6. Deut. 33:27.
7. Acts 20:7.
8. Wolfgang Simson, *Houses That Change the World: The Return of the House Churches* (Waynesboro, GA: OM, 2001), 84.
9. Ibid.
10. With thanks to Joseph O'Hanlon, "Questions, Questions," *The Tablet* (December 2012), 29, for helping me see that "Let's talk" in Jesus' day meant more than a monologue.
11. Bill Cosby, as referenced in Robert J. Kriegel and Louis Patler, *If It Ain't Broke . . . Break It* (New York: Warner, 1991), 18.
12. See http://gavinortlund.wordpress.com/2012/05/03/browns-biography-of-augustine-4-augustine-the-preacher/
13. Gamaliel's counsel in Acts 5:38.
14. 1 Cor. 14:26 NEB.
15. Coupons' and checkbooks' and crackers' perforations control failure. Fuses are designed to fail. Concrete has its well-placed "cracks." See Henry Petroski, "Designed to Fail," *American Scientist* 85 (September–October, 1997): 412–16.
16. James Walvin, *The Trader, the Owner, the Slave: Parallel Lives in the Age of Slavery* (London: Jonathan Cape, 2007), 77.
17. The lobster catch is called "bugs" for good reason. Turn over a cockroach. A lobster is just a cockroach on steroids. Lobsters are closer to insects than anything. When you eat a lobster, you're eating an arthropod invertebrate—in other words, an insect.
18. For an accent on dialogic preaching, as opposed to what he calls "speaching," see Doug Pagitt, *Preaching Re-Imagined: The Role of the Sermon in Communities of Faith* (Grand Rapids: Zondervan, 2005). But Pagitt's dialogue is less a part of the sermon itself than an adjunct to it, either after the presentation or on some day of the week when people gather to help form the sermon for the following week.
19. See http://quotationsbook.com/quote/23023/#sthash.odrX7Z0q.dpbs.
20. For example, "Therefore go and make *disciples* of all nations" (Matt. 28:19, emphasis added).
21. John 14:26.
22. Again, refer to chapter 3 for the meaning of EPIC.
23. David L. Blow Sr. and Frank A. Thomas, "I Wish I Had Somebody: The Rhetorical Devices of Black Preaching," *African American Pulpit* 5 (Summer 2002): 25.
24. For a book about "pastoral listening," see Frances M. Moran, *A Pastoral Style* (Harrisburg, PA: Morehouse, 1997).
25. Michael Oakeshott, "The Voice of Poetry in the Conversation of Mankind," in his *Rationalism in Politics and Other Essays* (New York: Basic Books, 1962), 197–98.
26. Ibid., 216.
27. Gabriel Josipovici, as quoted by Gordon L. Fuglie, *Representing LA: Pictorial Currents in Southern California Art* (Seattle: Frye Art Museum, 2001), 79.
28. John R. W. Stott, *Between Two Worlds: The Art of Preaching in the Twentieth Century* (Grand Rapids: Eerdmans, 1982), 198–201.
29. Jonathan Edwards, *A Faithful Narrative of the Surprising Work of God* (Elizabethtown, NJ: Shepard Kollock, 1791).

CHAPTER 16: BLOOD DRIVES: THE CLOSURE OF ALTAR/ALTER CALLS

1. Wayne Brouwer, "How to Land the Sermon," www.preaching.com/sermons/11567362/page–5/.
2. See http://news.google.com/newspapers?nid=1310&dat=20020731&id=QL5YAAAAIBAJ&sjid=1OsDAAAAIBAJ&pg=5767,7254920.
3. Ex. 17:15–16 nrsv.

CHAPTER 17: BLOOD VESSELS: SACRAMENTALITY

1. Quoted in Albert Rouet, *Liturgy and the Arts* (Collegeville, MN: Liturgical, 1997), 162.
2. Acts 2:17.
3. See Mark 8:17–21.
4. Robin Baird-Smith, "Keeping the Devil at Bay with Laughter," *The Tablet* (April 22 2006), 23.
5. For more along these lines, see my *Strong in the Broken Places* (Akron, OH: University of Akron Press, 1998).
6. Gen. 15.
7. Gen. 17.
8. 1 John 5:7–8.
9. John 19:34.
10. Deborah Sawyer, "Water and Blood: Birthing Images in John's Gospel," in *Words Remembered, Texts Renewed: Essays in Honour of John F. A. Sawyer*, ed. John Davies, Graham Harvey, and Wilfred G. E. Watson (Sheffield, UK: Sheffield Academic Press, 1995), 300–309.
11. Pierre Boulez, in *A Life in Music*, by Daniel Barenboim (New York: Arcade, 2013), 119.
12. John 7:37–39.
13. Dom Hugh Gilbert, OSB, *Unfolding the Mystery: Monastic Conferences on the Liturgical Year* (Herefordshire, UK: Gracewing, 2007), 86. See also Leonard Sweet and Frank Viola, *Jesus: A Theography* (Nashville: Thomas Nelson, 2012).
14. Gen. 2:6, 10; Isa. 35:6.
15. Ezek. 47:1.
16. Zech. 12:10; 13:1.
17. Marina Warner, *Signs and Wonders: Essays on Literature and Culture* (London: Chatto & Windus, 2003), 193.
18. Terry T. Tekyl, *The Presence Based Church* (Muncie, IN: Prayer Point, 2003). I disagree with Tekyl in one area, however: in Tekyl's theology, you create an atmosphere in your church with prayer that will "attract" God. I would disagree with that part, saying, God does not need attracting, but is there always, and prayer makes us aware of God's presence. The church by its nature should wake up to the presence of the Holy Spirit of Christ and his sanctifying power.

CHAPTER 18: BLOOD CHILLS AND THRILLS: IMPACT AND DELIVERY

1. Haddon W. Robinson, "Introduction," to *Biblical Sermons: How Twelve Preachers Apply the Principles of Biblical Preaching*, ed. Haddon W. Robinson (Grand Rapids: Baker, 1989), 8.
2. Gardner C. Taylor, "Healing Our Homelessness," *African American Pulpit* 10 (Spring 2007): 87.
3. Al Fasol, *A Complete Guide to Sermon Delivery* (Nashville: Broadman & Holman, 1996), ix.
4. Austin Farrer, "The Burning-Glass," in *Austin Farrer: The Essential Sermons*, ed. Leslie Houlden (Cambridge, MA: Cowley, 1991), 19.

5. Paul Scott Wilson argues that by means of the sermon "a relationship with God is begun and maintained, not just a relationship with ideas about God." See Paul Scott Wilson, *The Practice of Preaching* (Nashville: Abingdon, 1995), 23.
6. Friedrich Nietzsche, "On Truth and Falsity in Their Extramoral Sense (1873)," in his *Philosophical Writings*, ed. Reinhold Grimm and Caroline Molina y Vedia (New York: Continuum, 1995), 92.
7. Colin S. Smith, "Keeping Christ Centered in Preaching," in *Telling the Truth: Evangelizing Postmoderns*, ed. D. A. Carson (Grand Rapids: Zondervan, 2000), 112.
8. Nicholas Vincent, *The Holy Blood: King Henry III and the Westminster Blood Relic* (New York: Cambridge University Press, 2001), 178.
9. Annie Dillard, *The Writing Life* (New York: HarperPerennial, 1989), 68.
10. Mary Kassian, *Conversation Peace: Improving Your Relationships One Word at a Time* (Nashville: B&H, 2004). See also Marie Armenia, "Talk Soup," *Christian Health* 2 (February 2002): 6–7.
11. Henry Mitchell, *Black Preaching* (San Francisco: Harper & Row, 1979), 163. See also Evans E. Crawford with Thomas H. Troeger, *The Hum: Call and Response in African American Preaching* (Nashville: Abingdon, 1995).
12. Janet Frame, as quoted in *Times Literary Supplement* (August 28–September 4, 1990), 1033.
13. The phrase "Sleep is an opinion" is attributed to "the French actor, Samson, said to the young dramatist," as quoted in Thomas Wentworth Higginson, "Americanisms in Literature" (1871), in *The Oxford Book of American Essays*, ed. Brander Matthews (New York: Oxford University Press, 1914), 224.
14. Calvin Miller, *Marketplace Preaching: How to Return the Sermon to Where It Belongs* (Grand Rapids: Baker, 1995), 19.
15. *Pirke Aboth: Sayings of the Fathers*, Ethics 2:21.

CHAPTER 19: BLOOD CLOTS: PREACHER'S BLOCK

1. As quoted in Neil Corcoran, "Back Home: Dylan, Now and Then," *TLX* (June 22, 2012), 15.
2. Mark Galli and Craig Brian Larson, in *Preaching That Connects* (Grand Rapids: Zondervan, 1994), recommend Timothy Perrin's five techniques that stimulate generative thought processes: freewheeling, clustering ("mind mapping"), heuristics (posing questions), conversation, and outlining.
3. In his day, St. Patrick's followers prayed 150 psalms a day: 50 in the morning, 50 in the afternoon, 50 in the evening.
4. Tom Peters, *Re-Imagine!* (New York: Doring Kindersley, 2003), 215.
5. Charles Haddon Spurgeon would challenge his hearers to greet the biblical narrative with all their senses: "See that man on the center cross.... Feel the cold shiver of darkness.... Hear the agonizing cries of the two thieves.... Smell the putrid effects of dying flesh amid the mounds of burning rubble.... Taste the blood dripping into the Savior's mouth coming from His thorny crown."
6. "Finding helpful images in the work of contemporaries like Matthew Prior (the 'nearer waters') and Pope (eyes 'diffusing rays'), the Wesleys wove them into others from Scripture to speak to the experience of all." See Andrew Bradstock, "Hymns for a Thousand Tongues," *The Tablet* (December 15, 2007), 16.

CHAPTER 20: BLOOD FEUDS AND BLOOD BATHS: HANDLING CRITICISM

1. Maxioms.com, www.maxioms.com/maxiom/48087/judge-not-the-preacher-for-he-is-thy-judge-if-thou-mislike-him.

2. Cf. 2 Tim. 4:3.

3. Jer. 7:27 NASB.

4. Acts 2:29.

5. Cf. 1 John 3:21.

6. Acts 4:13, 29, 31.

7. Acts 9:28.

8. Acts 13:46.

9. Acts 14:3.

10. Acts 19:8.

11. Acts 26:26.

12. John 18:33, 37, my paraphrase.

13. When the interaction becomes particularly intense with one person who hogs the criticism, I try this: "Look, it seems that everybody here wants to give me a hard time, and I just can't let you have all the fun."

14. Winkie Pratney, *Fire on the Horizon: The Shape of a Twenty-first Century Youth Awakening* (Ventura, CA: Renew, 1998), 71.

15. For more on this, see my article "The Sacrament of Failure," *Theology Today* 34 (1977): 143–49.

16. Quoted by Daniel Medin, "Decisive Days," *Times Literary Supplement* (April 24, 2009), 7.

17. Austin Farrer, "Grace and Resurrection," in *Austin Farrer: The Essential Sermons,* ed. Leslie Houlden (Cambridge, MA: Cowley, 1991), 136.

18. So estimated William Riley Parker in his *Milton's Contemporary Reputation: An Essay Together with a Tentative List of Printed Allusions to Milton, 1641–1674, and Facsimile Reproductions of Five Contemporary Pamphlets Written in Answer to Milton* (Columbus: Ohio State University Press, 1940), 70.

19. "Judge nothing before the appointed time; wait until the Lord comes" (1 Cor. 4:5).

20. I borrow this metaphor from Joseph Sittler, "The View from Mount Nebo," in his *The Care of the Earth and Other University Sermons* (Philadelphia: Fortress, 1964), 75–87.

21. Norman Vincent Peale, *The True Joy of Positive Living: An Autobiography* (New York: Morrow, 1985), 81.

CHAPTER 21: BLOOD HEMATOMA: AVOIDING BRUISING

1. Loren Niemi and Elizabeth Ellis, *Inviting the Wolf In: Thinking about Difficult Stories* (Little Rock, AR: August House, 2001), 7.

2. Ibid.

3. Ibid., 55–60.

4. Ibid., 55.

5. Ibid., 58–59.

6. Ibid., 59–60.

CHAPTER 22: BLOOD PRESSURE: THE NERVOUS PREACHER

1. Martin Luther, as quoted in Fred W. Meuser, *Luther the Preacher* (Minneapolis: Augsburg, 1983), 52.

2. Heinrich Himmler, officer in charge of the Nazi death camps, fainted dead away at the sight of blood.

3. There are two classics on preaching in times of hypertension. My favorite is H. Beecher Hicks, *Preaching through a Storm* (Grand Rapids: Zondervan, 1987). The second is Haddon Robinson's essay "Preaching with a Limp," a true classic on how you "preach through pain," when "you don't feel like it," when people are spreading

false rumors about you. See chapter 4 in *Making a Difference in Preaching: Haddon Robinson on Biblical Preaching*, ed. Scott M. Gibson (Grand Rapids: Baker, 1999), 48–57. Robinson's text *Biblical Preaching: The Development and Delivery of Expository Messages* (Grand Rapids: Baker, 1980; 2nd ed., 2001) is probably the most widely used and influential preaching text in existence today.

4. As referenced by John Piper in *The Supremacy of God in Preaching* (Grand Rapids: Baker, 1990), 14.
5. Archibald Naismith, *2400 Outlines, Notes, Quotes, and Anecdotes for Sermons* (Grand Rapids: Baker, 1991), 89.
6. See Lam. 3:21.

CHAPTER 23: BLOOD DOPING AND BAD BLOOD: FALSE PROPS AND BAD LEADS

1. Warren Wiersbe, *The Patented Preacher*; see www.sermoncentral.com/pastors -preaching-articles/warren-wiersbe-the-patented-preacher-1046.asp.
2. "A Conversation with Margaret Avison," *Image* 45 (Spring 2005): 71.
3. When competing hypotheses are equal in other respects, the principle recommends selection of the hypothesis that introduces that fewest entities while still sufficiently answering the question. It is in this sense that Ockham's razor is usually understood.
4. Paul Valéry, as quoted in Iris Murdoch, *The Book and the Brotherhood* (New York: Viking, 1988), 581.
5. For the benefits of randomization rituals, see Leonard Sweet, *Nudge: Awakening Each Other to the God Who's Already There* (Colorado Springs: WaterBrook, 2010), 98.
6. Eph. 1:18.
7. James Denney, as quoted in George Sweazy, *Preaching the Good News* (Englewood Cliffs, NJ: Prentice-Hall, 1976), 126.
8. 1 Cor. 2:4–5.

CHAPTER 24: BLOOD POISONING: DEALING WITH HERESIES

1. Quoted by Alan Dershowitz in *The Genesis of Justice* (New York: Warner, 2000), 78.
2. For more on seeker sensitivity, see Marva Dawn, *How Shall We Worship? Vital Questions* (Carol Stream, IL: Tyndale, 2003).
3. Ernest T. Campbell, "The Friend We Have in Yahweh," in *Preaching as a Theological Task: World, Gospel, Scripture: In Honor of David Buttrick*, ed. Thomas G. Long and Edward Farley (Louisville: Westminster John Knox, 1996), 110.
4. Luke 9:26.
5. Mark 8:38.
6. 2 Tim. 1:8.
7. For more on JDD, see Leonard Sweet and Frank Viola, *Jesus Manifesto: Restoring the Supremacy and Sovereignty of Jesus Christ* (Nashville: Thomas Nelson, 2010).
8. Jonathan Benthall, *Returning to Religion: Why a Secular Age Is Haunted by Faith* (London: I. B. Tauris, 2008).
9. Eph. 4:15–16.
10. Mark 5:25–34, emphasis mine.
11. Luke 6:46, emphasis mine.
12. Luke 10:27.
13. Matt. 15:11.
14. Matt. 28:18–20.

Notes

CHAPTER 25: RED-BLOODED REALITIES: THE PREACHER'S HUMILITY AND HUMANITY

1. Phil. 2:3 (Jerusalem Bible).
2. Samuel Bradburn was a popular and successful London preacher. Something he said had apparently displeased Charles Wesley, whose complaint to John resulted in this critical evaluation of Bradburn's preaching:

   I fear you think of yourself more highly than you ought to think. Do not you think too highly of your own understanding? Of your gifts? Particularly in preaching, as if you were the very best preacher in the Connection? Of your own importance, as if the work of God here and there depended wholly or mainly on you? And of your popularity, which I have found, to my surprise, far less even in London, than I expected?

   May not this be much owing to the want of brotherly love?... I fear there is something unloving in your spirit—something not only of roughness, but of harshness, yea of sourness! Are you not also extremely open to prejudice, and not easy to be cured of it?...

   I am afraid lest your want of love to your neighbours should spring from want of love to God, from want of thankfulness. I have sometimes heard you speak in a manner that made me tremble; indeed, in terms that not only a weak Christian but even a serious Deist would scruple to use.

   I fear you greatly want evenness of temper. Are you not generally too high or too low? Are not all your passions too lively, your anger in particular? Is it not too soon raised? And is it not too impetuous, causing you to be violent, boisterous, bearing down all before you?

   Now, lift up your heart to God, or you will be angry at me. But I must go a little further. I fear you are greatly wanting in the government of your tongue. You are not exact in relating facts. I have observed it myself. You are apt to amplify, to enlarge a little beyond the truth. You cannot imagine, if others observe this, how it will affect your reputation.

   But I fear you are more wanting in another respect: that you give a loose to your tongue when you are angry; that your language then is not only sharp but course and ill-bred. If this be so, the people will not bear it. They will not take it either from you or me.

   See Letter to Mr. —— ——, December 1786, in *The Works of the Reverend John Wesley, A.M.*, 1st American complete and standard ed., from the latest London ed., ed. John Emory (New York: Waugh and Mason, 1835), 7:229. See also *The Letters of the Rev. John Wesley, A.M.*, ed. John Telford (London: Epworth, 1931), 7:355–56.
3. Humbert of Romans, *Treatise on the Formation of Preachers*, in *Early Dominicans: Selected Writings*, ed. Simon Tugwell (New York: Paulist, 1982), 195.
4. Ibid.
5. In the words of Dominican theologian Simon Tugwell, "It is not apart from [Humbert's] preaching that he discovers what it is to enjoy God; it is precisely as a preacher." Simon Tugwell, "Humbert of Romans," in his *Ways of Imperfection: An Exploration of Christian Spirituality* (London: Darton, Longman and Todd, 1984), 142.
6. John Piper, *The Supremacy of God in Preaching* (Grand Rapids: Baker, 1990), 37–38.
7. Haddon Robinson, "Preaching to Everyone in Particular," in *Making a Difference in Preaching: Haddon Robinson on Biblical Preaching*, ed. Scott M. Gibson (Grand Rapids: Baker, 1999), 127. It's been said of Robinson that "God made Haddon Rob-

inson and then he made all the rest of us—two runs of production." Quoted in Keith Willhite's foreword to *Making a Difference in Preaching*, 9.

CHAPTER 26: BLOOD TIES: LEARNING FROM PEERS AND RELATIONSHIPS WITH COLLEAGUES

1. William Arthur Ward, "The Wisdom of Laughing at Yourself," *Science of Mind* (May 1970), 104.
2. Gen. 2. See Leonard Sweet and Frank Viola, *Jesus: A Theography* (Nashville: Nelson, 2012).
3. For more on this, see Leonard Sweet, *What Matters Most: How We Got the Point but Missed the Person* (repr. ed., Colorado Springs: WaterBrook, 2012).
4. Nikos Kazantzakis, *The Saviors of God* (New York: Simon and Schuster, 1960), 73.

CHAPTER 27: BLOOD TESTING: INTERPRETING EFFECT AND RESPONSE

1. Acts 20:9.
2. Leonard Sweet, *11: Indispensable Relationships You Can't Be Without* (Colorado Springs: WaterBrook, 2012).

CHAPTER 28: LIFE BLOOD: FOOD FOR THE BODY

1. Austin Farrer, "Consecrated Bread," in *Austin Farrer: The Essential Sermons*, ed. Leslie Houlden (Cambridge, MA: Cowley, 1991), 81–84.

CHAPTER 29. GIVING BLOOD: SALVATION AND RESURRECTION

1. Gary B. Pillersdorf, "Sweet Visuals to Sway Jurors," *Trial* (June 2007), 56–60.